PRAISE FOR ANN RULE'S BRILLIANT *NEW YORK TIMES* BESTSELLERS

EVERY BREATH YOU TAKE

"Affecting, tense, and smart true-crime. . . . Rule digs up details . . . that form a case study of the classic American con man crossed with the more exotic strains of the sociopath."   —*Washington Post Book World*

"Ann Rule has outdone herself. . . ."

—*The Orlando Sentinel* (FL)

"Rule, in classic form, meticulously re-creates the . . . lives of her characters."   —*Publishers Weekly*

"Troubling but absolutely riveting. . . . A sober, nonsensational account of Sheila's murder, the mind-boggling series of events preceding it, and the nail-biting sequence of twists and turns in the investigation of the crime. . . . As usual, Rule excels at painting psychologically perceptive portraits of all the characters in this stranger-than-fiction but nevertheless real-life drama."   —*Booklist*

. . . AND NEVER LET HER GO

"Most people like to think they recognize evil when they see it. But as this gripping story makes clear, most people are wrong. Much more than the profile of a handsome, insidious killer and the young woman he murdered, . . . *And Never Let Her Go* is also the story of three close-knit families and how 30-year-old Anne Marie Fahey's death strengthened or destroyed them. . . . In Rule's capable hands, [this is] the raw material for a modern-day tragedy."   —*Publishers Weekly* (starred review)

"[A] truly creepy true-crime story. . . . This portrait of an evil prince needs no embellishment." —*People*

"In her selection and treatment of the Fahey murder, [Rule] might have created her masterpiece." —*The Plain Dealer* (Cleveland)

"Even crime buffs who followed the case closely are bound to gain new insights. . . . The courtroom scenes of *Capano* are especially compelling." —*The Orlando Sentinel* (FL)

"[Rule] tell[s] the sad story with authority, flair, and pace." —*The Washington Post*

"[A] compassionate portrayal of the victim and a chilling portrayal of her killer. . . . This is a true page-turner." —*Booklist*

BITTER HARVEST

"A must-read story of the '90s American dream turned, tragically, to self-absorbed ashes." —*People*

"Impossible to put down. . . . A tour de force from America's best true-crime writer." —*Kirkus Reviews*

"[A] tension-filled, page-turning chronology and analysis of a psychopath in action. . . . It is Rule's expert attention to detail that makes this Medea-incarnate story so compelling. . . . [A] gripping saga of sin and murder most foul." —*Publishers Weekly* (starred review)

EMPTY PROMISES
AND OTHER TRUE CASES
ANN RULE'S CRIME FILES: VOL. 7

"Fascinating, unsettling tales. . . . The shortest article here is deeper, and tells us more about the nature of crime, than a whole stack of full-length books written by less talented competitors. Among the very small group of top-notch true-crime writers, Rule just may be the best of the bunch."
—*Booklist*

A RAGE TO KILL
AND OTHER TRUE CASES
ANN RULE'S CRIME FILES: VOL. 6

"Her telling of the [Seattle] bus-crash saga is filled with those trademark touches that make Rule's readers feel like they were there."
—*The Seattle Times*

"Gripping tales. . . . Fans of true crime know they can rely on Ann Rule to deliver the dead-level best."
—*The Hartford Courant* (CT)

THE END OF THE DREAM
AND OTHER TRUE CASES
ANN RULE'S CRIME FILES: VOL. 5

"[The] stories take on a poignancy that goes far beyond mere cops-'n'-robbers stuff. Without resorting to psychobabble, Rule tells us—through exhaustively detailed interviews with lovers, friends, and families—what led three such talented men to such tragic ends."
—*Seattle Post-Intelligencer*

"Rule's true-life crime stories read better than most fiction murder plots."
—*St. Petersburg Times* (FL)

Books by Ann Rule

Without Pity: Ann Rule's Most Dangerous Killers
Heart Full of Lies
Every Breath You Take
. . . And Never Let Her Go
Bitter Harvest
Dead by Sunset
Everything She Ever Wanted
If You Really Loved Me
The Stranger Beside Me
Possession
Small Sacrifices

Ann Rule's Crime Files:
Vol. 8: Last Dance, Last Chance and Other True Cases
Vol. 7: Empty Promises and Other True Cases
Vol. 6: A Rage to Kill and Other True Cases
Vol. 5: The End of the Dream and Other True Cases
Vol. 4: In the Name of Love and Other True Cases
Vol. 3: A Fever in the Heart and Other True Cases
Vol. 2: You Belong to Me and Other True Cases
Vol. 1: A Rose for Her Grave and Other True Cases

The I-5 Killer
The Want-Ad Killer
Lust Killer

ANN RULE

ANN RULE'S
MOST
DANGEROUS
KILLERS
WITHOUT PITY

POCKET BOOKS

NEW YORK   LONDON   TORONTO   SYDNEY   SINGAPORE

An *Original* Publication of POCKET BOOKS

The names of some individuals in this book have been changed. Such names are indicated by an asterisk (*) the first time each appears in the book.

POCKET BOOKS, a division of Simon & Schuster, Inc.
1230 Avenue of the Americas, New York, NY 10020

ISBN: 0-7434-4867-7

First Pocket Books paperback edition December 2003

10 9 8 7 6 5 4 3 2 1

POCKET and colophon are registered trademarks of Simon & Schuster, Inc.

Cover design by James Wang

Manufactured in the United States of America

For information regarding special discounts for bulk purchases, please contact Simon & Schuster Special Sales at 1-800-456-6798 or business@simonandschuster.com.

DEDICATION

To my friends, a thousand homicide detectives from at least a hundred different departments around America. For almost thirty years, I have watched them work under circumstances that most people could never imagine. When the rest of us are enjoying holidays, spending time with our families and sleeping, they are often out in the field, slogging through rain, mud, snow, and sometimes blood. They are coping with the devastation that violence can do to the human body. They come to know and care for the victims they never met in life, and they strive to find who took their lives away even if it means working twenty-four to thirty-six hours without sleep. They are skilled, dedicated, dogged, tough, perceptive, tender, inquisitive, compassionate, hard-nosed, meticulous, and sometimes even clairvoyant. We all hope we will never need their services, but if we should they will do their best to deliver justice. Yes, the homicide guys are sometimes full of black humor—but I have also seen most of them cry.

And a salute to Detective Sergeant Don Cameron, thirty years with the Seattle Police Department's Homicide Unit, on his retirement. A better homicide detective never served. And to Chuck Wright, who retired in 1999 after three decades with the Washington State Department of Corrections. Chuck has helped rehabilitate the thousands of people who have been assigned to his case-load, and he has also worked tirelessly for victims' rights.

And, finally, to the memory of Seattle Police Homi-cide investigators Detective Sergeant Ivan Beeson, De-tective Dick Reed and Detective Don Strunk.

CONTENTS

CONTENTS

AUTHOR'S NOTE

I have chosen a dozen cases for this collection that would probably be too unbelievable for publication if they were fiction. We don't like to think that human beings can be so consumed with greed, jealousy, revenge, or obsession that they evolve into homicidal rage. Although in these cases, the perpetrators are not all beautiful or handsome—or rich—they have many characteristics in common. Some are wealthy and some are drifters, but they all have a special gift with words, a rather negative talent that lets them hide what they really think from friends, enemies, victims, and even detectives—for a while.

In each of these stories, I was acquainted with at least some of the characters mentioned. Sometimes it was the victim or grieving survivors and sometimes the detectives, the prosecutors, or the defense attorneys. Probably hardest for me to accept were the few times when I actually knew the killer. Considering that I write in the true-crime genre, I suppose that is to be expected—all these people move in part of my world.

More and more, I've arrived at a place where stories come to me, rather than my having to go out to look for them. I cannot begin to write the thousands told to me every year, and so I have always chosen those that baffle and intrigue me most. Murder is never routine, but the cases that follow are truly exceptional. They may well haunt you as they have haunted me down through the years.

Ann Rule

WITHOUT PITY

The Tumbledown Shack

After writing more *than a thousand articles about homicide cases, I suppose it's natural that some of them blur slightly in my memory. However, there are those that I recall vividly, and I even remember my own life at the time I first researched their tragic details. The story that follows brings back gloomy recollections of four days when I was trapped by a blizzard in Wenatchee, Washington. The sheriff of adjoining Okanogan County had given me a ride from Seattle over the Cascade Mountains on November 16, 1978, and I planned to take the bus back after I'd talked to Chelan County homicide detectives. But a huge snowstorm clogged the mountain passes and no car, bus, train, or plane could get through. That meant I couldn't get home until the road thawed.*

All the sidewalks in Wenatchee were covered with four or five inches of ice that weekend and many stores had closed. Stuck in a little motel, all I had to read was the police file of this horrifying case. I found no diversion from horror when I turned on the television set. The news had just broken that Reverend Jim Jones, the cult leader of the Peoples' Temple from San Francisco, had forced his hapless congregation to drink poisoned Kool-Aid at "Jonestown," in Guyana. Of his 1,100 followers, 973 were dead, and so were California state representative

Leo J. Ryan and most of the staff and film crew who had gone with him to Guyana to investigate Jones. There was nothing for me to watch beyond blanket coverage of that story on every channel and a screen filled with a sea of bodies.

I spent those days completely alone in the dead of winter only thirty-five miles from where the case I was studying had happened in the blazing summer heat. By the time the ice thawed, I knew this story of two vulnerable young women by heart and it stays in my mind to this day.

Like those who died in Jonestown, the Chelan County victims had been lulled into the false belief that they were safe, and they too trusted enough that they failed to see the evil behind a pleasant facade.

It would seem that a double homicide that happened almost thirty years ago would have been solved by now. It has certainly not been forgotten. I still meet people who were closely connected to the victims, people for whom time has no meaning. Technically, it is an open case. Yet, over and over again, one man confessed to the murders of two beautiful young women. Was he telling the truth, or was he only throwing up a smokescreen that clouded the investigation so that the *real* killer was never caught?

You be the judge.

Chelan County, Washington, is only a two-and-a-half-hour drive from Seattle, but it lies on the other side of the mountains in eastern Washington, in a climate where the landscape is completely different. The weather, the vegetation, and the topography of Chelan County might as well be three or four states away. Chelan County is fruit-growing country, particularly Delicious apples, and vacation country, a place far away from the congestion of the increasingly industrial west sides of Oregon and Washington, where Portland and Seattle traffic rivals that of L.A. and New York City, and where new housing developments cover fertile valleys with cement streets and perfectly landscaped yards.

The town of Chelan is forty miles north of Wenatchee, and it exists mostly because of expansive Lake Chelan, the second largest inland lake in America. Tourists flock to Lake Chelan, where deep blue water cuts through dry hills for a hundred miles or more, ending at the isolated hamlet of Stehekin, accessible only by boat or seaplane. Visitors board the *Lady of the Lake* in Chelan for a four-hour leisurely cruise to another world. Vacationers and those attending conferences fill the myriad resorts curving along Lake Chelan.

The road between Wenatchee and Chelan winds through quite beautiful country. To the east, poplar trees stand like sentries and as windbreaks for the apple orchards close to the mighty Columbia River. Close to the town of Entiat, roadside stands sell fresh produce, honey, candy, pickles, and flowers. The water thundering from Rocky Reach Dam is awe inspiring, and its grounds thrill little kids; every thatch of spreading junipers provides shelter for rabbits and other little creatures, the descendants of Easter bunnies and abandoned pets released there decades before. Park rangers feed and watch over them.

It all feels very safe and benign.

But farther north, the land becomes much more rugged. In high summer and early autumn, rolling hills burn brown, and tumbleweeds, wild daisies, and sagebrush are the only plants that grow. Too often, forest fires erupt and the land burns black as the wind carries flames from tree to tree and across roads. Animals—and humans too—can be trapped with no way out. Many come to Chelan County for reasons other than vacationing. When harvest time comes, migrant workers and young people with the stamina to work hard for several weeks head up U.S. Highway 97 to find jobs bringing in the crops.

In the mid-seventies, nobody gave a second glance to

the strangers and teenagers who stood beside the roads with their thumbs out. They were such a familiar sight that they became part of the environment. It was past the time of peace, love, and hippie beads, but many young people still clung to those beliefs, and they continued to hitchhike.

At various spots, the road north to Chelan suddenly disappears into black tunnels cut into the rock cliffs, only to emerge into blinding sunlight. There are well-maintained homes along the road to Chelan, but there are also gray pioneer shacks, long deserted and leaning toward the ground. In September and October, the fruit pickers arrive, followed in late fall by hunters stalking deer and elk.

Chelan County deputies expect extra work in autumn because so many transients swell the population. Sometimes the officers are called out for homicides, but the vast majority of calls are the result of drunken fights, over a bottle of "Mad Dog" or "Night Train" wine, among the nameless drifters who follow the crops.

It was 2:35 on Tuesday afternoon, September 30, 1975, when Deputy D. B. Mayo received a call from the radio operator at the Chelan Police Department. Someone had gone to the farm-labor office in town wanting to report a "possible rape." The attack had apparently occurred somewhere out in the county.

Mayo contacted Bill Myer,* who was staying in a pickers' cabin at the Hesperian Orchards. Myer appeared agitated as he tried to explain what he'd seen.

"Me and my friend Hal Oxley* were out hiking in the hills behind the orchards when we found a couple of

---

*Some names have been changed. The first time they appear, they are marked with an asterisk (*).

chicks in a shed. . . . I think they've been raped," he said hurriedly.

Myer said he had been spooked by what he'd seen and didn't stay around long enough to check to see if the victims were alive or dead. If they *were* dead, Myer and his friend would become the first suspects, but Mayo didn't mention that. He simply studied the excited young man.

"But I'm afraid they might be dead," Myer said. "I can lead you back there where I saw them if you want."

Deputy Mayo urged the young picker to hop into his patrol car. They picked up Oxley, and the deputy sped to the area the witnesses pointed out. They directed him to Old Downey Road, which leads off U.S. 97, and headed up that road for a little over a mile, passing some weathered ranch buildings. The man who owned the ranch verified that there was, indeed, an old shed about two miles further on.

Since Oxley and Myer said they had stumbled upon the shack while they were walking in the rugged hills, they were a little disoriented and had trouble figuring out how to get back to the spot where they'd seen the girls.

Mayo drove along the increasingly rutted dirt road and was just about to turn back, when they suddenly spotted an old A-frame shed that weather must have battered for half a century. It was about to collapse.

"That's it," Myer said. "That's where I saw them."

The deputy eased out of his patrol car and started to walk toward the pile of weathered boards when suddenly a large gray dog—or wolf—bared its teeth at him and barked ferociously. He paused, and saw that it *was* a dog, probably a husky–German shepherd mix, that was barring the way.

"I'm pretty good with animals," Myer called out from the car. "Let me try."

For a fleeting moment, Mayo wondered if he might have walked into a trap. He was far from backup with two scruffy-looking strangers, and now Myer seemed able to get closer to the dog than he had. Maybe the dog already knew Myer. The deputy wondered if there really *were* two girls inside the shack.

But Myer seemed sincere as he talked calmly to the dog, and grudgingly the animal finally let him approach and allowed himself to be tied to a post.

Mayo peered into the old shed through some gaping one-by-eights, his eyes slowly adjusting to the darkness inside. The girls were there, all right. At this point, he had no idea if they had been raped, but they were most certainly dead. And they probably had been dead for days.

Even in death, the two girls—one flaxen-haired, the other with brown hair—showed signs of their former beauty. Their bodies were tanned and slender.

Mayo backed away from the terrible sight and ran to his patrol car to radio for help from the sheriff's headquarters in Wenatchee. There was no possibility that the girls had perished accidentally. From the mote-filled beams of sunlight that filtered into the shack, Mayo saw bruises and dried blood on their bodies. Either they had been attacked here in the shed or someone had carried their bodies here to hide them.

While the three men waited for help, they filled a battered metal dish with water from their canteens for the dog, which had stationed himself loyally next to his owners' bodies, possibly waiting there for days.

Right after receiving Deputy Mayo's call, Chief of Detectives Bill Patterson and detectives Jerry Monroe and Tillman Wells had left their offices in Wenatchee and headed north along the Columbia River.

Careful not to step on physical evidence that might have been left behind at the murder site, the Chelan County investigators squinted into the dilapidated structure. The brunette lay closer to the entrance than her companion. She was partially clothed, wearing hiking clothes and boots. And dried blood covered what they could see of her body. Someone had apparently tossed her backpack on top of her, perhaps in a hurried attempt to hide her body, perhaps as a gesture of remorse for what he had done to her. Most of her wounds appeared to be in the upper portion of her body.

The second girl's body was nearby. She was nude, and her jeans, thick-soled hiking boots, and backpack were beside her. The blond girl had fought her killer: her hands had wounds from a sharp object.

Who were they? The dead young women looked so much like the hundreds of girls who moved through the Chelan County area in picking season. They were obviously experienced campers and their gear had been well used. How they had come to be in this lonely shed so far off the main road was a puzzle. It would seem that they would have to have been familiar with the region to even know the ramshackle structure was here. Either that or they had been led here by someone who knew about it.

Not knowing the victims' names, the three detectives temporarily dubbed them "Victim Number One" and "Victim Number Two."

They lifted the blond girl's backpack carefully from the shed. Maybe Victim Number Two's belongings would help identify her. The bag contained the usual: clothes, makeup, camping gear. But they also found two prescription pill bottles from a pharmacy in Lincoln City, Oregon. The name "Pat Weidner" was on one bottle; the other prescription was for "Brad King.*"

They found a purse in the shack, and it contained $59.08. The detectives also fished a tin can from one of the packs, and it had two $10 bills in it—emergency money perhaps. Robbery was an unlikely motive for double murder.

The purse held a Social Security card and an Oregon driver's license, both in the name of "Beverly Mae Johnson." Her birth date was listed as May 14, 1952, and her description was 5 feet 3 inches and 110 pounds. The address was also in Lincoln City, a resort town along the Oregon coast. She'd been very young, only twenty-three.

Tentatively, Patterson figured that the petite blond girl was Johnson, and the taller brunette was almost surely Weidner. That was much easier to deduce than whatever reasons had brought the victims hundreds of miles from home to a rundown shack in the wilderness.

Dr. Robert Bonafaci, the Chelan County Medical Examiner, arrived at the scene with Detective Don Danner. Bonafaci said that it appeared that both women had died from having their throats cut. Patty Weidner, who had been taller and huskier than her friend, had probably had no warning of danger. Either she had been asleep or she hadn't expected to be attacked because she apparently had put up no fight at all. But Beverly Johnson, who looked to weigh no more than a hundred pounds, had fought valiantly. She had the deep cuts in her hands—defensive wounds. Whether rape had been the motivation for such violence would have to be determined at the autopsy.

Dr. Bonafaci gave his OK for the bodies to be transported to Wenatchee to await postmortem examinations. Now the Chelan County detectives could move in to work the crime scene.

Patterson felt both girls had been killed in or near the shed. Blood droplets marked the sandy soil and led them to a spot about six feet from its entrance. Here, there had been a large puddle of blood, long dried now into a dark brown segmented splotch. They found even more blood fifty-six feet away, and in several areas where the dog had dug frantically into the soft soil. These too bore traces of his mistresses' blood.

Had the victims screamed for help? It would have done little good. They were miles away from anyone who could have rescued them. No one on the ranch two miles down the road could have heard their screams.

Patterson and his crew of detectives wondered if the dog might prove to be their best—albeit silent—witness. He had been very protective of the victims' bodies, and he must have tried to defend the girls when they were attacked. If he had managed to bite the killer or killers, his bite marks in their flesh could be compared to his teeth with a scanning electron microscope.

Now that the bodies he'd guarded were gone, the dog paced nervously.

The investigators searched the second backpack. There was nothing in it that would help identify its owner. They did find a pocketknife with the initials "G.B." scratched on the handle. That didn't match either victim's initials.

By 7:00 P.M., the shadows of the hills encroaching upon the crime scene cast it in odd purplish light. But the Chelan County probers had managed to bag and label the last of the evidence before sundown. The detectives had sketched the scene and photographed it, and even made moulage castings of tire tracks in the area. Still, they feared the moulages would be of little use; the earth was baked so hard and dry that little dust devils whirled.

Now Detective Chief Patterson and his men would have to seek positive identification for the two young victims, and somehow backtrack on their journey to Chelan. It was a long way from the Oregon coast to these isolated hills.

Their trail was relatively cold; Dr. Bonafaci felt the

girls had been dead for more than thirty-six hours. He believed they had probably been killed on Sunday, September 28, but the exact time could vary by a few hours either way, depending on the temperature outside. Rigor mortis had come and gone, making time-of-death estimates a little difficult.

Bonafaci performed the autopsies. He found that the blond victim, now confirmed to be Beverly Johnson, had died as a result of exsanguination (bleeding to death) from her neck wounds. He detected no significant trauma to her brain, chest, or abdomen. Oddly, there were no positive signs of rape beyond her nakedness—no bruising on the inside of her thighs or tearing of her vagina or rectum. The second girl (who was still called "Jane Doe") had also succumbed to exsanguination, although she *did* have two scalp bruises, suggesting she had been struck on the head. There were, however, no signs of underlying brain damage. Apparently, this victim hadn't been sexually assaulted either.

Still, Beverly Johnson's nudity and the fact that "Jane Doe's" clothing was in disarray certainly suggested that rape had been attempted.

It was sick and ugly. They hadn't been robbed, they might not have been raped, yet someone had coldly slit their throats. Were the detectives looking for someone who got his thrills merely from the act of killing? They hoped not, because that was the most dangerous breed of killer of all.

The only living witness to what must have been terrifying violence was the now-crestfallen dog. He was housed in the county jail, wolfing down dog food and water as if he were starved. Even if he recognized the killer, he wouldn't be able to tell anyone. If he did snarl or the hackles raised on his neck when confronted with a suspect, it was doubtful that any judge would allow that as testimony.

* * *

As soon as news of the double murder hit the media, Bill Patterson and his men were deluged with tips from citizens. One migrant worker reported that three or four men he had never seen before had offered him a ride from a tavern in Chelan. "They drove me up to Knapp's Coulee and said if I didn't give them everything I had, they'd kill me on the spot," he said. "I gave them my wallet with all my I.D. and thirty-five dollars. They dumped me and left me out there. They left driving down towards Entiat."

He described the thieves as "hippie types" with full beards, and said they were driving either a two-door Chevy or a Pontiac. Knapp's Coulee was quite close to where the bodies had been found, but the incident had happened days before the victims' probable time of death.

An elderly couple reported that they'd driven past Old Downey Road on September 25. They had noticed a plume of dust as if a vehicle had just gone up the road, but they saw no one. When they came back some time later, they had seen a 1969 or 1970 light green or blue Ford pickup with a canopy turning from Old Downey Road. There wasn't a lot of traffic there, so they remembered it. They had heard a dog barking somewhere too, but hadn't thought anything of it at the time.

The dog couldn't have been the dead girls' gray dog; he was miles away, at the crime scene, and Patterson couldn't make a case out of a dust trail and a pickup truck. More important, the witnesses had seen the truck five days before the bodies were discovered. The victims would still have been alive on the 25th, although it was possible they might have been camping back down Old Downey Road at the time.

Another lead seemed to have no connection—at first. A bank teller who commuted down Highway 97 called to say that she had seen a reddish brown dog that looked to be an Irish setter mix north of Knapp's Tunnel three or four times during the week. "I saw him first on Sunday—the 28th—and then on Monday and Tuesday. He was pacing up and down beside the road as if he was lost. He had a red bandanna tied around his neck."

The dog found with the victims couldn't possible be described as "reddish brown" in color, but it too had been wearing a red bandanna around his neck. Was it possible that the girls had been traveling with *two* dogs?

That question was answered when Lieutenant Harvey Coles from the Lincoln City, Oregon, Police Department called with information on the dead girls. As their I.D.s indicated, they had both lived in the "Miracle Mile" resort area along the Oregon coast. Coles said that Patricia Weidner had a boyfriend there, who might have known of her plans, although he hadn't yet been able to locate the man.

As it turned out, both young women had friends and family in Lincoln City who had begun to worry about them. His voice trembling, Pat Weidner's father told the detectives that she had a scar on her forehead and a surgical scar on her left knee.

And so did the unidentified victim. There was no question that Pat Weidner and Beverly Johnson had been found. Their friends said they had planned to hitchhike to the Wenatchee area to find jobs for the apple harvest.

Early on the morning of October 2, friends of the dead girls arrived to identify their bodies and offer whatever help they could to the sheriff's investigators.

"They had their dogs with them," one young woman said. "Charlie is a husky mix, and Silas is a kind of retriever-setter mix. Those dogs wouldn't let anyone near Beverly or Patty. They felt safe because of the dogs. Patty's dog would tear anyone apart who tried to hurt her!"

Well, Charlie had stayed with them, but the investigators

hadn't seen anything of Silas. There *was* the red dog the bank teller had seen close to the road, but he was gone now.

The victims' friends from Oregon identified Beverly Johnson's purse and said, "Both of them had knives with them—to use in camping out."

They recognized the one knife in evidence, but the other knife was missing. Beverly and Pat were experienced at camping. In fact, Patty had been living with her boyfriend in a tepee near Lincoln City. According to her friends, Patty Weidner always traveled with her backpack, sleeping bag, spices to cook with, pots and pans, and extra clothes. Beverly had had her backpack and she carried a four-man tent. They had planned to come back to Lincoln City after apple-picking season.

They were described as independent young women who made their own way. Patty had been working as a waitress in Oregon, while Beverly clerked at a health food store. But they'd reportedly become bored, and thought the trip to Washington sounded like fun and a chance to make quite a bit of money in a short time.

The detectives learned that a friend had driven the women about ten miles out of Lincoln City on Wednesday, September 24, leaving them at a good spot to catch a ride hitchhiking. Their destination in Chelan County, Washington, was more than three hundred miles away.

The investigation took an odd turn when Patty's boyfriend was located—not in Lincoln City—but in jail in Chelan, arrested on October 3 for being drunk and disorderly. That put him in the top spot as a suspect.

Detective Tillman Wells interviewed Brad King and found him very upset, though no longer drunk. "I saw Patty and Bev* on September 24," King said in the interview. "It was a week ago Wednesday, and they asked me to come with them—but I wasn't ready yet. So I told them maybe I'd see them up here. I did come up, but I didn't get to Wenatchee until Tuesday the twenty-ninth. I couldn't find them, so I went ahead and got a job up at the Lucky Badger orchard and I worked there through the week. I didn't even know what had happened to them because I was out in the orchards working until Saturday night."

He sighed and stared at his hands. "I went into this tavern and I heard some guys talking about what happened to Bev and Patty. I just lost my head and went nuts. It's my fault—if I'd gone with them when they asked me, they'd be alive now."

No matter how much Patty's boyfriend appeared to be grieving, Wells didn't take his story at face value. He checked with the Lucky Badger orchard and with the victims' friends in Lincoln City. He was able to verify Brad King's alibi absolutely. It would have been impossible for him to be in both Chelan and Lincoln City on the Sunday that detectives believed the young women died. They'd already been dead for at least a day when Patty's boyfriend left Oregon for Wenatchee.

After the *Wenatchee Daily World* ran a story about the double homicide asking for help from the public, more leads began trickling in. One witness was sure she had seen the two young women on Thursday. The woman worked as a waitress at the Mineral Wells lodge restaurant near the summit of Blewett Pass. Most people driving to Wenatchee from Seattle take I-90 east, crossing Snoqualmie Pass and then veering north to cross Blewett Pass, which comes out about 18 miles from Wenatchee. The rustic Mineral Wells restaurant is the only place to eat near the summit.

"It was Thursday when I saw them," the waitress told

Bill Patterson. He showed her several photos of young women, and she picked out Beverly Johnson easily. "That's her—the blonde," she said. "She and another girl spent the night of September twenty-fifth in the campgrounds here. They ate dinner here on Thursday night and then had an early breakfast on Friday morning."

"Were they alone?"

"They were for dinner. But they were with two men for breakfast—"

"Can you describe the men?"

She shrugged, searching her memory. "All I can say is they were white, maybe in their early twenties—both about five feet ten with dark hair. One of the men paid for breakfast. The girls' two dogs waited outside."

"So the women left with these two men?"

"No. I think the men drove off toward Seattle, and the girls waited outside for at least an hour, trying to catch a ride. I never saw the men again," she said. "I got busy and I didn't see the girls get picked up. They were just gone the next time I looked outside."

Who were the two men, and was it possible that they had come back to pick up Beverly and Patty? Patterson had a stroke of luck this time—or so it seemed—when he got a call from Deputy Tony Fitzhugh of Okanogan County, Washington. Fitzhugh had received a call from a man named Jeff Hunt.*

"He's willing to talk with you," Fitzhugh said. "He was evidently with the girls for a while."

Jeff Hunt turned out to be a hitchhiker himself, and said he'd met the women out on the road. "I was hitching out of The Dalles, Oregon," he said, mentioning a town on the north side of the Columbia River, where it divides Washington from Oregon. "I met these two girls on Thursday at the intersection of the road that goes to Vancouver, Washington. They were headed to central Washington too, and they had two dogs with them. We all caught a ride with a fellow from Vancouver and he took us to Mineral Springs. We got in the campgrounds there around seven that night and decided to camp."

Patterson nodded, but he wasn't sure about this guy. Beverly and Patty were sure taking the long way around if they were going to Wenatchee. They could have caught a ride north on 97 to Wenatchee. Vancouver meant backtracking—but then, hitchhikers can't be choosers.

"So," Patterson continued, "did the girls talk to you much?"

"Not really. They were quiet—almost antisocial— until I said I knew about apple picking, and then they had a lot of questions. But they told us what their names were: Bev Johnson and Patty Weidner."

Maybe the man from Vancouver—whose name Hunt didn't know—had been a nice guy and driven them more than 200 miles from his home to be kind, or maybe he had expected "repayment" for his trouble. If the latter were true, he had been disappointed. Hunt said they all slept in their own sleeping bags, and the girls' dogs growled at anyone who came close to them.

There were no hard feelings apparently. "I bought breakfast for all of us Friday morning," Hunt said. "The guy who gave us a ride headed back to Vancouver. I think he said he worked in some kind of factory there. The girls said they wanted the spot in front of the restaurant, so I walked about a mile up the road. I had to wait an hour, but I got a ride into Cashmere. I never did see the girls come by, so I don't know who they got a ride with."

"Do you think it's possible the guy from Vancouver changed his mind and came back?" Patterson asked.

"I don't think so. He was pretty mellow, and he

seemed anxious to get to work. They were going about 70 miles north and he wouldn't have wanted to take them that much farther. And those dogs wouldn't have let him get near Patty or Bev."

In the end, the friendly driver's whereabouts didn't really matter. Someone else had seen the girls later on Friday.

Detective Tillman Wells talked with a long-haul truck driver who felt sure he'd seen Patty and Beverly on Friday, September 26.

"It was right about a quarter to one in the afternoon," the witness told Wells. "I was on Maple Street in the north end of Wenatchee and I saw these two pretty girls with backpacks, and their dogs were with them."

"Could you describe them?" Wells asked.

"One girl was blond and the other had kind of brownish hair. See, I read about them being killed, and I saw that picture of their dog in the paper. It was the gray dog. But when I saw them, they had a kind of reddish dog with them too. Both dogs had red bandannas around their necks. I saw them all close up because the girls crossed the street right in front of me."

He gave Wells information that hadn't been in the paper. It placed Patty, Beverly, Charlie, and Silas in Wenatchee on Friday afternoon.

After that, there was only silence. The calls of actual sightings dried up. If anyone had seen the girls between Friday afternoon and Tuesday, no one came forward to talk about it. The Chelan detectives got calls all right, but they were all about weirdos who either lived in the Wenatchee-Chelan area, or who were rumored to have traveled through. None of the calls had even tenuous links to Patty Weidner and Beverly Johnson.

Who picked them up near Highway 97 and gave them a ride 35 miles up the road? And how did they end up miles off that road? It was true that camping spots thinned out as the highway wound its way north, but the girls should have gotten a ride all the way into Chelan. They still had six or seven hours of daylight after the trucker saw them, plenty of time to travel only 40 miles.

Patty and Beverly had probably believed in their own invincibility because they'd never gotten into trouble before and counted on their ability to judge character and their dogs' fierce loyalty. But no one can really discern who is "normal" by looking at outward appearance. Between Wenatchee and the Old Downey Road, the girls had met someone who looked safe, which, of course, is the terrible danger in hitchhiking. Some of the most sadistic creatures on earth look normal, drive new cars, and troll for hitchhikers.

A few days later, the final lab reports came in. One of the victims had had a single dead sperm cell in her vagina, but that could have come from consensual intercourse back in Lincoln City. It might or might not mean that she'd been raped. As far as comparing it to a suspect's blood type, it was 1975 and DNA matches were unheard of—still something out of science fiction.

But just when the case appeared to have reached a brick wall, information came from an unexpected source. On October 7, Detective Jerry Monroe took a phone call from Constable Keith Johnson of Calgary, Alberta, Canada. Johnson said his department had a man in custody who had been talking about murdering two girls near Wenatchee.

"You have anything like that down there?"

"Yeah," Monroe said. "We sure do. What's he saying?"

"The guy first said his name was Maneto Minelli*— but he's actually Jack Stolle. We have him on forgery and possession of stolen property charges. He says he and a friend from Albany, Oregon, killed two girls by cutting their throats. . . ."

Monroe signaled to Bill Patterson to pick up a phone.

"We've got him up here," Johnson said, "because he tried to open up a bank account with checks stolen from a man in Vancouver, Washington. Then he started talking about killing some girls near Chelan. He gave us four different names and he claims to be the son of some family living in Chelan."

"Don't let him loose," Patterson said. "We're going to have men on the road up there in about five minutes."

"Don't worry. We'll keep him right here for you."

Detectives Tillman Wells and Jerry Monroe drove to Calgary the next day, and they were led to an interview room where Jack Lee Stolle, 34, waited. Stolle had a long "rap sheet" for arrests in Washington, Oregon, and California, but he didn't look like a hardened criminal. He was a slight blond man with rather feminine features and a "cookie duster" moustache.

Stolle's recollection of meeting Beverly Johnson and Patty Weidner warred with what the Chelan investigators already knew.

"Me and this guy I know—Rudy Snell*—met these gals near Portland and we drove them west to Hood River, Oregon. The four of us spent the night together, but when Rudy and me woke up, they were gone and so was fifteen hundred dollars in cash that belonged to us."

It was possible, Wells and Monroe knew, that there was some truth in Stolle's story. The victims *had* been in The Dalles, which was 15 miles east of Hood River. But that was where they got a ride with the Vancouver man who drove them all the way to Blewett Pass. Wells and Monroe didn't say anything, but let Stolle keep talking.

"We decided to go and look for them and get our money back. We crossed the Columbia at Biggs Junction and drove into Washington. And we saw them again at a rest stop, where they were trying to hitch a ride. It was somewhere between Yakima and Ellensburg. We picked them up again."

"What day was this?" Wells asked.

"Lemme see. That was the twenty-eighth. We all smoked pot, drank beer and wine. We were in Wenatchee and then we went to this tavern in Entiat."

Stolle had wound his story around so that he was only about 30 miles from the homicide scene, even though the first part of his statement seemed to be a patent lie. The victims *had* found a ride in The Dalles, but not with him—or Snell.

"What were their names—these girls you met?"

"Maude and Frannie."

The wrong names. Wells and Monroe exchanged glances, but they didn't comment. The girls from Lincoln City might have deliberately given strangers made-up names. "So, what did you do when the tavern closed?"

"It was Rudy who thought of it. He whispered to me that we should 'off' the girls because they stole all that money from us. Me, I thought he was only kidding."

Jack Stolle said they had driven north on 97 and found a spot near Chelan where they decided to camp out. They had all spread out their sleeping bags as Rudy got angrier and angrier about being ripped off. "He was really mad at Maude and Frannie," Stolle remembered.

"Me, I was so stoned on weed and booze that he was already slashing them before I knew what happened. One girl was dead already, and he made me help him kill Frannie."

It was a weird confession, but Stolle had just enough of the details and times right to be believable. Still, Wells and Monroe wondered if there *really* was a Rudy Snell, or if Stolle was making him up to take the blame off himself.

Patty and Beverly had been in Wenatchee on September 25, so why would they have retraced their steps 300 miles back to Hood River, Oregon? They'd almost reached Chelan on Friday, but Stolle was telling the detectives that he had met them way back in Oregon on the 27th. It just didn't make sense.

They were sure, however, that he had been at the crime scene in the tumbledown shack. He knew too much not to have been there. His work boots closely matched a blurred print they had found in the sand outside the shack and cast into a moulage, but the edges weren't sharp enough to make it a positive match.

The investigators suspected that Stolle was probably "confabulating"—taking things that were true and mixing them up with some other time in his life or in his imagination. At any rate, they needed to get him back into the U.S. and to Chelan County to figure out what part he really *had* played in the death of the two young women. Extradition proceedings began.

Bill Patterson's team of detectives found that Jack Stolle was, indeed, familiar with the area where the girls had been found. He had worked for a family named Minelli who owned a farm near Chelan. They had a son named Maneto, but he was accounted for. Stolle had simply taken his name as an alias.

The Minellis said that Stolle and his uncle had come to work for them four years earlier. He had been a good worker, and they hired him again the next summer. "He worked until late August," Nick Minelli said, "and he said he had to go into town to see to some legal papers. And he was gone for a whole month! The next time we heard from him, he was calling from Idaho. He needed eighteen dollars for bus fare to get back to Chelan. We sent it to him."

"Where did he say he'd been?" Tillman Wells asked.

"He didn't talk much about that. Later, we found out he'd spent twenty-eight days in jail in Jackson Hole, Wyoming. He never did say what for."

The Minellis were a very forgiving family and they hired Stolle again. He'd then worked until November 1972.

"So the next time we heard from him was in February 1973, and he was calling from Boise, Idaho. He said he'd been sentenced to twenty years in prison for forgery. He wrote to us from prison because he wanted to apologize to us for stealing one of our radios."

"You ever hear from him again?"

"Three years later—in July, this year. He wanted to come back and work for us, but we'd had enough. We turned him down—and that's the last we heard from him."

So Stolle had known the area between Wenatchee and Chelan very well, and he'd been there as recently as late July. One sad discovery indicated that he may have been very close around the time Beverly Johnson and Patty Weidner were murdered. Silas, the missing red setter mix, was finally found dead. Maybe Stolle had taken the dog with him when he left the dead girls, or maybe the frightened animal had followed the only human alive out from the desolate hills. Railroad workers found the remains of the dog on the railroad tracks near Stayman Flats, very close to the Minelli farm. Although, weeks later, there was little left of the dog's body, the detectives were able to identify it by its hair and scraps of the red bandanna, which had the same print as the one Charlie wore.

Detective Chief Bill Patterson called the Hood River, Oregon, Police Department to see if there might really be a man named Rudy Snell. To Patterson's surprise, Snell turned out to be an actual person. A Hood River investigator located him and reported back that Snell knew Jack Stolle and had worked in the orchards in Hood River—*not* in Chelan—with Jack Stolle.

When Patterson checked the Hood River orchard, he learned that Stolle and Snell had been hired as temporary pickers, and that they'd worked on September 26 and 27. They had, however, failed to show up on Sunday the 28th.

"They came in on the 29th," the orchard foreman said, "but they only picked up their checks and left. We haven't seen them since."

Rudy Snell told the orchard foreman that he lived in Albany, Oregon, and that his wife was sick, so he'd had to go home. Oregon State Police verified that Snell did live in Albany. Armed with a search warrant, they brought in criminalists from the Oregon State Police Crime Lab to process his vehicle. Snell didn't protest. Actually, he couldn't; he was in jail in Albany on drug charges.

While Jack Stolle was short and slight, Rudy Snell was a huge man who weighed more than 250 pounds.

Detective Don Danner flew to Oregon to interview Snell, who was very cooperative. He said he'd met Jack Stolle for the first time in early September, and they'd picked fruit together in Hood River off and on during the month. They had picked on the 26th and 27th, getting off about 3 P.M. on that Saturday.

"We never left the Hood River area Saturday or Sunday," he said.

That seemed to shoot down the Chelan County investigators' firm belief that they had found the killer or killers of Beverly Johnson and Patty Weidner. But they weren't ready to give up.

They weren't sure Rudy Snell was telling the truth, or even if he had his mental timetable right. He did remember that he and Jack Stolle had met two girls, but his description of them didn't sound at all like the two murder victims. "We drove over to Biggs Junction and spent the night, but we were back in Hood River before noon on Sunday. I worked on my car on Sunday afternoon, and we started picking again on Monday morning."

The orchard foreman, however, had said the men had come in on Monday only to get their paychecks. And he wasn't sure of the time.

Rudy Snell hadn't actually *seen* Jack Stolle, according to his story, at least, from before noon on Sunday, September 28 until sometime Monday. "Jack quit the orchard on Monday—he said his stomach hurt. He told me he might go to California or Wenatchee. I left him at the bus stop about eight Monday night, and I went home to Albany."

The results of the processing of Snell's car were startling. The state police criminalists found many dog hairs as they examined the contents of their vacuum cleaner bags. The hairs were gray or white. Snell explained that away easily enough; he owned a Samoyed, and the hairs were from his own dog. Hair comparisons rarely yield absolute results, even under a scanning electron microscope. They can only be deemed microscopically alike in class and characteristics.

Rudy Snell acknowledged that he had once picked apples in the Wenatchee area. "But that was seven years ago," he said, "and I haven't been back there since."

He willingly took a polygraph test and Oregon State Police experts said the results indicated he was telling the truth about not being in Washington State for years. Nor did his blood pressure, breathing rate, pulse, or galvanic skin response suggest that he had killed Beverly Johnson or Patty Weidner, and he clearly didn't know who had. He showed no deception at all during any questioning about the Chelan County murders.

That left Jack Stolle as the lone suspect. Even so, Stolle would have to have adhered to a very tight schedule if he *had* killed the young women. It was about 170 miles from Hood River to the murder site. If Snell was remembering accurately, Stolle had been out of his sight from sometime Sunday morning until sometime Monday. Sunday was the 28th of September, the date Dr. Bonafaci believed the women had died. Stolle would have had to have caught a good hitch that took him all the way to Chelan. It was possible that he knew about the shack and had gone there to sleep Sunday night, hoping to go to the Minelli farm in the morning to ask for one more chance to work for them. But he would have found Beverly and Patty asleep in his secret camp. . . .

The detectives found the motel in Biggs Junction where Stolle had stayed Wednesday and Thursday nights, September 24 and 25, paying for his stay with stolen checks. He checked out the morning of the 26th but he'd picked apples nearby that day and the next.

One thought kept coming back to the Chelan County investigators. It had to be more than mere coincidence that Jack Stolle had been within 15 miles of where Beverly and Patty caught their ride north on September 24. It *was* quite possible that he had spotted them and stopped to talk as they waited for a ride. Nobody knew how long they had stood there before they met Jeff Hunt and the man who gave them a ride to Mineral Springs.

Hunt had told the detectives that the women weren't friendly until he brought up the subject of finding orchard jobs. Jack Stolle was also an old hand at apple picking, and he might well have told Beverly and Patty about the Minelli farm and the shack.

The thought of two pretty girls alone out there so far from civilization could well have festered and churned in Stolle's mind over the next three days, enough to draw him back to his old stomping grounds.

Stolle's stories to the detectives were a strange interweaving of sexual fantasy and fact, and it was difficult to tell where one stopped and the other began. And, unlike Rudy Snell, Jack Stolle "blew ink all over the walls" when he took a lie detector test. His responses were so emotional and chaotic that it was difficult to interpret the tracings on the polygraph. That, combined with his knowledge about details of the girls' murder and the shack where it happened, was enough for the Chelan County Prosecutor to charge him with murder. He was scheduled to go on trial in March 1976.

Given Stolle's ramblings, the public defender who represented him was inclined to offer a plea of innocent by reason of insanity. However, he first decided to ask for another lie detector test. Washington State's legendary polygraph expert, Dewey Gillespie, of the Seattle Police Department, agreed to administer it. Both the prosecution and defense stipulated that the results could be used in Stolle's trial.

The results of the second test hit like a bombshell. Stolle passed. Where only a few months before he had seemed to have extensive guilty knowledge of the victims' deaths, Jack Stolle now barely reacted to Gillespie's questions.

Lie detector tests aren't foolproof. Some subjects learn to control even their autonomic body responses, keeping their blood pressure and pulse steady. Other subjects cannot perceive right from wrong, and questions evoke neither fear nor remorse. And some subjects are simply insane, impervious to the mysterious machine with its moving stylus.

Jack Stolle seemed psychotic, a man bent on self-destruction. His history was appalling. Born in California, Stolle was one of nine children. His first trouble with the law came when he was fourteen. He was incarcerated and then paroled on four different occasions by youth authorities. Early on he was deeply involved in drugs and had been diagnosed in California as suffering from schizophrenia. His rap sheet eventually listed burglary, forgery, assault, vagrancy, parole violation, grand theft, possession of marijuana, and auto theft.

He married when he was twenty-five and fathered two children, but soon left his responsibilities behind him.

Jack Stolle had been overtly suicidal for most of his adult life. Two years before the double murder of the young women from Oregon, he tried to commit suicide with a razor blade he'd hidden under his tongue while in jail. When taken to a doctor, he attempted to hide a scalpel in his bandages. At other times he had swallowed hypodermic needles and had to be operated on to remove them.

In jail in Chelan County, Stolle slashed his wrists with another razor blade he'd managed to secrete on his person. Sent to Eastern State Hospital to determine if he was fit to stand trial for Patty's and Beverly's murders, he had complained of abdominal pain, and admitted that he'd swallowed glass and metal. Five days later, he hung himself with a leather strap, but he was found quickly and jailers were able to get him breathing again.

Two days after that, Stolle broke the toilet in his cell and threatened to slash his wrists with the sharp porcelain edge if anyone came close to him. He had to be coaxed out by jailers. He hadn't cut his wrists, but he'd severed a tendon in his hand and had to be operated on and wear a cast on his wrist and hand. A day later, he managed to pry the cast off and reopen the incision. As he was rushed back to the hospital, he attempted to jump out of the car.

He was either insane or trying very hard to make authorities believe he was. In the end, the threat of a murder trial was moot. Because he had passed the second lie detector test, the Chelan County Prosecuting Attorney decided not to pursue the murder charges against Stolle. He had enough existing forgery charges hanging over him to send him to prison as it was, and they could always bring murder charges later.

It was a decision that Stolle would not accept. He kept up a lively correspondence with Chelan County detectives, court officials, and even the media. He wanted to confess to the murders of Beverly Johnson and Patty Weidner. He insisted that he was guilty and that he should pay for his crimes.

Detective Jerry Monroe made several trips to the Washington State Penitentiary in Walla Walla to talk to Stolle. He concluded that Stolle had either studied the case so meticulously that he knew as much about it as the investigators did, or he had been there on that night in September 1975. Indeed, he knew details that had never been published in any media coverage about the young women's deaths.

The problem, however, was that Stolle always veered away when Monroe began to bore in, getting too close for the suspect's comfort. It may well be that Jack Stolle knew so much about the horrifying scene at the forlorn shelter off Old Downey Road because he had been there and had committed the senseless murders. It may be that he knew the real killer and had gotten the details from him.

After a while, Stolle "cried wolf" too many times. The detectives backed away to give him time to think about it, hoping he would finally tell them the whole truth. Maybe that was what he wanted, after all.

But no one will ever be able to question him now. Jack Stolle died in prison at Walla Walla on October 2, 2001, apparently of natural causes. He was sixty years old.

Mike Harum is the current sheriff of Chelan County, and some twenty-eight years after Beverly Johnson and Patty Weidner were murdered, there may still be a definitive resolution to the mystery of their deaths. In conjunction with several other law enforcement departments, Harum has put together a cold-case squad to study victims who have been lost in the mists of time, who have never had justice done in their cases. With the tremendous advances in forensic science, cold-case investigations now have tools like DNA, AFIS (Automated Fingerprint Identification System), and advanced hair and fiber identification, all of which are successfully helping close decades-old unsolved cases once and for all.

Sometimes, when I am signing books or lecturing, I meet women who knew Bev and Patty on the Oregon coast. They still ask me about their lost friends, but today these women are not in their early twenties. They are in their fifties—just as Bev and Patty would be, had they not made a fatal misjudgment: trusting the wrong man.

Dead and on Tape

Readers often ask me which case I have written about has made the biggest impression on me, and that is virtually impossible to answer. Even so, I think that the stories that stand out most in my mind are the very few where I knew the killer or the victim before the crimes occurred. In thirty years as a crime reporter, I have met literally thousands of police officers and written about hundreds of killers. Sometimes the lines blur. Of course, I will never forget the Ted Bundy case. But there was another homicide case that involved someone I thought I knew well, a case that rocked the Seattle Police Department to its foundations, bringing with it one of the most publicized trials in Washington State history.

When I was a stringer for True Detective Magazine, the detective who was critically injured in the following case was a friend. He was always very cooperative in giving me photographs to accompany my early fact-detective articles. I was in my thirties at the time, divorced less than a year, and during the years that this detective was single, I occasionally had lunch or dinner with him. He was polite and quite handsome, a popular officer in his department, and he worked on many of the cases I wrote about. He was quiet, even a little moody at times. But he was definitely one of the good guys.

31

Never in a million years would I have expected to listen to him testify, defending himself in a packed courtroom, or that I would be writing about him.

I remember telling him that I would be as fair as I could be, and I believe I was. Indeed, I ran into him one night after the trial was over and he thanked me for showing all sides of this baffling case.

November 20, 1973, was a Tuesday, and it rained all day and all night, standard for Seattle in November. The wind howled and the streets were dark well before supper time. Seattle is so far north that, in November, the sun begins to sink toward the horizon shortly after three.

Most Seattle Police Department Crimes Against Persons detectives worked from 7:45 A.M. to 3:45 P.M., with only a sergeant and four investigators on duty from 3:45 to 11:45 P.M. After midnight, the lights would be turned out on the fifth floor of the Public Safety Building and if an emergency came up, the on-call detectives would respond from their homes. Weekend nights and full moons seemed to spawn the most violent crimes, so a moonless, stormy Tuesday night should have meant a calm interval in the Homicide Unit.

Each quintet of detectives worked the night shift every third month, and Homicide Sergeant Bruce Edmonds's crew was on during November: George Marberg, Jesse Cook, Al Gerdes, and Bernie Miller. They usually ate dinner at one of the restaurants where cops are a familiar sight; the food was good and the service quick, in case they got a call. Ironically, that night they didn't expect much to happen.

Edmonds was in his car heading back to the Public

Safety Building when he got the worst call any police officer can hear: "Officer down in alley at Boren and Pike. Officer down."

Edmonds immediately notified his crew and asked them to meet him at the location given. Homicide detectives are only rarely the first to arrive at any crime scene. Uniformed officers in patrol cars invariably handle the initial response to a call for help. When the call concerns one of their own, every unit in their sector is on the scene in minutes.

In this case, Patrol Officers Milton McClelland and Richard Duval were working in the 2-George-1 sector of Seattle. In the mid-seventies, "First Hill," the area around Boren and Pike, was partially commercial, with short blocks occupied by small businesses and shops, running east up the steep hills of Pike and Madison. Along Boren, there were a few banks and a number of large old houses that had long since been chopped up to make low-rent apartments. The patrol partners were used to being summoned to break up fights or quiet drunks who lived in the drab rooms left over from Seattle's glory days when millionaires outdid themselves building mansions.

"Pill Hill" was nearby, with its plethora of hospitals and clinics.

The area was in transition; by the year 2000, most of the aging mansions were gone and expensive condominiums and hotels had begun to dominate the skyline. But on November 20, 1974, the skyline was hidden in the dark, rainswept night and even the lights of the ferry boats traversing Elliott Bay to the west were fuzzy and muted.

It was a few minutes after 6 P.M. when a woman called the police radio's emergency number. "One of your detectives has been shot," she blurted.

"Where did this happen, ma'am?" the operator responded in the calm, even voice he'd been trained to use, even though his heart lurched.

"In an alley—first one south of Pike, off Boren." And then she hung up.

McClelland and Duval raced to the location, and pulled into a business parking lot between an older hotel and the detox center where they'd often brought alcoholics. They could make out the silhouettes of what appeared to be three people leaning against a low wall. Two of them seemed to be supporting the third. And, as the patrol car's headlights swept over the parking lot, the officers caught a glimpse of a fourth person, who lay on his back in the pounding rain.

Duval hurried to the fallen body with great apprehension, worried that he was going to recognize a fellow officer. "Is this our man?" he called out to the trio standing nearby.

He looked down at the man and knew that he had to be dead. He had a gaping hole in the middle of his forehead and the puddle beneath him was not water, but blood. To his relief, Duval didn't recognize him.

"Your guy's over here," someone yelled. "He's hurt bad."

Duval whirled and this time he did recognize someone. It was Burglary Detective Stan Tappan,* a familiar and popular investigator who worked out of the Burglary Unit in the downtown precinct. Tappan was bleeding profusely from wounds to both his left hand and his abdomen, but he had somehow managed to stay on his feet with the help of passersby.

Patrol Officers Alan Smalley and Leonard Hayes were only thirty seconds behind the first officers, and Stan Tappan lurched over to them, holding his left hand in his right, trying in vain to stop the bleeding.

"Get me to a hospital," he gasped. "I've lost a lot of blood."

They didn't stop to ask questions but helped Tappan into the backseat of their patrol car, and sped away, headed for Virginia Mason Hospital, which, fortunately, was only a few blocks away. As Smalley drove, Hayes knelt backward in the passenger seat and applied pressure to Tappan's injured hand.

"It looked as if his hand had exploded," he recalled later. "There was a through-and-through wound at close range. His skin was blackened and torn very badly. It seemed to me that his hand was mutilated."

At the hospital, emergency room personnel helped Stan Tappan remove his clothing and discovered another terrible-looking wound. It too was a through-and-through bullet wound. It looked like a contact wound, with gunpowder burns and debris visible. The skin around this injury was discolored in a five-inch circle of dark purple bruising.

Alan Smalley and Leonard Hayes stayed with Stan Tappan as he waited for X-ray results. They could see he was in great pain, and that his left hand "looked like raw meat." But he kept his jaw clenched to stop his teeth from chattering. His police training helped him to stay focused and rational, and he was able to answer their questions. They didn't want to hammer him, but they knew he might have critical internal injuries; they had to try to find out what had happened while he was still conscious.

Stan Tappan told them he'd been working at his second job as a security officer for a mortgage company that evening. There were two parking lots connected to the company. The one directly in front of the entrance was for customers, while employees parked in the side lot off the alley. The mortgage company had considerable cash on hand, and female employees were hesitant to walk to their cars in the dark alley lot during the winter months, so having an armed security guard relieved their anxiety considerably.

Scores of local law enforcement officers worked off-duty jobs at banks, stores, and athletic events. The bank jobs could be dangerous, and indeed a Seattle detective had been fatally shot by a bank robber only a few years earlier.

Stan Tappan said he'd worked in the Burglary Unit that day until his shift was over at 3:45. When he walked out of the police garage, he saw that it was raining fiercely, and he had gone back to his locker to give a friend an extra raincoat he'd stored there. That delayed his leaving the Public Safety Building by ten minutes. He wasn't due at his second job until 4:30, so he had stopped for a beer at a restaurant that was kitty-corner from headquarters, a spot popular with off-duty cops. Then he had walked several blocks up the Cherry Street hill to where he'd parked his pickup truck, and driven to the mortgage company.

Everything had gone normally, Tappan said, until a man named Nick Kyreacos had shown up in the alley looking for him. Stan Tappan said he knew Kyreacos because he'd been the arresting officer when Kyreacos was charged with credit-card theft. Bizarrely, the man whose card was stolen had been murdered only a few weeks after his arrest. Aware of that, Tappan said he'd been afraid for his *own* safety when he spotted Kyreacos in the alley.

There had been a struggle, gunfire, and now Kyreacos was dead and Stan Tappan was badly wounded. Good cops hate to have to fire their guns. It's a familiar saying in law enforcement that "A cop who has to fire his gun is usually wounded more than his target." When he is forced to kill someone, an officer almost always suffers from prolonged post-traumatic stress disorder.

* * *

Back at the scene, Emergency Medical Technician George Barnes walked toward the supine body and leaned over, placing the tips of his fingers against the carotid artery at the side of Kyreacos's neck. There was no pulse. Despite the near-contact wound in the center of Kyreacos's forehead, Barnes inserted a plastic airway into his mouth and tried to force air into his lungs with a bellows-like device. There was no response other than the mechanical expansion of his chest.

Not yet ready to give up, Barnes ripped open the man's jacket, preparing to give him a closed chest massage. But as he did this, he saw a gunshot wound in his chest, too close to his heart and other vital organs for him to have survived. It was far too late for even heroic measures to bring the man back.

John Lombardini and Robert Ryan, investigators for the King County Medical Examiner's office, were notified that they could pick up the body as soon as the homicide team was through working the crime scene.

Detective Sergeant Bruce Edmonds and his crew had had no difficulty finding the alley where one man lay dead. Blue lights cast their whirling shadows over the drenched black asphalt, and the street was blocked off by patrol cars.

They were shocked to learn that Stan Tappan was the detective who'd been rushed to the hospital. He was not only a fellow officer, Tappan was also a good friend to many homicide detectives. The Burglary Unit was located right next to Homicide and Robbery, and investigators who worked in those units saw each other every day. Stan went elk hunting east of the mountains with several homicide detectives, and usually had a drink after work with them. He was an expert photographer and he often took pictures at homicide crime scenes.

Stan Tappan was a cop's cop who loved his job. He

was thirty-two, handsome, 6 feet 1 inch, weighing close to 210 pounds.

Born in New Mexico, Tappan, whose family included five siblings, had moved to Roseburg in southern Oregon when he was a child and he graduated from high school there in 1959. He worked as a logger for a few months and then enlisted in the navy. It was a wise decision for him, and he did extremely well in the service. Tappan mastered two skills that would be especially important in law enforcement, and he'd wanted to be a cop as far back as he could remember.

First, Stan Tappan became a navy diver, trained to swim under cover of darkness on reconnaissance missions. He was fearless in the water, at home as any fish. Like most navy divers, he got a tattoo, one that led into a little deliberately shocking joke he liked to play—a guaranteed conversation stopper.

"Would you believe," he would say with a sly grin, "that my cock goes down to my ankle?" As faces reddened and people stuttered, Stan would slowly pull up his pant leg to reveal the tattoo of a rooster on his ankle. And then he would explain, "They say that King Neptune protects all creatures who are helpless in the water, and a rooster is about as helpless in the water as anything you can think of."

Stan Tappan stayed in the service for four years, and was stationed in Florida, Saipan, and Japan. He had a chestful of overseas ribbons, a good conduct medal, and an honorable discharge when he was mustered out just before Christmas, 1963. He went back to logging for a while and then joined the North Bend, Oregon, Fire Department. After working as a firefighter for eighteen months, he still wanted to be a cop. He passed the civil service test for the Springfield, Oregon, Police Department and hired on. He was twenty-four years old, and he knew that *this* was the profession where he belonged.

Two years later, Stan Tappan joined the Seattle Police Department. Like all new hires, he worked in a two-man patrol car, assigned to Seattle's bustling Asian neighborhood. Rated an expert marksman on the police firing range, he never had to draw his gun on anyone for three years. On the occasion when he finally did, he and his partner were in hot pursuit of a stolen car. His partner was driving and shouted to Stan to "Take a shot!" as the high-powered Buick pulled away from them toward the freeway. Stan's shot hit the left front tire of the Buick and it went into a sideways skid and stopped.

Stan Tappan moved up through the department when his expertise with a camera became apparent. He was transferred to the crime lab and he often accompanied the lab director, criminalist Dr. George Ishii, to homicide investigations. It was vital to memorialize the crime scenes, as grotesque as some of them were, and Tappan's clear photographs were a tremendous help to detectives in their investigations and in preparation for trial.

There were even times when Stan was called upon to take pictures in the waters of Lake Washington, Lake Union, Green Lake, or Elliott Bay, where corpses were often discovered floating. He was, perhaps, the only "swimming photographer" in America working for a police department.

Stan Tappan took photographs outside the police department too: some portraits and nature scenes, some pin-ups, and even nude shots of women. He was working toward his associate's degree in police science and at the time he was shot, he was only three hours short of a diploma. He himself taught classes in crime-scene photography at several community colleges.

Finally, after six years on the Seattle Police force, Stan Tappan realized his fondest dream: he was appointed to the Burglary Unit as a detective. Anyone who knew him felt he was driven by two consuming passions: his career and his two small children, who lived with one of his former wives in Oregon. Every two weeks, he drove 500 miles to see them, and he never missed a visit.

For all of his success on the job, Stan Tappan hadn't had much luck with women. His relationships had been stormy and short-lived. He was in his fourth marriage when he was shot, although he had married one wife twice—for the sake of their children. He held high hopes for his current marriage, but Stan had a wandering eye and he was so good-looking that women flirted with him, and he flirted back. That wasn't unusual for a cop; a lot of women are police groupies, drawn to the uniform.

Now Stan Tappan had been admitted to Virginia Mason Hospital for observation. If his hand was permanently crippled, it would mean the end of his days as a working cop. His X-rays hadn't shown any internal injuries, but he *was* in a great deal of pain from his hand and stomach wounds.

There was no rush to move the man who lay in the parking lot. He would have died instantly when Tappan fired at him in self-defense. The cops knew who he was—twenty-six-year-old Nicholas Kyrcacos. Tappan had been correct in his identification of the victim.

Nicholas George Kyreacos was no stranger to the police, but he wasn't a big-time felon either. Detectives had considered him a fringe person, a penny-ante thief. He was a short man who was handsome in a pouty, soft way. Born on May 25, 1947, Kyreacos worked as a waiter at one of Seattle's finest restaurants. Detectives figured that wasn't his *only* occupation, however—more likely, that was his only legal occupation.

When Kyreacos was fifteen, he was charged as a juvenile for extortion and burglary and released to his parents. Two years later, he was picked up for illegal discharge of a firearm and sent to the Youth Service Center, Seattle's juvenile "jail." Almost as soon as he was released, he was charged with driving a motor vehicle without permission. As an adult, his crimes were more serious: second-degree burglary, car theft, and robbery. He drew a fifteen-year sentence on the burglary and ten years for car theft. He actually served a fraction of that.

When he was released from prison, Nick Kyreacos got a job as a waiter in the popular upscale restaurant, a job he held for several years. He usually worked in the cocktail lounge from 11 A.M. to 3 P.M., but sometimes he worked in the dining room. He got great tips and was considered a good employee, although he was sometimes prone to outbursts of temper. He had married an attractive blond woman who was quite a bit older than he was, and seemed to get along with her teenage children.

During the summer of 1975, however, Nick ran into trouble with the law. He had been picked up and charged with car prowling on July 23, and three months later Stan Tappan and his partner from the Burglary Unit arrested Kyreacos on the credit-card theft. The card belonged to Kyreacos's fellow waiter, fifty-three-year-old Branko Ellich. Ellich said that his card had been stolen from his home in July during a burglary.

These crimes still sounded like fairly small-time offenses. As far as anyone knew, Stan Tappan had never met Nick Kyreacos until the moment in October when he arrested him in the restaurant where both he and the burglary victim worked. Kyreacos had bailed out of jail, and his trial date had been set for early November.

But Nick Kyreacos's criminal history took on a more ominous tone on the night of November 10. Branko Ellich was standing on his own front porch, fitting his key into his front door, when someone shot him in the head. He died before he could tell anyone who might have shot him.

On the surface, detectives had no difficulty connecting Kyreacos to Ellich, but why would Nick have shot Ellich over something as minor as credit-card theft? Killing Ellich might have taken away the complaining witness, but the trial would have gone ahead anyway; burglary detectives had a paper trail linking Nick to Branko Ellich's credit cards.

The day before the shooting in the alley, homicide detectives Dick Reed and Don Strunk were stymied in their probe into Ellich's murder. They had no witnesses and virtually no physical evidence. The *only* person who might have wanted to silence Ellich was Nick Kyreacos. From the information they had gathered so far, they concluded that something had been frightening Kyrcacos. Maybe it was that he *was* Ellich's killer. Reed and Strunk met with Nick in their offices. He was polite and cooperative but insisted he had no idea who had shot his fellow waiter. His trial on the credit-card charges had been postponed until November 27. He was somewhat concerned about that, but he seemed far more nervous at the mention of the Ellich homicide.

When Dick Reed heard that Nick Kyreacos had been shot by Stan Tappan, he was dumbfounded. Stan was a good friend of his, a fellow elk hunter, a guy he often had coffee with. Reed, who had been in the Homicide Unit for almost fifteen years, simply could not make the connection that might explain why the two men had been in the dark alley.

Stan Tappan had also been frightened by the Ellich homicide. The night of the incident, he'd told officers Smalley and Hayes that he'd been alarmed to see Kyreacos show up in the alley beside the mortgage company.

"He said he was looking for me," Tappan recalled. Tappan said he'd been checking the parking lot after walking an employee out to her car when he spotted Kyreacos. "I chased him and put him up against a building."

"Did you frisk him?" Smalley asked.

Tappan shook his head. "I heard something metal fall on the pavement while I was chasing him and I figured he'd lost his gun—if he had one—and was unarmed.

"And then," Tappan said, "Nick reached into the waistband of his trousers and pulled out what looked like a .45. We struggled to get control of that gun, and then I pulled out my service revolver."

That would have been a .38 caliber police-issue revolver.

During the struggle, both men had been shot. Stan Tappan said he saw Kyreacos lying on the ground, while he himself had managed to stagger over to a courier who had just pulled into the mortgage lot and beg her to call the police.

After Tappan was taken to a private hospital room, Smalley and Hayes bagged his bloodstained clothing into evidence. Back at the shooting scene, Patrolman Richard Duval had chalked carefully around every piece of physical evidence that remained as he'd waited for the paramedics to respond and pronounce the shooting victim officially dead. He hoped the rain wouldn't wash the bright lines away.

Duval had found a .45 caliber semiautomatic with a spare clip and several empty casings near the body. There was also a .38 caliber revolver with a two-inch barrel lying just under the dead man's right armpit. Several segments of an expandable metal watchband were scattered on the pavement.

Duval looked twice at something in the victim's right hand to be sure he was seeing correctly. When he did, he recognized a very small piece of physical evidence that would take on gargantuan proportions in the months to come.

Clenched tightly between the dead man's index and middle fingers was a half-burned cigarette. It looked as if he'd been caught unaware by the gunfire that had ended his life. Certainly, if he'd seen a weapon, he would have dropped his cigarette.

The homicide crew working the scene thought they knew what had happened, but homicide detectives never take anything at face value. One of their own had come so close to being killed, and it looked at first as if a small-time punk had shot him, ending up dead because he'd taken on one of the best sharpshooters in the department.

Detective George Marberg placed each gun in an individual evidence bag. He did the same with the spent bullets and casings, marking the bags with the date and his initials. He and Jesse Cook used tweezers to retrieve fibers from the fenders of Stan Tappan's truck, dropping the tiny fragments into cardboard boxes. They did the same with the cigarette from Nick Kyreacos's hand. It was a Marlboro 100, smoked down to two-and-a-half inches.

Al Gerdes photographed the body where it lay, several feet in front of Tappan's truck. His legs pointed toward the truck's grill, his head toward the detox center on the other side of the alley. His arms were stretched out like wings.

The investigators could see where their fellow detective had bled too, the rain now thinning the scarlet stains. Many of them had worked with Stan Tappan for more than three years, while *he* had been the investigator taking the pictures. They couldn't allow themselves the luxury of emotion at this point. They had to gather as much physical evidence as they could before the pounding rain washed it all away.

There was such a massive police presence at the shooting scene that no one noticed a teenage boy who ran past an X-rated theater on the corner, up Pike Street, and into the alley. He stopped, shocked, as he saw the blue lights spinning crazily atop more squad cars than he could count and the circle of a half-dozen cops who had formed a phalanx to shut out onlookers.

Slipping up to them, the teenager approached officers Robert Vanderway and Gary Allenby. "I know that guy on the ground," he gasped. "It's Nick Kyreacos. I was with him. See that broken walkie-talkie? That's his. I've got one too. I was supposed to back him up."

The boy was obviously scared to death and very emotional. He seemed on the verge of hysteria and wasn't making a lot of sense. The officers led him over to a police car until detectives could question him. In the meantime, he huddled in the squad car, shivering. It would take a while to sort out any real witnesses from the curious gawkers drawn by the lights and sirens.

Another passerby walked up to Officer David Bruckbauer and held out a knife. "Hey, man," he said, "I found this shiv out on the sidewalk on Pike Street. I was going to keep it, but then I saw all the cop cars and I figured it might be something important."

It might well be. They slipped the knife into an evidence bag, and took the man's name so detectives could call him.

Stan Tappan said he'd heard something metal clatter to

the pavement as he pursued Kyreacos. Stan's gun was a police issue .38 revolver, and the investigators figured that the .45 had belonged to the dead man.

Finally, word reached those at the shooting site that Tappan was in serious condition, but that doctors were cautiously predicting that his hand had not suffered nerve damage, nor would he lose any fingers. His abdominal wound wasn't nearly as bad as it had looked; it was only a flesh wound and, miraculously, none of his internal organs were damaged.

Worried police officers had gathered at Virginia Mason Hospital to find out how Stan Tappan was doing. Sudden death was always a possibility for any cop, and that didn't change when they became detectives. Dick Reed, who was investigating Branko Ellich's murder, was very concerned about Stan Tappan. They'd hunted together in eastern Washington only a month before. The doctors assured those in the waiting room that, although he was in a great deal of pain, Stan Tappan was going to live.

Now, the homicide nightshift crew spread out to backtrack on Nicholas Kyreacos. They learned that he had worked his usual shift at the restaurant's cocktail lounge from 11 A.M. until 3 P.M. Asked if anything unusual had happened that day, the receptionist told the detectives that Nick had received a phone call from a woman at about 2:40 P.M. "He was in the kitchen and he picked up the phone there. The call lasted about five minutes—and I recognized the woman's voice as the person who had called him the day before too."

Something about the call had upset Kyreacos. "He came out to the front desk and he was really pale and looked shaken," the receptionist continued. "I asked him what was wrong—but he wouldn't tell me. He kind of ran into the cocktail lounge and he came back with Florrie*—she's a cocktail waitress and they're close friends. And then she stood by while he made a call from the public phone in the lobby."

In talking with Florrie Pappadopolis,* Bruce Edmonds's detectives learned that the woman on the phone had asked Nick to meet her in the alley off Boren between 6 and 6:15 that night. "She told him something that scared him," Florrie said. "I don't know all the details, but she said that she had things to tell him about Branko Ellich's murder."

Of course, the petite waitress said, Nick knew Branko. They were both waiters in the restaurant, but she didn't know how close they were or what business they might have together.

"Tell us about Nick," George Marberg said.

"Well, he was very impulsive and dramatic. He could be irritable in a childish way, like he might throw down a dish or a tray if something went wrong. He was so upset today that I told him not to go meet the woman. I said, 'I hope you're not stupid enough to take any kind of a weapon with you.'

"And Nick promised he wouldn't. But then he said, 'I won't go unprepared either.' I have no idea what he meant by that."

The case was becoming murkier. Despite his claim, it seemed that Nick Kyreacos had known something about Ellich's murder. He'd been to see Dick Reed and Don Strunk in their offices only the day before. Now, Florrie Pappadopolis said that she thought Nick had called his attorney before he went to meet the woman in the alley.

He had, and he had also called Detective Don Strunk. Strunk remembered that the phone call had come in about 3:45 P.M.—just as he was leaving the office at the end of his shift. Kyreacos said his lawyer had told him not to meet with a stranger in an alley, and Strunk told him that was good advice. He and Dick Reed were investigating the Ellich killing, and Kyreacos should stay out of it.

As Don Strunk was talking with Nick Kyreacos, Stan Tappan was walking up the Cherry Street hill to get in his truck and go to work at the mortgage company. He and Kyreacos were at least a dozen miles apart, two men on different errands.

Dick Reed questioned the witnesses who had come forward. A clerk in a Ballard area radio and electronic store remembered Kyreacos well. He had rushed in about 4:30 P.M. that Tuesday. Although there were several customers waiting in line, he pushed his way to the head of the line. He told the clerk he was looking for a small tape recorder. Then he picked out a unit about four by seven inches, tested it, and slipped it into his coat pocket, asking, "If I don't like it, could I return it later?"

"I told him 'Yes, until seven,' " the clerk told Dick Reed.

Next, Reed talked to the teenage boy who had appeared at the shooting scene, claiming that he knew Nick Kyreacos. He was calmer now, but still seemed frightened.

"You knew Nick Kyreacos?" Reed asked.

"Yeah—he lived in my neighborhood. He called me about 5:30 Tuesday afternoon and told me he needed 'a favor.' "

The boy recalled the odd conversation he'd had with the man who was dead now. "He said, 'Look kid, I've got to meet this woman in an alley downtown. It's got something to do with a guy I knew who got murdered.' He needed me to go along—but all I had to do was be a witness."

"How can I be a witness if I don't know anything about it?" the teenager had asked warily.

"You don't even have to be right there. I've got walkie-talkies," Kyreacos had told him.

"Why does this woman want to see you?"

"I've got some theories on that," Kyreacos had said excitedly. "Either she really wants to give me some information about Branko or maybe she's some kind of relative of his and she wants to set me up—or have the police set me up. Maybe she's going to blackmail me."

"That sounds dangerous," the boy recalled saying. "I wouldn't go if I were you."

"Nahh," Nick had said. "I've got this knife and this pistol—it's a starter's pistol but it looks real. I'll scare him with it."

The kid told Dick Reed he had wondered why Nick was talking about a *man* when he'd said before that it was a woman he was meeting.

Nick and the kid had driven through the rain to downtown Seattle; as they neared the alley at Pike and Boren, Nick pulled over to a small grocery store and said he had to make a phone call. "I gotta call in to work to be sure they don't need me for the night shift," he'd explained to the boy.

As Nick grabbed his coat, the teenager had seen the tape recorder under it. Apparently, they were going to use that as well as the walkie-talkies. Nick said something into it, and then played it back—to be sure it had recorded. It had. He slipped the tape recorder under his lavender shirt, tucking it a little behind and to the left side of his body. He'd clipped a small, round $1.98 mike to the collar of his tee-shirt, and then put his bulky, fleece-lined jacket on. The tape recorder was completely hidden.

Surprisingly, Nick Kyreacos hadn't seemed too apprehensive, but he'd warned the boy, "If anything happens, you just call the police and then drive my car home and tell my wife."

"What's going to happen?"

"Just do what I say," Nick had said.

It was almost right at 6 P.M. as he told this witness to stay behind the Cadillac dealership so he would be out of sight. Although the battery-operated walkie-talkies had worked earlier, the teenager wasn't able to get a response from Nick as he strode toward the dealership. Nick was still close enough to hear a shout so the boy said he'd called out, "Nick! Nick! I can't hear nothing!"

But Kyreacos kept on walking, and the boy paced behind the building as he had been told. A short time later, he heard sounds like a car backfiring. "I thought that was what it was," he said. "We were pretty close to the freeway entrance on Pike."

Back in the days of film noir, there were a number of detective movies that were filmed from the viewpoint of a man about to die. In 1946, there was even an eerie imaginative movie starring Robert Montgomery called *The Lady in the Lake* in which the camera was focused as if it were, indeed, the eyes of the main character.

On the night of November 20, the real story would be played out through the *voice* of a dead man and the *ears* of those who ministered to him.

When the medical examiner's investigators Lombardini and Ryan wheeled the gurney carrying Nick Kyreacos's body into the morgue—at the time a shadowy edifice located on Queen Anne Hill—they went about what seemed a routine procedure.

It was anything but.

On the morgue scale, the body weighed 170 pounds and measured 5 feet 6 inches. As Nick Kyreacos's clothing was removed, a battered and spent slug tumbled out. The investigators were quite sure that it was the .45 bullet that had pierced his forehead, going through his brain and exiting four inches behind his right ear. Finally it had become entangled in his jacket. They also found a small black pistol, loaded with blanks, in his pants pocket.

But that wasn't the most startling thing they found. Medical examiners occasionally discover all manner of secrets that the suddenly dead can no longer hide—men wearing women's underwear, men *and* women who have lived as the opposite sex, thick rolls of money secreted in shoes, socks and belts, wigs, glass eyes, penile implants, foreign objects inserted in the body during kinky sex acts. Fortunately, the dead can no longer be embarrassed and secrets discovered in the morgue are kept there.

Now, Lombardini and Ryan were amazed to see that the shooting victim had a tape recorder nestled in the small of his back. There was a wire, almost shredded now, leading to a dented round microphone clipped to Nick Kyreacos's tee-shirt. Recording devices were bulky and awkward three decades ago; the "state of the art" then was far from the minuscule mikes and recorders available today. This tape recorder was the size of a hardcover book and not that easy to hide.

The M.E.'s investigators stared at it for a full minute, tempted to listen to the tape, and then Lombardini muttered, "The detectives at the shooting site probably have no idea about this. We need to tell them pronto—we can't take a chance of messing this up or breaking the tape."

They immediately notified Sergeant Bruce Edmonds and his men, who had returned to homicide headquarters. Even though it was very late, they were still working on the fifth floor of the Public Safety Building, sorting out the evidence they'd collected in the alley.

It was 2:40 A.M. when Edmonds and George Marberg arrived at the morgue. They tried to rewind the sixty-minute tape but, anticlimactically, found its four batteries were dead. The detectives rushed to an all-night drugstore and purchased new batteries, racing back to the medical examiner's office.

Finally, the four investigators—two from the morgue and two from the police department—watched as the tape rewound to its beginning. They pushed PLAY and held their breath, wondering if anything caught in the tape would be meaningful to the shooting investigation.

Detective George Marberg would eventually listen to the tape a dozen times. "It still sends chills up my spine," he remarked later.

The tape began with Nick Kyreacos identifying himself, his voice sounding upbeat and cheerful, as if he was enjoying whatever adventure he was about to undertake. He was talking to someone else, someone with a young male voice.

"We are now recording. Stay around the general area. I'll just talk a little bit. When I say 'Out,' don't talk anymore."

The tape caught sounds of traffic, car tires on wet pavement, horns honking far away, someone coughing. Kyreacos spoke again, "Can you hear me?"

There was no answer.

"Can you hear me?" There was still no response. It must have been at this point that the walkie-talkie signals between Kyreacos and the boy were blocked by buildings.

Kyreacos kept talking anyway, obviously intent upon commemorating what was happening, perhaps still trying to contact his witness. "I'm approaching—time by my watch is six nineteen. I don't see anything out of the ordinary. Girl coming down the street, going south. Waiting on the corner. Girl did not come down here.

"There appears to be an Indian woman coming down the street, wearing a raincoat. Walks very masculine. A little short lady. No one's approached. No one coming

53

near. I'm walking slowly up toward the alley now. Someone is peering at me from the hotel across the street from the car place. Man in orange coveralls coming up street. Car slowing down. No sign of anyone. Everything looks normal."

The tape counter read five and a half minutes. It sounded as if Nick Kyreacos wasn't sure *who* had summoned him to the alley but that he had powerful motivation to be where he was, suspicious and feeling the need for evidence of whatever might be said. It was almost as if he expected someone wearing a disguise—perhaps a man dressed as a woman?

"Walking in the upper part of the alley now," his voice continued, a new nervous tautness apparent.

Suddenly, another voice cut in. *"Hold it, Nick!"*

There were sounds of a chase, feet thudding and sliding, and heavy breathing. Kyreacos sounded surprised. "Hey! Cop chasing me. Stan Tappan—"

A shot rang out, a sharp crack on the tape. "Hold it!" a male voice called from some distance. And then the second male voice was closer to the tape recorder again. "OK, Nick—back around here."

Edmonds and Marberg exchanged glances. They recognized the new voice. It was Stan Tappan.

"What's the deal?" Kyreacos asked.

"You know what the deal is. I'll tell you one thing, baby. *You have . . . had it.*"

"You got a charge?"

"We'll get a charge."

"If you wanted me, why didn't you come and see me?"

"Because—I'll tell you why—"

Without warning, four or five shots sounded on the tape, and the men listening jumped as if a gun were firing right there in the morgue. Kyreacos's voice was no longer deep, but the high-pitched scream of a creature in agony.

"Don't!" he cried out. "Ahhhhh . . . Ahhhh . . . Ahhh! Don't! God! Tappan, don't. You're wrong, man. You're wrong. Don't. Please, don't—"

Five seconds ticked by. There was another shot, muffled. It sounded almost like a champagne cork popping.

The silence on the tape was palpable. No more screams. No more pleading from Kyreacos. And then there were two more shots, five seconds apart.

The tape ran on, recording emptiness. A minute. Two minutes. George Marberg looked at his watch, unconsciously timing the tape whirring without sound. None of them moved. Was it over?

No. There were more voices on the tape, but now it was as if the investigators were listening through the dead man's ears.

A different male voice spoke: "We've already called the police. This guy is dead. He got shot right in the top of the head. You don't think he's still *alive?* Don't touch him."

Sirens caterwauled through the night, growing closer and closer.

Another voice: "They're taking some guy to the hospital. Is an aid car coming?"

"One of *our* officers?" The policeman speaking sounded shocked.

"Yeah."

There was a new sound, air whooshing into the body's throat. And then a crackling, and they realized that it was paramedic George Barnes who had tried to "bag" the victim with his own breath and was now pulling Kyreacos's jacket open, brushing the microphone—all unaware.

"Yeah," Barnes's voice said to someone. "He's got one right in the chest."

A young officer's voice: "OK, Sarge—I got a .45 over here. The *fucker* is cocked and ready to go."

Sergeant: "Leave it right where it is."

Steadily, accurately, the mindless tape rolled on, recording shouts, sirens, police calls coming in to the squad cars blocking the shooting site. The man was dead, but the device on his body continued to record his surroundings until the hour of blank tape ran out and the batteries faded. It had gone with him to the morgue and then stopped.

Edmonds and Marberg were shocked at what they'd heard. Even as dozens of police officers still gathered at Virginia Mason to show support for Stan Tappan and his wife, displaying the camaraderie and concern that binds police officers, the two homicide detectives who had heard the damning tape knew that things were not at all what they seemed.

There was no question that Tappan knew Kyreacos better than he had said. Tappan had chased the waiter, and as much as they hated to accept it, it appeared that he had deliberately shot him. It was all there on tape. It would take ballistics tests and a lot more questioning to find out what the real connection had been between the two men.

Detective Sergeant Ivan Beeson assigned two of his day-crew—Don Strunk and Dick Reed—as the prime investigators in Stan Tappan's shooting of Nick Kyreacos. They had been afraid that this might happen. It wasn't a matter of a conflict of interest—they were much too professional for that—but neither had ever found the main suspect in an inexplicable murder to be an old friend. Don Strunk and Dick Reed listened to the tape and their faces went white. It was clear that Tappan didn't know that the whole shooting had been recorded, and they couldn't tell him so until they had taken his full statement.

According to Stan Tappan's first brief statement to the patrol officers, it was Kyreacos who brought the .45 to the alley. When Sergeant Beeson, Reed, and Strunk went to the hospital to talk with Tappan, he was recuperating from plastic surgery on his injured hand and assured them that he would be able to use it again, well enough to shoot a gun accurately.

They asked him to go back over the shooting, and Stan Tappan reiterated that it was Kyreacos who had had the .45. He said he had been forced to defend himself against a convicted criminal who had a lot more firepower than he did.

Only they knew that wasn't true. They had already talked to a detective who was once Tappan's patrol partner. Although he and Tappan had ridden as partners together for two years, the man was troubled. He told Dick Reed that Stan had been extremely apprehensive about Nick Kyreacos. "He said Nick threatened both him and Branko Ellich—and then Ellich was ambushed and shot. He said he was really afraid of Nick."

Apparently, Stan Tappan had seemed so afraid that he met his old partner in the police garage on November 13 and told him that Kyreacos was hanging around his off-duty job at the mortgage company, and he needed a gun more powerful than a .38.

"I loaned him a gun that used to belong to my brother—a .45. He said he'd give it back to me."

Frank Lee was the Seattle Police Department's ballistics expert. He attempted to find the history of the .45, but found it was virtually untraceable. All he could be sure of was that it was a government model 1911 semiautomatic pistol. The bullet casings found at the scene had been manufactured in 1931 and 1967. The .45 was clearly used as what police call a "drop gun," a weapon that can be deliberately left at a shooting scene to confuse an investigation. It cannot be traced either by manufacture or ownership.

Seattle police regulations at the time forbade personnel from carrying a weapon more powerful than a .38.

King County Medical Examiner Patrick Besant-Matthews performed the six-hour postmortem examination of Nick Kyreacos's body. Besant-Matthews once shocked a courtroom during a homicide trial when he explained that he had honed his knowledge of the damage done by different caliber guns by actually shooting at corpses, as well as pigs.

However he had learned, he was expert at identifying the etiology of gunshot wounds. Kyreacos had been shot many times. He had a through-and-through wound in his left forearm, a wound to the front of his chest caused by a bullet that entered near the left nipple, coursed through the third rib, and ended in his right lung.

"That was fired from above," Besant-Matthews commented, "and it would have been rapidly fatal unless he had immediate care."

The forehead wound had been instantly fatal, and Kyreacos could not have spoken a word after that. There was no question that both of the fatal wounds had been caused by the .45.

But Stan Tappan had said that the .45 belonged to Kyreacos—not to him. Dick Reed and Don Strunk visited Tappan again in his hospital room. He was glad to see them, but he looked a little disconcerted when their sergeant, Ivan Beeson, walked into the room behind them. The faces of all three were grim and they didn't respond to his welcoming smile.

The homicide investigators dreaded what they had to do next.

"Stan," Dick Reed said, "I hate to do this but I have to tell you that Kyreacos had a tape recorder on him. The whole shooting is on tape. We've listened to it."

It was clear from the look on Stan Tappan's face that he'd been caught completely off guard. He was, if anything, more shocked than his fellow detectives had been when they listened to Kyreacos's tape. He said nothing as he digested this information. Up until this moment, it had been his word against that of a man with a long reputation of breaking the law. Tappan had been a hero, a good cop who had suffered grievous wounds in a gun battle with a punk.

"You're under arrest, Stan," Reed said. "The charge is murder in the first degree. You have the right to—"

"I know. I know. I know that by heart."

Reed finished the Miranda warning anyway, and then put a handcuff on Tappan's uninjured right hand. He was transported at once to the infirmary at the King County jail in the upper floors of the courthouse. He was right across the street from his old office in the Burglary Unit of police headquarters, but his whole world had changed.

Dick Reed and several other homicide detectives went out for stiff drinks after their shift ended, but liquor didn't help the sick feeling they had. Arresting a fellow officer is a terrible thing to have to do—but Reed had had no choice.

Chief of Police George Tielsch dismissed Stan Tappan from the department. His career as a police officer was probably over, even if he should be acquitted of the charges against him.

In a case that was already complicated enough, the FBI entered for a time. Although it seemed ludicrous, Tappan's attorneys asserted that his civil rights had been violated. In Washington State, it is illegal to tape-record someone without his or her permission. If indeed Tappan had deliberately shot Nick Kyreacos and Kyreacos had recorded his own murder without informing Tappan that he was being taped, the defense team maintained, the former detective had been deprived of his civil rights.

Soon enough, that argument was tossed out, although the defense attorneys would bring it up again at trial. For Dick Reed and Don Strunk, the investigation was far from over. They sought anyone who might have been a witness to the shooting, *and* they looked for the mysterious woman who had twice called Kyreacos at the restaurant, the last time a few hours before he died.

They didn't find the woman, but they did find Arthur Glidden,* a young construction worker who had been on his way to attend classes at Seattle Community College shortly after six on the night of November 30. He had stopped for a red light at Pike and Boren streets and he'd glanced idly at two men on the sidewalk. Something about their body language caught his interest.

"The tall man in the dark raincoat looked like he was holding a gun on the small guy," Glidden told Reed and Strunk. "And then they disappeared into the alley. I was curious enough that I circled the block twice. The second time around, I heard gunshots. Now, I had to see what had happened and I circled back one more time. This time, I saw the guy in the dark raincoat kind of staggering or weaving out of the alley. I stopped my car then, and went over to some cops who had just arrived."

Glidden was haunted by the face of the small man. "He looked right at me when he was being led around the corner. I recognized him lying there on the ground."

The witness was something of a gun buff himself, and he said he owned both a .45 and a .38. He was positive that the tall man had been holding a .45, with a six-inch barrel against the short man's arm.

There was another eyewitness, an elderly woman who lived on the third floor of the apartment house that abutted the alley. "I was watching the six o'clock news," she recalled. "I thought the shots were on the news—and then I realized they were outside. I pulled my curtains back a little and peeked out. The man in the black raincoat had the smaller man's right arm in his left hand. There was some 'object' in his right hand too."

"Could you see what it was?" Reed asked.

"I'm not sure. I guess I looked away for a few moments, and then I heard more shots—maybe four or five. When I looked again, I saw the man in the raincoat limping into the parking lot at the mortgage company."

As they made their way door to door around the shooting site, the detective team found a number of witnesses who had heard the shots: the woman courier for the message company, the manager of the Cadillac dealership, and medical personnel from the detox center who had rushed out to help the wounded men. But none of them had actually viewed the scene during the few moments when shots were fired. They had only heard the gunfire echo in the alley.

Stan Tappan was a confirmed womanizer, and, despite his marriage, the investigation turned up a few dozen women who were close to him in one way or another. Some of them had posed for him for nude shots, some worked with him, and some had dated him before his most recent marriage. But Dick Reed and Don Strunk never located the mysterious woman who had lured Nick Kyreacos to his death. They realized that even the woman herself might not have known why she was calling him; she might only have been doing Stan a favor.

More likely, she had read about Stan's arrest, and didn't want to become involved in the case.

Stan Tappan's trial began four months after Kyreacos's death. He had lost close to thirty pounds in jail, and he strode past a circus of reporters, microphones, and television cameras with his eyes straight ahead and his jaw clenched tightly. Interest on the press bench was so intense that the sought-after location next to the prosecutor's table—designed to hold seven—often had a dozen reporters packed so closely together that we could barely take notes.

Spectators lined the marble hallways and overflowed the available seats. Court deputies allowed new onlookers in one at a time, only as others left.

Bill Lanning was the lead defense attorney. A deceptively folksy, garrulous man who had many friends in law enforcement, he could be as clever as a fox in cross-examination. Lanning was assisted by Bob Bryan. Senior Deputy King County Prosecutor Michael Ruark spoke for the State, assisted by Deputy Prosecutor Marco Magnano.

Everyone in the courtroom was there to hear "the tape," which had been held in a locked safe-deposit box in a Seattle bank. King County's Chief Criminal Deputy Prosecutor David Boerner and Seattle Police Homicide Lieutenant Patrick Murphy had taken it there together, and both of them had to be present for it to be removed. The defense wanted it excluded from the trial, arguing that it would be inflammatory if the jurors should hear it. They likened it to a "television set with the picture blacked out," hinting that Nick Kyreacos could have "pre-recorded" the tape, or edited it at the scene.

"There is a tremendous danger of convicting a man on a tape that can't tell us what it hears," Lanning and Bryan submitted.

Mike Ruark said the tape should be allowed to speak for itself. All the voices had been identified by credible witnesses and the chain of custody was impeccable. "This is not a vacuum situation," Ruark said. "We have presented witnesses who verify every step of that tape and what it is purported to have recorded."

The prosecution's theory about what happened on November 20 was that Stan Tappan had arranged for an unknown woman to lure Kyreacos to the dark alley where Tappan had waited with *two* fully-loaded guns: his police issue .38 and the untraceable "drop gun," the .45. Tappan had, they submitted, then accosted Kyreacos, chased him, and forced him back up the alley away from the street, where he had shot him quite deliberately as Kyreacos pleaded for his life.

That would account for the first spate of gunshots on the tape. The single shot might have been the coup de grâce, causing either the wound in Kyreacos's forehead or that in his chest, more likely the former. And then, after the pause, there had been two more shots—some distance away from the microphone. Stan Tappan had suffered two wounds that turned out to be essentially flesh wounds. The .45 wound to his left hand had sliced only through the web of skin between his thumb and forefinger, taking with it some tissue and muscle. The prosecutors felt that the injury in the area of his waist looked as if he had intentionally tugged the fatty layer there away from his ribs and muscles to be sure a self-administered bullet wouldn't damage any vital organs.

Painful? Certainly—probably far more painful than he had expected. Life threatening? No.

Stan Tappan maintained the same stoic mien throughout his trial, glancing occasionally at witnesses who had been close friends, and at reporters who knew him. Even as Judge David Hunter began to rule on whether the mystery tape would be admitted, Tappan betrayed no emotion.

Hunter said he did not believe that the Kyreacos tape contained a "private conversation," as stipulated by statutes governing tape recording without the permission of both parties.

"I suspect the victim was going to have a conversation about bribing someone—something that he intended to record. He didn't plan to tape his own death. The interpretation of the tape is open for both the defense and the prosecution. I find, therefore, that the state has laid a proper foundation for the admission of this tape."

The press bench was on alert. Hunter specifically warned members of the media that the tape was not to be recorded. Just as Nick Kyreacos had carried a book-sized recorder to the murder, anyone in the media would have needed a very hard-to-hide device to capture the words about to fill the courtroom. One radio reporter had, of all things, a rubber chicken in his coat pocket, a running gag he perpetuated during courtroom breaks. Some of us wondered if he had somehow managed to hide a recorder inside the chicken. A local TV anchorman sat bolt upright, his attaché case balanced on his knees. He guarded his briefcase so carefully that he seemed the most likely suspect. The rest of us had only yellow legal pads and pens clutched in our hands, ready to write.

It was 11:40 A.M. on a gusty Wednesday morning.

We realized suddenly that Nick Kyreacos's widow and his stepchildren were in the room, and it was too late for them to leave. They sobbed quietly as the tape began. Stan Tappan scribbled on his own legal pad, expressionless.

Nicholas Kyreacos had his day in court, and this was the only time I have ever heard a deceased victim actually speak as he realized he was going to die—and speak at the moment of his death. Perhaps it *was* akin to a blacked-out television, but there was no mistaking what was happening on the tape. It was an awful thing to hear.

As the tape rolled ahead to silence, the courtroom was absolutely quiet, as if everyone had ceased to breathe. When it was over, Judge Hunter dismissed the jurors for a lunch break, instructing them to return at 1:30 P.M.

Bill Lanning had only one witness to present for the defense: Stan Tappan himself. Tall and handsome despite his weight loss, he seemed at ease. He was familiar with the witness stand; he had testified as a police officer numerous times. Although his complexion was the familiar yellowish-white of prison pallor and his three-piece suit was now too big for him, he spoke firmly, respectfully, and with assurance. He often stood or used his hands to describe what had happened the night of the shootings.

In answer to Lanning's questions, Tappan recalled arresting Nick Kyreacos earlier in the fall on suspicion of credit-card forgery. "I was driving an unmarked police vehicle when I took him to jail. As I got into the driver's seat, he said, 'You're not busting me for this. Somebody's gonna get killed over this matter.'"

"I said, 'Is that a threat?' and he said, 'I don't make threats—I make promises.'"

In the interrogation room at police headquarters, Tappan said he had informed his prisoner of his Miranda rights and asked him if he was ready to cooperate. "He said, 'I don't cooperate with anyone who's gonna send me back to the joint.' I said it would help him if he would cooperate, and he said he might get the 'Big Bitch' [life in prison], as he'd been arrested three times at that point. He had fifteen years hanging and he could get life."

At that time, Kyreacos had allegedly told Tappan that anyone who tried to put him back in prison would be buried. That had worried the tall detective when he saw

Kyreacos hanging around his off-duty job at the mortgage company. He had indeed discussed his fears of a possible gunfight with his ex-partner, Tappan testified, and asked to borrow the .45.

"I didn't even know if it would shoot, and I planned to take it out to the range and try it out. It was in my glove compartment of my truck along with the extra clips because I was going to the range."

On November 19, Kyreacos had come up behind him as he sat at his desk in the Burglary Unit, Tappan said. That had scared him more. "I asked him if he was looking for me, and he said 'Not yet.' I asked him again if that was a threat, and again, he repeated that he made promises—not threats."

At that point, Tappan said he had taken Kyreacos to the homicide offices, which were next to his, to talk with Don Strunk. When Tappan later asked Strunk what he'd talked to Kyreacos about, Tappan recalled that Strunk said it was about the shooting of Branko Ellich.

"I asked Don if Kyreacos had mentioned me, and he said, 'Not directly.' But he warned me to 'Watch yourself. That guy is dangerous and he doesn't like you at all.' "

(On rebuttal, Don Strunk said he could not remember warning Tappan about Kyreacos.)

Lanning led Stan Tappan into his theories on the mysterious shooting of Branko Ellich and why Nick Kyreacos had been so menacing to Tappan.

Tappan said that he thought it was because both he and Ellich had been named as witnesses against Nick in the credit-card case. "I believe that Nick killed Branko Ellich," the defendant said, turning to the jurors. "The day before Ellich was murdered, I talked to him and I told him that Kyreacos might kill him."

"Why didn't you tell the detectives immediately that

the .45 at the scene belonged to you?" Bill Lanning asked his client. It was a heavy question for the defense, and would not go away by being ignored.

"I was scared," Tappan said, explaining that he was afraid he'd lose his job for carrying such a high-powered weapon.

There were some big gaps in the defense's case, and Stan Tappan moved forward to sew up the ragged seams, reconstructing the crime scene as he remembered it.

"I got to work at four thirty. It was raining and the wind was blowing—gusting up to thirty or forty miles per hour. I parked my truck in the first or second stall in the upper parking lot—facing out. I was walking between the two entrances to the parking lot. Around six fifteen or six thirty, I was checking out the garage under the detox center to see if all the cars were gone. There was one car left, and I had just seen two girl employees still at work upstairs in the office. I decided to sit in my truck until they left.

"I observed several people in rooms at the hotel and I knew there would be people going in and coming out of the detox center at all hours. I noticed a man walking up the alley very slowly, looking at the alley very, very carefully. He looked at me, then quickened his pace. I thought he might be a car prowler. Then I thought about the situation with Kyreacos and I replaced new bullets for old in the clip of the .45."

Tappan was talking to the jury, and Lanning allowed him to continue his almost stream-of-consciousness testimony.

"Three or four or five minutes later, a man entered the parking lot, and then walked out of my sight. A few seconds later, I saw him again. He was flattened against a wall and peering around the corner of a building. He walked sideways for about twenty feet with his back against the wall.

"I recognized him. He wasn't looking at me. I opened

the door of my truck and stepped out. Nick had a gun in his hand, pointed down at the ground. The .45 was sticking in my belt. I drew my .38 because I didn't even know if the .45 would shoot. I pointed it at Nick, and I said, 'Hold it right there, Nick!' "

Stan Tappan described how Kyreacos had run. Tappan himself jumped over a retaining wall and chased him, firing one warning shot as he shouted at him to stop. As Kyreacos rounded the corner of a building, Tappan said, he'd heard something metal hit the pavement. Kyreacos had stopped and asked what was going on.

"I said, 'You know. You're under arrest.' "

It was a difficult spot for a defendant to be in. The jurors had heard the actual conversation between the two men. If Tappan varied from the true words, the jurors would not believe him. He either had to tell the absolute truth or fit his description of the shooting into the scenario played out on the tape.

Now Stan Tappan told the jury that he had feared *another* person might be in the area, might at that moment be drawing a bead on him with a rifle. He had walked Kyreacos back through the alley to get out of firing range, intending to go into the mortgage company to call for police backup. But he suddenly remembered he didn't have a key to the office. He testified that he started back to his truck, where he'd planned to handcuff Kyreacos to the steering wheel and take him to jail—just as soon as he'd gone back to get the waiter's gun.

"I had my left hand on his right arm." Tappan stood to demonstrate. "I was going to lean him over the hood to search him. I put my hand in the middle of his back to signal to him to bend over. I meant to say, 'I'll tell you about it when I get you to the station'—but I don't know if I did or not. I started to put my gun in my holster so I could search him. Both my jacket and my raincoat were open and he looked down at the gun in my belt. I was slightly behind him. He leaned forward—then he dropped and spun around."

Bill Lanning acted out Kyreacos's part as Stan demonstrated. "He grabbed the .45 and pulled it out," Tappan continued. "I brought my gun up. I don't know whose gun went off first. I felt his bullet hit me in the side. I felt like I'd been knocked ten feet, but I was still up. I grabbed his gun with my left hand. I pushed it toward him. We were spinning. It was all so fast. I believe it fired twice more.

"It was over. And we were almost on the ground. There was no more struggle."

Tappan testified that he somehow managed to call for help and then, sure that he was terribly injured, he sat on the retaining wall and tried to stop the blood from his hand and side.

Stan Tappan was one of the most confident witnesses I've ever watched. He had woven almost all of the questions into a tapestry that seemed to explain the recording of the scene. When he stepped down from the witness stand, I wondered what the jurors were thinking. They had heard the tape just before noon, and four hours later, they had heard Stan's explanation.

The next day, all of western Washington heard that tape.

Someone on our press bench had indeed recorded it, and it was played over and over on the news. It was heard on the station where the anchorman with the attaché case worked. He had sat aloof from the rest of us for most of the trial *until* the tape was played, and then he had vanished. Stan Tappan's defense attorneys were outraged and demanded that the anchor come back into court to explain how he had gotten the tape. Instead, the station sent a female reporter to cover the verdict deliberation.

The jurors retired to deliberate at 3:45 P.M. on a Friday afternoon. By late Saturday, they signaled that they had arrived at a verdict. Twenty-four hours after final arguments and Judge Hunter's instructions, the four woman–eight man jury found Stan Tappan guilty of first-degree murder. Considering the sentence parameters at that time, he would serve at least thirteen years and four months in prison, with a mandatory five-year consecutive sentence for using a deadly weapon in the commission of the crime.

He was freed on $50,000 bond to await sentencing two months later.

It should have been over then, but there are questions that remain. Why would Stan Tappan, who had never evinced fear about anything, be so frightened of a small waiter who was much more afraid of *him?* Tappan had all the power, unless Nick Kyreacos knew something about Tappan that he could use to blackmail him. The connections between Branko Ellich, Nicholas Kyreacos, and Stan Tappan seemed inordinately intertwined. Why would a credit-card fraud case cause so much terror?

Over the years, various detectives have had theories—none proven—that the three men were tied together by a burglary ring, or fencing of stolen property, or a pornography setup, or sex, or payoffs, or bribery.

Was the mystery woman caller helping Tappan set Kyreacos up by summoning him to the alley? Perhaps he went because *he* had something to hide and was afraid that Tappan would blow the whistle on him.

Maybe none of these theories is true. Perhaps the testimony that Stan Tappan gave in his hours on the stand was the truth, and he paid dearly for something he didn't do. Was it believable that he was forced to shoot Kyreacos during a struggle for his gun? He'd had *two* guns and the waiter had only had a starter pistol full of blanks. In addition, Tappan was eight inches taller and forty pounds heavier than Kyreacos. Even so.

Perhaps the damning tape itself can be explained away. But one small bit of physical evidence always bothers me when I think about this case. If Kyreacos was struggling so violently with Stan Tappan, who wanted to handcuff him, why was his cigarette still clenched in his hand when the paramedics arrived?

Despite Bill Lanning's appeals, Stan Tappan went to prison. He was sent far out of Washington State to a federal prison and given a new name; ex-cops live extremely perilous lives in prison, trapped among a population they once hunted. The world moved on, and eventually Stan Tappan was released. Tappan is in his sixties now, and many of the men who arrested him are gone: among them, Ivan Beeson, Dick Reed, and Don Strunk have passed away. The other homicide detectives who worked on the case have long since retired.

Stan Tappan would like to write a book, and it would indeed be a fascinating read. He need no longer fear that he would be arrested. He has paid his debt to society, and double jeopardy would apply if any agency tried to arrest him again.

So it's still possible that the whole truth about that stormy night thirty years ago will be told.

Fatal Obsession

Sometimes the solution *to mindless murder is too close for even skilled detectives to see. When the obvious answers are too appalling for the rational mind to contemplate, the mind skitters away, unable to accept the horror.*

As I chose cases from my thirty-year career as a crime writer, I considered the true story that follows many times—and then quickly moved on because it still troubles me . . . a lot. It is as close to a horror tale as anything I've ever encountered.

Still, this particular case contains answers that could help us understand similar cases that burst onto the headlines every year. I doubt that I could ever again write about such madness and pain, the insanity hidden behind the facade of a killer who seemed to be the perfect citizen.

No one ever knew the churnings of this dangerous mind—until it was much too late to stop the carnage. Perhaps it won't be too late now to prevent tragedies that begin to bloom into dark fantasies in the disordered consciousness of someone who has not yet acted them out. To be aware of danger is to disarm it and prevent it.

For many years, brilliant criminalist Dr. George Ishii headed the crime lab for western Washington State. Ishii had overseen so many bizarre homicides that nothing really surprised him any longer. He taught classes in crime-

scene investigation and kept all of his students—myself included—enthralled with the forensic details of cases that seemed unimaginable.

In the case that follows, Dr. Ishii told us, "The deaths represent the classic example of a case where detectives had to completely reconstruct events through evidence and interrogation. It is precisely this kind of crime that could lead to countless 'confessions' in years to come, unless Kitsap County officers were able to finally and completely lay the blame on the guilty party or parties at once."

Thirty-four-year-old Kip Rennsler* and his beautiful blond wife, Lori,* twenty-eight, were living what seemed to be the ideal life on Bainbridge Island, Washington. The island was—and still is—one of the most desirable places to live in America. Ferries traverse Puget Sound every half hour, carrying the island's residents to their jobs in Seattle and, later, home to a serene world that is much more than ordinary suburbia. Ten miles long and five miles across, Bainbridge, when the Rennslers lived there, had affordable waterfront property, strawberry fields, and evergreen woods. Farther back—in the forties—when Betty MacDonald wrote her classic novel, *The Egg and I,* about her wonderfully humorous life on Bainbridge, the island was still rural and seemed more distant from the bright lights of Seattle or Bremerton.

That isn't true any longer, nor was it *entirely* true when the Rennslers moved to the lovely island. The strawberry fields, Japanese produce farms, and stands of fir, cedar, and madrona trees have shrunk and expensively appointed houses have sprung up. Bainbridge now attracts well-known authors, attorneys, and executives. To buy a house on Bainbridge, one (or, more likely, a couple) has to have an income in the upper ranges. Still, the main street of Winslow, Bainbridge's historic village, remains quaint and friendly.

When Kip and Lori Rennsler bought their house on Bainbridge Island, Kip's career was soaring upward. In his early thirties, he was already vice president of personnel at the Seattle headquarters of the Old National Bank. He'd met Lori when she worked at the bank, and they had been happily married for six years, the last three while living in their waterfront home. By working hard and investing in upgrades for the house, they soon turned it into a lovely home. Their only child, Steven "Stevie" Daniel* Rennsler, was born on September 26, 1968.

Each year, Kip's fortunes rose. His competence and thoroughness in dealing with the problems of the diverse personalities who worked for Old National Bank did not go unnoticed by his superiors. His salary increased enough so that Lori could resign from her job and be a stay-at-home mom. The couple adopted a stubby-legged dachshund pup and joked that he was their watch dog.

Even though Kip often worked overtime and Lori was alone in their somewhat isolated house, she wasn't afraid. Bainbridge Island had a very low crime rate. Most burglars and rapists preferred to stay on dry land, where they could escape by freeway instead of ferry.

The sixth Christmas Lori and Kip shared together seemed to be happy. Lori had time to hang decorations and lights all around the house, and Stevie was old enough to be terribly excited about Santa Claus. On Christmas Day, they entertained relatives and everyone went home tired but happy.

If Lori—or Kip—had reason to be worried about anything, no one perceived it from their outward behavior. And yet, only nine days later, something terrible would happen in the Rennslers' home.

* * *

At 2:21 on the afternoon of January 3, a frantic woman called the Kitsap County sheriff's office. Max Abrams, the daytime dispatcher, caught the call as most of the sheriff's deputies were preparing for a shift change.

"*Please* get someone out here right away," a tremulous female voice pleaded. "We just found our neighbor inside his home. His chest has a terrible wound. I'm sure he's dead—"

Abrams kept his voice steady and reassuring, trying to keep the woman from lapsing into complete hysteria. "Please stand by, ma'am. I'm going to get our deputies in your area on the way."

"Please hurry! We're in the Ferncliff area. It's horrible."

Abrams managed to get an exact address from her, and then dialed the intercom line to alert Bill Clifton, the chief of detectives.

"We're not sure what it is yet, Bill," he said, "but the woman who called is really shook up. I've already started units on the way."

By land, it was a forty-mile trip from the sheriff's headquarters in the town of Port Orchard to the Ferncliff area. Clifton sent Sergeant Don Hamrich—who was stationed in Winslow—to check on the situation, and dispatched two detectives from Port Orchard, followed by his identification chief, Les Cline, a crime-scene expert.

There were six officers en route to the scene, whatever the scene was. It wasn't that unusual to get hysterical calls over dogfights and family beefs, but this complainant had talked about someone with a critical chest wound. Clifton paced as he waited for Don Hamrich to call back.

"You'd better get up here as fast as you can, Bill," Hamrich reported, his voice tight with shock. "It looks like homicide—*triple* homicide. The man's in the front room with stab wounds in his chest. They're all dead,

Bill. The woman and the baby are in the bedroom. Maybe there's more—I don't know."

"Close up the house," Clifton said. "I don't care what you have to do, but don't let *anyone* in that house until my identification crew gets there."

Bill Clifton grabbed his coat and headed for his car, stopping only long enough to tell Abrams to alert every commissioned officer on the sheriff's staff. "If they're not in a car, call them at home. I don't know what we're going to find up there."

The detective chief was only a mile away from Bainbridge Island—but that was by water. He wished he had access to a boat or even a helicopter, but he didn't, so he raced toward the island along the Puget Sound shoreline with his bubble lights twirling and his siren wide open. He navigated around Liberty Bay, past Silverdale, Keyport Junction, and finally across the Agate Pass Bridge.

Already deputies from the north end of Kitsap County were stringing yellow tape around the Rennslers' yard. Curious neighbors, drawn by the wail of sirens and the sight of police units, stood respectfully back from the crime-scene tape, hovering a good distance away from the neat yard, far down the long driveway. It was a gloomy day, already getting dark, and from the looks on the deputies' faces, Clifton knew that something really shocking had to have happened inside the pleasant yellow house.

Hamrich stationed himself on the porch. He knew how important it was that the scene inside be left *exactly* as it was. A careless step, a hand closing a door, a stubbed-out cigarette, even flushing a toilet or turning on a faucet could destroy vital evidence.

As Bill Clifton pulled up, he was relieved to see only squad cars near the house itself. It was necessary to negotiate the long driveway down to the yellow house, where it sat surrounded by evergreens. Even then, the parking area was separated from the residence by a wide gully that ran all the way down to the saltwater beach. To get to the front porch of the house, the investigators had to cross a four-foot-wide bridge that angled up to a series of cement slab steps.

It was eight minutes after three. Clifton had somehow managed to travel forty miles in less than forty-five minutes since the first call for help had come into the sheriff's office.

The sheriff's officers stepped into the living room. It was nicely decorated in a rustic manner with a freestanding Franklin stove serving as a fireplace and providing heat on stormy nights. There was a combination breakfast bar and room divider between the living room and the kitchen. At first glance, everything seemed normal. A woman's purse rested on the divider along with some notebooks, a birthday card, and a phone. But on closer examination the investigators could see faint red smears on the phone, dried now.

The sheriff's men moved around the divider and another room came into view. It was a combination dining room and den. Now all semblance of normalcy vanished. They were looking at a male body so grotesquely displayed that it might have been part of an Aztec torture-sacrifice ritual. The man was completely naked, and he lay on his back on top of a child's table. His heels barely touched the floor, his arms were outstretched, and his head tilted back.

"My God, look at his chest," one deputy breathed.

They all stared down at the man, who had obviously been in perfect physical shape, his muscles toned and powerful. But now he had four wounds in his chest, one of them gaping as if someone had been intent on reaching in and ripping his heart out.

Experienced as they were, none of the four men had

ever seen anything like this. As dispassionately as he could, Les Cline took photographs of the dead man.

The other investigators followed Bill Clifton as he moved toward the doors of two bedrooms that were now visible. They saw the woman, who lay facedown on the rumpled king-size bed. She was very slender and wore a red and white quilted satin robe, belted tightly at the waist. She was positioned crosswise on the bed, with her feet dangling over the edge and her hands tucked beneath her. There was a large knife to the left of her head, its blade slightly bent at the sharp end, its handle crusted with blood.

Les Cline was the last into the bedroom and his eyes were drawn to a small form, half under the bed. The bedspread flounce covered the upper part of a child's body. His feet and legs were covered with baby pajamas. The little boy appeared to be two or three years old and he lay on his back.

The child was dead too, with a puncture wound to the left side of his neck. The investigators wondered why on earth it had been necessary to kill the child. What possible harm could he have been to anyone?

The bedroom was a chamber of horrors. As the team looked more closely at the woman's feet, they saw the small brown dog, the dachshund puppy, lying on its side a few feet away. It too had been stabbed.

Like men moving through a nightmare, placing one foot deliberately in front of the other, Clifton and his detectives moved around the bed. They stared down at the woman who lay atop the expensive flowered spread. Unlike the little boy and the naked man, there were no bloodstains on her body or clothing beyond a faint mark on the collar of her robe. Bill Clifton knelt very carefully on the edge of the bed, and lifted the robe's collar at the back of her head.

"Les," he said with his jaw clamped tightly. "Her neck is *gone*. This looks like the exit wound of a contact shotgun blast. She may be lying on a shotgun. What else could have caused this kind of damage?"

Gingerly, the two men turned the once-pretty blonde over. There was no gun beneath her, but something had virtually severed her head from her body. Only her fragile cervical spine was intact. Someone had methodically hacked away with the knife in an effort to decapitate her.

Chest wounds were evident now—perhaps four or five. The investigators told themselves that she must have already been dead when the neck wounds were inflicted.

Three of the bedroom walls were splattered with cast-off blood, probably from the knife as it had been raised again and again, flinging red droplets on the wallpaper. However, some of the irregular smears had surely come from a human hand sliding over the wall's surface.

Oddly, the only signs of a struggle in the bedroom were some items that had been knocked from the dresser near the end of the bed.

"I hope to God there aren't any more," a deputy muttered as they all walked carefully toward the second of the three bedrooms in the house.

They found no more bodies, but this bedroom—obviously the little boy's—was an abattoir too. A bunk bed was placed alongside one wall, and the top bunk clearly hadn't been used. For some inexplicable reason, the bottom mattress lay on the floor next to its box springs. All the sheets and blankets were soaked in blood, and so was the cover of the box springs.

"This is strange," Bill Clifton said, his voice no longer firm. "I don't see how anyone could have bled enough to soak through a mattress into a box spring. The human body just doesn't *hold* that much blood—especially a child's body. But I think it was the little boy who was here on the mattress. That would account for the fact that there isn't any blood under his body now. He had no more left in him."

Apprehensively, they walked to the third bedroom, and as the door creaked open, they were vastly relieved to see no sign at all of violence. That room had apparently been used only for storage. The bathroom was clean too, but they did find a gauze and tape bandage, shaped like a finger, in front of the refrigerator in the kitchen.

Otherwise, the kitchen was neat. Two or three cups with sodden tea bags in them and a few glasses were stacked by the sink. A garbage strainer floated on one side of the divided sink. A dripping faucet had filled the sink with water.

Shaken but determined, the detectives held a hurried conference. "We're going to be flooded by demands from the media and thrill seekers as soon as this gets out—which is probably about now," Clifton said, "and we're going to have to have enough men out there to keep them on the *other* side of the gulley."

The Kitsap County investigators had not even positively identified the dead yet. They found boxes of papers and more notebooks in the living room and the den. Each had the name the neighbor had given them, and from the paperwork it did appear that the dead man was undoubtedly Kip Steven Rennsler, a vice president at the Old National Bank.

Although they were in deep shock, the neighbors who had seen the body were quite sure the naked man *was* Rennsler. "I went over there," one woman said, "because one of Kip's coworkers at the bank called me. He'd been calling the house many times—and was either getting no answer or a busy signal. That kind of scared me, so I went and got a neighbor man to go over there with me. Well, we went in, and the first thing we saw was the phone hanging down by its cord. The gentleman with me went further in, and he saw a man's body. He just turned around and came back out."

"The phone wasn't off the hook when we got here," Clifton said.

"I know. The neighbor man hung it up, just kind of a reflex," the woman said.

That was disappointing news for the detectives. If there had been fingerprints left on the phone, they might have been matched to a suspect's. Chances were that they were smeared and useless now.

The question that screamed the loudest was *"Why?"* These people had been a nice little family, living in a nice little house that they'd fixed up themselves. Why would anyone want to savage them in this way? These weren't normal murders—if, indeed, there was such a thing. This was maniacal overkill, something straight out of a nightmare.

Detectives and deputies were out canvassing door to door, asking neighbors if they knew anything about the Rennslers or *anyone* who might want to hurt them. So far, no one did. Asking neighbors if they'd heard anything wasn't helping. The Rennslers' house was isolated enough that their screams or calls for help couldn't have been heard. Waves washing onto their beach would also muffle sounds.

The neighbors who'd called for help said that the front door of the yellow house had been ajar when they arrived. It was January and it was cold. Why would their door have been partially open? Would they have felt safe enough in their house, cut off from the road by a ravine and a little bridge, that they didn't bother to lock their doors? That hardly seemed likely. Probably the killer or killers hadn't bothered to close the door when they left.

Searching for a motive, Bill Clifton kept returning to Kip Rennsler's occupation. "He was vice president of a bank. It wouldn't be the first time somebody who wanted the combination to a bank vault went to a bank officer's home and held his family hostage. Maybe Rennsler had that kind of information, but probably he didn't. But that doesn't matter. If someone *thought* he did, it wouldn't be hard to chart his movements."

The detective chief tried to find a scenario that fit this tragedy. "OK," Clifton began, "the neighbors say that Kip Rennsler took the seven ten A.M. ferry like clockwork every day. By a quarter to eight, he was in downtown Seattle. But suppose he was sick today and he stayed home? Suppose somebody came to the house expecting to find only the woman and the little boy, planning to hold them hostage, while they called Rennsler and forced him to come home by threatening their lives? But Rennsler was *in* the house today, so that would have thrown their plans into chaos.

"The woman and the boy were in nightclothes, and Rennsler was nude. Maybe he just got out of the shower. He could have come rushing out and put up one hell of a fight."

That was true. Rennsler was muscular and strong, but he would have been taken unaware. He probably could have subdued one man, but there might have been more.

There was another possibility. Lori Rennsler was a beautiful woman. She might have been the target. Somebody could have watched her on the beach, stalking her as she went into Winslow for groceries or to the library, and become obsessed.

"Erotomania," one detective said. "That's what they call it. People fixate on someone they don't even know. And some of them don't quit until they have that person in their power."

According to their usual schedule, Lori and Stevie were alone in the secluded house after 6:30 every weekday morning. It was a perfect setup for a sexual psychopath—a woman alone before dawn, a little boy, and a small puppy, in a house far away from everyone at the end of a long driveway.

But on this Monday morning, they hadn't been alone; Kip had been home. The entire family had perished together.

"Why didn't Rennsler call in sick?" a detective asked.

"I don't know," Clifton said, "but we're going to talk to his coworkers, and see what they have to say."

"And Lori Rennsler is fully clothed. There's no indication that she was raped."

"It's weird," Clifton agreed. "I gotta tell you this is the weirdest thing I've ever seen in my life."

It was almost dawn when the crime scene technicians—led by Les Cline—had finished processing the house. They were looking for fingerprints, hairs, fibers, shoe prints in blood, matchbooks, cigarette butts, torn bits of cloth, *anything* that didn't seem to fit. Before they finished, they had thirty envelopes for George Ishii to examine at the crime lab. They took scores of photographs, recording ghastly tableaus that might be very important in a courtroom one day.

They found Kip Rennsler's clothing in his son's room. His blood-spattered athletic shoe rested next to the mattress on the floor, and when they lifted the mattress, there was a pile of men's clothing underneath: trousers with jockey shorts still inside, a tee-shirt and a dark-colored wool sweater, as well as Kip's other shoe. The clothes were saturated with blood. Oddly, this blood was still wet, where the blood in the other rooms had dried. Perhaps the attack in Stevie Rennsler's room had occurred sometime after the other violence. The room was stifling hot; a space heater glowed red in the wall, turned to its highest setting.

Les Cline held up the white tee-shirt and studied the stain on it.

"Check Rennsler's chest again for me," he murmured to no one in particular.

"Why?" his assistant, Jay Mossman, asked.

"Just check it closely and count the wounds."

"Four," Mossman answered as he returned from the den/dining room area.

"Then something doesn't add up," Cline said. "If you'll look at this tee-shirt, there are only *three* holes. Two on the right and one on the left. Rennsler was stabbed three times with his clothes on, and then for some reason, his shirt was taken off and he was stabbed again."

"Why?"

"You tell me. What kind of a nut would stab a man three times, take all his clothes off, lay a mattress on them, and then stab him again? It would make more sense if they'd forced Lori Rennsler to disrobe, but they didn't."

"Unless the killer was a woman," a deputy said.

"No way. There isn't one woman in a thousand who has the strength to use a knife the way it was used here."

The investigators believed that Stevie Rennsler had been stabbed in his bed as he slept—and died there. Someone had then carried his body into his parents' bedroom. His father had probably collapsed for a time on the bunk's box spring and somehow managed to crawl or stagger into the den where the killer found him. There were more red stains on the dinette table—in a peculiar pattern, as if a man's hairy chest had slid across the table. A chair in front of the dinette set had been knocked over.

"Rennsler made it to the table, knocked over the chair, then reeled over to the child's table and collapsed on his back and died," Clifton said. "He may have been trying to make it to the phone. Maybe he *did* make it, knocked it off the hook—but was too weak to talk by then."

A deputy stationed on the bridge came to tell the investigators that three of Kip Rennsler's coworkers were waiting in the parking area beyond the small bridge. They had caught the first ferry they could to Bainbridge Island after being notified of the tragedy.

They were almost mute with shock, but said they wanted to help in any way they could. Then, for the first time, the sheriff's detectives had to look at a suspicion they hadn't even considered, something so seemingly alien to human nature that their minds hadn't even gone there.

"Kip hasn't been himself lately," one of his close work friends began. "I've known him and worked with him for about eight years. Something's been worrying him, and I can't say what. I guess I could say that he's been overly preoccupied with really minute details. He seemed to just worry them to death, obsessively. He missed an important appointment this morning at nine. Some men might do that—but not Kip. He was always on time and he scheduled everything. That's why I kept calling him."

Another coworker recalled that when Kip Rennsler had left the bank on Friday night—three days earlier—he had carried with him two cardboard boxes, "about the size of a case of beer," and a white paper bag.

They weren't full of money. The crime-scene investigators had already found those boxes and the bag; they held office items like mimeograph paper, address labels, and staples, things he often used to do bank work at home. His co-workers said that he also edited a magazine for his antique bottle collectors' group. He might have been taking slight advantage of the bank by bringing home office supplies, but that paled in contrast to what had happened in his home.

The third bank employee said he was the one who had tried in vain to call the Rennsler residence twice that morning, between 9 and 9:30. The phone rang, but there was no answer. "When I tried again at eleven thirty, the line was busy. I tried several times over the next few hours, and I finally asked the operator to check. She said the phone was off the hook."

At that point, the coworker was alarmed enough to call the Rennslers' neighbor. He considered himself a close friend of the Rennsler family, and things just weren't adding up.

"Kip and Lori—and Stevie too—were supposed to have Sunday dinner with my family at my house yesterday," he continued. "But Kip called and canceled on very short notice. That wasn't like him."

None of Kip Rennsler's fellow employees knew why he'd been so nervous lately. He was doing well at work, and as far as they knew, he and Lori were very happy together. He wasn't in debt and his health seemed excellent. And yet he had been jumpy and preoccupied.

A check of Old National Bank records showed no irregularities at all. Kip Rennsler most certainly was not an embezzler. His accounts were accurate to the penny.

The man who had found Rennsler's body said he had given Kip and Stevie a ride the day before—on Sunday afternoon. "I saw them walking quite a ways from their house, and I offered them a ride. Kip seemed upset and he was acting kind of strange. He seemed very tired and he told me that he and Stevie had been walking for a long time."

The woman who had called the sheriff's office called

again to say that she remembered seeing a car parked close to the Rennslers' footbridge sometime Sunday afternoon. "It was Sally Newland's* car," she said. "Sally is a good friend of Lori's."

Detectives contacted Sally Newland, who was shocked at her friend's death. Shocked, it seemed, but not totally surprised. "I saw both Lori and Kip yesterday," she began slowly. "It was very, very odd. First, I met Kip and Stevie walking along the road. I asked Kip if he wanted a ride home, but he said no, and then he told me he was taking Stevie for a 'long, long, walk.'

"I asked him if anything was wrong, and he said there wasn't but that Lori was very upset. He asked me to stop by their house and tell her that everything was all right."

Sally had driven to the Rennslers' house right away, and found Lori in tears. "She told me that Kip had been acting 'funny,' and he had asked her to take Stevie to the neighbors' house. He said he wanted to ask her one question, and she could answer either yes or no. She said she'd told him to just forget it.

"Lori told me that Kip had been behaving very bizarrely for about a week. She had tried to get him to talk with her, but she just couldn't get through to him. I had to agree with her about Kip. I wish I could put my finger on it exactly—but he was just *different* somehow."

One thing had occurred that might have upset Kip Rennsler. He had been trying to put together a deal to buy a historic lodge in a rainforest near the Washington coast. He didn't have the full down payment, and he'd been seeking a large loan to cover it. He'd been trying to finance the hotel for almost a year.

The investment would be a huge step for the young couple, and Lori wasn't enthusiastic about his quitting his job and moving them to Quinault, where they would probably have to live in the huge old lodge. But Kip had been very high on the project, and had been terribly depressed when he couldn't make it come together.

For most people, that would have been a disappointment—not a cataclysmic event. But Rennsler had taken it hard.

Bill Clifton received a phone call from a woman who lived in Poulsbo, a community with a mostly Scandinavian population, about fifteen miles north of Winslow. Solveig Hanson* told Clifton that she'd become acquainted with both Lori and Kip Rennsler within the last few months.

"I need to talk to someone about Kip," Solveig Hanson said. "There are some things that have worried me."

The attractive woman seemed relieved to talk to Clifton, but her hands shook slightly as she lit a cigarette. She said she had had various business dealings with Kip Rennsler and that they were friends. "But, before you ask, it was purely platonic. Kip was completely in love with Lori."

She shook her head, trying to find a way to describe her concerns. "But something changed with Kip. In the last two weeks, he's visited me half a dozen times. The thing is that each time, his actions became more complex and peculiar than the last. He became obsessed—I guess you'd call it that—to the point that he was beginning to frighten me. He seemed to be seized by the idea that he wanted to help others, and he would go into some detail about people—"

"In what way?"

"Well, he came to my house on Christmas Eve, and he absolutely insisted that I go shopping with him to get groceries for a needy family," she said. "I agreed to go with him to a supermarket, and he must have spent about $200 buying groceries. Then we drove to a house where he said a poor family lived and he carried the groceries to the front door."

Solveig said she had been touched by the gesture, and she had attempted to praise Rennsler for doing such a generous thing. "But he became very upset and wouldn't let me even mention it," she said.

Since Christmas, Solveig said she had heard often from Rennsler, and he had seemed to grow more disturbed all the time. "The last time he visited me at my home, he was talking irrationally—very fast—and not making any sense. He seemed to have so much to get out that he wouldn't let me answer or say anything at all. It was just a shower of words coming from a pressure cooker.

"Finally, I got up and left the room to go to the bathroom, just to get away from him for a moment. But he followed me and pounded on the door with his fist, insisting that I hurry out because he had so much to tell me. He had me scared."

Solveig Hanson said she had finally pushed Kip Rennsler gently toward the door and locked it behind him.

However, on the Sunday night before the murders, her phone had rung six or seven times. "Each time I answered, no one spoke—but I could hear hard, labored breathing. I can't say for sure it was him, but I just felt it was Kip."

It was easy enough to check. At that time calls from Bainbridge Island to Poulsbo were toll calls. The phone company pulled up the Rennslers' records and found that eight calls had been made to the Hanson residence after midnight on Monday morning.

It was beginning to look as if Kip Rennsler himself might have been the monster who erupted in his own home. Any number of people who believed they had known him well referred to how he "wasn't himself," and to the bizarre way he had begun to act during the holiday season and afterward. He had functioned well in his job and in the community, although it must have become an enormous struggle for him to keep whatever demons were driving him from surfacing. If he'd bombarded Solveig Hanson with ideas that didn't make sense, had he also frightened his wife with his distorted thoughts?

The new information wasn't nearly enough to mark three brutal deaths as "Closed" in the sheriff's files. Somehow, investigators would have to do a psychological autopsy of a dead man if they had any hope of understanding the enormous "Why?" that still existed.

What had caused Kip Rennsler to implode?

He had no business pressures because he was doing extremely well at his bank job—but he had become extremely morose and frustrated when he couldn't get the loan to buy the lodge in the rainforest. He was said to be in love with his wife, but he had certainly spent a lot of time with Solveig Hanson in Poulsbo. Perhaps she wasn't interested in him, but he had called her repeatedly in the wee hours of the morning when he had either just killed his family or was about to. He may well have felt tremendous guilt at even contemplating an extramarital affair.

Then again, it was beginning to look as though Rennsler had succumbed to a psychosis, perhaps one triggered by some recessive gene buried far back in his family tree. His recent actions certainly seemed insane. All his manic ravings might have ended in utter horror for so many other people.

A Seattle doctor said he'd treated Kip Rennsler for a duodenal ulcer in the recent past. He had found Rennsler to be under some tension, but hadn't found that unusual for a businessman in a fast-paced world. The physician had prescribed a mild tranquilizer, a routine drug for someone under stress. The drug carried no risk for mania or psychosis as negative side effects.

One of the other vice presidents at Old National Bank recalled that he had gone to lunch with Kip Rennsler on December 31. They were coworkers, but not really close. The officer recalled that Rennsler had asked him, "Have you seen a change in me lately?"

"I finally said, 'Yes, you seem much more happy and outgoing.' "

Rennsler had then gone into a complicated explanation of his new attitude and how happy he was because he had decided not to let things worry him as he had done in the past.

"I feel I'll be a better person to work with," he confided. "I'm not going to let finances bother me as much."

The other bank officer had assumed at the time that they were talking about New Year's resolutions and hadn't been too concerned that Rennsler had suddenly chosen him as a confidant. He knew that Rennsler's efforts to buy the hunting and fishing lodge had failed spectacularly, and figured that was what he was talking about.

Apparently, Kip Rennsler had talked to numerous people about buying the Quinault property for more than a year. When the news of the Rennsler family tragedy became public, a number of regular ferry boat commuters called sheriff's headquarters. Kip had buttonholed a lot of people to talk about his grand plans. More intimate friends came forward to say that Kip Rennsler had been completely devastated when the deal fell through.

"He told me," one man said, "that if he wasn't able to buy that place, he didn't know how he could face the future. I thought he was exaggerating, of course."

Rennsler's usual personality was that of a strong competitor, his friends told detectives. "He was the ultimate competitor," an acquaintance said. "You know, the kind of guy who had to be the best and the first at *everything*. He had to win at games, and when we went on camping trips, he was always the first to get his tent pitched. A winner all the way."

Lori Rennsler's friends said that Kip had always been the absolute head of the household, and that he could sometimes seem domineering. "But he loved her—and Stevie—and she never complained. She accepted him the way he was."

Perhaps Lori could *not* accept her husband the way he had become in the days before her death. Or perhaps she didn't know how far his mind had slipped over the edge of madness.

The postmortem examinations of the Rennsler family took place as their friends and family made funeral plans. The pathologist looked especially for some kind of defect in Kip Rennsler's brain that might have caused him to behave so bizarrely and violently, perhaps a tumor or a tangle of blood vessels that had caused an aneurysm or even a stroke. But there was nothing. The cause had not been physiological; it had been psychological.

Although it seemed unthinkable, Rennsler had apparently committed suicide by stabbing himself in the chest. Suicide by repeatedly slashing oneself is not without precedent, although it is extremely rare. The body tends to pull away from pain, and "hesitation wounds" are to be expected.

Rennsler had succumbed to the last of four stab wounds to his chest. The first three—which had stained his tee-shirt—were remarkably deep, but not deep enough to penetrate his heart or any other vital organ. The fourth thrust, however, had severed the intercostal artery on his right side, and his lung had filled with blood and collapsed, a condition called hemopneumothorax.

He would have lived several minutes at most after the fourth self-administered stab before literally drowning in his own blood.

He had a cut on one finger, but that was several days old, and probably accounted for the bandage detectives had found in the kitchen.

There was some—though not much—comfort to be taken in the findings on Lori and Stevie Rennsler. They had probably been asleep when they were stabbed fatally in their chests. There was no evidence at all of defense wounds on their arms or hands, and no bruising on their bodies.

The crime scene was cleared, and grieving family members were allowed to enter the yellow house to collect keepsakes and other items. All the evidence had been evaluated, and there was nothing at all to indicate that anyone other than the Rennsler family had been present on the Monday night they all died.

One relative came across a mass of torn paper fragments in Kip Rennsler's sports jacket. She brought it to the detectives.

Tediously, they laid the ragged pieces of paper out on a flat surface, arranging and identifying them as though working on a jigsaw puzzle. At first, the combined scraps looked like a jumble of scribbled letters on wrinkled paper, but slowly, slowly, a pattern began to emerge.

The investigators realized they were looking at a letter, a twenty-five-page letter, judging from numbers on the bottom of some of the pages.

The letter made a horrible kind of sense, despite its rambling tone, and the fact that some sections were missing. It had obviously been intended for Lori to read, even though there was no salutation on the first page. No one will ever know if Lori Rennsler read the letter, but the chance is that she did not. Had she read this careening jumble of thoughts, she might have been forewarned of the depth of her husband's mental illness. More likely, Kip Rennsler wrote the letter and then tore it into bits, believing that he could explain his thoughts to her verbally.

The letter was handprinted and many words and phrases were underlined heavily for emphasis.

It began:

Now, you will realize why I am doing all this. What I have to do is so simple it's unbelievable. It is something that will never hurt anyone—even you or Stevie or Me. However, it's so shocking that even when I tell you, you won't believe it. PLEASE READ THIS ALOUD! That means that although you and I can live out our entire lives VERY HAPPY—NO DOUBT ABOUT THAT—the rest of the world will never get a chance. Everyone that ever lived in the past and everyone that will ever live in the future.

You are not going to believe what I have to go through. It's so simple yet so tough. Please put Stevie to bed—no matter what he says.

There was a section missing, and then it went on:

But that kills the whole deal. You made the decision. Now I have to stick to it. I'm about to tell you what it is. But you must first provide me two things out loud and on paper and really mean them. They are very simple but so weird that you will probably wonder if I'm still around this world.

Remember. I have to do this the rest of my life. You must believe me immediately. No hesitation. Are you ready? I have to remain silent the rest of my life.

And here the note trailed off into a stream of consciousness as Kip Rennsler struggled to make his mind do his bidding:

I forgot one of the things. I can't go ahead without that one, even though I remember the other one. However, I can't tell you what the thing I have to do is until I find that simple thing.

You still have the <u>hardest</u> part because I know all this to be absolutely true, but you have only my word for it. I will tell you something. You and I and Stevie were meant to do this out of all the people past, present and future. Why were we picked? Because God thought we were the very best out of all people, past—present—future. I am, and if he didn't know this, he would never have picked me for this final or final things.

"IT IS UNBELIEVABLE TO ME TOO!!!"

An explanation for the tragedy lay on the table in front of them, scattered thoughts on scattered notes. Kip Rennsler had completely lost touch with reality, and he believed that sacrificing himself and his family would save everyone in the world. On the last day of his family's lives, he had undoubtedly been completely delusional, believing that he was making a noble sacrifice.

Perhaps the preposterous things he mentioned in the torn note became the verbal questions he asked his wife on the night of January 2. Expected to answer instantly, the horrified woman must have faltered in her shock. She may have asked her husband to face reality. Such hesitation would have spurred the final maniacal attacks.

Lori and Stevie probably died first, and Kip Rennsler may have been alive for hours afterward. Someone made the eight phone calls to Solveig Hanson, long after midnight. Someone carried Stevie's body into the master bedroom so he could be with his mother.

One psychiatrist felt that the torn note was an indirect suicide note. Perhaps. Another diagnosed Rennsler as being a paranoid schizophrenic. Not likely. Thirty years ago, the term *schizophrenia* was a catchall phrase to diagnose all manner of aberrant behavior. It is more likely that Kip Rennsler was a manic-depressive whose disease had moved into a psychotic phase.

His "highs," or the mania that gripped him, had soared with his vision of owning a hunting and fishing lodge, and he believed he would be very rich and fulfilled. But the higher the highs, the lower the lows when his disease hit the depressive cycle. He had become devastated by his inability to bring his purchase of the Quinault property to fruition, but he bounced higher again. Only this time, the mania made no sense.

It was perfectly clear to Kip Rennsler that he was meant to be the salvation of the world. He could not understand why Solveig Hanson wouldn't sit still and listen to his amazing theories and visions. And he must have seen the shock and disbelief in his wife's eyes as he pointed out how easy the solution to all the world's problems was.

No one wants to believe that someone they care about is slipping into mental illness. It is easier to find other explanations and blame aberrance on fatigue or stress or anything that isn't "crazy." But "crazy" is nothing to be ashamed of, and there are treatments that can help the mind come back to reality—just as the body can be healed.

Every year, there are bleak headlines about fathers and mothers, husbands and wives, and even grown children who, for their own unfathomable and distorted reasons, destroy their entire families. Many of these tragedies can be prevented in the future if we pay attention to symptoms that are like tiny red flags just beyond the periphery of our vision.

Campbell's Revenge
(from *A Rose for Her Grave*)

"Don't the stories *you write frighten you?" It is another predictable question that I have heard two hundred times. Usually my answer is that I am rarely afraid, even though I have written about some of the most heinous criminals of the last three decades. But sometimes I must admit that a case cuts too close to the bone and triggers fears that all women have. We fear first for our children and only second for ourselves.*

Charles Rodman Campbell is a killer straight out of a nightmare. There should have been some way to keep him locked up forever. But he slipped through the loopholes of our justice system, and he was allowed freedom to stalk his unknowing victims. If ever there was a case that pitted innocence against pure evil, it is this one. He was out of his cage, and he was aware of every facet of her life, and yet his potential prey felt only a chill premonition of danger. He was a man consumed with rage and the need for revenge. Because of a neglectful bureaucracy, Campbell was allowed to take not one life—but three.

Clearview, Washington, is little more than a crossroads, a tiny neighborhood in Snohomish County, twelve miles south of Everett, the county seat. Travelers headed for Stevens Pass, one of the northern routes over the Cascade Mountains, pass through Clearview and scarcely realize it.

After it was over, Clearview residents cried, "This sort of thing doesn't happen here—not in Clearview." *Why* do people say that? Is everyone who lives outside a major metropolitan area convinced that he or she lives in a safe zone, under a kind of glass bubble where violent crimes never break through? Possibly—if the nightly news is any barometer. The cold fact is that tragedies and terror happen everywhere, no matter how sylvan the landscape, how slow the pace of life is, or how loving and protective the friends and neighbors. Psychopaths move among all of us, their motivation usually hidden behind a winning, clear-eyed smile and sincere promises. Many of them are handsome or beautiful, successful—at least for a time—and persuasive. And sometimes all of us trust too much, too soon.

He was not like the smoothly handsome predators. He frightened most women just by the way he looked. He was so big—almost six feet five—and his bushy mustache and tangled Afro hair were reddish brown and seemed to bristle with electricity. But it was his eyes that caught them in a steady, mind-altering stare. They were like the entrance to a tunnel, the dark orbs fixed above an expanse of white beneath. *Sampaku,* the Japanese call them: "eyes of death." Like Rasputin's—the mad monk who mesmerized Russian nobility, another huge man who seemed impervious to his enemies—Charles Rodman Campbell's eyes had a life of their own. They were often glazed and a little crazy. To the cons in the Monroe, Washington, Reformatory, he was a "bad-ass," and to his guards, he was trouble. To his victims, he was the devil himself.

Renae Ahlers Wicklund was a beautiful woman— dark-haired and big-eyed, with the high cheekbones and symmetrical features of a model. Her career was beauty—the art of bringing beauty to other women. She was kind, responsible, and gutsy. She must have been gutsy to endure what she did.

After she graduated from high school, where she was a drum majorette for the band, in Jamestown, North Dakota, Renae Ahlers moved to California and then to Washington State. When Renae met her future husband, Jack Wicklund, she was working in a beauty parlor in Seattle. She was nineteen, and Jack was fourteen years older, divorced with two children from a previous marriage.

In 1972 they fell in love and got married. Renae was expecting her first baby when they moved into their own home, a neat one-story rambler set far back in a stand of fir trees near rural Clearview. Lots were acre-sized, and being neighborly required some effort. Running across the street to have coffee meant almost a quarter-mile jog. But Renae and Barbara and Don Hendrickson grew close right away. Don was forty-three and Barbara forty-one.

They had lived there for ten years, and they became almost substitute parents; their children—Peggy, Susan, and Dan—were family, too.

Jack Wicklund spent much of his time on the road, and as Renae neared term in her pregnancy, she was more grateful than ever for the Hendricksons. When she went into labor, Jack was out of town, and it was Peggy Hendrickson who drove Renae to the hospital on that day in 1973 when Renae gave birth to a baby girl she named Shannah. Shannah looked just like her mother—she had the same huge brown eyes and chestnut hair. Renae adored her, and everywhere Renae went, her baby went along.

It is impossible to know if Shannah remembered the first bad time. Probably not. She was only a year and a half old when it happened. It is likely, though, that the toddler sensed her mother's frantic terror, that the feeling surfaced in bad dreams through the next eight years. The first time, Shannah lived only because her mother did what any mother would have done to save her child: Renae Wicklund gave in to a rapist to keep him from harming Shannah.

December 11, 1974, was an unseasonably warm and sunny day for western Washington, where December usually means rain, rain, and more rain. Taking advantage of the weather, twenty-three-year-old Renae Wicklund decided to wash her windows. Knowing that darkness comes near four on a winter afternoon in the Northwest, Renae hurried to gather rags, vinegar, and water to accomplish the task. It was about 1:30 P.M. when she carried Shannah out and plopped her down on the grass in the sunshine, talking and singing to the baby while she worked on the windows.

On that Wednesday afternoon, Renae Wicklund suddenly became aware of someone walking toward them along the long driveway that led through the trees to her house. She saw a tall figure out of the corner of her eye and turned to stare directly at a youngish man with a copper cast to his hair. When she did that, he turned and walked back out to the main road. She thought he had probably been lost and realized when he saw her that he had the wrong house.

Leaving Shannah on the grass, she stepped into the house to grab some more rags. Moments later she returned and stood at the front door. The man was coming back, and this time he was moving fast.

As she would testify later in court, "He was running. Toward the house. Up our driveway. I thought that he was after Shannah, so I ran outside to grab her. And before we could get inside the house, he was pushing the door."

Renae, dressed lightly because of the balmy December day, tried to hold the front door shut with her body, but the man was much too strong, and she had Shannah in her arms. When he burst through the door, she saw that he had a knife in his right hand. Keeping her voice determinedly calm, she asked if there was something she could do for him—thinking that if she pretended she hadn't seen the knife, it still might not be too late.

It was too late. "Yeah," the intruder said. "Get your clothes off right now or I'll kill the kid, and I mean it."

He was holding the knife terribly close to Shannah. Renae Wicklund didn't have to decide what she would do. She put Shannah down at the stranger's order and slowly removed her boots, her purple corduroy shorts, her black sweater and vest, then sat down in a chair, waiting for what she feared would come next.

But he didn't want intercourse; he wanted oral sex. While her baby daughter screamed, she complied until her attacker was satisfied.

She prayed he wouldn't hurt them and was relieved to hear him mutter "Thanks" and saw that he was leaving. Sickened, she ran to the bathroom and washed out her mouth. Then she flung her clothes back on, grabbed Shannah, and ran across the street to the Hendricksons'. Barbara Hendrickson took one look at Renae's face and pulled her inside.

"Renae said there was a man outside and she was afraid he was going to come back," Barbara told deputies later. "And she looked out the window, and I promptly locked the door and got out my shotgun."

Both Renae and Shannah were very, very upset. The women barricaded themselves inside the Hendricksons' home with a loaded shotgun and called the Snohomish County Sheriff's Office. A deputy arrived at 2:25 P.M.

Renae Wicklund was able to give a good description of the man who had sexually assaulted her and threatened to kill her baby. She said he was very tall, with frizzy reddish hair, and that he'd worn blue jeans and a red and black plaid shirt. She thought he was in his early twenties. She had detected a faint odor of alcohol on his breath.

With her description, Snohomish County detectives narrowed in on Charles Rodman Campbell, twenty, as a possible suspect. He was tremendously tall, and his hair stuck out around his head like a dandelion gone to seed. He had been in trouble since he was old enough to leave his own yard.

Charles Campbell was born October 21, 1954, in Hawaii. His parents soon moved to Snohomish County. Campbell's early problems were not his fault. He was always *different*—and in so many ways. Because of his Hawaiian descent, the kids at his school teased him. Perhaps more damaging, Charles Campbell's sister was crippled, and some of the thoughtless kids not only tormented her but teased him about it, too, shouting cruel epithets at him. He fought to protect her, and out of sheer rage. Charles Campbell's parents tired of the responsibility of children early on and had long since defected, leaving the boy's grandparents to deal with him and his sister. They didn't know where to begin, and they were not particularly interested in raising another generation of children anyway.

Charles Campbell was an angry child from the very beginning, large and clumsy for his age with a chip on his shoulder. He was always fighting or running away. Detectives at the Edmonds, Washington, police department had dealt with him since before he hit junior high school. Even then they doubted that he would stay out of prison long. He had always seen the world as out to get him.

His first arrest came when he was sixteen years old after he stole a car. According to different sources, he stayed in school either through the ninth grade or the tenth—or the eleventh. Whichever, he was not a diligent student. He was too preoccupied, apparently, with drugs and alcohol.

Chuck Campbell married when he was nineteen, eloping with a twenty-two-year-old woman. His new in-laws were not impressed with him. The couple did not celebrate even a first wedding anniversary, divorcing after ten months. One month before their divorce, his wife gave birth to a child. He was ordered to pay $75 a month in child support, but his visitation rights were revoked after a judge decreed that he "poses a serious threat to the welfare of the child and the petitioner in that he has physically abused the child and petitioner in the past and neglected them." Since Campbell went to prison shortly thereafter, his ex-wife and child were assured that he would not visit.

* * *

That was why Snohomish County police were familiar with Charles Campbell. Once you saw a man six-and-a-half-feet tall with wild reddish hair and a kind of rage that almost vibrated, you didn't forget him—especially if you were a cop. They had a mug shot of him in their files. This photograph was included in a "lay-down," which they showed to Renae Wicklund two weeks after she was attacked.

Trembling but resolute, Renae Wicklund picked Campbell's picture immediately. "That's him."

Finding Charles Campbell would prove far more difficult than identifying him. It would be more than a year before Campbell was arrested and placed in a police lineup. On March 1, 1976, Renae Wicklund looked at the line of men through one-way glass and instantly picked Campbell from the lineup. He was the man who had forced her to perform fellatio sixteen months earlier.

Campbell argued that he could not possibly have been in Clearview on December 11, 1974. He claimed that he had been living and working as a cook at a pizza restaurant in Renton, Washington, almost 30 miles away during the period in question. He insisted he had punched in to work at 3:30 P.M. on December 11 and stayed in the kitchen throughout his shift.

A closer look into Campbell's background, however, brought forth information that stamped him as more than the average hardworking pizza cook. He was wanted for a drug violation in Snohomish County in late December 1974, and he had been working in Renton under the alias Dan Leslie Kile to avoid apprehension. He had quit his job at the pizza parlor very suddenly on December 14, 1974, the day Renton police began their investigation into the apparent theft of $1,200 from the restaurant's cash register.

Campbell admitted that he could not say exactly what he had done earlier in the day that the Wicklunds were attacked, but said it was his pattern to drink in the morning—"just enough to get a buzz on"—and that he had probably done so on that Wednesday. He said he didn't even know where Clearview was for certain and that he had never had any reason to go there—despite the fact he had lived in Snohomish County for fifteen years until he moved into his mother's home in Renton a month before the sex attack.

Charles Campbell's juvenile record showed arrests for auto theft, burglary, and resisting arrest, and that he had spent time at a juvenile detention center. In 1973 he had been charged with defrauding an innkeeper, and the 1974 drug charges had stemmed from his alleged possession of sixty tablets of amphetamines. And that was just in Snohomish County. Far across the Cascade Mountains, in Okanogan County, Campbell had been arrested in the fall of 1974—before the attack on Renae Wicklund—for violation of the federal firearms act, resisting arrest, criminal trespass, burglary, two counts of grand larceny, carrying a concealed weapon, and second-degree assault. Those charges were still extant.

All in all, Charles Campbell was not someone any woman would want to see running up her driveway.

Renae Wicklund was vastly relieved when Campbell was arrested after she identified him in March 1976. He was charged with one count of first-degree assault with intent to kill and one count of sodomy. By reporting what had happened to her, she had become one of the small percentage of women who have the courage to turn a sex criminal in to the police. Law enforcement authorities agree that statistics on sex crimes are almost impossible to chart accurately, that perhaps only one out of ten victims makes a police report. Women who have been raped and sexually molested are afraid and embarrassed. They are naturally hesitant to get on the witness stand and tell strangers in a courtroom the intimate details of an aberrant sexual attack.

But Renae Wicklund reported Campbell, and she got up in court and told it all. Her neighbor, Barbara Hendrickson, went on the stand, too. There was no way they could refuse to testify and face their consciences knowing that a monstrous criminal might go free to harm other women. Still, the ordeal was agonizing.

Under our justice system, the suspect has the right to face his accusers, and Renae had to testify about the sexual appetites of her attacker as Charles Campbell stared at her, this huge man with the piercing dark eyes.

Renae Wicklund's testimony was bolstered by testimony from a young woman who had once lived with Campbell. The woman said she lived near the Wicklunds' home and that Campbell had visited her often—including the week of the rape. Campbell's former lover said that he carried a knife and that he had told her, "You never know when you're going to need it."

The seven-woman, five-man jury found Charles Campbell guilty of both the assault and the sodomy. They also found that he had committed those crimes while in possession of a deadly weapon. At his sentencing, his prior record was introduced, and the consensus was that he was not fit to be on the streets for a very long time. Campbell had already pleaded guilty to second-degree burglary in the Okanogan County cases and had received up to fifteen years in prison with a five-year minimum. In Snohomish County, Judge Phillip Sheridan sentenced Campbell to another thirty years in prison with a seven-and-a-half-year minimum for the attack on the Wicklunds.

Charles Campbell's trial in the attack on Renae and Shannah lasted only three days. It didn't even rate a headline in the Everett papers.

The headlines would come later.

Renae Wicklund went home to pick up the pieces of her life, scarred as all sexual attack victims are by a pervasive fear that never quite goes away. Her marriage to Jack Wicklund broke up, partially from the lingering emotional trauma of the sex attack and partially for personal reasons. She and Shannah remained in the modest little white house in the woods, and Renae worked hard to support them. She worked as a beautician and also as an accountant for beauty parlors. She was a very intelligent woman and a single mother who wanted to be sure Shannah had everything she needed. Her own mother, Hilda, had always worked, and Renae's life was solidly grounded in the work ethic.

Renae remained on friendly terms with Jack after he moved out. She also stayed close to her in-laws, who lived in a little town in Kitsap County across Puget Sound. Jack's parents had always liked Renae. She joined their family get-togethers happily; her own mother and her sister Lorene were more than a thousand miles away in North Dakota. Renae was a great cook and brought food to every Wicklund holiday gathering, and she was a wonderful mother to Shannah, their granddaughter. Even though Renae was divorced from their son, she made sure that Jack's parents saw Shannah often.

Once they got used to Jack's being gone, Renae Wicklund and Shannah seemed to do all right. Don and Barbara helped out with chores Renae couldn't manage, and both the Hendricksons adored Shannah.

* * *

Jack Wicklund was the one who now became a target for violence. In December 1977 he was almost killed in a bizarre attack. Wicklund was found in his West Seattle home, tied to a chair and severely burned over most of his body. He was rushed to a hospital, but it was a long time before doctors would cautiously say he might live and even longer before Wicklund could give a statement. All he remembered was that a stranger had walked into his home carrying a package and wished him Merry Christmas. He insisted he had never seen the man before. The stranger then tied Jack to a chair, poured gasoline over him, and struck a match.

Miraculously, Jack Wicklund didn't die, but he was horribly scarred and lived with constant, unyielding pain. He was forced to wear a kind of rubber suit to minimize the formation of scar tissue.

In April 1978 Jack Wicklund left his parents' home in Hansville, Washington, after a visit. They were worried about his burns, and it had been awful for them to see their son in his strange rubber suit, but he was alive. A few hours after Jack left to go home, a Kitsap County coroner's deputy came to his parents' home and broke the news that Jack had been killed in a one-car accident on the Hansville Road. His car had left the road and crashed into a tree, killing him instantly. There were no witnesses. The ensuing investigation into Jack Wicklund's death never produced any definite answers as to why the crash had occurred. After surviving what should have been a fatal torching, Wicklund had met his fate on a lonely road. The curve where the car had left the road was known to be dangerous, but Wicklund had traversed the county road countless times before, and he knew the curve was there; he should have been prepared for it. Perhaps he had been temporarily blinded by oncoming headlights. If so, the other car hadn't stopped. Perhaps he had been run off the road.

Seattle police have never solved the murder attempt on Wicklund. Perhaps he was suicidal and it took him two tries to succeed in destroying himself. Perhaps he was involved in something unsavory or dangerous—or both. Or perhaps Jack Wicklund was only a very unlucky man.

The shock of the deliberate torching of her ex-husband and then his accidental death coming so hard on the heels of the murder attempt only served to heighten Renae Wicklund's constant anxiety. The attack by Charles Campbell had made her think that the world was a terribly dangerous place where tragedy waited just ahead. She could not help but wonder if the incidents were somehow connected, if they were more than just random misfortunes. She told friends and co-workers that she lived and walked in terror that something awful was going to happen again. And who could blame her?

Still, Renae Wicklund put on the facade of a cheerful, outgoing woman who was confident that she could take care of fatherless Shannah. Maybe trouble came in threes; people always said that. If that was true, then her three were all used up: the sexual attack, the burning, Jack's fatal car crash.

Renae Wicklund didn't know much about the workings of the justice system. She knew that Charles Campbell had been sent to the Monroe Reformatory—Washington's mid-level penal institution. Security was not as tight there as it was in the state penitentiary at Walla Walla, but it was much stronger than at Green Hill Academy, the boys' training school in Chehalis. Renae didn't care where Campbell was as long as he was locked up. All together, he had forty-five years hanging over him. That seemed like a safety net. Renae assumed that Campbell would be over sixty-five when he finally got out. By then Shannah would be middle-aged and Renae would be an old woman. They would probably have moved far away, too, maybe even back to North Dakota.

To a layman, forty-five years does sound like a long, long time. However, Charles Campbell's two sentences would run concurrently, not consecutively. Although it wasn't likely, it was within the realm of possibility that he could serve only the seven-and-a-half-year minimum and be released in 1983 or 1984. He would, of course, have to have some time off for good behavior to do that.

Renae had no idea that forty-five years didn't really *mean* forty-five years.

She and Shannah stayed in their old neighborhood, and Renae worked to keep the house and yard up. Shannah grew through the toddler stage and became a pretty little girl with straight shiny brown bangs, a pageboy haircut, and big brown eyes. Tall for her age, she was quiet and a little shy. She went to the Shepherd of the Hill Lutheran Church Sunday school and they teased her fondly about being their "little missionary" because she was always bringing a new friend along with her.

Renae had played the flute as a girl, and Shannah had ambitions to master it, too. She invited Don and Barb over for "a recital," and they clapped as if she were a child prodigy. She took dancing lessons, and Don Hendrickson took pictures of her in her costumes. Her grandpa Wicklund helped her learn how to ride a two-wheel bike.

The neighborhood in Clearview was a good place for a little girl to grow up, even though it might have been easier for Renae to live in a city apartment where she didn't have to cope with leaking roofs and broken plumbing and keeping a yard clear of weeds. She really counted on her neighbors. She and Shannah shopped at the Clearview market, and everybody knew both of them. Barbara Hendrickson's grandchildren grew up along with Shannah, and they often played together.

Renae proved to be a really clever businesswoman. She operated her accounting business for beauty parlors out of her own home, and her clients were pleased with her know-how and efficiency. She was expert in helping students get grants and loans to help them through beauty school. In early 1982 Renae was only thirty-one, but she was shouldering her responsibilities with great maturity.

If she thought about the man who had broken into her home eight years earlier—and those close to her say she did—the scary memories crept up full-blown only when the moon was hidden behind scudding clouds and the wind sighed in the tall trees around her little house. He was part of a nightmare she couldn't quite forget, but his image was gone when the sun rose again.

Renae bought a large dog, an Afghan hound, more to keep her company than for protection. Afghans are not particularly territorial or effective as watchdogs. But it would bark if anyone came around her property.

Less than 25 miles away, Charles Campbell was locked up in the Monroe Reformatory. He had earned the nickname "One Punch" because his fist was so powerful. He was a bully, and weaker inmates toadied to him, fearful of that fist. Guards were aware of Campbell's drug trafficking—*inside* prison—and his infraction record grew thicker and thicker.

Renae was serene in her belief that her attacker was locked up in prison and still had years and years to go on his sentence. Nevertheless, she was super-cautious, because she knew what could happen. Charles Campbell wasn't the only man who attacked women. Renae had strong locks on the doors and windows, and she warned Shannah never, never to go with strangers.

It snowed in early January 1982, and Don Hendrickson noticed footprints one morning outside the side windows of his home. Later that day, Renae told Barbara that she too had found footprints beneath her windows. Since her house stood so far back from the road, the large prints in the snow upset her.

Hilda Ahlers had been visiting Renae over Christmas, as she almost always did. Renae had never told her mother about the man who had attacked her seven years earlier.

"Renae was so strong," her mother said. "I never knew. She didn't want me to worry." But with the clarity of hindsight, Hilda would come to see that something was wrong that winter. "I remember one night when Renae's dog—who normally never barked at all—went wild and began barking fiercely. I thought there was something horrid outside, but I was afraid to look."

Not long after that, the Afghan nipped a neighbor's child, and Renae decided to give it away.

Looking back, Hilda Ahlers remembered more. "Another time, I saw Renae looking out the window at the road with the strangest look on her face. I said, 'What do you see out there?' and Renae just answered, 'Oh, nothing.' She didn't seem frightened; she was just watching so quietly."

Renae didn't know that Charles Campbell had been out of prison that weekend in January. Incredibly, and despite a stack of infractions, he had somehow earned time off for good behavior. He had served less than six years in prison, and he was already going out on furloughs.

Neither Renae nor the Hendricksons were aware of that. No one had bothered to tell them. Nor did anyone tell them when Campbell was transferred a month later to a work-release facility located less than ten miles from Clearview.

Renae missed the Easter service at church on April 11, 1982. She had a terribly sore throat. Don Hendrickson finally coaxed her into seeing a doctor. "I'll go with you; I'll hold your hand," he kidded. And he *did* hold her hand while an emergency room doctor examined her. She had strep throat, and she had to stay in bed for days, taking penicillin and trying to swallow the soft foods that Barb Hendrickson brought over to her.

April 14 was a Wednesday—just as it had been a Wednesday when Charles Campbell attacked Renae and Shannah in 1974. It was sunny but blustery, and the bright periods alternated with overhanging clouds. Daffodils, dogwood and fruit trees were in bloom, and spring had almost arrived. Except for the fact that Renae was sick, everything was normal. Barbara ran over in the morning to see how she was and found her a little better. She promised she would be back in the afternoon. Renae watched television and tried to read a little.

"Barb went out to the end of our driveway to get our mail that afternoon," Don remembers. "She met Shannah coming home from school and told her to tell Renae that she'd be over soon to make Jell-O. I remember it was 4:20 when Barb asked to borrow my watch; she wanted to use it to check Renae's pulse."

Barbara Hendrickson then headed toward Renae's house. There were no loud sounds from the Wicklund home, nothing to alarm any of the neighbors. She was gone for quite a while, but Don didn't think anything of it. She and Renae and Shannah often visited for hours.

It seemed to get dark earlier than usual that evening. A gale-force wind battered the Hendrickson house. Don glanced at the spot on his wrist where his watch usually was and then got up from his chair and checked a clock. He discovered that it was almost six. His wife had been gone for an hour and a half.

Don put on a jacket and walked down his driveway, across the street, and up Renae's long driveway. He usually went in through the sliding glass doors to the kitchen area. The glass doors were partly open and he paused. *That's odd,* he thought, and then he slid the doors open more and stepped into the house.

"The house was *so* quiet," he said later. "It was unlike anything I'd ever heard before—or since. Totally still. And then, as I got further into the house, I heard something—water running from a faucet somewhere."

It was the faucet in the kitchen sink. He turned the spigot off and listened for some other sound. There should have been three of them in the house—Barb, Renae, and Shannah—and they always made enough noise for six. He listened again, but he heard nothing. Don looked around the kitchen and shuddered involuntarily when he saw that a chair had been knocked over near the dinette set. That wasn't right. Renae always kept everything so neat. The silence kept Don from calling out to his wife or Renae or Shannah.

Donald Hendrickson found them in a few moments of horror that he will never forget.

He had left the kitchen and moved slowly toward the short hallway that led to the bedrooms. He found Barbara first. His wife of thirty-four years lay motionless in the hallway, her throat slashed, the arteries severed. Even as he knelt beside her, he knew she was gone. A halo of blood soaked the carpet beneath her head and stained her beautiful prematurely silver hair. It was a scene that Don Hendrickson would never, ever be able to erase from his memory.

His wife's throat had been slit from one side to the other with a razor-sharp knife, allowing the blood to course out of her jugular vein and carotid arteries. She could have lived only moments before she bled to death.

Numb with shock, Don got up from Barbara's side and continued to make his way down the hall. He didn't want to, but he had to see what was behind the other doors. Shannah's bedroom was empty. He moved to Renae's bedroom next, pausing at the door before he made himself turn and look inside.

They were both there on the floor. Renae was nude—her body hideously bruised and her throat slashed with macabre efficiency. Shannah lay across the room from her mother. She had been almost decapitated by a knife's merciless edge. Nine years old, with her throat cut. All of them dead.

Automatically Don Hendrickson picked up the phone with nerveless fingers and dialed 911. Then he walked outside to try to make his mind function. "I heard a car engine start up," he said. "It was Renae's next-door neighbor and her daughters, and I ran out and shouted at them, 'Shannah and Renae are dead!' But they just looked at me, and then they got out of their car and ran back into their house. I think they were afraid of me because I was acting so wild."

Snohomish County deputies arrived shortly. They took one look at the carnage inside the Wicklund home and radioed in for the homicide detectives. What they encountered on April 14 would mean days of working almost around the clock. The public had no idea at first how ghastly the triple murder was. The Clearview story hit the media as a very short, deliberately succinct news bulletin.

The detectives released almost no information: "Three people were found dead on April 14 in south Snohomish County. . . ."

Lieutenant Glenn Mann and Sergeant Joe Belinc would head the probe. If anyone could sort out the real story behind what had happened in the little rambler in Clearview, these men could. In addition, they would have twenty-nine investigators working on the Wicklund-Hendrickson case before it was finished. Belinc had been the driving force behind the apprehension of Washington's infamous Bellevue Sniper in the early 1970s. Now he had another headline case to work.

Someone had gotten into the Wicklund home, someone strong enough to overpower two women; the youngster could not have been much of an adversary. It appeared that Barbara Hendrickson had broken free and was, perhaps, running for help when she was struck down in the hall. It was even possible that Renae Wicklund and Shannah were already dead when Barbara Hendrickson entered the home. She might have called out to them, or she might have felt the same dread that her husband felt an hour later, might have heard the same thundering silence and been afraid—only to encounter the person with the knife and realize at the last moment that she had walked into horror.

The Snohomish County investigators spent hours at the scene, looking for bits of physical evidence that the killer might have left behind. The bodies were photographed where they lay before they were released to the Snohomish County coroner's deputies. Saddened and shocked neighbors stood at the edge of the crime-scene search area, along with cameramen from the news media who shot footage of the body bags being loaded into a station wagon–hearse for removal to await autopsy. It did not seem possible to them that Renae and Shannah and Barbara were dead. This couldn't have happened, not so suddenly and so quietly on an April day. One neighbor murmured how frightened she was, wondering if some madman was on the loose, waiting somewhere in the thick trees to strike again.

The investigators began a door-to-door canvass. They found no one who had heard or seen anything—but they did hear again and again that this was not the first time that Renae Wicklund had been the victim of a madman. Everyone knew that Renae had been attacked eight years before, and those close to her recalled that she had lived in a state of quiet terror ever since. She had feared that he might come back one day and wreak revenge upon her for testifying against him. No amount of reassurance that she had probably been a random victim, that he had probably forgotten all about her, could convince her.

She had seemed to know that she was doomed, that he—or someone—would destroy the safe walls she'd tried to build around herself and Shannah. And yet everyone described Renae as a wonderful person, a good friend, an intelligent hard worker. The extent of her friends' and neighbors' grief demonstrated just what a good person she had been. And so had Barbara Hendrickson. Once, Barbara had loaded a shotgun to protect Renae and Shannah. This time, she hadn't had the opportunity to seize a weapon to fight back. The slash wounds across each victim's throat stamped the killings as executions—cold-blooded, effective, designed to kill as if that was the murderer's only mission. He had wanted them dead. It seemed that simple. The child? She couldn't have harmed the killer, but she was old enough and smart enough to describe him, and so she had to die too. It seemed impossible that anyone could have had a grudge against a nine-year-old girl.

The detectives questioned Don Hendrickson, asking who he thought might have had reason to kill his wife and neighbors. He finally said, "The only person I could imagine that might have done this is the man who raped Renae."

At the time, he could not even remember Charles Campbell's name. Campbell was history, or he was supposed to be. But when the detectives checked on Campbell's whereabouts, they were shocked to find out that he had been living and working a short distance from Clearview, *without supervision,* almost every day.

The word from the Department of Corrections was not only startling; it was appalling. Records showed that in October 1981—less than six years after his conviction for raping Renae Wicklund—Charles Campbell had been moved to a minimum-security facility known as Monroe House. He worked there as a cook, and he was still confined, but eligible for furloughs. On February 24, six weeks before the triple murders in Clearview, Campbell moved even closer to complete freedom: he was released from the prison itself and assigned to an Everett work-release residence two blocks from the Snohomish County Courthouse. This meant that he would work outside during the day, sleep in the facility at night, and had to follow strict rules. In his case, particularly, he was to abstain from alcohol and drug use.

Even though Campbell was literally free for much of each day and within a dozen miles of the Clearview home where the 1974 attack had occurred, even though he was housed two blocks from the Snohomish County Courthouse, there was no notification to the sheriff's office.

Some might say it was like dumping a fox in the chicken house without letting the farmer know.

On the night of the murders—April 14—Charles Campbell returned to the work-release residence obviously under the influence of alcohol. His blood alcohol reading was .29—almost three times higher than Washington's legal level for intoxication. Tests also detected the presence of morphine, codeine, quinine, methadone, and cocaine!

Because he had broken the cardinal rule of the halfway house, Campbell was taken back to the Monroe Reformatory. Of course, by then, Renae Wicklund, Shannah Wicklund, and Barbara Hendrickson were dead. They had neither been consulted nor informed about Campbell's early release in February. What happened to them was shocking, but the most shocking part of the horror was that it was preventable. There were so many ways the inexorable path to violent murder could have been blocked.

Back in the Monroe Reformatory, Charles Campbell was charged with three counts of aggravated first-degree murder on April 19, 1982. With the news that Charles Campbell had been charged with the three murders, citizens of Snohomish County—and, indeed, citizens all over the state—began to react with disbelief and anger. The owner of Rick's Clearview Foods, Rick Arriza, placed a petition in his small grocery store, where the victims had shopped, asking for signatures from residents demanding the death penalty for Campbell if he was convicted. People came from all around the state to sign it.

Along with the anger, there was fear. The number of women reporting rapes and other sexual assaults dropped dramatically. Women were afraid to report rapes. If they couldn't be sure that the men who had attacked them would be put away for a long time, if they had to fear violent reprisal, then they decided that it was safer just to forget what had happened—and try to live with it.

Sheriff Bobby Dodge, Lieutenant Mann, Sergeant Belinc, and their crews of detectives worked under great constraint. They had a job to do which required an orderly progression to bring a solid case against Campbell. They would not—could not—talk to reporters, and they took the flak stoically. Snohomish County sheriff Bobby Dodge did appear on television decrying the system that had allowed a man like Campbell, with all the crimes he'd been convicted of, back into the same community where the crime against the Wicklunds had occurred—and without any notification to law enforcement authorities.

On May 1, 1982, Charles Campbell, now twenty-seven, appeared before Judge Dennis Britt and entered a plea of innocent. He was ordered to undergo psychiatric testing. Possibly a defense attorney would use the results later to enter a plea of innocent by reason of insanity. The hugely tall Campbell wore handcuffs and leg irons, and spectators were searched with metal detectors before they were allowed into the courtroom. Campbell wanted to go to Western State Hospital for testing, but the roster of sex criminals who had escaped from that mental hospital to do more damage to innocent citizens was too long already. Judge Britt ordered that Campbell would meet with psychiatrists in his jail isolation cell.

The first reports on Campbell's six years at the Monroe Reformatory indicated that he had a good record there. Parole board members were aware that Campbell had made a suicide attempt in custody in 1976, and he had been watched closely by the board, but they refused to comment on the prisoner's psychiatric records. Campbell's attorneys said he had acknowledged that he had a problem with alcohol and drugs and that he thought himself a "borderline case" who "snapped" when he was drinking and blacked out.

In a case that grew steadily more bizarre, the *Seattle Times* reported that one of the witnesses interviewed by homicide detectives was a drug and alcohol counselor who had participated in a program in the Monroe Reformatory until about 1980. According to records of her former employer, the young female counselor had resigned because she had broken one of the first rules of counseling by becoming romantically involved with her "patient." The patient was Charles Campbell. The woman refused to comment, but a relative admitted that Campbell had been a visitor in their home in early 1982 while he was on a furlough from prison.

Campbell's alleged close personal relationship with the woman was borne out by a notation in the Monroe House files on January 28, 1982. Campbell had returned from a furlough and said he was in a car that had hit a pole northwest of Monroe. The car, a 1974 Volkswagen, was found, abandoned, by a Washington State trooper. It was totaled, and the pole was heavily damaged. The trooper checked with the Department of Motor Vehicles for the car's registration and found that it belonged to the woman who had been a counselor at the prison. She later told her insurance agency that it had been wrecked, but no charges were ever brought because troopers could not determine who had been driving the Volkswagen.

Campbell may have had charm for one woman, but another, his ex-wife, seemed unimpressed by his charisma. She reported to a detective in the town where she lived that Campbell—whom she, too, believed was still in prison at the time—had come to her home on Christmas Day 1981 and raped her. She said he had returned twice to rape her again. She had finally gone to the police on March 16 and attempted to make a formal complaint of rape against Campbell but the police had advised her the case seemed too weak to bring to court.

This was the man who Renae Wicklund believed was safely behind prison walls. He had only been 12 miles away, working days in a landscaping firm, apparently maintaining some kind of romantic relationship with his former drug counselor and allegedly assaulting his ex-wife. There was another factor. He had come to the attention of work-release authorities on March 18 for "having possession of or consuming beer at Everett Work Release." A female officer found a partially filled can of beer on his bed and noted that the room smelled of alcohol.

This report enraged Campbell. He hated having the female officers at the facility write him up, and he showed his resentment openly. He argued with them about even the slightest order they gave him. He said he had much more freedom in his social outings when he had furloughs from the reformatory. He felt he should have complete freedom to do what he wanted while he was in work release.

A hearing had been held about his "poor attitude and behavior" toward two women officers, but he was allowed to remain in work release. He was given a second chance primarily because of his good record while in prison.

But *was* his record that good in prison?

A look at Charles Rodman Campbell's "good behavior" was startling. For some reason, when Campbell came up before the parole board seeking work release, the paperwork that came with him cited only three minor infractions during his first year at Monroe and referred to him as a "model prisoner" thereafter. The infractions mentioned were not that bad: mutilating a curtain; possessing "pruno" (an alcoholic beverage that cons distill from yeast and any fruit or vegetable matter they can get their hands on: potatoes, apples, oranges); and refusing to allow a guard to search him for a club he had hidden under his jacket. He said he carried the club to ward off attacks by bullies in the yard.

After these minor incidents—more indicative of the behavior of a bad boy than a dangerous con—the superintendent of the state reformatory indicated to the parole board that Campbell's record was spotless.

Not quite.

After Campbell had won his furloughs and his work-release assignment, *after* Renae and Shannah Wicklund and Barbara Hendrickson had their throats slit, and *after* Campbell was charged with those crimes, the head of the guards' union at the reformatory said that Campbell had used drugs as recently as the year prior to his work release.

It was obvious that someone had been covering up for Charles Campbell. Shortly after Campbell was transferred to the work-release program, the Washington State parole board discovered that the Monroe Reformatory had failed to forward copies of prison infractions to them. Hundreds of prisoners had been released without having their behavior in prison evaluated. And Charles Campbell was one of those prisoners who had slipped through the fissures in the justice system.

KIRO-TV in Seattle managed to obtain additional infraction reports on Campbell, incidents that occurred between December 31, 1977, and June 13, 1978; these infractions were never revealed to the parole board beyond a cursory notation in a counselor's report, which mentioned that Campbell had threatened a nurse and gotten into a beef with another inmate. According to the records, the huge bushy-haired con had lunged at the nurse on New Year's Eve 1977, when she refused to give him his medication because he was an hour late reporting to the hospital. "When I refused to give him the medication late," the nurse had said, "he jumped to his feet with his fists clenched and moved toward me in a threatening manner, as though he intended to hit me."

A staff member had stepped between Campbell and the female nurse, and a guard had dragged Campbell away while he shouted obscenities at her. On May 8, 1978, Campbell had kicked another inmate in the groin and ignored a guard's order to move on in a stand-off that lasted until additional guards arrived. Later that month, Campbell had cut into the chow line and angered other prisoners. He refused to move on and broke a tray in half in his hands. The situation was fraught with tension in the mess hall full of convicts. On May 24, Campbell was discovered high on drugs. He fought guards like a tiger until they got his jacket off and found an envelope in it containing three empty yellow capsules.

A month later Campbell again balked at a body search and tossed an envelope to another con. Guards recovered it and found a syringe and needle inside. He was punished with the removal of privileges for these infractions, but even his guards were afraid of him. They asked administrators to transfer Campbell from Monroe to the state penitentiary at Walla Walla. Nothing came of this request.

None of this information was available to the parole board when it came time for Campbell's parole hearing.

When the news of Charles Campbell's actual prison behavior reached the media, Washington State legislators immediately scheduled an investigation. One state senator put it bluntly: "Somebody obviously held back information that caused the death of three people." Prison administrators argued that the parole board had asked *not* to see all the minor infractions, and that they had held back the reports for that reason.

Charles Campbell apparently scared the hell out of a lot of people, guards and fellow prisoners alike. He was so big, so muscular, and so quick to erupt into rage. Guards who had reservations about Campbell's suitability for parole didn't want their names published, but said off the record that they thought he should have been sent back to prison.

Even more frightened of seeing his name in print was an ex-convict who had served time with Campbell; the label "snitch" is a sure way to commit suicide in or out of prison for an ex-con. But the anonymous man recalled that Charles Campbell had ruled his fellow inmates with terror, forcing the weaker cons to obtain drugs for him and to submit to sodomy. Prison "prestige" belonged to the physically strong.

It is quite likely that no one will ever know what really happened on April 14, 1982. The victims are dead, and the murderer chose not to speak of his crimes.

Charles Campbell went on trial in November 1982. If he was convicted of aggravated murder in the first degree, he could be sentenced to death. To accomplish that, the state had to prove that Campbell's crimes fit within the parameters of the statute as follows:

- He was serving a prison term in a state facility or program at the time of the murders.
- The victims had previously testified against him in a court of law.

- Campbell allegedly committed the murders to conceal his identity.
- There was more than one victim and the murders were part of a common scheme or plan.
- The murders were committed along with other crimes, including first-degree rape, first-degree robbery, and first-degree burglary.

They were all true. Renae Wicklund had been raped as her stalker wreaked his revenge. Her jewelry was stolen. Allegedly Charles Campbell attempted to sell the missing jewelry hours after the slayings. The burglary charges would indicate that the defendant made illegal entry into the home—by force or subterfuge.

Charles Campbell asked for a change of venue to another state, claiming that he could not receive a fair trial in the state of Washington because of the media coverage. His request was denied.

On November 26, 1982, the day after Thanksgiving, the jury retired to debate the question of Campbell's guilt or innocence. They returned after only four hours. They had found the defendant guilty. Guilty on three counts of aggravated first-degree murder.

In the penalty phase of his trial, Charles Campbell was sentenced to death. At first he refused to cooperate with his attorneys' efforts to have his life spared. They appealed, but he said it was against his wishes.

He would spend years on death row in the Washington State penitentiary in Walla Walla, a fearsome figure who spat at Governor Booth Gardner when he had the temerity to peer through the bulletproof-glass window in Campbell's cell. For a man who one day soon might beg Gardner to stay his execution at the last minute, it was an incredibly stupid show of temper.

Campbell was visited regularly by his mistress, the ex-alcohol counselor and her child—Charles Campbell's son. They seemed a strangely mismated couple.

As the years passed and his attorneys continued to appeal his death sentence, Campbell was disdainful of their efforts on his behalf. All the while, he was drawing nearer and nearer to the hangman's noose. In March of 1989 he came within two days of being executed when his attorneys won a stay from the U.S. Ninth Circuit Court of Appeals. The three-judge panel agreed to listen to Campbell's attorneys' appeal, which contended he had been denied his right to a fair trial because he was not present when his jury was selected. (*He* had refused to come to court.)

The second issue was that having to choose the means of one's death was cruel and unusual punishment. (When Washington State added death by lethal injection to its roster of execution methods, Charles Campbell had balked. He would not choose, he insisted. In essence, the state was forcing him to commit suicide by saying which method of execution he preferred.) "That's against my religion," he said smugly.

The Ninth Circuit Court panel heard arguments in Campbell's case in June 1989, but the judges did not hand down their decision for two and a half years. In April 1992 they rejected Campbell's arguments—but later granted his request to have the same issues reheard by an eleven-judge panel. In addition, Charles Campbell and his team of attorneys filed another federal petition, his third. He lost the latter, but the second is still pending.

In the decade since his conviction, Charles Campbell has apparently come to believe that he too is mortal and that there is a fairly good possibility that the state of Washington *is* going to kill him. By the time Charles

Campbell began to cooperate in the endless series of appeals, it may have been too late.

When Westly Allan Dodd, a murderous pedophile, was executed on Washington State's gallows on January 5, 1993, the state broke its thirty-five-year pattern of not carrying out the death penalty. Charles Campbell is expected to be executed before 1993 is over. Whether the execution will be by hanging or lethal injection is the only question left.

Few tears will be shed.

Renae and Shannah Wicklund are buried side by side in Jamestown, North Dakota, far from Clearview, Washington. Hilda Ahlers came to Clearview to settle their affairs, and grocer Rick Arriza drove her to the Clearview Elementary School to pick up Shannah's belongings. There wasn't much, because nine years is not enough time to gather much—beyond love. "I took her up to the school," Arizza recalled. "We picked up Shannah's things—glue, storybooks, an umbrella, notebooks. She just started crying."

Hilda Ahlers rarely sleepwalks anymore, but she did for years, reliving the moment she first learned of Renae's and Shannah's deaths.

"There was a light tap on my door at three A.M.," she recalls. "And I said, 'Who is it?' and this small voice said, 'It's me,' and I knew it was Lorene. I was so frightened when I opened the door, wondering which one of my grandchildren I'd lost. But Lorene was standing there holding her littlest one, and her husband, Jerry, was standing beside her with their other two children.

"I remember saying to myself, Thank God, they're all there, and then I looked behind them and I saw our pastor, and I knew it had to be Renae.

" 'Airplane accident?' I asked.

" 'No.'

" 'Car accident?'

" 'No . . . murdered.'

"My mind flew to Shannah. Who was looking after Shannah? And then I heard Lorene say, 'Shannah too.' "

Update, December 2003

After twelve years of appeals, Charles Campbell finally came to the end of the road. His last chance to have his death sentence commuted was to obtain a reprieve from the governor of Washington State. In 1994, Mike Lowry was one of the most liberal governors in the state in recent years, and, ironically, he did not believe in capital punishment. Lowry did, however, meet with Campbell face-to-face, aware that Campbell had spit in the face of his predecessor.

Mike Lowry had read voluminous information on Campbell's crimes, and he stared directly in the eyes of the strutting convicted killer. Seeing the danger there and remembering what he'd read of the last moments of Renae and Shannah Wicklund and Barbara Hendrickson, Governor Mike Lowry refused to commute Campbell's sentence.

Late on the night of May 27, 1994, guards came to bring Charles Campbell to the gallows. Witnesses staring nervously at the window of the hanging room knew there was a delay, but they didn't know why. Behind the scenes, Campbell was so frightened at the thought of his own death that he had to be carried from his cell. His legs would not support him.

When he entered the execution chamber, it was obvious that he could not stand to have the noose slipped over his neck. Finally, his legs were strapped to a board so he could stand atop the trap door.

A curtain fell over the window as the trap sprung, and minutes later, Charles Campbell was declared dead. He was the second person to be executed in Washington in thirty-five years.

Although the money was only a small measure of justice for Campbell's three victims, Hilda Ahlers's and Don Hendrickson's civil suit against the state for failing to notify Renae Wicklund that he was on work release, living so close to her home, was successful. The grieving families were awarded $2.3 million.

For several years, Don Hendrickson was active in Friends and Families of Violent Crime Victims and Missing Persons, one of the first victims' support groups in the country. There, he met Doreen Hanson, who had lost her daughter, Janna, eight years earlier to homicidal violence (see "The Runaway" in *A Rose for Her Grave,* Ann Rule's Crime Files, Vol. 1).

Don and Doreen got married and it seemed to be a happy ending after so much tragedy. But the things they had in common—grief and regret—were burdens instead, and they couldn't sustain their marriage. They divorced a few years later.

Don Hendrickson died several years ago.

One Trick Pony
(from *You Belong to Me*)

Most of us believe that there is no such thing as a perfect murder. And we have good reason to; literature down through the ages has told us that. Shakespeare said it in many of his plays: "How easily murder is discovered!" "Truth will come to light; murder cannot be hid long." "Murder, though it have no tongue, will speak."

Cervantes wrote in Don Quixote that "Murder will out."

In the seventeenth century John Webster wrote, "Other sins only speak; murder shrieks out."

Not really. There are, unfortunately, hundreds of perfect murders. Some are never discovered. More are never solved.

Donna Howard's death was listed as accidental in dusty records for a dozen years. But Donna didn't die the way detectives and coroners originally believed she had, and it took the determined efforts of her own sister, Bobbi, to bring belated justice. Bobbi Bennett never gave up until the truth about Donna's death was exposed to light like the underside of a muddy rock turned over in the bright sun. With a singleness of purpose that defied fatigue and despair, Bobbi fought to avenge Donna. Only when she did could she go on with her own life.

This case, I believe, is a classic example that things are not always what they seem to be—particularly when it comes to murder.

The state of Washington is cut in half by the Cascade Mountains; Seattle and its environs are termed "the coast" by eastern Washington residents, even though the actual Pacific coast is many miles away. The west side of the state is moderate and lush, green, often sodden with rain. Eastern Washington has fertile fields, arid desert, the rolling Palouse Hills covered with a sea of wheat, and orchards as far as the eye can see.

Ellensburg and Yakima are in the middle of orchard country, of horse country. You put an apple or cherry twig in irrigated land there and it will take root overnight. Or so it seems.

These are western towns where even the bankers and the grocery store managers usually wear cowboy boots. There are rodeos, horse shows, and county fairs. Just as it does in every medium-sized town in America, an occasional scandal surfaces. Sometimes the scandals are homegrown: a love triangle exploding into deadly violence, or a family fight that ends in death. The shock waves that follow seem to occur only in small towns. Perhaps it is simply that big cities have so much violence that individual crimes don't stand out as much as they do in small towns.

* * *

Donna Bennett was born on Flag Day—June 14, 1932; a few years later, her sister Blodwyn—who would always be called Bobbi—came along. Their parents were older, at least for that era, both over thirty when their girls were born. The Bennetts and their forefathers had lived near Ellensburg at the upper edge of the Yakima Valley for generations. They were horse people—not fancy-schmancy horse people, but genuine cowboys.

Possibly because they had waited longer to have children, Donna and Bobbi's parents adored their two little girls. The Bennett girls were pretty, with shiny brown hair and huge brown eyes. Both Donna and Bobbi were born to ride horses, galloping joyously with the smell of sagebrush and apple blossoms in their nostrils. They grew up together, as close as sisters are meant to be.

Donna was already standing bareback on a horse at the age of three, her balance perfectly attuned to the horse's gait.

When Donna was five she was chosen the "best-dressed junior cowgirl" at the Ellensburg Rodeo parade.

Donna and Bobbi attended Ellensburg High School. Donna was in the class of 1950, and her friends from those days remember her as clearly as if they had seen her only yesterday. She could be very serious and a little straitlaced, but when she was your friend, she was your friend forever. She didn't have a lot of time for after-school activities because she had chores to do on the farm. She usually rode the bus right home after school, and she didn't date much in high school.

But Donna's dad had played the drums, and she did, too—the slender girl marching along in the Bull Dog band, keeping time on the bulky drums. Jean "Tex" Turner Parsons was the drum majorette, and Fay Griffin Moss and Gail Kelly Sether were flag twirlers. They were

Donna Bennett's best friends. Fay and Donna had known each other since fifth grade. They would stay close for all of her life.

All through high school and for years afterward Donna and Bobbi rode their horses in parades. "They rode in the Ellensburg Rodeo—and in the other parades," Fay Moss remembers. "They were never in the royal court, though. I think it's because their family wasn't rich—and that's what it took to get in the court. But they were so classy, sitting straight in their saddles. They were *real* cowgirls."

When she was eighteen and graduating from Ellensburg High School a local newspaper picked Donna as the graduate with the prettiest eyes. It was true; she had huge doe-like eyes.

Donna and all her closest friends exchanged pictures. On the one she gave to "Tex" Turner she wrote, "Hi Tex, I can't forget all the good times we've had. Parties and the jokes on our band trips. I wish you all the luck and happiness in [the] future and be good!! Love and Kizzes, Donna."

Summertimes and after she had graduated high school, Donna performed as a trick rider at rodeos all over eastern Washington. She was wonderfully talented. Beautiful and slender, Donna wore bright satin shirts in rainbow colors, with sequined embroidery and pearl studs, tight pants, boots, and cowboy hats. Her picture brightened up many a county fair poster.

But Donna wasn't just pretty; she was a superb equestrienne. An action photo from those days in the fifties shows Donna standing *atop* Bobbi's white steed, Dana, her perfect body leaning tautly into the wind, her arms flung out exultantly as she performs a stunt called "The Hippodrome." Bobbi is on the horse, too, her feet hooked into the stirrups as she drapes herself *backwards* down over Dana's hindquarters, so close to the ground and the horse's hooves that her long hair actually trails along the ground of the arena.

Both Bennett girls were as confident with horses as most people would be with a puppy. They were alternately atop, underneath, dragging, and cavorting as the horse trotted so fast that the wind whipped their hair. They were exquisitely coordinated, in their glory.

But they weren't daredevils. They knew that horses could be skittish, and they took no chances. "Donna knew that you never put your head down to work on a horse's hooves," Fay says. "That you *back* up to a horse and present your least vulnerable part."

Donna figured she would meet a cowboy one day and settle down. That was her world, and she met dozens of handsome young men at the rodeos. But another kind of man came along, and Donna Bennett was attracted to him in spite of herself, and in spite of her friends' and family's reservations. She met Noyes Russell Howard at Yakima Valley Community College and began dating him sporadically.

Russ Howard was handsome then—not a big man, but he had a good, compactly muscled build. He was about five feet nine—two inches or so taller than Donna. He combed his thick hair into a wave in front. The best thing about Russ was his gift of gab; he was a riot at parties. You could never predict what Russ would do next.

"He was fun, and he was crazy," Fay Moss remembers. "I could see how she could be attracted to him."

Donna and Russ dated off and on. For a while in 1954 Donna and Fay moved to Seattle and lived together in a little apartment on Republican Street—on what would become the site of the 1962 World's Fair. Donna got a job as sales clerk at Best's Apparel in downtown Seattle. By the time Best's became the flagship store of Nordstrom's, Donna had moved back over the mountains. Her picture often appeared on fashion pages in the *Yakima Herald*. She was so photogenic that department stores often asked her to pose, wearing their newest lines.

After college Russ worked in a number of jobs—selling shoes at first. Eventually he worked, in one capacity or another, with seeds, sometimes as a salesman for a seed company in the Yakima Valley and later as a seed inspector for the State Department of Agriculture. He was only two years older than Donna, but far more worldly. When they met Russ was already a pretty good drinker, and that put Donna off. She didn't drink at all and didn't want to raise a family with liquor in the home. She was young; she thought he would change his bad habits in time.

When Russ proposed Donna hesitated. But she kept going out with him, and it was soon obvious that the quiet rodeo rider was in love with the glib party guy. They were very different, but often opposites *do* attract. Donna finally said yes, and though she delayed the wedding a few times, Donna finally married Russ Howard as the fifties eased into the sixties. She was almost thirty; all of her friends had been married for years.

Donna's family smiled determinedly at the wedding, but they worried. Donna's friends could see that she wanted desperately to make a go of her marriage, and that she ached for a secure home in which to have children. Apparently it took her a long time to feel secure; Donna Howard was into her thirties before her two daughters, Lisa and Marilyn, were born. Even though things weren't perfect and Russ was drinking, she wanted so much to have children.

Donna's family, well-known and respected in the valley, helped the young couple buy a home and some acreage on Galloway Road a few miles northwest of Yakima on the Naches River. Yakima is only about forty miles south of Ellensburg, so Donna still saw her family often. There was room for a stable; Donna couldn't imagine living without a horse or two.

Russ's job with the State of Washington meant he had to be on the road a good deal. That gave him the opportunity to imbibe away from his wife's disappointed eyes. It also gave him the chance to date other women. He would one day refer rather obliquely to his wife's "changing sexual needs" as the impetus that "drove" him into affairs with at least eight other women. It was an easy and ambiguous excuse for him, and Donna never had a chance to tell her side of the story.

Did Donna know that Russ was cheating on her? Probably. But she was loyal, and she was a very private person. Many women would have run crying to friends or, in Donna's case, to family. But for years Donna Howard kept her problems to herself. Her pride wouldn't let her admit how hellish her marriage had become.

Why any man would want to cheat on Donna Bennett Howard was a puzzle in itself. She was warm and friendly, and her family came first with her. Into her late thirties and early forties she remained a startlingly beautiful woman. She was as slender as she had been during her days as a rodeo queen, her face unlined, her eyes as lovely as ever, and her hair free of gray strands. Russ, on the other hand, had begun to show the effects of years of hard drinking. His face was seamed with deep wrinkles. But he had taken up weight-lifting, and that made him as strong as a man twice his size. He was still a barrel of laughs at a party or in a bar, however—and it was true that he had little difficulty attracting women.

The class of 1950 of Ellensburg High School stayed in

close touch. Originally there had been 107 in that graduating class. Although their numbers dwindled, at least half of them showed up at the class reunions they held every five years.

"Donna only came once," "Tex" Parsons says. "And she came alone. I think we all knew that she was afraid that Russ might get drunk and embarrass her. As much as she wanted to come to our reunions, she missed most of them."

"Tex" and Gene Parsons, who had moved to the Seattle area after they got married, stopped by to visit the Howards once when they were in Yakima for a Toastmasters convention. Russ seemed the same as he always had—maybe a little bit cockier. Gene Parsons, who stands well over six feet, found Russ something of a swaggering show-off. "He had several guns, and he took me out on the porch to show me what a marksman he was," Parsons recalls. "He would toss aspirin into the air—ordinary aspirin tablets—and then blast them to pieces before they fell. He was good, and he must have been practicing a lot. It never rains over in Yakima, and his yard was sprinkled with all those little white bits of aspirin. Must have been a thousand or more of them."

Donna Howard apparently tried every means she could think of to save her marriage. She prevailed upon Russ to go to an alcoholic treatment center. He went, but he began to drink again after he was back home. Feeling that his friends exacerbated his drinking problem, Donna put her foot down and barred them from her home, and that irritated Russ. She herself joined Al-Anon (the group for families of problem drinkers), and she talked almost daily with members of the group, seeking some way to help Russ stay sober. When nothing seemed to work she went so far as to consult an attorney about a divorce. But she changed her mind. She worried that she couldn't support her daughters alone, and she really wanted them to have a father as well as a mother.

If there was one thing that the Howards were both concerned with, it was their daughters. The little girls were eight and ten, and Russ and Donna loved them.

Even so, his children were not enough to keep Russ Howard home much. Donna never knew where he was for sure. Once she was injured in a car accident, and nobody could find Russ for hours to tell him she had been hurt.

When Russ was in town he was a frequent patron at the bar at the Yakima VFW Club. The bartender there had been the attraction for a year or more. She was a cute little blonde with a sprinkling of freckles across the bridge of her nose and just the beginning edges of hardness. Her name was Sunny Riley,* and she was about a dozen years younger than Donna.

Sunny and Russ Howard had been involved in a sizzling affair for a year. Sunny liked the same characteristics in Russ that had drawn Donna to him twenty years earlier: he was fun, he was exciting, and he made her laugh. She wanted to marry him. But of course, he was already married. Sunny turned the screws a little. She simply told him that if he didn't get a divorce, he'd better not expect her to wait around; she was going to date other men.

By December, 1974, Donna Howard could no longer hide the strain of living in a house torn apart. Here it was the Christmas season, and her family was living a sham. Russ was hardly ever home; he'd slacked off the alcohol treatment and gone on as before.

Donna had tried so hard to do whatever Russ seemed to want, hoping that they could get along better. One of the things he had wanted was to buy a new house. Donna hadn't wanted to move, but she'd gone along with it. They bought a house on Tieton Drive, and they would be moving in January. It seemed ridiculous when the marriage was so shaky, but she thought a new house *might* shed a happier light on the marriage—kind of a geographical remedy to a seemingly insoluble situation.

In mid-December Russ got home very late one night, and he was drunk. An argument ensued, and he hauled off and belted Donna twice in the head, practically knocking her out. That scared her. When her head stopped spinning she called the sheriff's office and filed a report. Donna told the officer responding that she was going to see her lawyer the next day, that she would be filing for divorce.

Russ hitting her was the deciding factor. Her lawyer was worried about Donna. He had advised her to file many times before, but Donna had always backed out. Now she was determined to divorce Russ and seek sole custody of her two daughters. She told Bobbi that she was resolute. "I was positive in my heart," Bobbi remembered, "that she was going ahead and getting the divorce."

Fay Moss suspected things had come to a breaking point, too. "Donna was always the kind that never complained. *She* was the one who would always go up to the rest of us, look us square in the eye, and say, 'How are you? How are the kids?' and she really wanted to know. But this one time in late December I said to her, 'Donna, how are *you, really?*' She just broke down and cried and responded, 'Not good. Just not good.' "

Russ Howard was between the proverbial rock and a hard place. If he didn't divorce Donna, Sunny was going to dump him. If Donna divorced him—as she was threatening to do—he might lose his kids, and the equity in their new home as well. Since the original down payment for the old house had come from Donna's family, he suspected a judge would award Donna the new house.

Perhaps to punctuate that she, too, meant what she said, Sunny had broken up with Russ as 1974 turned into 1975. Both women in Russ's life were fed up.

What he really wanted were his kids, the new house, and Sunny. On January 9, 1975, Russ Howard had a long talk with Sunny, and he confided an idea he had. She didn't really believe him; she thought it was the liquor talking.

On that same January 9th Donna's friend Fay Moss was visiting in Ellensburg. "I was talking to a friend who went to Yakima often, and I said, 'Ellie, call Donna. She *really* needs a friend right now.' "

Fay remembered her phone conversation with Donna Howard in December, and it had left her with anxiety over her old friend. Donna had cried during that call, and Donna *never* cried. "She had told me that she was sorry that she hadn't been able to make it over to Seattle to visit. Then she said, 'I'm changing a few things in 1975. We're moving to Selah on January first. This should prove very interesting. I'll let you know more.' "

Fay Moss didn't think the real changes in Donna's life had anything to do with the new house. She knew Donna, and Donna was talking about something that would mean far more upheaval in her life than simply changing addresses. It had something to do with her marriage. Fay worried about Donna all day on January 9th, and she made up her mind to drive on down to Yakima and see her the next day. "But I didn't. A winter storm blew in, and the roads were so bad that I turned around and came home. When I got home I learned that Donna was dead."

* * *

Donna Howard was forty-two years old when she died on January 10, 1975. It happened so quickly; it was 9:27 on that bitter, icy morning in Yakima, Washington, when Russ found her. Emergency medical technicians pronounced her dead at 9:47.

How ironic that Donna Howard of all people should die in a stable, when she had loved horses since before she could walk. It just didn't make sense. It would take almost a dozen years before it did.

Donna and Russ and the girls hadn't quite finished moving everything out of the house on Galloway Road. Russ and Donna took their girls to school, and then they headed back to the old house. They passed some of their neighbors, and Russ and Donna waved.

Russ told the medics that they had put on a pot of coffee, and a little later he went into town to the hardware store to buy a mailbox for their new house. Then he stopped at a doughnut shop and picked up a dozen fresh doughnuts, explaining that he was taking them back to share with Donna. He talked to a number of people at the hardware store and the doughnut shop that morning. He had even written a check at the hardware store. Always talkative, Russ had seemed particularly gregarious.

His call for help came in just minutes before 9:30. A woman had been injured out on Route 8, Box 741. A fire department medic responded along with Yakima County Sheriff's Office Patrolmen Jerry Hofsos and Ron Ward.

A worried Russ Howard led them out toward the loafing shed where the family's two horses were kept. He explained that he and Donna were doing some last-minute moving and repairs. He had gone into town to get some supplies they needed, and he'd thought he would surprise Donna with some fresh doughnuts. But she hadn't been in the house when he got back, nor had she responded to his shouts. He figured Donna was over at the neighbors' house because she often visited there—but they hadn't seen her either. He felt as if he had wasted precious minutes looking in the wrong place.

When Russ trudged through the deep snow out to the barn area he had found Donna. She lay in the loafing shed, just as she still was—except for the quilt, which he'd placed over her. The fire department medic knelt beside her and removed the quilt.

Donna Howard lay on her back with her left arm raised, her face turned to the left. Her right hand was pinned palm down beneath her right buttock. The medic felt for a pulse in the carotid artery in the neck. There was none. Donna Howard's eyes were slightly open, but the pupils were already fixed and dilated. Her body was warm, but she was dead.

The immediate cause of death seemed to stem from some manner of head injury; there was blood streaking Donna's forehead, running back into her thick brown hair, which was virtually soaked with blood from some terrible head wound. Mere inches from her head one wall of the two-sided shed had thick scarlet stains, as if someone had taken a paint brush and daubed on two swaths. Almost directly opposite and a foot or so above Donna's left elbow one swath was horizontal, the other vertical.

Donna wore bell-bottom jeans, rubber galoshes much too big for her feet (unzipped), a white sweater, a dark quilted jacket (open), and gloves. Her sweater was pulled up, exposing flesh at her waist. Her jeans were wrinkled oddly, too, pulled up slightly toward her knees. Her clothing looked almost as if someone had dragged her by her feet. Her galoshes nudged a salt block placed there earlier for her two horses.

"I found her like this," Russ Howard explained. "I covered her with a quilt, and I called for the medics." He had not moved her at all, he said, fearful of injuring her further.

The fire department and the responding deputies had, of course, called detectives for backup. In all cases of violent death—accidental or deliberate—detectives must investigate. Detective Sergeant Bob Langdale and Detective Ray Ochs responded to the scene to assist in the initial probe.

The sheriff's men took pictures of the scene, but that was all. The barn and the house were a good distance apart. There was nothing in the house that seemed out of place. There wasn't much to photograph. The cause of death seemed obvious: one of Donna Howard's beloved horses had spooked and kicked her in the back of the head. She had lain there until Russ returned.

Pictures remaining in police files show a pretty woman with a lithe, perfect figure lying stretched out on the icy ground of the loafing shed. Over toward the slatted open side there is a plaid quilt and a Bekins Movers' blanket. Beyond, a blizzard has kicked up, and the snow and sky meet in never-ending white.

Neighbors rushed to comfort the bereaved widower, who blamed himself for not being home when Donna needed him. "One of her horses must have kicked her," he said. He couldn't describe his feelings. "I don't know how you describe something like that. I felt a combination of grief and rage, not knowing where to vent the rage."

One of the first things Russ did after Donna's body was removed was to contact Sunny Riley. He told her that Donna was dead, and he explained the events of the morning. Sunny was appalled, even terrified by what he related. But Sunny still loved Russ despite what he had told her. She kept her knowledge to herself.

Donna's family was stunned by the news of the tragedy. That Donna should be killed by the very animal she loved was incomprehensible to them. She had been around horses her whole life; she talked to them in some unspoken language, and she trusted them more than she trusted most people. Moreover, she was no neophyte who didn't know how to approach horses.

Dr. Richard Muzzall, the Yakima County coroner and a local surgeon who had gone to Ellensburg High School with Donna, performed her autopsy on January 11th. Although he was a board-certified surgeon, Muzzall had no special training in forensic pathology. He noted the back of the skull where it had been shattered and found the damage consistent with a blow from a horse's hoof. He also found a second fracture of the skull, on the upper right side, a small ovoid (oval-shaped) depressed fracture. That puzzled him, given what Russ Howard had told him about the accident. Muzzall was not as sure about the cause of that wound as he was about the occipital fractures, and he made a note to go to the loafing shed and find out what had caused that.

When he went back to the horse shed Muzzall spotted three stacked railroad ties that made up part of the wall adjacent to where Donna Howard's body was found. The top tie had been broken off raggedly at some time and had a sharp, jagged piece of wood protruding. That might have caused the small single fracture.

Muzzall deduced that Donna had been bending over, cleaning a horse's hoof, and that she had been kicked by one of the horse's other hooves, knocked headlong into the tie, and then propelled backward, her head sliding across the side of the shed, leaving the two bloody swipes. She had finally come to rest flat on her back with her legs stretched out. That scenario might explain how her skull was fractured both in the back and on the top, and why the smaller top fracture's shape bore no resemblance to a horse's foot size.

Muzzall's postmortem report was only a page long, and the conclusion was death from multiple skull fractures due to horse kick. He noted the two areas of fracture and a third finding—a bruise on the webbing between the thumb and forefinger of the right hand. That bruise bore the imprint of the fabric of the glove Donna had worn. At the bottom of the autopsy report the summary diagnosis listed the fabric-pattern bruise as having been found on the *left* hand. A minor oversight, but one that would have been *very* important to a forensic pathologist.

A bruise in the webbing between the thumb and the forefinger is a classic defense wound. What part of a horse could have given Donna Howard such a bruise? And why hadn't Muzzall proofread the autopsy report?

Outside of major metropolitan areas there are few trained forensic pathologists, and even the best sometimes disagree with one another on a close call. Indeed, in many rural and thinly populated areas coroners are not even required to be physicians. Muzzall had drawn his conclusions from the information available at the time and with the training that he had. Later several forensic pathologists would agree with him; others would not.

Neither Detectives Langdale and Ochs nor Yakima County Prosecuting Attorney Jeff Sullivan could come up with enough probable cause to arrest anyone for killing Donna Howard. It was, they were forced to conclude, a tragic and ironic accident.

Donna was buried, and Russ Howard and his daughters pulled their lives together, living in the new house. There wasn't much insurance on Donna's life—only $17,000—but Russ would receive social security benefits for the minor children.

* * *

Only Donna's family could not accept the cause of death on the death certificate. Nothing added up. One might attribute the family's doubts to grief and denial. And yet . . .

Bobbi Bennett sought—and found—refuge in her religion, but her growing faith only heightened her conviction that it was her duty to Donna to see that the real killer was punished. Bobbi knew how unhappy Donna had been, knew of her decision to divorce Russ, and knew that he had physically attacked her sister less than a month earlier—an attack so violent that Donna had been left almost unconscious. Bobbi Bennett was convinced that Russ Howard had killed Donna, but she had no idea in the world how to prove it.

With her family's backing, Bobbi hired a private detective.

One of the startling pieces of intelligence the private investigator reported was that a young woman named Sunny Riley was living with Russ and his daughters. Donna was barely in her grave when Sunny moved in during February. Ostensibly she had been hired as a baby-sitter to care for the girls. Since Russ was a traveling seed salesman, it made sense that he had to have household help, but Donna's family was suspicious. The private investigator pretended to be a real estate agent and talked with Sunny. There was no question that she was living in Russ's home full-time. And she didn't strike him as the baby-sitter type.

Four months later, in June—the month when Donna would have celebrated her forty-third birthday—Russ Howard and Sunny Riley were married, ending the arguments among townspeople over whether Sunny was a baby-sitter or a girlfriend.

There were reasons that the June wedding was not as

romantic as it might have been. Sunny Riley was a woman tortured by conflicting emotions. She *did* still love Russ no matter what her suspicions were, and she had wanted to marry him for a long time. But she was frightened, too. Russ had confided things to her that she wished she had never heard. Whatever he might or might not have done, Sunny was absolutely convinced that she was just as responsible under the law as he was. Indeed, Russ often reminded her of her complicity, and she believed him when he said she would be in terrible trouble, too, if she ever revealed what he had told her.

She had been afraid to marry him and afraid *not* to marry him. She had gone along with the wedding plans, she would say later, because she kept hoping something or someone would intervene before she and Russ made it to the altar. For his part, Russ was quite aware that a man's wife cannot be forced to testify against him in a court of law.

No one intervened, of course, and the wedding went off without a hitch. Sunny did her best to block her fears out of her mind; at times she was able to completely submerge her doubts. Once they were married Russ didn't seem to worry much at all about the law. He seemed quite secure. The coroner had agreed with his version of Donna's death, and so had the prosecutor and the sheriff. Let the past bury the past.

But Donna's sister Bobbi was not about to let that happen. She knew nothing about how to investigate a murder when she began her quest, but she read voraciously, and she soon gleaned a great deal of information. One afternoon while she was sitting in a beauty parlor chair she read about Thomas Noguchi, then chief medical examiner of Los Angeles County.

Bobbi Bennett got in touch with Noguchi and asked him and an associate to review Donna's case. After doing that they agreed that it at least warranted a more complete autopsy.

Yakima County D.A. Jeff Sullivan agreed to an exhumation order, and a second postmortem examination was performed on Donna Howard's body in late 1976. Forensic pathologist Dr. William Brady—then the Oregon state medical examiner—performed the autopsy with Dr. Bob Bucklin, an ex-assistant medical examiner for Los Angeles County, assisting. Dr. Muzzall, Jeff Sullivan, and Sergeant Langdale observed.

At length Dr. Bucklin concluded that he could not say with *absolute medical certainty* that the damage to her skull had not been caused by the kick of a horse. His inclination, however, was to *disagree* with Dr. Muzzall's findings.

Dr. Brady prefaced his written report with the comment that pathological conclusions must take into account what was known to have been at the scene of a death—i.e., common sense combined with autopsy findings. A badly fractured skull and horses would tend to go together; unless other circumstances were known, Brady said he could not say what had caused the damage to Donna Howard's skull.

The lack of a definitive decision on the part of either pathologist was a crushing disappointment for Donna's sister. She had fought so hard to get the exhumation order and the second postmortem examination. It had been agonizing to go through, too—and now it seemed all for nothing.

For D.A. Jeff Sullivan there was still not enough probable cause to issue an arrest warrant charging anyone with murder. For the second time he declined to prosecute.

The world moved on. Donna Howard was dead, and that's the way it was—to everyone but Donna's family. Her parents grew older, their will to live weakened by the loss of their beloved daughter. Donna's father would not live to see the end of the case.

Bobbi Bennett, however, never gave up. She read. She phoned. She wrote letters to anyone who might help her avenge Donna's death. "Some people might say it took over my life," she would recall later. "I made up my mind that I was not going to let her go until they did something."

Over the years Donna's family would spend thousands of dollars on the case, a case everyone else seemed to consider closed.

The marriage between Sunny and Russ Howard was a bumpy one. Perhaps it was inevitable that it would be. Sunny had fallen in love with Russ because he was fun, and she loved fun. But there was little hilarity once they were married; Sunny was scared and guilty about what she knew, Russ was gone a lot, and he continued to drink a great deal. For all intents and purposes the marriage ended in 1978.

Sunny left Russ and ran off with another man. But Sunny was adept at picking the wrong men. She found herself in an abusive relationship. Periodically things got so bad that Russ looked good, and she would phone him and beg him to come and rescue her. He would pick her up, bring her back, and help her get set up in an apartment or in his house. Until 1979 Sunny and Russ had some manner of a relationship, however tenuous.

Donna Howard had been dead for almost five years, but Sunny's conscience still bothered her. If her niggling doubts hadn't gone away by then, she figured they weren't going to. In early July, 1980, Sunny went to a Yakima County deputy sheriff, an old friend from high school, and asked him a hypothetical question: "If I knew information about somebody that was going to be murdered, and then they were, and somebody told me more things—and I never said anything—would I be in trouble, too?"

Her deputy friend stared at her quizzically for a few moments, and then he assured her that *she* would not be the focal point of a sheriff's probe.

Sunny replied that in that case, she had some things to say. However, she told him that if she *did* get charged with a crime, she was going to deny everything. Her friend took her down to the county detectives, who took a taped statement from her.

Bob Langdale had retired, but Ray Ochs was still in the detective unit, and Jerry Hofsos had moved up from patrol. What Sunny Riley had to tell them was riveting, to say the least.

Sunny began by reviewing late December, 1974. She said Russ Howard had told her that he planned to kill his wife. He had told her he was going to lure Donna out to the barn of their old house on the pretext of making some repairs that had to be done before the new tenants moved in. It would be only natural, he had said, for him to have a hammer with him. Then he planned to strike Donna with the side of his hammer because he thought that would make a wound resembling a horse's shoe. His alibi would be that he had been in town at the time Donna died. He would go to town right after the crime, and he would make sure people in town remembered him.

On the day Donna died Russ had told Sunny he'd done it—but he said it had been more difficult to kill his wife than he expected. He confided that he'd had to hit Donna in the head three times before she died. The rest of his plan had been carried out just as he had outlined it to Sunny earlier.

The information that Sunny gave might well have been enough to indict Russ Howard for the murder of his wife. There were some problems, though; the things he had told her before marriage would be admissible in a court of law, but the confidences after marriage probably would not be. And then there was the fact that Sunny had gone right ahead and *married* a man she believed to be a murderer. A jury might wonder about that and find her a less than credible witness.

A polygraph exam administered by an expert from the Washington State Patrol indicated that Sunny Riley was telling the truth.

The Yakima County Prosecutor's Office continued to mull over whether to charge Russ Howard. So much of the original physical evidence was gone. Donna's blood-stained clothing, the quilt, the Bekins blanket had all been destroyed. The loafing shed had been repainted, obliterating the blood smears there. No investigator had ever found a hammer or, for that matter, even looked for one.

The railroad tie that Dr. Muzzall believed to be the instrument that made the oval fracture in the victim's skull was now anchored in cement, part of a fence. No one had ever searched the barn or the house thoroughly for signs of violence; it hadn't seemed important back in 1975 when the autopsy decreed accidental death.

Now it was too late.

Sunny ran scared. She moved around from place to place, fearful of reprisal from Russ. She moved to California with a new man and waited for word from Yakima authorities. Impatient now, she couldn't wait for Russ to be arrested. But months passed, and nothing happened—at least nothing she could see.

The case was already more than five years old, and authorities were doing their best to make it as solid as possible before they moved on it. They figured Russ Howard wasn't going anyplace.

It was 1981. Sunny was worried, and she was drinking. A few more drinks and Sunny was not only worried, she was angry, too. Russ had her furniture. She called him one night and suggested that they get married again. She pointed out that he was going to be charged with murder sooner or later, and if they were married, she couldn't testify against him. Sunny figured this might make him give back her furniture. After the trial was over they could split up again, she reasoned.

The next day Sunny was sober, and she changed her mind about the plan that had seemed so good the night before. Russ had rejected her proposal anyway. But she had tipped him off that something might be happening that he didn't know about. Still, he didn't move from the Yakima area. He didn't seem the least bit worried.

Russ Howard continued to have bad luck with women in his life. In the early 1980s he was living sporadically with a new woman and working part-time at a local tavern. One afternoon the couple came home together and talked for a few moments with Russ's daughters and a friend of theirs who was visiting.

Russ left a little while later to go to work at the tavern, and his girlfriend went upstairs, apparently to take a nap.

A few minutes later the three teenagers heard a loud noise upstairs. They went up to investigate and found the woman dead on the bed, shot in the stomach. She clutched a gun in her hand.

The nearly hysterical girls called Russ at work, and he rushed home, managing to arrive even before the police did. When the police got there they found Russ standing next to the dead woman, the gun in his hand.

The bartender at the tavern told investigators that Russ had been there when the phone call came in from his daughters. His most recent girlfriend's death was ruled a suicide.

* * *

This was the situation when two of the Washington State justice system's most prominent figures entered the case. A special investigative unit of the State Attorney General's Office was mandated by a new law in 1981 to conduct independent inquiries into criminal cases around the state, to offer assistance to counties, and indeed to prosecute in some instances. (At the request or with the concurrence of the governor or the county prosecutor.) It was to be basically a two-man operation, but those two men were quite probably the equal of a half-dozen less-skilled investigators and prosecutors. Greg Canova would head the unit as senior assistant state attorney general, and his sole investigator would be Bob Keppel, late of the King County Police's Major Crimes Unit.

Greg Canova worked as a deputy prosecutor in the King County Prosecutor's Office from 1974 to 1981, ending up as the senior deputy criminal prosecutor in that office. Canova was brilliant, honest, and persistent. He rarely lost a case, and he garnered respect from both conservative and liberal factions. Greg Canova had helped draft Washington State's new capital punishment law. Tall and handsome, with a luxuriant mustache, a quick legal mind, and a deep, confident voice that served him well in the courtroom, Canova had been so successful a prosecutor that he was already something of a legend at thirty-five. Canova candidly attributed some of his wins to luck. "Luck plays a part. In the past I've won some cases I probably should have lost and lost some I figured to win. You can never be sure with juries.

"I always go in thinking I can win. If you don't think you can prove guilt beyond a reasonable doubt, then you shouldn't ever file a case."

The other half of the new team—Bob Keppel, Canova's investigator—is one of the smartest detectives this reporter ever knew, respected all over America for his intellectual approach to investigation. A former track star, Bob Keppel was a young homicide detective in the King County Police Department with only one case under his belt when he found himself plunged into one of the biggest cases of his—or any other homicide detective's—career: the "Ted Murders" that began in the Northwest in 1974 and ended in Florida in 1978.

("Ted" turned out to be Ted Bundy, who died in the electric chair in Starke, Florida, on January 24, 1989. Just a day before he died, Bundy, who was suspected of murdering anywhere from twenty-five to three hundred young women all over America, confessed some of those murders to Bob Keppel. He viewed Keppel as his intellectual equal, and the two had jousted many times. Indeed, many experts suspect that Bundy's offer to "advise" Bob Keppel and several F.B.I. special agents on how to second-guess serial killers was the basis for *Silence of the Lambs.* Keppel let Bundy *think* he was a respected advisor—just to keep dialogue open between them.

In 1975, using what now seems to be an archaic computer system, Keppel narrowed a field of 3,500 suspects in the "Ted Murders" to only five, and Ted Bundy was one of those five. Keppel's methods were right on target when Bundy was arrested for similar crimes against pretty dark-haired women in the Salt Lake City area. The rest is, of course, criminal history.)

With the expertise he gained in being one of the lead detectives in the "Ted Task Force," Bob Keppel has been called upon by probers in dozens of serial murder investigations in this country. When Canova recruited Keppel away from the King County police, he knew what he was doing. Even so, he had to lend Bob Keppel back to the Green River Task Force for two years.

Greg Canova and Bob Keppel were just what Donna Howard's family had needed for a long, long time; they had become disheartened by years of butting their heads into bureaucratic brick walls. Bobbi Bennett would not give up until someone was convicted for what she believed to be Donna's murder.

Bobbi carried her campaign to reopen the investigation into Donna's death to the governor's office, and her arguments were cogent and persuasive. Then-Governor John Spellman asked the Attorney General's Office (specifically Canova's unit) to look into the Howard investigation in late 1981.

At that time it was a moot point. Canova *had* no investigators. In March, 1982, Bob Keppel came aboard, and the probe began in earnest. Keppel would practically wear a groove in the I-90 Freeway across the mountains to Yakima, interviewing and re-interviewing. He talked to the original detectives, and to Ray Ochs and Jerry Hofsos, who were more than eager to continue the probe. He questioned the paramedic who had been at the scene of Donna's death. He found neighbors and hardware store employees, and perhaps most important, Keppel questioned Sunny Riley.

Meticulously Bob Keppel reconstructed a case that was already seven years old and seemed to be as dead as the victim. In truth, it was about to have a whole new life.

The problem, Greg Canova felt, had begun with the first autopsy. The report was only one page long, and that page stated that the wrong hand bore the defense bruising. Moreover, it had not been a complete autopsy because her death was deemed accidental. The investigating stopped, any physical evidence was tainted or obliterated, the body was buried, and the case collapsed like a straw fence in a windstorm.

What Greg Canova and Bob Keppel *did* have was a witness who had passed the lie detector test with no signs whatsoever of deception. Sunny Riley had come forward even though she was scared to death of being implicated. She was a woman whose life-style had changed from hedonistic to responsible. Sunny knew she would probably face some uncomfortable questions from Russ Howard's attorneys—if this case ever got as far as a courtroom—but she was prepared to answer them.

Bob Keppel's efforts to talk with Russ Howard himself were met with scorn. "I was amused," Howard said later. "I never dreamed it would get this far, that anybody would take Sunny seriously."

Howard confided to reporters that he felt he had antagonized Greg Canova and Bob Keppel by "laughing at them."

Not so. He only intrigued them more.

The physical evidence came down to a few precious items that remained. There were the pictures taken by investigating officers that icy morning of January 10, 1975. Blow-ups of the photographs and the recall of the Yakima deputies who were there indicated that there had been absolutely no hair, blood, or human tissue on the sharp end of the railroad tie. Some experts felt that since the ovoid fracture was a depressed fracture, the instrument causing it would have pierced the brain itself, however briefly, and probably come away with blood and tissue residue, and probably some hairs from the victim's head.

Beyond that, Dr. Muzzall's re-creation had Donna Howard kneeling to clean off her horse's hoof. If that was true, why didn't the pictures show dirt or snow on the knees of her jeans? In the photographs the knee portion of her jeans was clean.

Greg Canova and Bob Keppel had a picture in their minds now of how and why the murder had occurred. Russ Howard had wanted out of his marriage and had wanted to keep his children and his financial assets. So, as he had told Sunny, he had, indeed, managed to get Donna out to the loafing shed on some ruse. There he had struck his wife once with the flat of the hammer, expecting her to go down. But Donna had fought him, fending off the hammer with her right hand, protecting her head. The force of the hammer's blows against the webbing between her thumb and forefinger had been so strong that it was not only bruised, but the actual weave of her glove was imprinted on her flesh. Twice more Russ had crashed the hammer against Donna's head.

Then he would have dragged her body along the frozen ground on the Bekins blanket, arranging the corpse in the loafing shed where the two horses were. If Donna Howard had been kicked and simply fallen back, her shirt and jeans would not have been pulled up as they were in the pictures. That rumpling was exactly what would happen if someone had pulled her by her feet.

Donna's body was warm when the sheriff's men and the paramedic arrived, covered tenderly with a quilt. Russ had probably done that deliberately—to keep her warm while he was in town creating his alibi. Either that, or he had gone to town first and returned to carry out the rest of his plan.

The problem for Greg Canova and Bob Keppel in 1982 was how they were going to prove their theory of what happened in 1975 to a jury's satisfaction.

The main piece of physical evidence was Donna Howard's skull. Cleaned and dry and reconstructed, it would be examined now by some of the most expert forensic pathologists in the country.

Dr. Donald Reay, chief of the King County Medical Examiner's Office, examined the skull in July, 1982, and agreed that the damage did not seem to be from a horse's hoof. The back of the skull, maybe—it had been shattered in nineteen pieces, and all manner of force could have done that. However, the much smaller ovoid fracture on the top right side of the skull was very unusual. An oval piece of bone had been broken clean through and forced through the skull against where the brain had been.

The skull was sent next to the Smithsonian Institution, where it was examined by a chief forensic anthropologist. He thought that the top single fracture looked as if it had been caused by a hammer. However, he said, "There's someone who knows a lot more about this kind of injury than even I do—and that's Clyde Snow."

Clyde Collins Snow, Ph.D., forensic anthropology consultant and something of a legend. Big, gray-haired, and deceptively casual, Snow lives in Norman, Oklahoma, but he is rarely there. He may be in South America working over skeletons or in the Philippines reconstructing skulls of massacre victims. He is a witty and jovial man whose manner belies the grimmer aspects of his profession. Snow can tell all manner of things from a skull.

Dr. Snow is not averse to checking out his findings with other experts, and in this case Snow showed Donna Howard's skull to Dr. Bob Kirschner of the Cook County (Chicago) Medical Examiner's Office, to Kirschner's associates, and to Dr. Fred Jordan of the Oklahoma State Medical Examiner's Office. They all agreed with Snow's conclusion that the small oval fracture had been caused by a hammer. Kirschner particularly pointed out that he felt the wood from the railroad tie would have left splinters in the wound, and the wound would have left tissue on the railroad tie.

When Clyde Snow reported his initial findings to Bob Keppel he commented, "This case shines like a herring left too long in the hot sun." That was Clyde Snow's way of saying things were not as they had been reported to be.

After a meticulous examination of Donna Howard's skull Dr. Snow sent a letter to Bob Keppel and Greg Canova. Donna Howard had not had a thin skull, easily shattered. Rather his exam had shown it to be slightly thicker than normal.

Snow noted, too, that the wood of the railroad tie would have been far too soft to have done the damage found in the ovoid fracture. "The fracture was caused by an object of high density with a flat face and a circular upper margin."

Snow continued, "The critical feature of the cranium is the depressed fracture of the right fronto-parietal region. It is a classic example of a 'fracture à la signature' of a hammer. To me, this finding reduces the arguments about the remainder of the injuries to academic quibbling. Whether it was the first or last blow, or whether there was one, two, or three blows is of little significance. . . . Of course, one might speculate that a horse kicked the victim and then administered the coup de grace with a hammer. I don't know about Washington horses, but Oklahoma horses have not shown that degree of dexterity. . . ."

Snow felt that the back blow (probably two blows, according to what Russ Howard had allegedly told Sunny) had been delivered while the victim was still standing, and from the rear, where she could not see it coming. The depressed frontal fracture had occurred when she was lying on her back with her head turned to the left. The killer would have been standing over the victim at that point, and she could well have tried to cover her head with her hand.

Snow's findings made a gruesome and pathetic mind picture.

Photographs of the blood patterns on the loafing shed wall were blown up to 11 x 14 prints and sent to Lt. Rod Englert of the Multnomah County Sheriff's Office in Portland, Oregon. Englert is one of the most respected experts in the United States on blood patterns. He spends much of his time traveling to testify in homicide trials and has presented over three hundred seminars on blood spatter analysis. Lt. Englert teaches detectives how to determine myriad facts from the silent testimony of blood—if blood is "high velocity" (gunshot wounds), "medium velocity," or "low velocity." Among the concepts he teaches are "bloodstain transfer" and "blood swipe." In both of the latter, bloody objects come into contact with a surface not previously contaminated with blood and leave distinctive patterns.

Englert examined the pictures of Donna Howard's body and the loafing shed and weighed the blood patterns he saw with the story told by Russ Howard and with the reconstruction of the "accident" by Dr. Muzzall.

Lt. Englert's opinion was that Donna's death simply could not have happened the way Muzzall had perceived. Donna Howard's curly brown hair had been sodden with blood from the head wounds. But *had* she been kicked, had she bounced off the jagged railroad tie and then fallen backward, the blood patterns would have been higher, more diffuse, and well beyond the body. The pictures didn't show that.

Instead, the two thick, bloody swaths in the picture looked as if they had been left as someone was lowering and re-positioning a body on the ground. Donna's hair, so heavy with wet blood, would have left exactly those marks photographed on the wall: one swipe up and down and another side to side. The laws of motion would not have allowed Donna Howard to have been kicked into the railroad tie with enough force to penetrate her skull and then let her fall back so gently that her hair left those two solid stains on the white wall a foot away. A powerful kick from a horse would have sprayed blood in a diffuse pattern all over that wall.

The layman would never have thought of that. A surgeon, trained for other kinds of medicine, might not have seen what Rod Englert saw.

Donna Howard might not have known what was about to happen to her. One would hope she was not frightened by the steps behind her as she concentrated on something in the barn. The first blow might have knocked her unconscious as her skull shattered, and the second might have come hard upon the first. Perhaps she fell neatly on an already-spread Bekins blanket, only to be smashed once more on the top of her head because she still breathed. Perhaps she was still able to use one hand to try to block the hammer coming down.

No one would ever know that except for Donna and her killer.

On November 8, 1984, the Washington State Attorney General's Office charged Noyes Russell Howard, fifty-four, with first-degree murder in the death of his first wife almost nine years earlier. Attorneys Susan Hahn and Wes Raber were appointed to defend him.

But the murder case was to be kept from the courtroom even longer. Challenges were made in pre-trial hearings asking who was going to pay for the defense, challenges that were ultimately appealed to the State Supreme Court. Eventually the state and not Yakima County was found liable for the cost of Russ Howard's defense since it was the state that had filed the murder charges.

In 1986 Washington's state legislature appropriated $50,000 to pay for Russ Howard's defense.

The trial finally began on October 13, 1986, in Superior Court Judge James Gavin's courtroom. Greg Canova was the sole prosecutor, and most of the State's witnesses would be experts in forensic science.

The only civilian witness Canova called was Sunny Riley. She made an excellent witness as she testified for hours. Yes, she had been told by Russ before the murder that he planned to kill Donna with a hammer and make it look as though a horse had kicked her. And yes, he had called her on the day of the murder and told her he had done it. The courtroom was hushed as Sunny related that Russ had complained it had taken him three blows with the hammer to do the job. Sunny said she hadn't wanted to believe it was true, and when she did allow herself to believe it she said she thought that something would happen to prevent her from actually marrying Russ. Yes, she acknowledged softly, part of her had still loved him even then.

In the end Sunny said she could not live with the thought that Donna Howard's murder had never been discovered.

Each side had its forensic pathology witnesses because the burden of the case rested ultimately on one small skull, its battered occiput reconstructed from nineteen shattered pieces.

It was hard going all the way. The defense would not even stipulate that the skull in evidence belonged to Donna Howard.

The forensic pathologists and anthropologists for the State agreed that the massive crushing at the back of Donna's skull *might* have been caused by a hammer, but that the fracture in the front of the skull *definitely* had been.

The defense team called Dr. Muzzall (then practicing in Alaska), Dr. William Brady, and Cyril Wacht, a world-famous forensic pathologist from Pittsburgh. They disagreed with the absolute statements the State's doctors had made. "Our position was," Defense Attorney Susan Hahn said, "[the injury] does look like a hammer [caused it]. But that's not the only thing that could cause that kind of injury, and the explanation that was originally given was still the best explanation."

Greg Canova questioned Dr. Muzzall carefully about the original autopsy. He asked Muzzall to step down from the witness stand and demonstrate just how the injuries could have occurred given the original autopsy's scenario. Greg Canova argued that a contortionist could not have gone through the sequence that Donna Howard's body was alleged to have completed. Dr. Muzzall resolutely disagreed, and maintained his original stance.

Seventeen days after the trial began the jury retired to deliberate. They went out on the evening of October 30, 1986, and returned in the early afternoon on Halloween. It took them eight hours to find Russ Howard guilty of premeditated first-degree murder.

"I had a feeling the jury wanted to find a way to find the man innocent," the jury foreman commented later. "Then there was the feeling, as one juror said, 'I know he did it, but . . .' We talked about what would follow that 'but.' There was nothing there."

Judge Gavin sentenced Howard to life with a twenty-year minimum term. That would make him eligible for parole in thirteen years and eight months, around the turn of the century—when he was almost seventy. Noyes Russell Howard, fifty-six years old in 1986, continues to maintain his innocence, as do his daughters, and he continues to appeal his conviction.

As this is being written it is January, 1994, almost two decades since Donna Howard walked out to the stable for the last time. In her case, the wheels of justice ground exceedingly slow—but they *did* grind. Without Bobbi Bennett's determination and dedication, without Greg Canova and Bob Keppel, Donna would have lain unavenged throughout time.

Update, December 2003

Noyes Russell Howard was paroled from prison as he neared seventy. He returned to Yakima, where he died on September 2, 2002.

The Last Letter
(from *You Belong to Me*)

When I was in college studying the works of great poets, there was one poem by Ocsar Wilde that puzzled me because it seemed to make little sense. My own experience in the years ahead and many of the murder cases I chose to chronicle would eventually make the meaning of these lines all too clear:

> Yet each man kills the thing he loves,
> By each let this be heard,
> Some do it with a bitter look,
> Some with a flattering word.
> The coward does it with a kiss,
> The brave man with a sword.
> —"The Ballad of Reading Gaol" (1898)

Almost ninety years after Wilde wrote this poem of bitter regret, I read through voluminous police files that unveiled every facet of the following case, and I was amazed. If ever a man killed the thing he loved, it was the murderer who tried to make amends for what he had done in "The Last Letter."

Whether his use of a "sword" was brave *is a question only the reader can answer, although I think not. Like a brilliant flame, love, too, can be smothered when it has no air to breathe.*

173

I have written about other cases of obsessive, possessive, love—but never one as hearbreaking as this story.

No one who knew them through the decades of their relationship would ever deny that Bill and Jackie were in love. Their years together—and apart—were full of longing and wonder, jealousy and ecstasy. They were, indeed, two people who embodied the kind of emotion we hear about in love songs. Songs of love lost, love regained, and sometimes love destroyed—forever. But popular songs seldom mention a kind of supremely selfish "love" that can hurt innocent people and smear even the most romantic love affair with blood.

This story troubles me. Why? I suppose it is because the ending was so pointless, so totally unnecessary. Quite probably thirty years of happiness were thrown away because one of the partners did not believe in love. And the other believed—and trusted—in love too much. There is an old adage: "Be careful what you wish for—because you just may get it, but your wish will never come about exactly as you planned . . ."

Detectives from the Bellevue, Washington Police Department, of necessity, viewed the "Bill and Jackie" story first as a forensic puzzle. Only later could they allow themselves to delve into the reasons why Bill and Jackie Brand's romance ended as it did. They had a bit of a head start. One of the principals in the love affair had written their story, possibly believing that theirs was a relationship too momentous not to be shared with the world, possibly feeling the need to explain what was unthinkable.

In 1958 Bill Brand lived in Fairbanks, Alaska, with his wife and small daughters. He was in his early thirties, a tall, sandy-haired man who was handsome in a rugged way that seemed to fit Alaska. He was involved in lumber and construction and was already on his way to a considerable fortune. Brand had had the foresight to see where Alaska was headed and had dug himself a solid foothold in the building supply business there. When Alaska became the forty-ninth state on January 3, 1959, Bill already had it made. The largest state in the union had the smallest population, but it was about to boom, and housing was in great demand. As the years went by Bill Brand would become an extremely wealthy man.

Jackie Lindall* was seventeen, pretty, dark-haired, and slender when she met Bill Brand for the first time. She had moved from her Minnesota home to go to the University of Alaska in 1958, leaving behind small-town life and a large, loving family. She had a sister two years older than she, and two brothers, seven and twelve years younger. Although it was hard for her to travel so far from home, a spirit of adventure burned within Jackie. And Alaska was about as adventurous a spot as Jackie could imagine.

Wherever she went, Alaska—or rather, what it meant to her—would always call her back and back and back.

Her family didn't worry about Jackie as much as they might have because she was going to live with the Brand family instead of in a college dormitory or apartment. She would be a nanny for the little girls and help around the house to pay for her room and board.

Bill Brand apparently found the willowy teenager absolutely enchanting. To a seventeen-year-old a man over thirty must have seemed far removed from her social sphere, and yet it is likely she found him a little exciting; he was dynamic, and much smoother than the college boys she met. Indeed, Jackie may well have had a crush on Bill.

Whatever Jackie's and Bill's relationship may have been in the late 1950s and early 1960s, nothing openly marred the surface of the Brand marriage. Although his work meant he was always busy and often away from home, Bill was a devoted father, and seemingly as devoted a husband. He and his wife had a third baby girl.

After a few years of living with the Brands Jackie graduated from college and returned to Minnesota. Jackie moved out of Bill's life. Or rather, she tried to. Bill Brand always managed to know where Jackie was and what she was doing. He never really let her go.

With her personality, poise, and beauty, Jackie Lindall quickly found a job with Northwest Orient Airlines. Jackie went through flight attendant's training in Minneapolis in 1962. (She was called a stewardess in those days.) Her first home base was in Washington, D.C.—all the way across the country from Bill Brand.

In 1963 Jackie shared an apartment with another stewardess from her training class, and she was caught up with a new social life, dating, and making friends. She refused, however, to date pilots or other airline employees. More experienced stewardesses had warned her that it usually brought only grief. But then, she didn't need to; Jackie met scores of men on every flight. One businessman, Dan Barret,* who flew regularly between Detroit and Washington, introduced her to his roommate in Washington, D.C., Cal Logan.* Jackie fell in love with Cal, and they were soon engaged. For a while she was able to relegate her life in Alaska to her past, and she was excited about her wedding plans.

Only months before her wedding day Cal Logan was killed in an automobile accident. That was the first time violent death wiped out Jackie's plans. Dan Barret had lost his best friend, and Jackie had lost the man she planned to marry. They comforted each other, and it strengthened their platonic friendship. For years Dan was special to Jackie—but she never loved him in a romantic way.

Whatever might have happened between Jackie and Bill back in Fairbanks, it was pivotal in his life. He had never forgotten Jackie, and he missed having her as a part of his life. She was no longer a schoolgirl. She was a grown woman now, and drifting farther and farther away from him. He had no intention of letting that happen. Bill Brand wanted Jackie—possibly he had from the first time he saw her—and he detested the thought that another man might touch her. Even though he remained in his marriage he kept tabs on her, calling her often, questioning her when she wasn't home for his evening calls. Brand comforted himself for a long time, convinced Jackie wouldn't have sex with anyone else because she had such a solid midwestern religious background.

It did not seem to occur to him that an affair with a married man—himself—might be far more alien to her moral upbringing than intimacy with a single man.

* * *

Jackie's friendships with the other flight attendants were solid, and she would keep in touch with many of them for the next two decades, just as she remained close to the friends she had grown up with in Minnesota, and with her brothers and sisters and parents. She was a very loving young woman; Jackie was "down-to-earth," according to friends. Despite her tragically short engagement to Cal Logan, most of her close girlfriends had realized even then that Jackie's real longing was for Bill Brand. Few of them would ever actually meet the man Jackie spoke of in such glowing terms.

Jackie compared every man she met to Brand, and none measured up. But instinctively she tried to pull away from the big man she had left behind in Alaska. Although she had probably loved Bill Brand since she was in college, Jackie wanted security. She wanted a home and a husband who could support her without worrying about bills. She had exquisite taste, and she hoped one day to be able to have the home she wanted without considering the cost.

Bill had taught her that. He had told Jackie over and over that *she* was like royalty—that she should never consider riding a bus or streetcar. That was for ordinary women, and she was special. She never believed that part—but subtly, cunningly, Bill had instilled in Jackie an appreciation of and desire for expensive clothes and lovely homes.

After Cal died Jackie began to date often, but in the back of her mind there was always Bill. And Bill was not free to marry her. Bill Brand was not an option for her.

After she had spent a few years in the East, Northwest Airlines transferred Jackie to Seattle. It was a promotion; now she would have a chance to fly to the Orient as well as the States. One of her best friends was transferred with her. They had lived a block apart in Washington, D.C., and they were delighted and surprised to find they had taken apartments just as close in Seattle.

Bill Brand would later claim that Jackie became pregnant in the summer of 1965. He suspected the father was either an Alaska state trooper or an airline pilot. He told people the "pregnancy" was aborted while Jackie was on a flight to Tokyo. The alleged father of that child was rumored to have committed suicide in Anchorage, Alaska. It was all very nebulous. It may have been true; more likely it was a vicious figment of Bill Brand's jealous imagination. Years later, as he looked back upon his life and Jackie's, he saw indiscretions that had never happened, and he hated vehemently anyone he thought might have come between him and Jackie.

Friends who knew Jackie Lindall since kindergarten and others who remember a younger Bill Brand believe the physical affair between Jackie and Bill probably began in the mid-sixties. He was, of course, still married, but his obsession with Jackie had continued undeterred by time or distance.

Although far apart in miles, Alaska and Seattle seem right next door to northwesterners, and commuters fly back and forth all the time. Brand frequently had business in Seattle, or he *made* business in Seattle. Jackie was flying out of Seattle, and he saw her as often as he could, seething with jealousy over her other suitors.

And still he did not plan to divorce his wife or leave his children. He offered Jackie nothing more than an affair. For the ultimately selfish man, it worked out well. Jackie would have her job to fill much of her time, and she would wait for Bill in the meantime. Brand couldn't see that she might need a life beyond that; he liked the thought of her in her Seattle apartment, waiting for his call.

He made vague promises to Jackie from time to time.

Someday, perhaps, they *could* be married, but not until his children were grown. He missed Jackie when he was away from her, but he was a very busy man, continuing to build his fortune in Alaska's booming construction era.

For Jackie it wasn't as easy; she wanted a *life*. She could see her twenties passing by with no man who was really her own, and she dreaded spending her life that way. Bill was always showering her with presents—but presents were cold comfort over lonely weekends.

Friends remembering Jackie recall that, of all things, Jackie seemed to need security the most—emotional security and financial security. Bill Brand was not in a position to give her either.

At that point, in the mid-sixties, Jackie probably truly loved Bill Brand. She clung to the same dream every "other woman" has—that someday Bill would be divorced and they would marry. He was even more attractive at forty than he had been when she first moved into his home, and he was quite powerful in the business world, making money hand over fist. As one of Jackie's friends said later, Jackie would have left any man for a chance to marry Bill Brand. "He personified all the things she admired in a man."

Jackie turned down scores of dates to keep her promise to be faithful to Bill.

But finally there were just too many days and too many long nights alone. Maybe Jackie intended to force Bill's hand; maybe not. More likely, in the end she simply couldn't bring herself to break up another woman's home. Jackie met another man, a good man who was free to be with her. Jud Jessup* was divorced and had custody of his two children. Worst of all for Bill Brand, Jessup lived on the East Coast.

By 1967 Jackie was twenty-six, and she had decided to marry Jud and help him raise his youngsters. It was a decision that Bill Brand deplored. He was incredibly vicious when he spoke of Jessup and his children. He could not imagine why Jackie would leave him to raise what he termed "another man's idiots." As he remembered the situation, the events were cunningly rearranged to suit his obsession. It was almost as if he believed that Jackie had been somehow *forced* to marry Jud Jessup, and that Bill had tried vainly to save her.

Bill Brand was a man who kept diaries, marked dates on calendars; writing down his thoughts helped him remember those things that were of great importance to him, both in business and in his relationships. He would one day write a long, long letter, the pages chronicling so many years of his feelings for—and about—Jackie. Many of his recollections were about the many rendezvous the pair had had.

During October, 1967, Jackie and I got together in Anchorage. I was there on business and she was on her way through on a trip to the Orient, and when she arrived, she found that we were staying at the same hotel. So she left word for me to call her. I did, and that night we went to dinner together at the hotel. Luckily, the next day her flight was delayed for twelve hours which gave her the chance to recover and we made plans to meet in Portland on December 12th.

I arranged for a suite at a hotel in Portland for that day, and that evening Jackie flew in from Seattle after having worked a flight from Tokyo that day. She was absolutely exhausted. . . . We went back to the room, she in one [bed] and I in another, and she immediately fell asleep. . . . During dinner that night at the hotel, I told her that I really loved her. There wasn't much of a response to that, but that night she came into the room where I was sleeping and laid down on the bed next to me and asked, "What are we going to do?" I knew that she was to be married, but it wasn't until then that I understood that the date was hard and fast.

Brand would not accept Jackie's marriage to another man.

The next day she turned, put her arms around me and told me that she felt she was in love with me . . . we had decisions to make.

My position was that I would proceed immediately with the business of a divorce because nothing would ever be the same between my wife and I. She objected to that, saying that was nothing for me to do because the girls were too young and their absence would make my life miserable for me. The indignity of aborting her wedding plans and the subsequent explanation to her family were repulsive to her, so much so that she would rather cast her lot with a life of unhappiness. It later developed that the decision was almost disastrous. . . .

Bill Brand had waited too long to be with Jackie. She had simply decided to take her life off hold and marry a man who loved her and was free to do something about it.

She must have had doubts. After a decade of being bound to Bill she must have wondered if she was doing the right thing. Even as she prepared to marry another man, Jackie gave Bill a silver letter opener inscribed "Somewhere, Someday, Somehow." Bill interpreted that to mean they would eventually be together.

Maybe she did mean it that way. Maybe she knew how Bill was hurting over her defection from their relationship, and she wanted to ease his pain. But she still went ahead with her wedding.

"The saddest day of my life took place while I was a continent away," Bill Brand wrote of Jackie's wedding day. "The marriage wasn't going to amount to anything from the beginning."

Despite the fact that she was married to someone else, Bill called Jackie Jessup three times a week. He gloated, "She was in his bed, and I was on his phone talking to her three times a week. . . ."

Jackie's best stewardess friend was married in late 1969, with Jackie as matron of honor. Bill planned to fly to meet her, but at the last minute his business in Fairbanks "went to hell" and he didn't go. He reminisced later, "Jackie felt betrayed. That pack (her new family) had been giving her fits, and she badly needed a renewal of hope."

That was only Bill's perception, and in retrospect at that. Jackie's stepchildren liked her, and would always remember her as "a 'mother' and our friend."

Bill considered Jessup a monster and his children "genetic cripples." They were impediments to his true love for Jackie. He fought constantly to break up her marriage. He urged Jackie to meet him and arranged to fly back to her home on the eastern seaboard to see her. In Bill Brand's mind Jackie was being driven nearly insane by her marriage and her separation from him. In actuality it was quite the other way around.

If Jackie was upset, it was undoubtedly because she was being pulled in two directions. Now that he could not have her, Bill Brand *would* not let go.

In October, 1973, Bill Brand was forty-eight years old. He was admitted to a Seattle clinic for a procedure designed to prevent a stroke. Tests had shown that his left carotid artery—the artery that carries blood to the brain—was ninety percent occluded (blocked). He had episodes of tingling and numbness in his hand and trouble with one eye. There was the very real possibility that his mental functions might also be compromised by the lack of oxygen to his brain. Delicate surgery removed the fatty plug that blocked the vital artery, and he recovered uneventfully.

In the years to come Brand would have frequent checkups and take a vast array of medications—to help him sleep, to relieve depression, and to control ulcers. He was clearly not a happy man; his ailments were those often triggered by anxiety and depression.

How could he be happy? Jackie was married to someone else, and even though so many years had passed he still struggled to find a way to bring her back to him. He called and wrote and sent tapes, cajoling, pleading.

She still cared about him, as much as she fought it. Time after time Bill's campaign to draw her back worked. He sent Jackie money to come to Seattle to talk with him in April of 1974. He rented a suite at an expensive hotel; he always got accommodations in the very best hotels. But he recalled later that Jackie's visit was not as wonderful as he had expected. Bill was convinced he had caught her in an assignation with another man—an airline friend she had known for years. Bill Brand was becoming shockingly paranoid in his thinking, at least when it came to Jackie. There were so many men he suspected of being Jackie's lovers.

There were not enough hours in the day for Jackie to have had that many lovers.

One day Bill Brand would document his years with the woman he loved so possessively in a missive he called "The Bill and Jackie Letter."

"The reason that I mention this incident," he wrote

many years later, "is because she displayed a vulgar capability that was so totally foreign to me according to my moral values."

Bill Brand was so righteous. He saw sin wherever he looked—if Jackie was involved. In reality, he manufactured sin out of whole cloth. Except for her meetings with Bill, Jackie was faithful to her husband.

"The week was memorable," he wrote of the 1974 visit, "and was the foundation for our being together. There were no hard and fast dates set because things in Fairbanks needed attention but things in Maryland were coming apart pretty fast by then and arrangements in Seattle were in order. . . ."

Bill constantly urged Jackie to leave Jessup as soon as possible and to come to Seattle to live. He would set her up in an apartment and take care of her completely. Then, in time they would be married.

Jackie Jessup was, as the song goes, "Torn Between Two Lovers." She was thirty-three years old in 1974, and whichever man she chose to be with she fully expected to *stay* with until she died. If she expected to have children of her own, she didn't have that many years left. Bill clearly wasn't going to go away unless she did something convincingly decisive. But did she truly *want* him to go away? She loved Jessup—but not with the fiery passion she felt for Bill. She had been in love with Bill for so long that he was part of who *she* was. And now, for the first time, he was promising that he really would marry her. He tugged at her continually, and finally he pulled her free of her husband.

He wrote proudly in "The Bill and Jackie Letter" that he had convinced her to leave Jessup and her stepchildren, and how "relieved" she was when he instructed her to be in Seattle by November, 1975.

Jackie really had no choice at that point. Jud Jessup had finally discovered Jackie's other love when he found a bunch of cassette tapes with long messages to Jackie from Bill. Not surprisingly, he gathered up his youngsters and left.

"He had gone into a rage and otherwise behaved like a jerk," Brand wrote happily. "He must have realized long before that his days with her were limited. . . ."

Jackie's marriage had lasted a little more than seven years. In reality, it never stood a chance. By sheer force of will Bill Brand had not allowed it to succeed.

Bill Brand was gleeful. He had won. He had his Jackie back. She packed her things and shipped them to Seattle.

"Then she got herself on an airplane and headed to Seattle to arrive here late in the day on November 1st. There was a suite ready for us at the hotel. We needed to stay there until we decided just where in the Seattle area it would be that we wanted to live."

Bill was a bit premature. They would not actually live together for a long time. Bill Brand was still married and living with his family in Fairbanks.

But he had wrenched Jackie free of her marriage, and she was once again waiting for his visits. Now she no longer had her career as a flight attendant to fill her time. Bill could not be with her for Christmas or New Year's, of course; he had his family. He bought her a ticket to fly to Minneapolis to be with her family.

Bill Brand had become her sole support. Jackie was his mistress. She loved him. She was faithful.

On November 14, 1977, Jackie Jessup moved into the apartment where she would live for the next eight years. It was a lovely three-bedroom unit in Bellevue, Washington, one of Seattle's posher bedroom communities. She signed the lease and listed her occupation as a "buyer's assistant" for a Fairbanks, Alaska, corporation. It was, of course, one of Bill Brand's corporations. In reality, Jackie didn't work at all.

She was a quiet tenant, and her landlady soon became familiar with the handsome man who often spent time with Jackie. "It was my observation over these years that Jackie was beautifully courted by Bill Brand," she recalled. "Although I didn't know the Brands socially, I was never aware of any domestic strife between them. I knew Bill Brand as a very gentle man with a gruff exterior."

Bill Brand still nursed his paranoid fantasy that Jackie was not true to him. For all his blustery gloating, he felt deep down that his main attraction for Jackie was his wealth. He believed that she wouldn't stay with him unless he could support her better than any other man. It was a premise that wasn't even remotely true. He was her "prince," her perfect man. She adored him. All Jackie sought was honesty and commitment.

The two things Bill would not give her.

Brand later recalled:

During late February, 1980, Jackie and I had some problems communicating. I wasn't spending enough time in Seattle, and according to her, I wasn't moving fast enough to get things done in Fairbanks so that we could get on with our lives. I was in my office one afternoon when the phone rang. She was on it, asking if I was sitting down because she had just checked into an inn in Fairbanks. The purpose of the visit was to talk and get our stuff together. She stayed overnight and the better part of the next day, and then left for Seattle.

The problem was simple enough. Bill Brand wouldn't make the break with his wife. Even so, he was furiously jealous when he found a rough draft of a letter on one of Jackie's legal tablets. She had written to a man—a friend of one of her brothers—thanking him for buying her dinner when they met accidentally in the airport. This had been the night she returned from her trip to urge Bill to divorce his wife. In the letter she invited the friend, his wife, and his daughter to stay in her apartment in Bellevue if they ever found themselves passing through Seattle.

"I never mentioned anything about it to her," Brand wrote in his "Bill and Jackie Letter"—"but it's another example of her morally loose style of life and her need to have something going on. I have no way of knowing how often he stayed with her, but I do know that she's spectacular enough in bed that any man would rig more than one Seattle trip to be with her if he was invited."

Bill Brand saw shadows of sex everywhere. If Jackie went to the beach with a friend and her husband during the time Bill was home in Fairbanks, he imagined kinky threesomes. He even suspected Jackie of having incestuous relationships with a male member of her family. He perceived her hand touching a man's as she passed a cigarette lighter as an overtly sexual signal.

It was all in Bill's own distorted perception, but frightening in its intensity. As he wrote out his evaluation of Jackie's morals, the skewed convolutions of his thinking show in his tangled prose.

She has always had traces of the hedonistic approach to things such as, "If it feels good and the consequences aren't that bad, do it." Sex to some people is like shaking hands, no more consequential than that. The most disturbing matter to this is that while I have been aware of it, I have never exposed my resentment to her behavior, expecting to be accepted on a normal social and moral level, while, because she isn't going to say anything different, she doesn't, in fact, belong at *any* level. When it's considered the number of men she has had sex with in her lifetime and then demands and receives acceptance of a moral and social level that most people have to earn, there is something very wrong.

There *was* something very wrong. Jackie Jessup had no hint of the rage in her lover. Bill never mentioned his jealousy to her. He never gave her a chance to convince him of her fidelity, of the truth. Jackie didn't realize Bill considered her "morally loose"; she would have been appalled had she known what was really festering in Bill's mind.

Bill Brand finally obtained a divorce and came to Jackie at last a single man.

On April 23, 1982, almost a quarter of a century after they first met, Jackie Jessup and Bill Brand were married. When Jackie married Bill she virtually gave up friends, family, and all outside interests. Jackie's role—a role she accepted gladly—as defined by her bridegroom was to live for Bill, and only for Bill. Their life together, realized after many years of frustration, was supposed to be one long honeymoon; the peak phase of Bill Brand's ecstasy must never be allowed to settle into a pleasant, comfortable marriage. It must be romance, romance, romance.

A devastatingly impossible goal.

Bill finally moved into the Bellevue apartment he had rented for Jackie so many years earlier. He opened a business, Alaska Marketing Industries, and rented an office on 116th N.E. in Bellevue.

It should have been a happy ending. It was anything but.

Bill wanted to know where Jackie was every minute, and who she was talking to. He resented it if she spent too much time with anyone else—even her own family. She had made scores of friends—but Bill was annoyed when they passed through Seattle and called her. If she did arrange a brief lunch with a girlfriend, he paced and grumbled until she came home again. She always seemed to be on edge during those quick meetings, explaining that she had to hurry home. She was too jumpy to enjoy herself.

Bill's pervasive jealousy was ridiculous. Jackie loved him; she never cheated on him. The only thing that could have made her leave her marriage to Bill Brand would be her death. She had given up so much to be with him, and she appreciated what he had given up for her. A quarter of a century of longing had finally led to their marriage, and she treasured it above anything else.

Barring an accident, however, Jackie Brand wasn't likely to precede Bill in death; she was much younger than he was—forty-three to his fifty-nine—and it was Bill who had a number of health problems.

All things being equal, Jackie would outlive Bill. That was a possibility she had considered and found unimportant when she married Bill in 1982. Whatever time they might have together would be worth the pain of widowhood later.

On February 22, 1985, Bellevue Police Lt. S.M. Bourgette received a phone call from the police dispatcher. They had received a worried call from Regis Caulfield,* Bill Brand's insurance agent. Caulfield had been alerted by another business associate of Brand's, Thomas Donley.* Both men had reason to be concerned; they had each received long identical letters from Brand which also contained his last will and testament. Caulfield had only recently tried to talk Brand out of changing his will. Bill had wanted to exclude Jackie completely and leave everything to his daughters instead. Besides that, Bill Brand had taken out an additional half million dollars worth of insurance.

After they received the bizarre letters from Bill Brand both Donley and Caulfield had attempted to phone his apartment, but no one answered. They had then contacted the apartment house manager. The manager went to the Brand apartment and knocked, and finally Bill Brand, his hair tousled, had come to the door. He assured the manager everything was "fine." The manager hadn't seen Jackie Brand but reported back that nothing was wrong at the apartment.

Not satisfied, Regis Caulfield had driven to Bellevue. It was nearly 4:30 when he got to the Brands' apartment house. Both Jackie's and Bill's cars, a Plymouth Arrow and a Mercury Cougar, were parked outside. He knocked at their door, but no one answered. He went to the manager's office and used the phone there. This time Bill's answering machine picked up his call.

Worried, Caulfield had called the Bellevue Police Department. Both he and Tom Donley had received an odd ten-page typewritten letter, with "Bill and Jackie" scrawled in Brand's handwriting across the top. It was mimeographed, and it was a scalding exposé chronicling the couple's twenty-five-year relationship, but mostly decrying Jackie Brand's lack of morals and her betrayal of Bill. Even to a layman's perception the letter was sick and full of rage. It was as if Bill Brand had attempted to obliterate Jackie with words, revealing the most intimate things about her to virtual strangers.

But what alarmed Caulfield and Donley were not the slurs on Jackie's fidelity. The document had ended, "Inasmuch as my wife has died with me, I direct that she shall be conclusively deemed not to have survived me."

Lt. Bourgette and Patrol Officer Dennis Dingfield arrived at the Northside Apartments at 5:30 p.m. on February 22nd. The day had been gloomy and cloudy, and it was almost full dark out.

Regis Caulfield pointed out the Cougar and Plymouth Arrow parked in the lot. "The first time I looked through the window," Caulfield said, "I saw a glass with some liquor in it—when I came back twenty minutes later, it had been moved. Somebody's in there."

Bourgette and Dingfield noted that the Brands' apartment occupied the entire lower half of the south side of the building. Apprised of the floor plan of the apartment by the manager, they could see light in the kitchen, the dining/living room area, and a back bedroom. And then they saw someone walking around inside. It was a tall man with silver hair.

Dingfield asked the police dispatcher to try to call the apartment and gave both of Brand's numbers. The phone rang, but the man inside didn't answer. The second number was the answering machine. The dispatcher left a message that the police were outside and wanted Brand to come to the door. Bourgette, watching, saw the man inside walk to the machine, rewind it, and listen to the message.

But he did not come to the door. The lights inside were turned off now, save for one in the back bedroom and a stove clock light.

Bourgette called for backup and got a key from the

manager. He could still see someone walking around inside the apartment, and then the tall man drinking from a glass.

He could not see a woman.

The Bellevue Police thought they might have a hostage situation, and they quickly surrounded the apartment building. Armed officers covered all its perimeters. Hostage negotiators Tom Wray, Cherie Bay, James Kowalczyk, and E.O. Mott, led by Lt. Mark Ericks, were briefed on the situation.

Thomas Donley, still surprised that he had been designated the executor of Bill Brand's estate, was convinced that Brand's will meant "There will be no tomorrow." Caulfield, the insurance agent, knew very little about Bill Brand. He knew only that Brand was married to a second wife, that he was a "self-made, very hardheaded man" whose huge Alaska business empire had collapsed, and that all he had left were real estate holdings. Brand was described by both informants as an awesome drinker.

They waited. Minutes and hours passed. If Jackie Brand was inside, perhaps unable to get past Bill and come out, they didn't want to rush the apartment and give Brand a chance to carry out the promise in his "will."

Dennis Dingfield had not taken his eyes off the dimly lighted rooms inside the apartment for even a minute. After hours of observation he spotted the man inside crawling on his hands and knees. He would crawl for a while and then either lie or fall down. He appeared to be injured, or perhaps about to pass out from an overdose of some kind. He no longer looked capable of harming anyone. Bourgette called for an aid car.

At the same time, 2126 hours (9:26 p.m.), the TAG (Tactical Arms Group) team advised over police frequencies that there was a Code 4 at the Brand residence. Code 4 meant that everything was stable. It did *not* necessarily mean that everything had turned out well.

And then the TAG team went in. The man inside was standing as they went through the door, but only with great difficulty.

It was Bill Brand. He was alive—but extremely intoxicated.

Dennis Dingfield looked beyond the man frozen in the TAG team's flashlights. Dingfield's breath caught in his throat. Beyond the man, down the hallway, Dingfield spotted someone else, a woman lying motionless on the carpet. There was a dark red circle spread out around her body.

Too late.

Maybe it had been too late four hours earlier when they first surrounded the apartment building. It would have made the police feel better, somehow, to know that.

Dingfield cuffed Brand and led him to a police car to drive him back to headquarters, where E. O. Mott and Tom Wray were waiting to talk to him.

The investigation at the apartment was handed over to the detectives. Sadly, there was no hurry now.

Detective John Hansen had worked some of the more bizarre homicide cases that had begun to proliferate in Bellevue, the sleepy little town of the 1940s that had become one of Washington State's largest cities. Hansen was a stubborn, even dogged, instinctive investigator with flashes of brilliance. Tall and husky, with a voice like a bear, Hansen rarely smiled—unless the conversation turned to hunting dogs or his wife and children. In repose his face was handsome, but closed off; no one ever knew what he was really thinking.

Bill and Jackie Brand and John Hansen moved in different worlds, even though they all lived in Bellevue.

Hansen was active in his church and spent whatever time he wasn't on duty with his family.

However, Hansen now began to be intimately acquainted with the tangled story of the Brands' lives, probably *better* acquainted than anyone else ever had. He would be the principal investigator assigned to Case No. 85-B-02260.

Hansen had stood outside the Brand apartment since 6:30. One paramedic from the Bellevue Fire Department had been allowed in to confirm that the woman inside was beyond human help, and then the scene had been sealed. As soon as Bill Brand was taken out Hansen and Detective Gary Felt stepped in.

The woman lay facedown on the hallway carpet. She wore a brown plaid skirt, a yellow silk blouse, and a brown corduroy jacket. She was also wearing high heels, stockings, and black gloves. Her makeup was perfect. A brown and tan comforter, which the fire department medic had lifted from her body, lay at her feet. A shiny briefcase was there, too.

John Hansen touched the calf of one of the woman's legs; the flesh was icy and stiff. The victim had been dead a long time. Hours at the very least.

The dead woman looked as though she had been headed for a trip; a camera on a red strap, a key ring, and a large blue purse rested on the floor beside her. A tweed suitcase was further down the hall. A capped container of tea lay where it had dropped from her hand. Her feet pointed toward the front door. She looked as if she had fallen straight backward, felled instantly by someone or something.

She could not have known she was about to die.

Although a layman might wonder why it was necessary to have permission to investigate what almost surely was a murder, the detectives needed a search warrant to move freely around the apartment. Hansen immediately listed his reasons for a search warrant and obtained one via telephone from District Court Judge Brian Gain. With this in hand Hansen and Detective Gary Felt began to search the apartment.

The apartment was impeccably furnished, as if it had been done by a designer—or by someone with natural talent and a loving hand. The living room was done in shades of red and white, with objets d'art, pillows, and paintings all carrying out the same theme.

Someone had apparently been sleeping on the floral and satin striped couch. There was a rumpled quilt there. A glass of scotch, its ice not yet melted, was leaving a ring on the shiny waxed surface of the teak coffee table. Beside the glass there was a cocked handgun. A .357.

Ironically, the walls of the hallway where Jackie Brand lay dead were hung with gentle pictures of children and fields of flowers. All the furnishings were expensive. All the pictures were of flowers and children and, of course, of Bill and Jackie.

Bill had been proud of his affluence and his expensive tastes; he had discussed that in "The Bill and Jackie Letter" that Regis Caulfield and Tom Conley had turned over to the investigative team. The letter would answer many questions, but it would leave more unanswered. Brand had written of the Bellevue apartment and of the time when Jackie first agreed to live there and wait for him to "take care of things in Fairbanks."

"We found the apartment that suited our needs, leased it, and headed for downtown Seattle to shop for the furniture to furnish it. On one day, we bought for three bedrooms, a devan [*sic*], patio furniture, and a new car. When we got home, she threw up because we spent so much money."

Bill Brand seemed to have liked to communicate by writing—of one kind or another. The apartment was littered with notes. Felt and Hansen gazed around the apartment and saw them. They were everywhere. Notes from Bill to Jackie hung from door jambs, and fluttered where they were taped on cabinets. Brand had even taped them to the wall above her body.

They were love notes of a sort. Some of them were requests for sex; others were weird affirmations of Brand's devotion to the woman who had apparently been his wife for almost three years, his lover for twenty.

One note dated February 11, 1985—ten days earlier— read: "My weekends are great because of you. Monday comes and that means I have to leave you—I hate that. I can barely wait for the next weekend. That tells you what my life is all about. Love is what you and I are all about and that's what makes us go. I'll see you this noon. Be kinky—wear it to lunch. Bill."

The detectives shook their heads. What had he meant? Probably some Frederick's of Hollywood piece of lingerie he had bought Jackie. If the note had been there ten days, that probably meant that no one but Jackie and Bill ever entered this apartment. They couldn't imagine that she would have left such an explicit note for someone else to read. She must have felt like a prisoner.

Hansen and Felt moved around the apartment. Hansen noted a scuff on the hallway of the kitchen area, just a slight gouge in the plasterboard, probably a bullet ricochet. He saw an ashtray and a calendar on the dining room table. Bending to read, he felt the hairs rise on the back of his neck. The last entry on the calendar was penciled neatly into the block for February 21st. Yesterday.

"Jackie passed away at 13:10 hrs."

There was a half-empty bottle of Johnnie Walker Red Label scotch and an empty bottle of Bulloch scotch in the kitchen, and at the other end of the counter a long row of vitamin bottles next to a pack of Winstons. That must have been Jackie Brand's choice. A last cigarette, a Winston, was stubbed out in a crystal ashtray, its filter scarlet with fresh lipstick.

Liquor, cigarettes, and vitamins. Everything in this place was a contradiction. Guns, flowers, blood, love notes.

Trying to look at it all rationally and with as little emotion as possible, John Hansen deduced what had probably happened. For whatever grotesque reason, Bill Brand had shot his wife in the back of the head as she was walking ahead of him toward the front door. The cup of tea in her hand indicated she had been totally oblivious to the danger behind her.

After she was dead Brand had apparently calmly jotted down the time of her death on his calendar, as if he were marking some business appointment.

Then he would have hit the scotch, trying, perhaps, to get the courage to shoot himself, too. He had indicated in the letters he sent out that they would *both* be dead by the time the letters reached their destinations. The .357 Magnum six-shot revolver was cocked and ready there on the coffee table, with three cylinder chambers empty.

Deputy Medical Examiner Corinne Fligner checked for the wounds of entry and exit. She determined that two .357 slugs had struck Jackie's head; one on the right side had entered between her ear and the top of the head and penetrated her brain. A fatal wound. At the back of the victim's skull a shot had simply grazed Jackie's head.

Barring an eyewitness, it is impossible to reconstruct

exactly how any homicide occurs—but John Hansen could almost visualize what had happened here.

The location of the wound at the rear of the head—plus the gun debris that surrounded it—indicated that this was the first wound, fired from a short distance away. The shooter would have been just behind Jackie in the hall. This bullet appeared to have deflected off the back of her skull and lodged in the hallway ceiling directly ahead of her.

The direction of fire of the fatal wound was different. Its path went from front to back, right to left and very slightly downward.

When the first shot was fired and it grazed Jackie Brand's head its force would probably have spun her around to face the man with the gun. Her Bill.

The second bullet was fired from farther away but had pierced her brain, killing her instantly. Would she have had time to form a thought? Had she looked into her killer's eyes when she spun around?

No one would ever know.

At Bellevue police headquarters Detectives E. O. Mott and Tom Wray observed Bill Brand. His face was flushed, and he appeared intoxicated. He wore a white dress shirt with blue pin stripes, buttoned at the cuffs and tucked into his dark blue slacks. His clothing had clearly cost a great deal; the labels showed the garments had been purchased at Seattle's best stores. He was shoeless, but he wore dark socks.

Alone with the detectives in the interview room, Brand suddenly began talking about football and the Seattle Seahawks as if nothing unusual had happened at all. More likely, he didn't want to remember the tableau he had left behind in the apartment he shared with Jackie.

Mott introduced himself and Wray and waited for directions from Lt. Mark Ericks before they proceeded. The guy seemed so drunk, they wondered if they would be able to get any sense out of him. Ericks and John Hansen called from the crime scene to ask that Bill Brand's hands be "bagged" and that he remain handcuffed until a neutron activation analysis test could be performed to determine if he had indeed fired the .357. They also asked that a nitrate test be done to see what would show up on swabbings of his hands, and that a breathalyzer reading be taken before Wray and Mott proceeded with any questioning.

Gary Felt had advised Brand of his rights under Miranda before he was driven away from his apartment. However, when Brand suddenly blurted to Mott and Wray that he had shot his "beautiful wife," both detectives tried again to advise him of his rights to be absolutely sure that he understood.

Brand commented that he understood his rights but said he was quite willing to talk and answer questions. He said he was sorry for shooting his wife. He had shot her, he recalled, about noon the day before. She had been headed for the front door, and he was following her when he shot her twice. She had fallen to the floor, and he had left her there.

"Why did you kill her?" Mott asked quietly.

Brand did not answer directly.

"He only indicated that she was a very beautiful woman and that I wouldn't understand things about her, nor would I understand things about him," Mott wrote in his report.

"I got nothing to hide," Brand blurted. "I murdered my wife. I shot the most beautiful woman in the world."

And then he had begun to drink scotch.

Bill Brand was still drunk, twice as drunk as required in order to be considered legally drunk in the State of Washington. His blood alcohol was .20; his breathalyzer was .19.

He rambled on about killing his "beautiful wife," interspersing his memories of Jackie Brand's murder with a chillingly calm discussion of football. He shook his head back and forth, and his eyes filled with tears. He acknowledged that he was intoxicated and promised he would give a written statement when he sobered up—"tomorrow."

Brand stared at Detective Tom Wray and blurted that Wray looked just like a Seattle Seahawks football star. Then he sat silent for long minutes, tears welling up and beading at the corners of his eyes. Brand finally looked up at Wray and said, "I murdered my wife about twenty-four hours ago. I just got bombed—Johnnie Walker Red. . . . I used a .38 or a .357 and shot [pointing his left index finger under his chin]. I loaded five rounds—.38s, I think. There are three left, the gun's on the table, you know. . . . Who were those guys who barged into my home?"

Brand confided to Wray that he had kept drinking because that was the only way he could sleep. He had slept on the couch, waking up every three hours or so and drinking more.

"I can't believe I really messed things up. She didn't deserve this. . . ."

Bill Brand was coming down from his alcoholic binge, and he began to confront the horror of what he had done.

None of the detectives yet knew why.

Back at the Brands' apartment Hansen and Felt, along with Ericks, Oliver, and a police photographer, worked until almost four in the morning gathering evidence.

Gary Felt found a single spent bullet lying on the ceiling light trim, just beyond where it had passed through the wall. They had to saw a square of plasterboard free to get at that one. Ericks discovered a small lead fragment on the hallway carpet. They knew that Brand had blown a .19 on the breathalyzer—that he had been legally intoxicated when he was arrested. But had he been intoxicated thirty-three hours earlier when Jackie Brand died?

The tenant who lived in the apartment above the Brands told Hansen and Felt that she had heard a "thud-like sound, like someone had dropped something heavy" the day before, confirming that Jackie had been dead more than twenty-four hours when police entered her home.

John Hansen realized he would have to work this case backwards. He knew who the murderer was; the killer had been waiting for the police. And the evidence they had gathered during the long night after Bill Brand was arrested only served to confirm what had happened. The question was why. Why on earth had Bill Brand shot his "beautiful wife" in the back of the head?

Some of the answers began to come in from a dozen or more people who had received "The Bill and Jackie Letter." With each passing day that monstrous document showed up in more and more mailboxes across the country. Bill Brand had spewed out his jealousy and suspicion, so long repressed, in the ugly letter, and then he had sent it to everyone he could think of that Jackie had known— her family, her friends, even men he suspected had cuck-olded him. It was not enough that he had killed Jackie; he had wanted to destroy her image, too. He had tried to wipe away every trace of the real, loving woman. Most of those who received the letter were horrified and sickened. Some were disgusted. Some—who had barely known Jackie Brand—were merely bewildered.

In talking with her relatives and friends, John Hansen found nothing to substantiate Jackie's alleged infidelities. Rather, friends who had received the letter gave statements that were just the opposite. Whenever they had come to Seattle and tried to spend some time with Jackie, her ex-stewardess friends said, she was always looking at her watch, anxious to get back to Bill. On the very rare occasions when they did meet Bill he was pleasant enough, but disinterested, obviously bored with their company.

"Jackie told me Bill unplugged their phone—so they wouldn't be bothered by outsiders," one woman remarked.

Bill had cloistered Jackie, keeping her just for himself, but she hadn't seemed to mind it. Hansen didn't find one witness who could remember that Jackie ever complained about her husband's suffocating affection. She still loved him. Nor could Hansen find anyone who believed Jackie had cheated on Bill Brand.

Two of Jackie's girlfriends had spoken to her a day or so before she died, and she had told them that Bill was going to fly to Alaska on the 21st—and that she would be taking him to the airport. That made sense. The suitcase found next to Jackie's body was packed with men's clothing.

Hansen read "The Bill and Jackie Letter" again and again. It was apparent, even with Brand's exaggerations, that the two had been a part of each other's lives for a long, long time.

They had, indeed, finally been married. Happy ever after.

It wasn't going to be easy for Hansen to ferret out what had gone wrong. Sobered up in jail, Bill Brand declined to talk. He would only say—as if John Hansen could give him some answers—"I'd just like to understand why it all happened."

Hansen was silent, and the room seemed to hum with tension. If anyone should know why it happened, it was the man in jail coveralls, the man who had known Jackie for almost three decades. But Bill Brand just shook his head as if he, too, was bewildered. Perhaps he was. Perhaps he was beginning to try to save his own skin.

Finally Brand sighed and said, "I'll be able to sort it all out in a few hours." And then he said he wanted an attorney. John Hansen ended the interview.

As John Hansen interviewed Jackie's friends and Bill Brand's business associates he was told that Brand had once been extremely wealthy in Fairbanks. At some point, however, his fortune had begun to slide. He had suffered severe business reversals in the late seventies when high interest rates began to cripple the construction business. Bill Brand had finally been forced to file for three separate bankruptcies—a personal bankruptcy due to his guarantees to his bank and supplier debts on behalf of his companies, and two business bankruptcies. Along with his own financial disaster, Brand's first wife sacrificed most of her holdings to settle Brand's debts.

From 1977 on, Bill Brand had suffered continual financial reverses. His vast fortune dwindled. The Alaskan oil pipeline had gone on line in 1975, and Brand had counted on a natural gas pipeline to follow. It never happened, though, and interest rates kept climbing.

Amid the ashes of what had once been a thriving business Bill divorced his first wife, moved to Seattle, married Jackie, and began a business that was scarcely more than a front to conceal his growing desperation. He had begun with high hopes that he could earn a good living again by helping Washington businesses that wanted to branch out into Alaska. He still had savvy; he still had contacts. But the only real money Brand had coming in was from leases he held in Alaska.

Jackie had no idea how bad things were. Bill had always showered her with jewelry and presents, and he worried that she would leave him if she found out how close he was to financial disaster. So he didn't tell her. Even though he wasn't doing any business at all, he left their apartment each day, carrying a briefcase. At the office he phoned friends or read magazines. Sometimes he chatted with people in neighboring offices. In truth, Bill simply marked time until he could rush home to Jackie.

If only he had confided in her, she would have understood.

Jackie knew they were living off his prior investments, but Bill had always had so much money, she assumed he had a stake that would see them through any hard times.

But failure bred failure. Bill Brand, stressed to the breaking point by his business losses, by the fact that he had almost reached the limit on his many credit cards, by his overriding fear that he would lose Jackie, became impotent.

Although she had seldom confided in anyone about her marriage, Jackie did mention Bill's sexual problems to one of her two Seattle friends. She also said it was no big deal. "I like so many other things about my Bill that it really does not matter to me."

One friend told John Hansen that Jackie Brand had always struck her as a woman so straight and puritanical that she was "almost sexless," and that she couldn't imagine Jackie in the role of the harlot Brand described in his final letter. No, she assured Hansen, a husband who could no longer make love wouldn't have been the end of the world for Jackie. Not at all.

But it had been for Brand. He had consulted sex therapists, trying to regain his potency. Hansen found a desk planner in Brand's office that went back two years, and its pages were full of coded notations about business meetings and about sex. He had listed both his failures and his successes. Bill Brand had been obsessed with his sexual performance. Perhaps in an attempt to prove himself, he had been unfaithful to Jackie, even during the times in his marriage when he had accused *her* of cheating on him.

Bill Brand's sexual notations and the derogatory notes about Jackie were all written in red ink. Every sexual encounter, however brief, had been noted in Brand's books. There were also a number of references to pornographic movies Brand had seen, right down to the titles and the dates he had viewed them.

Along with all of this Hansen read through medical records that showed that Bill Brand had consulted physicians more and more frequently, worried about his eyes, his lungs, his heart, his blood pressure. The business and sexual performance strain Brand felt had quite clearly converted into physical symptoms. Beyond that, there was the very real possibility that Brand *was* falling apart physically. He overindulged in everything; that had worked when he was younger, but he was almost sixty, and his body was failing him.

It was easier now for Hansen to see what had gone wrong. Bill Brand had feared he was losing those things that *he* perceived Jackie wanted from him—money and sexual performance. He was no longer the vigorous young man she remembered from 1958.

Brand had been gripped in a nightmarish midlife crisis blown all out of proportion. Despite all the years they had been involved with each other, Brand clearly hadn't known Jackie at all. He didn't know his wife well enough to trust her with his pain. And she obviously had known virtually nothing about what was going on in his head.

Something had to happen, some explosion, some end to it.

And tragically, something had.

John Hansen met another of Jackie's friends a week

after Jackie died. This friend had known Jackie, she said, since they grew up together in Minnesota. She said she had not approved when Jackie married Bill. He had been overly possessive, and rude and overbearing toward her family and friends.

"I realized I could not enjoy Jackie's company when Bill was around. I resorted to meeting her for lunch or talking with her on the phone. But if you called and left a message for her with him, he wouldn't pass it on."

Jackie had called her friend at 5:00 p.m. on either the 19th or 20th of February to say that Bill was flying to Fairbanks on Thursday for business and wouldn't be back until Sunday. Jackie had invited her friend over to the Bellevue apartment for dinner, but the woman said she had other plans. They had agreed to meet at a restaurant for lunch the following week.

Instead of having dinner with Jackie Brand in her apartment on February 22, the friend had received "The Bill and Jackie Letter" by Priority Mail and read it with growing horror.

Two of Jackie's other friends said that they had always felt that Bill treated his wife tenderly. One friend had last seen Jackie only six days before she died. During this last meeting she had been a little surprised when Jackie commented, "I would like to have had somebody more handsome, but you know, Bill is so good to me."

It had been almost as if Jackie was trying to convince herself that she *had* made the right choice when she committed her life to Bill Brand.

This friend received the letter on the 22nd, too. "When I read it I knew instinctively that Jackie was dead; I immediately called their house, starting at 6:25. I left messages on the tape machine, but never got an answer. . . ."

* * *

February 21, 1985, had been Bill Brand's cutoff day. He had told Jackie he would be flying to Fairbanks. He bought a ticket, but he never really expected to fly to Alaska that day. He had hoped against improbable hope that he would make a deal, extend a lease, do *something* so that Jackie wouldn't know they were flat broke. If nothing happened by the 21st, they would both have to die. To Bill Brand it was that simple.

Nothing happened. All Brand's money was gone. He couldn't even charge a meal on a credit card. Jackie didn't know. He had lived a lie for so long that Bill was able on this one last day to paste a serene look on his face so that she *wouldn't* know. He mailed his hate-filled letters, a dozen or more of them.

There was no turning back now.

When Thursday morning came they both dressed. Jackie packed Bill's bag, stubbed out her cigarette, grabbed a cup of tea for the ride to the airport, and walked down the hall ahead of Bill on her way to drive him to SeaTac Airport.

Bill raised the gun. He fired. Jackie spun around, a look of pain and shock on her face, and Bill thought for one crazy second that she might be having one of her headaches. She had terrible headaches. He fired again.

And Jackie died. She never knew that Bill had no more money. For a man who had failed at so many things, Bill Brand had managed to succeed in this one tragic effort. This one useless, senseless act of cruelty.

Bill's note to his executor was succinct. He wrote that he had supported Jackie since November 1, 1975.

It was Brand money that purchased all the furniture and appliances that are in the apartment. That includes a Maytag washer and dryer and a Sears freezer. . . . Also, I brought to the marriage a Unigard policy. . . . At the time we were married, I made my wife beneficiary, but on the 12th of December, I signed the enclosed change of beneficiary statement. . . .

I should make clear to you . . . that my wife never adopted the Jessup children which will severely limit any claims they might think they have for any of her possessions. . . .

Bill had never accepted Jackie's stepchildren. He saw them, too, as interlopers, and he wanted to be sure they got nothing. He wanted his body cremated and sent to relatives. He left Jackie's remains to her family.

Bill Brand would have preferred that Jackie's family received nothing more. But John Hansen made a decision to give the victim's family the few pieces of gold jewelry that the medical examiner had removed from her body. That was all they would have left of her—that and the despicably savage letter from Bill.

It was over.

But of course, it really wasn't. Bill Brand had had the courage to kill the woman he claimed to love beyond life itself, but he had not had the courage to commit suicide.

John Henry Browne, his defense attorney, had Bill Brand examined by a psychiatrist to see if he had been, under the law, responsible for his actions on February 21, 1985.

Brand's diagnosis was that he was in the grip of a major clinical depression and that his responses were indicative of a narcissistic personality disorder. The former was understandable, given the circumstances; the latter had probably been a part of Bill Brand his whole life. The narcissist focuses always on himself. He is not crazy, either legally or medically; he simply cannot empathize with other human beings. He expects special favors and views those around him as extensions of himself—his to summon or to send away at will. Jackie's main job was to admire Bill and offer him unconditional support. As all narcissists do, Bill alternately overidealized and devalued her.

Jackie made Bill whole. He owned her, and he could not let her find out that he was a failure. "Unconsciously," his examiner wrote, "his need to kill her represented his need to protect himself from her harsh judgment. His life . . . was dominated by her attentions and approval, from which he sustained his major—if not his sole—emotional support."

No one would ever say that Jackie had not done her best to make Bill Brand happy. She shut herself away from everyone but Bill. It wasn't enough. Nothing ever could have been.

Bill Brand had a profound personality disorder, and he was depressed—but he was not crazy. His examiner, a physician from the University of Washington School of Medicine, determined that Bill Brand had indeed been aware of his actions when he shot his wife in the head, and that he had had the ability to distinguish right from wrong. He could not hope to plead innocent by reason of insanity.

Bill Brand was convicted of second-degree murder in King County Superior Court Judge Jim Bates's courtroom in February, 1986. Sentencing was delayed as Defense Attorney John Henry Browne argued that medical tests had revealed a degree of brain damage. It was a defense that might have worked six or eight years later, when medical experts understood how devastating steroids could be to both the physical and mental health of men who took them. Bill Brand, panicked by impotence, had been taking steroids. He had also been taking Halcyon pills to sleep. The synergesic (cumulative) effect of combining those

THE TUMBLEDOWN SHACK

Beverly Johnson left the Oregon Coast with her best friend, Patty Weidner, to hitchhike hundreds of miles. Neither girl ever came home.

Beverly Johnson and Patty Weidner were much too isolated to call for help when they desperately needed it.

THE TUMBLEDOWN SHACK

Two young women from Oregon chose this
abandoned shack to spend the night in.

Jack Stolle told
detectives a number
of scenarios about
what had happened
in the lonely shack.
He went to prison for
forgery, but he had
a much worse crime
on his conscience.

Pretty Patty Weidner (bottom) and Bev Johnson thought joining the Washington State apple harvest would be fun and lucrative. Instead, they encountered a deadly stalker.

THE TUMBLEDOWN SHACK

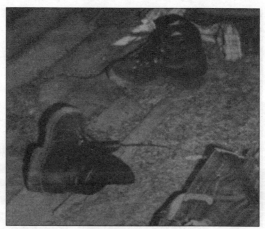

Beverly Johnson's jeans, shirt, and boots were on the floor next to her body.

"Charlie," one of the victims' dogs, tried to protect them. Their other dog was not at the crime scene when Chelan County investigators arrived.

DEAD AND ON TAPE

Nick Kyreacos, 26, prepared for a mysterious meeting in a dark alley with walkie-talkies, a tape recorder, a knife, and a gun filled with blanks. It wasn't enough.

This alley was dark as ink during a November storm. Nick Kyreacos crept along the building walls while someone watched him from a truck parked where the white car is pictured. Seattle police officers were stunned to learn who the shooter was.

DEAD AND ON TAPE

Counterclockwise from upper left: Detective George Marberg, Detective Sergeant Bruce Edmonds, Lt. Patrick Murphy, and Detective Dick Reed and Detective Don Strunk. They solved a murder case, but this time they wished they were mistaken about the killer's identity.

A former Seattle burglary detective walks to a trial where his testimony will keep an entire courtroom in suspense. Stan Tappan*, right, was playing an unfamiliar role.

Kitsap County Chief of Detectives Bill Clifton will never forget the most horrifying case of his long career. Not even an experienced detective could have predicted the identity of the killer of a perfect little family.

FATAL OBSESSION

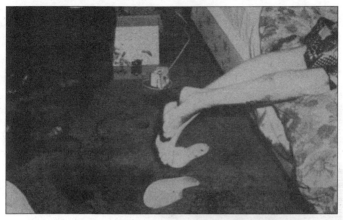

The New Year had barely begun when sheriff's officers were summoned to a virtual house of horror. Lori Rennsler's body lay across her bed; her small son's body was nearby, and so was the body of their dachshund puppy. There was one more victim in a case of multiple murder that defied explanation.

Lori Rennsler was fully clothed in a red and white satin robe when detectives found her. The investigators didn't know who could have destroyed her entire family in their picturesque waterfront home.

CAMPBELL'S REVENGE

Snohomish County detective Joe Belinc worked tirelessly
to track down the killer of Shannah and Renae Wicklund
and Barbara Hendrickson. (Ann Rule)

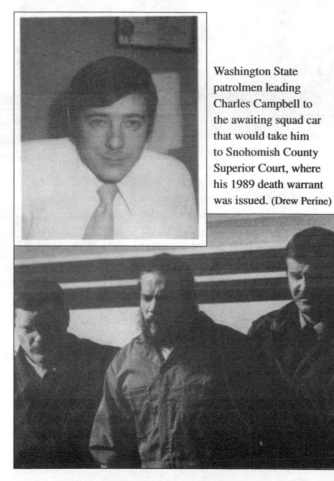

Washington State
patrolmen leading
Charles Campbell to
the awaiting squad car
that would take him
to Snohomish County
Superior Court, where
his 1989 death warrant
was issued. (Drew Perine)

CAMPBELL'S REVENGE

Renae Wicklund, a beautiful drum majorette in high school in Jamestown, North Dakota. After graduation she moved to the West, where she found great happiness and stark tragedy.

Shannah Wicklund was too young to remember the first time the huge red-haired man came to her house.

Washington State Senior Assistant Attorney General Greg Canova, who successfully prosecuted Russ Howard for the murder of Donna Howard.

Bob Keppel, investigator for the Washington State Attorney General's Office, who would not quit until he uncovered what *really* happened to Donna Howard.

ONE TRICK PONY

Donna Bennett, around 1950, a few years before she met her future husband, Noyes "Russ" Howard. Her sister felt they had little in common, but Russ's charisma caught Donna, and she forgot her dreams of marrying a cowboy. She married him, knowing she was taking a chance on love. (Bobbi Bennett)

The Bennett sisters in the early 1950s. They were as close as sisters could be. Donna is on the left, and Bobbi is on the right. (Bobbi Bennett)

ONE TRICK PONY

This is how Russ Howard said he had found Donna after he'd returned from town with warm doughnuts and a new mailbox. Note the "paintbrush" swipes of blood just above her left elbow. Lt. Rod Englert, nationally renowned blood-spatter expert, said these were made as someone repositioned Donna's body, not by medium velocity blood spatter from a horse-kick wound. Donna's shirt and jeans are pulled up as if she had been dragged by her boots.

Noyes "Russ" Howard on trial in 1986 for the murder of his wife, Donna, a dozen years after her death. The years since Russ met Donna are etched on his face.

THE LAST LETTER

Jackie and Bill Brand. He pursued her for years,
but when he won her for himself he still wasn't happy.

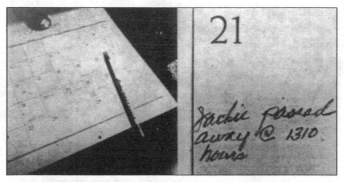

21

Jackie passed
away @ 1310
hours

Bill Brand was nothing if not precise. He noted
the minute of Jackie's death in military time.

I'LL LOVE YOU FOREVER

From the magazine "Dr." Anthony Fernandez raises a glass of champagne to toast his new bride, Ruth Logg. Their perfect love did not survive for long. (Ann Rule collection)

Roger Dunn (below), King County, Washington, homicide detective, worked with Detective Ted Forrester to prove that Ruth Logg had not died in a tragic driving accident. (Ann Rule)

Anthony Fernandez was so angry at Detective Ted Forrester (above) for pursuing him on a murder charge that he sued Forrester for a million dollars. He did not collect.
(Ann Rule)

MURDER AND THE PROPER HOUSEWIFE

This is "Nancy Brooks," the modest housewife who became involved in a bizarre murder plot. (Ann Rule Collection)

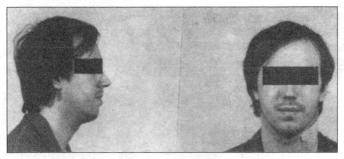

"Bennett LeClerk," who seemed to mesmerize the women in his life. (Ann Rule collection)

MURDER AND THE PROPER HOUSEWIFE

The rear entrace to the Acadia Health Center. Deputies
were stationed on the roof of the auto body shop to the left,
and Seattle police officer Mike Crist waited at the alley entrance.
He faced down a bleeding gunman. (Police file photo)

Seattle homicide
detective Benny
DePalmo, who—
with his partner
Duane Homan—
broke one of the
most puzzling
cases they had
ever encountered.
(Ann Rule)

THE MOST DANGEROUS GAME

Detective Doug Englebretson, Snohomish County Sheriff's Office, discovered the identity of the mysterious sniper who stalked two teenagers in the snowy wilderness. (Ann Rule)

The tiny cabins with a foot of snow on the roofs, where the runaway girls "played house," until fear of a roving monster scared them. (Police file photo)

The Snohomish County Sheriff's Department often has to cope with blizzards and deep snow, as their territory includes mountain foothills.

THE MOST DANGEROUS GAME

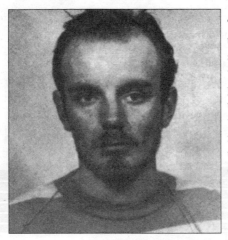

The runaways were thrilled that "Al" spent so much time with them and promised to protect them in the snowy woods. He was not who they thought he was. (Police file photo)

Snohomish County sheriff's vehicles parked near the main road. The cabin where Maeve lay injured was far away, in deep snow; the only way to bring her out was with snowmobiles. (Ann Rule collection)

THE KILLER WHO NEVER FORGOT . . . OR FORGAVE

Lee Yates, who has one of the highest conviction rates in the King County Prosecuting Attorney's Office, behind the wheel of his Porsche in a race at Portland, Oregon's, International Raceway. (Lee Yates collection)

Arne Kaarsten ran to neighbors for help after finding his wife, Judy, strangled under blankets on the floor and seven-month-old daughter Peri Lynn under blankets on the Bathinette (inset). (Court photo)

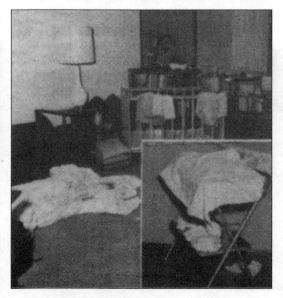

THE KILLER WHO NEVER FORGOT . . .
OR FORGAVE

Deputy Ken Trainor, King County Police, was one of the first officers on the scene of the double murder at the Kaarsten home in Kent. (Ann Rule)

The house where Arne Kaarsten's wife and baby were strangled during the night. A neighbor saw someone standing in the living room an hour or more before Kaarsten called for help. The baby's room was to the right of the door; the Kaarsten's two-and-a-half-year-old daughter's room was at the far right. Why did she live and the baby die? (Court photo)

Photo of Marcia Moore as a bride in November 1977. She was thrilled with her new life and her new husband. Sadly, her happiness wasn't fated to last long.

Barbara Easton, noted Northwest psychic consultant, came to a tragic conclusion when she read several spreads of cards about the fate of Marcia Moore. (Ann Rule collection)

Author Robin Moore, famous for *The French Connection* and *The Green Berets,* knew his sister would never have disappeared willingly. (Publicity shot: *Court Martial,* Robin Moore)

THE STOCKHOLM SYNDROME

Investigators found the body of the victim where it had rolled down an embankment with a helping push from the man who shot him. (Police photo)

Reporting the "accident," the suspect told probers that he shot Rusty, the victim's collie, when the dog tried to attack him. (Police photo)

The prosecution's tightly prepared case was ably assisted by Oregon Assistant Attorneys General Bob Hamilton, shown holding up the bullet from the antique gun used in the slaying, and Stephen Keutzer (right). (Ann Rule)

Jim Byrnes, the attorney general's investigator, found a way for the brainwashed victim to tell her story. He is a sensitive and intelligent detective, and Robin came to trust him. (Ann Rule)

drugs—not to mention his excessive use of alcohol and other medications he was taking—might well have heightened the paranoia he felt over losing Jackie.

It would have been an interesting courtroom battle. Crimes committed while someone is under the influence of so-called recreational drugs and/or alcohol do not usually go unpunished. A "diminished capacity" defense doesn't usually work because the defendant has *chosen* to render himself less than capable. Might an insanity plea have convinced a jury, given the new information that has come out on steroids? Perhaps. But then there was the whole quarter of a century of background of Bill Brand's possessive hold over Jackie—a thread going back to the days when he was young and alert and vigorous.

At any rate, John Henry Browne, who is one of Seattle's most sought-after defense attorneys, did not yet have the final decision on the negative effects of steroids to argue with in 1986.

In the late summer of 1986 Bill Brand was sentenced to thirteen years in prison. Due to his increasingly poor health and diminishing mental capacity his sentence was appealed, and he was released on October 11, 1991. He was suffering from chronic obstructive pulmonary disease, better known as emphysema.

In the summer of 1993 Bill Brand, now sixty-eight, was admitted to the Veterans Administration Medical Center in Seattle. He died there at ten minutes past eleven in the evening on July 16th. Brand's death certificate listed him as a widower, and he was indeed that. Jackie had been dead for eight years.

Jackie had told him long before that they would ultimately be together. And they were—but for such a bitterly short time.

"Somewhere, Someday, Somehow" had come and gone.

I'll Love You Forever
(from *A Fever in the Heart*)

I learned about this story of ultimate betrayal long after it was too late to save the victim. Ruth Logg's daughters and other relatives could not save her either, but they prevailed and saw a certain kind of justice done in a landmark court decision.

This is the kind of nightmare case that speaks to every woman on her own. Each of us can identify with Ruth Logg. Each of us would like to think that we would never fall for the blandishments of a man like Ruth's "Tony." And yet, inside, I think we must admit that any woman who hopes to find permanent love risks meeting the perfect liar instead of the perfect lover.

When I researched this case many years ago, I found Ruth Logg's "perfect lover" so sinister that I actually changed my usual pen name to a completely different pseudonym so that he wouldn't be able to find me.

For this story only, I became a mysterious female author named "Dierdre Fox." The convicted killer had threatened detectives and their families, and filed numerous million-dollar suits. I didn't want him to know who I was.

Although he was a charming, take-charge man who seemed larger than life when he seduced the victim, he *was much diminished when I first saw him in a courtroom, on trial for murder. He didn't look dangerous at that point. Rather, he appeared to be a small, gray man with pale skin and dark circles beneath his eyes. Still, his mistress was there, sitting just behind him, wearing the lavish gifts he had given her, probably using largesse from his victim's insurance policy. I could see glimpses of the powerful, conniving man he really was beneath his humble-for-the-jury demeanor.*

And when I looked at the police photographs of the dead woman who had adored him and read report after report of his lifetime as a con man, I realized how crafty and dangerous he was. Even today, when I visit the small Washington town where he began his machinations, people remember him and tell me stories I've never heard before about even more of his fraudulent schemes.

Yes, I was right in remaining anonymous when I wrote about him.

I think you will see why as the story of the man who promised to love Ruth "forever" unfolds.

When her life was viewed in terms of worldly goods, Ruth Logg had everything. The lovely blond widow had been well provided for by her late husband, Les. She lived alone for several years after Les's death in her sprawling house in Auburn, Washington. The grounds were impeccably maintained and there was even a huge swimming pool. Ruth's home was valued in the early seventies at $85,000. Today, it would be worth well over a million dollars. Les Logg's business holdings had amounted to something over a quarter of a million dollars at the time of his death. Again, that $250,000 would be worth ten times as much in the economy of the nineties. Ruth herself had a good business head. She had moved smoothly into her new place as owner of a business.

Unlike many women who are suddenly widowed, Ruth Logg was able to manage. Her two pretty teenage daughters, Kathleen and Susan, lived with her and she loved them devotedly. But Ruth was only in her early forties, and she sometimes dreamed of finding a man to share her life. She was lonely and the years ahead often seemed to stretch out bleakly.

Ruth knew that her girls would soon be moving away to start their own lives, and that was as it should be. She accepted that. But she couldn't bear the thought of rattling around her huge house alone once Kathleen and Susan were gone. In March of 1971, she put the house on the market. Perhaps she would buy a condominium or take an apartment where she wouldn't have to worry about yard work. Her personal safety was on her mind too. A woman in a house alone wasn't as safe as one who lived close to other people in a security building.

Most single women hold on to a romantic dream that a special man will come along one day and change their lives. Ruth Logg was no exception. She was far too young to give up on love, even though her prospects looked slim. She hated the idea of dating services or Parents Without Partners, or blind dates set up by well-meaning friends. She sometimes wondered why it had to be so difficult to meet someone.

And then Ruth Logg *did* meet someone in such an unexpected way. It was a blustery March afternoon when she first encountered the man who would suddenly launch her world in exciting new directions. A sleek luxury car pulled up in front of her home and a compactly muscled, impeccably dressed man emerged and knocked at her door. He had a great voice. He introduced himself as "Dr. Anthony Fernandez."

No one would have described Dr. Fernandez as handsome, and yet he had an undeniably charismatic quality. He had wide shoulders and thickly muscled arms and wrists, and he looked at Ruth with warm dark eyes under thick brows. Ruth could sense that he was gentle. His manners were wonderful; he was almost apologetic for interrupting her schedule, but he did want to see her home. Ruth assured him that she would be delighted to show him through the house.

Dr. Fernandez explained that he was forty-eight years old and divorced. He said he had just opened a family counseling clinic in the Tacoma area and that he was hoping to buy a house within easy commuting distance to his business.

Ruth Logg was quite taken with Dr. Fernandez, who urged her to call him "Tony." They talked as she led him through her home and he seemed impressed with the floor plan, the way she had decorated the rooms, and with the lawn and gardens. It wasn't long before they stopped talking about the house; they discovered that they shared many interests. Dr. Anthony Fernandez asked Ruth Logg if she would join him for dinner and she accepted, a little surprised at herself for agreeing to a date with someone she really didn't know.

Tony and Ruth had such a good time on their first evening that they both knew they would see more of each other. More dates followed and Ruth suddenly found herself caught up in a whirlwind courtship. After so many years at the edge of other people's lives, she found it incredibly exciting to have this fascinating man pursuing her. And Tony Fernandez *was* pursuing her. At first, Ruth questioned her great good fortune, but then she accepted it. She was, after all, a good-looking woman with a lush figure and a pretty face. She had forgotten that in her years as a widow. Now, Ruth became even prettier with her newfound happiness.

It never occurred to Ruth that Tony might be interested in her because she was wealthy. In fact, she believed that what she had was chicken feed compared to what he owned; Tony had told her that he was a man with substantial assets. He spoke of timber holdings and real estate, and, of course, he had his counseling practice. He didn't *need* her money.

Ruth didn't know that the plush car Tony drove was rented, nor did she know much about his life before they met. None of that mattered. Ruth Logg was totally in love with Anthony Fernandez.

Ruth's family and friends were not as enthusiastic about Tony. They wanted her to be happy, of course, because she had devoted many years to helping other people, but they were worried. They had checked into Tony's background, and they soon heard rumors that "Dr." Fernandez had spent time in prison for fraud. They doubted that Ruth would believe the rumors, so they pleaded with her to check into Fernandez's background before she considered marriage.

Ruth only smiled and reassured them that she knew all about Tony. He had told her that he had had a little bit of trouble in the past. He had been honest with her, she said, and his past didn't matter to her. Ruth's philosophy was that everyone deserves a second chance. Why should she dredge up unhappy memories? Ruth's sister was particularly persistent in trying to coax Ruth off her rosy cloud.

When Tony Fernandez discovered that, he told Ruth's sister that if she didn't like his plans with Ruth, then she could just consider herself excluded from their social circle and future family gatherings. Amazingly, Ruth went along with Tony's decision.

No one is blinder than someone in the first stages of romance, and Ruth refused to listen to one detrimental word about Tony. By September of 1971, Ruth and Tony were engaged. She gave up all thoughts of selling her house; she and Tony would need it to live in. At his suggestion, Ruth and Tony drew up new wills. Although the will Ruth had drawn up three years earlier had left everything she owned—$250,000 plus her home—to her daughters, her new will left it all to Tony. She was confident that if anything should happen to her, Tony would provide for her girls. In turn, Tony left everything he owned to Ruth in his will.

What Anthony Fernandez actually owned was debatable. Despite his grandiose boasting to his fiancée, Tony's assets were negligible. When he met Ruth, he had seventy-five hundred dollars in the bank, a thousand-dollar bond, and some mining claims and real property that would one day sell at a tax sale for less than four thousand dollars. Beyond that, Tony had substantial judgments filed against him. His financial statement would have been written entirely in red ink.

Despite objections and pleadings from the people who truly loved Ruth Logg, she and Dr. Tony Fernandez flew to Puerto Rico on January 5, 1972, where they were married. She had only known him ten months, but it seemed as if they were meant to be together. They toasted their new life with champagne, and Ruth was blissfully happy. Her honeymoon with her new husband was everything she had hoped. She was confident that, in time, her family would come to see Tony for the wonderful man he was.

While she had left Tony everything in her will, she didn't plan on dying for at least four more decades. She had too much to live for now. When Tony casually mentioned that it would be easier for him to help her manage her affairs if he had her Power of Attorney, Ruth didn't hesitate. They went at once to a notary and Ruth gave her husband the power to sell her property or do any other business in her name.

In retrospect, it is easy to see that Ruth Logg Fernandez knew pitifully little about this man who was her husband. Even her worried family had no idea.

It would not have been difficult for Ruth to have found out about Tony's recent and remote past. Reams of newspaper copy had been published about Tony Fernandez's checkered career. In his home territory, he had been at first famous—and later *infamous*.

In the early 1950s, Tony Fernandez had been an important player in the timber industry of Washington and Oregon. When he was in his twenties, he had made a killing in the logging business. He operated mainly out of Longview, a city of twenty thousand in southwestern Washington. The Longview *Daily News* frequently carried reports of Fernandez's new and massive timber buys. Some of his deals involved millions of dollars worth of virgin timber.

Tony Fernandez was listed as a partner in many companies, and he was considered one of the more solid citizens in Longview. He was headline material: "Fernandez Buys Timber at Dam Site in Oregon" (this was on July 19, 1954, when Tony had purchased 40 million board feet at thirty-two dollars per thousand feet); "Chinook Region Logging Planned" (this was on October 4, 1954, when he had bought eight million board feet); "Fernandez Buys Pacific Timber" (on March 9, 1956, when Tony Fernandez estimated his newest contract would eventually cost $300,000).

At the time Tony Fernandez was only thirty-one, but he was on a roll and he didn't stop at timber. On March 22, 1955, the Longview *Daily News* told of a new mining company being incorporated in Cowlitz County, Washington. Tony Fernandez was its president. The purpose of the company would be "to mine, mill, concentrate, convert, smelt, treat and sell gold, silver, copper, lead, zinc, brass, iron and steel." The new company also expected to obtain oil rights. Stock valued at $100,000 had been authorized.

Tony Fernandez maintained a high profile. He drove new Cadillacs. As an honorary deputy sheriff, he was allowed to install a siren in his car. He lived in a big house on the hill above Longview with his wife and four children. He was a Boy Scout leader and a Longview city councilman.

In April of 1957, Fernandez announced that he was

branching out into Canada and that he had purchased a *billion* board feet of timber—an early land grant by the British Royal family—near Nelson, British Columbia for $1,500,000. He said he was considering setting up a branch office near the Canadian border.

In reality, Tony's business empire seemed to have been built on shifting sands. Several huge timber companies brought suit against him, saying that he had logged off areas long after his contracts had expired. He was also accused of selling sections of timber by misrepresentation; he had identified the wrong sections of trees to prospective buyers. They thought they were buying acreage thick with timber when in reality Tony had simply shown them property that he didn't own. They had signed purchase agreements without checking legal descriptions.

It wasn't only the big corporations who were after Tony Fernandez. Several elderly landowners claimed they had been cajoled into signing their names to blank contracts, only to find to their regret that they had signed quit-claim deeds to their timberland.

Tony Fernandez couldn't juggle his books forever. By July 1958 the IRS began to look at him with a jaundiced eye. The Internal Revenue Service filed notice of a tax lien of $95,246.31 against him for taxes that he hadn't paid in 1951, 1952, and 1953. The IRS filed what was known as a "jeopardy assessment" against Fernandez's assets. This amounted to a lien against all his property. It followed two Superior Court memorandums saying that the wheeler-dealer logger had to pay two logging firms over half a million dollars as the result of civil suits.

Still, Tony Fernandez drove his Cadillacs, lived in his nice house, and kept up the facade of a highly successful businessman and a pillar in Longview.

Individuals who had done business with Fernandez were nothing if not confused. An Oregon man, Bill Belcher, was foggy about a trip he had made to Nelson, British Columbia, with Fernandez in March of 1958. Tony had offered to "fly over" his timber holdings there so Belcher could have a look. But the clouds had been so thick that Belcher couldn't tell whether he was looking at fir, pine, spruce, hemlock . . . or tumbleweed. When they attempted to reach the woods later by Jeep, they were forced back by deep snowdrifts.

While they pondered their predicament, Belcher stepped behind the Jeep to light a cigarette. The next conscious memory he had was of lying beside a railroad track; his head felt as though a train had run over it. He was found by railroad workers who called for medics. Belcher was hospitalized with severe head injuries for ten days.

Later, he learned that Tony Fernandez had returned to the guest cabin where the two men had been staying. He had told the managers that Belcher had decided to stay up in the woods in a miner's cabin.

The Royal Canadian Mounted Police notified Bill Belcher's family that he had been critically injured. His wife left at once for Canada. After assuring herself that he would survive, she followed Belcher's instructions to retrieve his briefcase in which he had carried important papers and money. She found the briefcase but Belcher could not explain a logging contract that had been tucked inside. There was also a receipt for $40,000 in payment for some land.

Bill Belcher had no memory whatsoever of what happened to him after he stepped out of Tony Fernandez's vehicle to have a cigarette alongside a snowy road. However, he was adamant that he would never have bought timber he had not even seen, and he would not have given someone $40,000 for trees hidden in fog.

While Belcher had lain unconscious, a bank officer in Grants Pass, Oregon, where Belcher had an account, received several phone calls from a man who identified himself as Bill Belcher. The caller directed the banker to transfer $40,000 to a Gresham, Oregon, bank to the account of the "Fernandez-Belcher deal."

Belcher, who had never suffered blackouts, fainting spells, or anything akin to them before his mysterious "attack" behind the Jeep in the snowy Canadian timberland, eventually recovered thirty-six thousand from Tony Fernandez's company in an out-of-court settlement.

In 1959 Tony Fernandez faced charges of another kind. He was arrested in March of that year and charged with three counts of carnal knowledge and indecent liberties after a teenage girl alleged that he had forced sex on her two years earlier. After many delays and a change of venue to Clark County, Washington, Fernandez was acquitted of the charges.

Tony Fernandez continued to remain active in timber commodities. In the latter part of April 1961, another bizarre incident took place when John Casteel, an elderly Cresswell, Oregon, lumberman, flew over the Canadian timberland with Fernandez. It was almost a replay of what had happened with Bill Belcher. Casteel couldn't see well enough to judge the quality or kind of timber far beneath him. All the while, Fernandez kept talking, mentioning that the syndicate he represented had recently purchased 1,800 acres in Wasco County, Oregon, for two million dollars. Casteel craned his neck to try to see the trees that Fernandez wanted to sell him, but the plane was much too high and the weather didn't cooperate.

After the abortive flight, Fernandez and Casteel stayed

in a Spokane hotel and Tony said it would take about $100,000 to protect the rights to the Canadian timber. Casteel said he didn't have that kind of money to invest in timber at the moment and wasn't interested. Tony knew, however, that the elderly man had plenty of money; earlier, Casteel had given Tony a three-day option at a price of three million dollars on some timberland Casteel owned.

When the two returned to Longview, Fernandez invited the old man to look at a tract of timber twenty miles east of Longview. After they had looked at one stand of trees, Tony suggested they check out another forest which grew at the end of a logging road.

They viewed the trees and Casteel wasn't very impressed. On the way out of the deep woods, Tony Fernandez had suddenly shouted that he had lost control of the Jeep.

"When I looked up, I saw Fernandez bailing out," said Casteel, who proved to be more resilient than Tony had figured. "He was still hanging on to the steering wheel."

Casteel himself had had no choice but to ride the out-of-control Jeep to the bottom of a sixty-foot grade, "bouncing like a rubber ball" inside the closed cab. To his amazement, he was still alive when the Jeep finally stopped against a tree trunk. He had clambered out of the wrecked Jeep and made his way painfully up the slope.

Fernandez was waiting at the top, towering over him as he climbed hand over hand. Casteel wasn't sure if he was in trouble, but Tony had snorted and said only, "You're a tough old devil—I couldn't kill you with a club."

Casteel hoped Fernandez wasn't about to try.

The two hitched a ride into town on a logging truck and Casteel drove himself two hundred miles to his home, where a doctor found he'd survived the crash with only some torn ligaments.

Later, when John Casteel opened his suitcase to show a friend a map of the Canadian timberland, he found copies of a memorandum of agreement between himself and one of Fernandez's companies. He had never seen it before, yet it was a deed conveying Casteel's timberland to Fernandez in consideration of an option on Tony's Wasco County property, *and* an assignment of the Canadian timber asserting that Casteel had offered $400,000 for it.

John Casteel was a sharp businessman and he immediately set about clouding the title to his three-million-dollar stand of timber so that Fernandez could not take it over. He eventually paid Tony fifteen hundred dollars to release all claims and considered himself lucky to have lost only that much.

It would take a book-length volume to describe the intricacies of Tony Fernandez's timber dealings. One would suspect that he had some successful incidents where would-be buyers "signed" papers without being aware that they had. There may even have been other "accidents" in the woods that were never reported.

Fernandez's financial world blew up finally in April of 1962 when he was indicted by a federal grand jury on charges of engaging in a multimillion-dollar timber swindle. It was the culmination of a four-year investigation into Fernandez's business machinations. The incidents involving Belcher and Casteel were cited in the charges along with many others.

Tony Fernandez was convicted of seven counts of interstate fraud and one of conspiracy in Judge William G. East's Federal District Courtroom in Portland, Oregon, in December 1962. Two months later, he was sentenced to eleven years and eleven months in prison. That April, his remaining property was sold to satisfy judgments against him. Despite appeals, Tony Fernandez remained in the McNeill Island Federal Prison until his parole on January 15, 1970.

Tony was far from idle during his years on the bleak prison island in Puget Sound. In 1968, claiming status as a taxpayer in the state of Washington, he sued Washington's Secretary of State Lud Kramer and U.S. Representative Julia Butler Hansen for a hundred thousand dollars on the grounds that Ms. Hansen was not qualified to serve in Congress because she was a woman. The suit was capricious, not to mention chauvinistic, and it got nowhere. However, it netted Tony Fernandez more headlines and he liked that.

Six months after he was paroled, Fernandez was awarded a degree from Tacoma Community College's extension program. He became the first convict in the State of Washington to earn a college degree through an innovative program that allowed prisoners to take courses while they were in the penitentiary.

And so, in 1970, Anthony Fernandez was free—both from prison and from his twenty-three-year marriage. His wife had divorced him in 1965 while he was in prison. Surprisingly, she said she had no ill feelings toward Tony. He had always been a good provider and never mean or abusive. She did mention his wandering eye, however. She just hadn't wanted to be lied to any longer. It had been a most civilized divorce. *So* civilized, in fact, that when Tony was paroled, he often brought his new girlfriends to visit his ex-wife.

Scattered accounts of Tony Fernandez's postprison activities boggle the mind. He reported to hometown friends that he was a senior at Pacific Lutheran University in Tacoma, majoring in psychology and ecology. This wasn't long after his release from prison. As part of his studies, he joined a student tour to Arizona and New Mexico to study Navajo Indian history, culture, and economy. In an article in the Longview *Daily News,* it was also noted that Tony was enrolled simultaneously in an MA and Ph.D. program in a Florida university. (As it happened, all this "college" required its students to do to get a "diploma" was to write a thesis of unspecified length.)

Tony Fernandez's doctorate had been awarded simply because he had submitted a paper entitled "The Innovated Navajo." And *voilà!* Tony Fernandez became Dr. Anthony Fernandez.

When he was heard from next, *Dr.* Fernandez reported he was attending the North American College of Acupuncture in Vancouver, British Columbia. Tony is quoted as saying he attended classes in Vancouver three times a week and would be spending fifteen weeks in Hong Kong and sixty days in Peking as part of his training.

It wasn't that Fernandez believed that acupuncture was particularly important in the Western world. "It is," he pontificated, "at best, a fad. But I'm going into this with the point of view that it is most likely a psychological tool. And even if I never use it, the experience and knowledge will be a benefit."

On March 30, 1971—the same month he met Ruth Logg—a small item appeared in the Longview *Daily News.* "Anthony Fernandez, formerly of Longview and a recent Pacific Lutheran University graduate, will open a counseling office complex next month at 8815 S. Tacoma Way. He is also negotiating for property in Kelso on which to construct a family counseling clinic."

Dr. Fernandez promised to provide a twenty-four-hour

answering service and said he had contracted to evaluate welfare recipients for the Tacoma office of the Department of Public Assistance.

On June 10, 1971, "Dr." Fernandez's picture appeared in the Wenatchee, Washington, *Daily World* beside an article about his plans to establish a "rehabilitation center" for drug addicts and alcoholics on eighty acres he owned in the rural town of Alstown. He promised that he would build a modern clinic but retain the flavor of the historic old cabins on the eastern Washington property. He assured nearby residents that his patients would not be "turned loose" in the community. He did not mention, of course, that he himself was a parolee from a federal prison.

None of Fernandez's new endeavors ever got off the ground. He didn't need them. He had Ruth Logg and the fortune her late husband had left her.

This was the man with whom Ruth fell madly in love. This was her soft-eyed, warm-voiced hero who was going to make the second half of her life a wonderful time of love and companionship. She had never known anyone with no conscience at all; she was naive about the world of the con man. Les had loved her and protected her.

Once married to Ruth, Tony Fernandez was kept busy overseeing her business interests and fortune. He encouraged Kathleen, her older daughter, to move out almost immediately after his marriage to her mother. He told Ruth it would be good for Kathleen to have an apartment of her own. Ruth's younger daughter, Susan, lived with them but was involved with her own friends.

At first, the Fernandez marriage seemed idyllic. If Ruth's former friends and relatives didn't call often, she didn't notice—she was so caught up in loving Tony.

The marriage turned bitter and disappointing far too

soon. While Tony's first wife had turned a deaf ear to rumors of his infidelities, Ruth could not. She suspected he was seeing other women. It tore her apart.

In May of 1974, when she had been married to Tony for just over two years, Ruth took a trip to Texas—alone. Tony remarked to one of her daughter's boyfriends, "When she comes back, she'll have to shape up or ship out."

While Ruth was gone, Fernandez used Ruth's Power of Attorney and sold some of her property without her knowledge for $100,000—far less than its actual value.

Only six months before, Ruth and Tony had vacationed at a plush resort in Mazatlan, Mexico, where they had impressed other couples as an "ideal couple." But that had evidently been the last try on Ruth's part to make the marriage work. One reason for the end of the perfect romance—and a good reason at that—was the fact that Tony reportedly had another woman he was seriously involved with. She lived in Centralia, Washington. Although Ruth didn't realize it, he had used *her* money to give the other woman an expensive fur coat and a diamond solitaire. He told the woman that they would be married soon.

While Ruth Fernandez was on her lonely trip in May, Tony also took care of some other pressing business. He took out a $100,000 accidental death insurance policy on Ruth through Mutual of Omaha. There was never any concrete evidence that Ruth signed the application for that policy.

To her everlasting misfortune, Ruth still loved Tony. She still believed she could win back his love and that he would be faithful to her. During the third week of July 1974, she was excited about a camping trip they were going to take together. It would be like another honeymoon. They had rented a fully equipped Winnebago

Brave motor home from a local dealer, and also took a four-wheel drive vehicle with them.

On Sunday afternoon, July 26, Ruth and Tony Fernandez stopped at the Mount Si Golf Course restaurant in North Bend, Washington, for cocktails and lunch. They lingered in the picturesque spot for a long time.

Just beyond North Bend, the I-90 freeway and back roads head east swiftly up toward the summit of Snoqualmie Pass. The land drops away steeply at the edges of the byroads. The Fernandez's campsite was eight miles up the mountain from North Bend.

According to witnesses, both Ruth and Tony had seemed somewhat affected by the drinks they had with lunch. They left, saying they were headed for their campsite. At 4:15 that July afternoon, the Fernandezes visited the Snoqualmie office of the Weyerhauser Lumber Company on a business errand. Employees there recalled that Ruth seemed to be unhappy and a little querulous, while Tony was reflective and quiet. Neither of them, however, seemed to be intoxicated. When they left, they said they were going on up toward Snoqualmie Pass to the place where they were camping.

The first hint that something might be wrong came at 8:30 that Sunday evening. Tony called the waitress at the Mount Si restaurant to ask if she had seen Ruth. She had not. Next, he called the Little Chalet Café in North Bend, asking the staff there if they had seen Ruth. They knew her, but they hadn't seen her that evening.

At 8:36 P.M. Tony called the Washington State Patrol station in North Bend, expressing his concern for Ruth's safety. When the trooper on duty asked him why he was worried, Tony said first that Ruth had left the campsite for a walk in the woods alone and she had not returned. But then he changed his story. He said she had driven in the

Winnebago, and he thought she had been heading for their home in Auburn.

"I followed her twenty minutes to half an hour later in my four-wheel drive Scout," he said. "But I couldn't find any sign of her."

Coincidentally, Susan Logg and her fiancé, Don Stafford, had headed up the Granite Creek Road toward the campsite between 8:30 and 9:30 P.M. that Sunday night. They had passed neither Ruth nor Tony along the way. When they got back to the big house in Auburn at 10:40 P.M., they encountered Tony, who had just emerged from taking a shower. He told them he had no idea where Ruth had gone off to. He figured she would come driving up any time, and there was no use to go looking for her. It was too dark.

The long night passed with no word at all from Ruth. The next morning, Don Stafford and Tony Fernandez drove back to North Bend and officially reported Ruth as a missing person to the State Patrol. Then they drove up the Martha Lake Road to the Granite Creek Road along the route to the vacated campsite. There was no sign of the Winnebago along the roadway. Suddenly, Stafford spotted some tracks in the dirt shoulder next to the Granite Creek Road. The tracks appeared to disappear over the cliff's edge. When Stafford pointed them out, Tony Fernandez asked him, "Do you think I should look here?"

Stafford volunteered to look. He walked to the edge of the precipitous cliff where rock had been blasted out, making it an almost sheer drop. Bracing himself, he looked down. Far, far below, he saw the crumpled mass of metal that had been the Winnebago.

Before he turned back to give Tony the bad news, Don Stafford forced himself to look along the cliff side between the wrecked camper and the top. About halfway down, he saw a body and he knew it was Ruth Fernandez.

In a very short time, the sunny mountain road was alive with King County Police and Washington State Patrol troopers. The wreckage was three hundred feet below. The investigators were able to approach it only obliquely by using a logging road farther down the grade. When they finally got to Ruth Fernandez, they confirmed that she was dead, and that she had been for many hours. Rigor mortis was almost complete. She appeared to have suffered massive head injuries. Oddly, her clothing was remarkably untorn for someone who had ridden the hurtling camper off the embankment and then one hundred fifty feet down the hill before she had fallen out.

Tony Fernandez complained about the hours the police were spending at the scene. It was perfectly obvious what had happened. He muttered to Don Stafford, "They are just creating red tape." Tony asked Stafford to leave with him. He didn't want to stay around there any longer, watching from above as the cops worked over his dead wife.

There were aspects of the accident that puzzled and bothered the investigators. Trooper Don Caughell of the Washington State Patrol's Fatality Investigative Unit looked with his discerning eye first at the road and then at the shattered motor home. The road had no defects that would make control of a vehicle difficult; there was no breaking away of the shoulder area where the rig had gone over. This indicated to him that the Winnebago had been moving slowly and that no one had stomped on the brakes in a desperate attempt to keep from plunging over. "Why?" he wondered. Why hadn't Ruth Fernandez tried to save herself?

Although the motor home itself was thoroughly crum-

pled, there was no sign inside it to indicate that a body
had bounced around during the terrible drop. No blood,
no torn flesh, no hair. Ruth Fernandez had been wearing a
loosely woven blouse which would have been likely to
catch on *something* during the terrible bucketing down
the steep hill. But her blouse had no tears or snags at all.

Ruth Fernandez's body was lifted with the use of a
carefully balanced litter, from the side of the cliff and
taken to the King County Medical Examiner's Office in
Seattle to await autopsy.

The postmortem examination showed that she had suffered two severe injuries, neither of which was typical of
a victim who had ridden a vehicle down a slope for almost two hundred feet. The first wound was caused by
some kind of blunt object striking her omentum—the
fatty, apronlike membrane that hangs from the stomach
and transverse colon in the abdominal cavity. The omentum is rich in blood vessels. Ruth's second wound—and
the fatal wound—was a fractured skull. She had died
sometime between 11:30 A.M. on the 26 and 11:30 A.M.
on the 27. The best clue to time of death is when the victim has last been seen. As Ruth was known to be alive at
4:30 P.M. on the Sunday she disappeared, the time-of-
death period could be cut to nineteen hours.

According to autopsy findings, she could have lived a
maximum of six hours without treatment and a minimum
of one hour. Blood alcohol tests indicated that Ruth had
been legally intoxicated at the time of her death, that is,
she had at least .10 of alcohol in her bloodstream.

Tony Fernandez was Ruth's sole heir, and he applied
almost immediately for her insurance benefits. Mutual of
Omaha declined to cut him a check, however, because

there was an ongoing investigation into her death. Indeed, King County Police homicide detectives Ted Forrester and Roger Dunn would spend months in their initial probe of the strange circumstance of Ruth Logg Fernandez's death. Those months would stretch into years.

Circumstantial evidence indicated that some outside force had caused Ruth's Winnebago to plunge over the cliff. Forester and Dunn suspected Tony Fernandez of killing his wife, but they could not prove it.

What did happen between 4:30 and 8:30 P.M. on July 26, 1974? No one but Tony saw Ruth during that time, and he insisted that she first took a walk in the woods and then decided to drive home alone from their campsite.

He liked to imply that Ruth had been out of control, hysterical, irrational—a woman who should not have been driving the big Winnebago rig. Tony even suggested obliquely that Ruth might have been suicidal. But was it consistent with human psychology that a healthy, forty-four-year-old woman, slightly intoxicated, perhaps upset at her failing marriage, would deliberately drive herself off a cliff? She had two daughters who needed her, family, friends, a considerable fortune. If she was so angry at Tony that she wanted to die, would she have done this knowing that it was Tony and Tony alone who would inherit everything she owned?

Probably not.

The case dragged on. No criminal charges were filed against Tony Fernandez. Fernandez himself pooh-poohed the theory that he might have killed his wife. He remained in the family home and gave frequent interviews to the media, appearing often on the nightly news television programs. He appeared affable and confident.

Tony Fernandez was *so* confident, in fact, that he

began to date publicly. He was a grieving widower, yes, but a man got lonely.

In February of 1976, a year and a half after Ruth Logg Fernandez died, her daughters, Mrs. Kathleen Logg Lea, twenty-two, and Susan Logg, nineteen, brought civil suit against Tony Fernandez, charging that he was not eligible to inherit any of Ruth's fortune. Under the Slayer's Act, no one shall inherit benefits resulting from the death of someone whose death they have caused.

Ruth's daughters were so frustrated to see Tony Fernandez going blithely on with his life that they felt they had to do something. Ted Forrester and Roger Dunn had explained that they had not yet come up with enough physical evidence to take to the King County Prosecutor's Office so that criminal charges could be brought. Criminally, guilt must be proved beyond the shadow of a doubt. *Civilly,* however, a judgment can be made on the "preponderance of evidence." Testimony on "prior bad acts" (of which Tony Fernandez had plenty) could be introduced.

Ruth's daughters decided to go for it.

Enraged, Tony Fernandez brought a million-dollar lawsuit against Ted Forrester.

It was a marathon four-week trial and received more press coverage than most criminal trials. Superior Court Judge George Revelle's courtroom became a kind of microcosm of the lives of Tony Fernandez and Ruth Logg Fernandez. Ghosts of Fernandez's past reappeared. John Casteel, the man who had bounced in a Jeep sixty feet down a cliff after Fernandez bailed out, was there. So was William Belcher, who wound up with a head wound in the snowy wilds of Canada. Neither man came right out and accused Tony of violence—they merely related what had happened to them.

Tony's ex-wife testified—for the defense—saying he

was faithful "in his own way" and that he had never thrown his other women in her face during their marriage. She smiled at him as she testified.

After the background of the couple's meeting, romance, and marriage was presented, both sides called experts in forensic pathology to the stand.

Dr. F. Warren Lovell, Chief Pathologist of Northwest Hospital, testified for Fernandez's defense. Lovell, who specialized in the study of fatal accidents and designed the autopsy program for the NASA flight project, said that it was likely that, when the Winnebago went over the cliff, Ruth Fernandez's body became an essentially weightless object, thrown against the motor, which would have yielded on impact. This, Lovell testified would explain why Ruth's injuries were not more extensive. He also said it was not unusual that her clothing was untorn.

On cross-examination, however, Dr. Lovell conceded that the fatal skull fracture could have been caused by a man taking her by the hair and striking her head on a rock. "But it would be very hard to do," he added.

Dr. Lovell did not agree with the plaintiffs that the injury to the abdomen was consistent with a blow from a fist. He said that it could have been caused by Ruth's belly hitting the steering wheel.

Detective Roger Dunn, however, testified that he had examined the steering wheel of the Winnebago and found no damage consistent with a great force pushing against it.

Dr. Gale Wilson, who had been the King County Medical Examiner for forty years before his retirement and who had done over seventeen thousand autopsies, testified that, in his educated opinion, Ruth was not in the motor home when it left the road. He was convinced, rather, that she had died from a blunt instrument applied with great force to her head. Dr. Donald Reay, the current medical examiner, testified that Ruth had died of a skull fracture and that it was possible—but not very likely—that she was in the motor home when it left the road.

The options open to the deciding judge were essentially this:

1. Ruth Fernandez, distraught and a little intoxicated, drove accidentally off the cliff without even applying the brakes of the motor home. Her body fell out halfway down.

2. Ruth Fernandez drove deliberately off the cliff and her body was thrown out halfway down.

3. Someone bludgeoned and beat Ruth Fernandez, pushed the motor home off the cliff and flung Ruth down after it. *Or* someone carried her body halfway down to make it look as if she had been in an accident.

4. Someone pushed the Winnebago over and persuaded Ruth to go down to it to help retrieve valuables. That someone then killed her where she was found.

Tony Fernandez himself did not testify in the trial.

Arthur Piehler, the attorney for the Logg sisters, summed up the plaintiff's case dramatically: "Tony Fernandez *did* fall in love when he met Ruth in 1971. He fell in love with her house, her five acres, her swimming pool, her stocks, her bonds, and other assets."

Piehler recalled that medical experts had testified that Ruth would have had broken bones, multiple cuts, lacerations, foreign objects in wounds, and torn clothing had she been in the Winnebago when it crashed. He theorized that Fernandez had somehow crashed the motor home and then persuaded Ruth to walk down the mountainside with him to recover items in it. It would have been easy for him to hit her on the head and in the stomach, and leave her there to die alone.

Piehler contended that Fernandez had forged Ruth's signature on the one-hundred-thousand-dollar accidental death policy two months and six days before she died. He said Tony had probably become concerned that his wife was considering a divorce. "He could see all his lovely property drifting away from him." Piehler told the court about the other woman Tony was seeing, the woman who had received the diamonds and furs.

John C. Hoover, Fernandez's attorney, argued that the couple had been happy and that they had taken a week's camping trip together. The Winnebago had crashed, he said, only because Ruth had had too much to drink. Hoover insisted that Ruth had been completely content with all the property agreements between herself and her husband. If she had not been satisfied with their arrangement, she had had plenty of time to change it.

In March 1976, Tony Fernandez's fortune evaporated when Judge Revelle read his oral decision to a packed courtroom, a decision in which he found the defendant without credibility. "I do not believe anything he says," Revelle began succinctly.

Revelle read his thirty-one-page decision and concluded, "I have examined many possibilities and numerous high probabilities of the cause and method of her death. Each such probability requires the participation of the only person I know who was with her; that's Anthony Fernandez. One of those methods or probabilities is a method suggested by Mr. Piehler, but I can't say that's it. I just know that under the burden of proof here—even stronger than necessary to be found—Anthony Fernandez, I conclude, participated as a principal in the willful and unlawful killing of Ruth Fernandez."

In his conclusions of law, Judge Revelle said, "Anthony Fernandez, as the slayer of Ruth Fernandez, shall not acquire, in any way, property or receive any benefit as the result of the death of Ruth Fernandez. Anthony Fernandez is deemed to have predeceased the decedent (under the Slayer's Act) Ruth Fernandez. All property which would have passed to or for the benefit of the defendant, Anthony Fernandez, by the terms of the Will of Ruth Fernandez, or any agreement of the defendant and Ruth Fernandez, under the provisions of RCW 21.16.120 shall be distributed as if the defendant had predeceased Ruth Fernandez."

With that, Tony lost the financial ball game. But he did not lose his freedom. He had only lost a civil case.

It took another court order to get Fernandez to vacate the home in Auburn. He had lived there since July of 1974 when Ruth died. Tony was ordered not to attempt to remove furniture, appliances, or anything of value that would be part of the estate. Judge Revelle also restrained Fernandez from using credit cards drawn on the estate. Counsel for Sue and Kathy said, "Fernandez has been dissipating everything he can get his hands upon and has spent about $155,000 that was part of the estate." Even as the trial had progressed, Tony was said to have been involved in a $200,000 land purchase.

Finally, Tony moved from the home that now belonged to Ruth's daughters. But, in the end, there was little of the estate left for the two orphaned young women. After lawyers' fees and Tony's free spending, they obtained less than 10 percent of the money their parents had put aside for their futures.

On June 3, 1976, Fernandez was charged in Lane County, Oregon, with forgery and theft by sale of timber valued at nearly $75,000 and was arrested on a federal parole violation warrant. He was not inside long. Yet another woman besotted with Tony Fernandez put up his bail.

On August 12, 1977, Fernandez was charged with seven felony counts in Thurston County, Washington—second-degree theft, two counts of unlawful issuance of bank checks, and four counts of first-degree theft alleging unlawful sale of timber rights that he claimed were his to a third party. These violations were said to have occurred in Thurston County in the winter of 1976–77. Convicted on all these counts, consecutive sentences could net him fifty-five years in prison.

On September 1, 1977, the charge for which Ruth's daughters and loved ones had waited so long was made. The King County Prosecutor's Office charged Anthony Fernandez with first-degree murder in the death of Ruth Fernandez. His trial, scheduled for January 9, 1978—almost four years after Ruth died on the lonely mountainside—was one where the evidence was mostly circumstantial, one of the most difficult cases for a prosecutor to press. It was lengthy, and full of surprises. Tony Fernandez's mistress, wearing her fur coat, was present at his trial every day.

Tony Fernandez was convicted of Ruth Logg Fernandez's murder in February 1978, and sentenced to life in prison. And that was exactly what he served.

On Christmas Day 1995, Anthony Fernandez, seventy-three, enjoyed a hearty holiday meal in prison. And then he dropped dead of a massive heart attack.

Who was the real Tony Fernandez? Was he a timber baron, a doctor of psychology, an acupuncturist, a historian of Navajo culture, a master of city government? A lover—a studied con man—or a methodical killer?

It doesn't matter anymore to Ruth Logg Fernandez. The man who promised to love her forever betrayed her. She lost her hopes for the perfect romance in the darkness on the steep mountainside along Granite Creek Road. She will never see her grandchildren and never know her daughters as mature women.

Perhaps she knows, however, that those daughters saw their quest through to the end and gave her the only gift they could: justice.

Murder and the
Proper Housewife
(from *In the Name of Love*)

There are myriad motives for murder, and there are almost as many co-conspirators—would-be killers who have virtually nothing in common but who form fatal alliances. Once their goal is accomplished, those who have seen homicide as the answer to their problems usually go their separate ways. I don't believe I have ever researched an odder partnership than the man and woman who joined up to carry out a hit. Neither was connected with organized crime; neither had much to gain from the murder they joined forces to plan. To this day, I am not sure why they did what they did.

One of them was merely doing a favor for a friend whom she dearly loved; the other fancied himself to be a force larger than life. Somewhere along the line, they both lost touch with reality.

We have all had friends whom we loved so much that we would have risked our money, our serenity, and even our freedom for them. Nancy Brooks* seemed like the last person in the world who would plot to kill another human being. But Nancy felt so sorry for her dearest friend that she did just that. She was quite willing to arrange a murder because she loved her friend.

She came within a millimeter or two of carrying it off.

"Murder and the Proper Housewife" remains in my "Top Twenty" list of memorable cases because it has every element of a good story—so many that it reads like fiction. It is horrifying, suspenseful, crazy, and even humorous on occasion. The would-be killers were bumbling and flawed, people right out of "America's dumbest criminals," but in their very clumsiness, they had the capacity to do great harm.

I have always maintained that what real people do to their fellow humans is often so much stranger than anything a fiction writer could think up. That has never been demonstrated more forcibly than in this case. If I had made it up, I could never have sold it because it would seem too far-fetched. But it is all true—as fictional as it may sound. I sat in a courtroom for weeks and watched it play out with my own eyes.

Nancy Brooks was a California housewife in the early 1960s. She married in an era when young wives strove to emulate the perfect television sitcom mother. Their floors were waxed, their children behaved, and they cooked healthy, nutritious meals. Their homes had orange shag carpeting, avocado-colored kitchen appliances, and daisy-print wallpaper.

Nancy and her husband, an engineer, lived in a large apartment with their son and daughter—the perfect 1960s family. One of their neighbors in the apartment house was a divorced woman, Claire Noonan,* whose son, Bennett, was in his late teens. Nancy and Claire became very good friends, and Bennett was also welcome in the Brooks home. He was a rather odd kid, lanky and gawky with stringy dark hair, who was considered a nerd by some of his contemporaries and just plain weird by others. Nancy was sympathetic when Claire confided that her former husband had been abusive to his stepson. Bennett had suffered so much physical abuse that he had problems with his self-worth and his own identity.

Nancy, a registered nurse, recognized that Bennett needed someone to listen to him, and she was kind to him. Her children adored Bennett, who was an accomplished magician. He would entertain them patiently for

ANN RULE

hours with amazing feats of magic. He had few social
contacts with people his own age, however, and Nancy
suspected he was lonely. He probably had a crush on
Nancy Brooks who was very pretty and only about a
dozen years older than he was. Claire was grateful that
the Brookses were so kind to her son.

Both families were transitory residents of California,
though, and they soon moved thousands of miles apart.
Claire married a physician and moved to Memphis, Ten-
nessee; Nancy Brooks's husband, Cal, got a job in Seattle
working for Boeing.

In the mid-1960s the Brookses moved to Bellevue,
Washington, a burgeoning bedroom community for Seattle
at that time and the best possible place for young Boeing
engineers to reside. Neighborhoods with picturesque
names like Lake Hills, Robinswood, Phantom Lake, and
Bridle Trails sprang up almost overnight. Houses were built
close together so that the developers could get the most out
of every piece of forest land they had snapped up, and bar-
becues and kaffeeklatsches were popular social events.

Nancy Brooks had always seen herself as a person who
helped others. That was why she had chosen nursing as a
career, and that was why she had done her best to help
Claire LeClerk Noonan with her problem son, Bennett. It
wasn't long, however, before Nancy found a new best
friend in Bellevue. She met Rose Stahl* through an interest
they shared: they were both animal lovers, and they entered
their dogs in local shows. Nancy and Rose raised show-
quality poodles, a breed that requires much grooming and
care. The women were the same age, thirty-nine, and they
had so much in common that they saw each other almost
every day and talked on the phone several times a day.

In California, Claire had had problems with Bennett
and Nancy had been a godsend to her. Now, in Washing-

ton, Nancy was a sympathetic listener as Rose confided the details of her unhappy marriage. Nancy and Cal Brooks appeared to have a solid marriage, and that made Nancy doubly sorry for Rose.

Rose and Art Stahl hadn't been married for very long, and they both had children from previous marriages, so they had a combined family of his-and-hers children, plus they had two baby sons together. But theirs was not a happy union. They had marathon fights over how to deal with their children. Rose resented Art's older children visiting and would not let him discipline her children. Their biggest arguments, however, were over how to spend, or *not* spend—a $780,000 trust fund that belonged to Art.

At the same time, Art had the best and worst of all possible worlds. On one hand, the fortune he had inherited from his father was enough to keep a man of modest needs comfortable for a long time. On the other, he found himself locked in a marriage that was not only destroying his peace of mind but which caused him constant anxiety. Stahl wanted it to last, if only for the children's sake, but nothing he did seemed to please his wife.

Although the interest on his trust fund was more than enough to support his family, Art Stahl chose to work. He was a teaching assistant in the Mechanical Engineering Department of the University of Washington. He was a very intelligent man, and he loved to teach. He also enjoyed the ambience of the University of Washington campus.

At age fifty-two, Art was five feet nine and weighed a trim 150 pounds; he was a dapper man with wavy dark hair, a beard, and a mustache that was waxed at the tips. He chose to dip into his near-million-dollar trust fund only sparingly. Rather, he wanted its interest to accumulate. He and Rose had signed a prenuptial agreement stipulating that she had no access to his inheritance; the only people who could touch it were Art and an attorney in New York. Rose fretted over the luxuries they could be enjoying if Art were less stubborn about their living on his teaching salary. She found him unnecessarily stingy.

There were times, of course, when the Stahl marriage seemed to sail on an even keel. At other times—which were becoming all too frequent—Art Stahl was a beleaguered man. Rose was nothing if not relentless. The children needed money, she needed money for her dog shows, and they needed a nicer house. To preserve even a modicum of peace, Art often gave in to her demands. Whenever he could compromise to glean even a little serenity in his marriage, he tried to do so.

Art Stahl's biggest sacrifice was to send his own teenage daughter to live in a foster home because Rose couldn't get along with her. He regretted having to banish his daughter from his home, and he visited her as often as possible. He was torn between his loyalty and love for her and his belief that his two baby boys from his marriage to Rose needed him more.

At Art's urging, he and Rose spent a lot of time talking to counselors about their problem marriage. He knew that Rose told even the most intimate details of their marriage to her best friend, Nancy Brooks, and got advice from Nancy. Art told *his* secrets to a journal that he had begun to keep. The more miserable he became, the more he spilled out his pain onto the pages of his journal, which was really a sheaf of loose papers filled with longhand notes.

Nancy Brooks seemed to be a sympathetic woman; Art didn't mind that Rose confided in her. Sometimes he too talked to Nancy about the problems in his marriage. But he soon regretted it; he found out that anything he told Nancy soon got back to Rose. It was clear that if Nancy had to choose sides, she would stand firmly behind Rose. Art wondered sometimes what kind of exaggerated complaints Rose was telling Nancy.

Nancy Brooks was not an animated woman, and it was hard to tell what she was thinking. Five feet seven and slender, she carried herself rather stiffly. This was not her fault—Nancy had been in a number of car accidents, which had necessitated three surgeries to fuse vertebrae in her back and neck. She was quite pretty—or would have been if she'd smiled more. She had dark hair, cut short and curling around her cheeks, big brown eyes, and a sweet mouth. Despite her physical problems, Nancy was always on the move, doing something for her children or her husband or her friends.

Nancy Brooks, with her PTA-mother facade, seemed like the last person in the world who would ever become involved in criminal intrigue. She was a wife, mother, friend, and dog trainer. She dressed conservatively, keeping her hemlines well below her knees—no matter what fashion dictated. She wore sensible shoes with Cuban heels, and she often wore dark-rimmed glasses.

As the Stahl marriage continued to come apart at the seams, Rose Stahl's good friend Nancy was beside her, listening to her complaints about Art and her worries about how she could support her children if Art moved out. The huge trust fund would go away if Art went away. Nancy patted her hand, poured her another cup of tea, and told her there had to be a way to work things out.

Meanwhile, Art's journal of marital misery grew thicker. There were times now when he actually felt afraid of Rose. He decided he could no longer keep his diary in the home they shared, so he locked the thick stack of pages in his desk in his office at the university. Sometimes he felt a little foolish about saving his writings and wondered why he even bothered to keep them.

But he *did* keep them. If anything ever happened to him, he would leave some kind of record behind of the shambles his married life had become.

By the middle of 1974, Art Stahl realized that there was no way he and Rose could ever live together in harmony. He wasn't so sure he would live at all if he stayed with Rose. He was not an aggressive man, but Rose was certainly a hostile and aggressive woman. One night in September, he had the temerity to change the channel on their television set. There was a show he wanted to see, but Rose, who was working in the kitchen, was angry that he had switched away from what *she* wanted to see.

According to his diary, Art looked up to see her storming toward him with a butcher knife in her hand. She shouted, "Some night I'm going to stick a knife between your ribs, and you won't know what night it is."

He stared at her, horrified at her rage and convinced she meant what she said. Art Stahl was a prudent man, and he saw that he no longer had a choice. He had tried reasoning and counseling, but now he knew he had to go. On October 3, 1974, he left the family home in Bellevue and moved into an apartment.

It was wrenching to leave his little sons behind. He had always intended to provide for Rose and their children, and he had been in the process of drawing up a will that would leave the principal amount of his trust to Rose, with substantial sums to all of their children—his, hers, and theirs. As it was, if he should die, Rose would take his place in the trust management. *She* would work with the financial adviser on the East Coast to decide how the money would be spent.

Stahl, of course, provided full support for Rose and the children, even while he maintained a separate residence.

Nancy Brooks and Rose Stahl continued to be best

friends and to hash over the state of Rose's marriage—
and they remained active in dog show circles.

Art Stahl was beginning to build new interests of his
own. He started taking a class in an obscure medical art:
reflexology. He enrolled in the evening course offered by
the Experimental College Program at the University of
Washington. It was held at a health center a block away
from the north precinct of the Seattle Police Department,
and it dealt with the healing techniques that reflexology
offered, the premise being that all the ills, aches, and
pains of the human body could be made well by the
skilled application of foot massage.

Instead of the needles used in acupuncture, a trained
hand on the right spot of the foot could allegedly cure almost everything. The once-a-week classes were to continue through November 26.

Whether Art really believed in the benefits of reflexology or not, it was an interesting concept, and he met new
people. Aside from his classmates in the science of the
human foot, the only others who knew he was studying reflexology were his estranged wife, Rose, and, through her,
Nancy Brooks, although Art might have mentioned the
classes to a few of his teaching associates at the university.

Nancy Brooks had reestablished her acquaintance
with Bennett LeClerk sometime in 1972. The awkward,
nerdy teenager she had known in California had meta-
morphosed into an entirely different person in the decade
since she had befriended him and his mother.

Bennett had called her Bellevue home and asked to
speak to Nancy. At first, she had no idea who he was. He
had changed his last name and was no longer using his
mother's name.

"Oh, I'm sorry," he said smoothly. "You would know

me as Claire Noonan's son. I used to do magic tricks for your kids in California."

"Of course," Nancy said. "You're *that* Bennett." It had been a long time, but she invited him to come and visit at the Brookses' home. He came over that very day and stayed for hours, reminiscing. He stayed for supper and long after.

Nancy stared at him, amazed. He had certainly changed. The skinny kid was now six feet two and weighed almost 200 pounds. He was dressed in a well-cut dark business suit. He said he lived in Everett, Washington; he had married a California girl, and they had moved up to Washington State. He told Nancy he had worked for a while as a jailer in the Snohomish County Jail and that he was studying to be a reserve officer.

Bennett had always been a little strange. Although she didn't bring it up, Nancy recalled that he had become upset if he heard about children being physically punished or abused—because he had suffered terribly as a child. He seemed quite urbane now that he was in his late twenties, but she wondered if his early insecurities still gripped him from time to time.

In the series of events that began to unfold in Bellevue, Everett, and Seattle in the mid-1970s, it is well nigh impossible to give complete credence to any of the principal characters' recall. The only way to tell the bizarre story is to give each person's viewpoint, and let the reader judge who was telling the truth—or perhaps came *closest* to the truth.

Nancy Brooks recalled that Bennett LeClerk came to see her frequently, always dressed in a dark business suit. He was not one to drop in for a quick visit; he invariably lingered for hours. He hung around until she was preparing supper for her family, and she felt that she had no choice but to invite him to stay. She began to hint broadly that she had things to do and places to go, but he never took it as a cue for him to leave. His presence became, she said, "intolerable."

At length, Nancy said she considered Bennett a nuisance and a pest. Her neighbors had begun to ask who he was, and her own children were puzzled about the man who came to their house so often and stayed so long. Apparently her husband was not jealous or suspicious. She never mentioned that he questioned her about the younger man who was becoming a fixture in their home.

Nancy led a busy life with her dogs, her family, and her friends, and she finally told Bennett LeClerk not to visit her again at her house when her husband was away. "My neighbors are talking," she said.

According to Nancy, he became enraged. "*We* know we're doing nothing wrong," he said, "and I don't care what society says!"

But Nancy Brooks said she remained adamant: she would not have him hanging around her house. She said that he had stormed off and never came back to her house—except for one final visit.

Who *was* this reborn Bennett LeClerk?

LeClerk was different things to different people. He had indeed been employed as a jailer in the Snohomish County Jail in Everett, Washington. Members of the sheriff's staff said he always wore green tennis shoes to work and that he liked to bounce off the walls with his feet to demonstrate his agility. He claimed to be a master in kung fu.

Others who met him said he told them that he was fluent in many languages, including Russian, German,

Japanese, and Sanskrit. He also said he was a speed reader who could read upside down and backwards faster than most people could read right side up and forward.

He was reportedly a devout Buddhist and considered himself a Buddhist priest.

None of these claims would make him undesirable as a jail guard; it was his attitude that cost him his job. According to fellow jailers, he was dismissed after a number of prisoners complained about his brutality and his propensity for choking them out.

With the demise of his career in law enforcement, Bennett LeClerk opened a business called the Cash Card Company. He apparently did well: he owned a home that would be worth $175,000 in today's real estate market. He was still married to his first wife when he moved a second woman, whom he *also* considered his wife, into the house and began a ménage à trois. His second "wife" had money, and she and LeClerk bought a tavern together. It was called the Iron Horse, and it soon became a thriving operation. In addition to being adept at Sanskrit and kung fu, Bennett made great fried chicken, which the Iron Horse served nightly.

His three-sided marriage lasted until Bennett's first wife gave birth to a son. Soon afterward she took the baby and left him, returning to California.

Bennett LeClerk, once a friendless teenager who put on magic shows for little kids, had become a kind of cult hero, even though his cult was small. Even when he had two "wives" living in his house, he wasn't satisfied; he was an accomplished womanizer, apparently insatiable when it came to conquests of new females.

He had an almost hypnotic effect on women. He met some of them in his various business enterprises, some came to the classes he taught in kung fu, and others attended Buddhist worship services, which he conducted in a shrine he'd had built in the basement of his home. Some said that he had his own little cult in his private shrine and that the religion he practiced was more like witchcraft.

One would think that a man with money, women, and business success would be confident, but Bennett wasn't. He could not bear to have even one of his women leave him or, worse, to have one of his seduction attempts fail. He could not take no for an answer without being plunged into depression.

It is quite possible that he'd had a teenage crush on Nancy Brooks and that he had hoped to seduce her during one of his many lingering visits to her home. If that happened, she never admitted it, and she sent him away, triggering in him a rage and quite probably an obsession. He could not endure rejection in any form.

Image was everything for Bennett LeClerk. He worked hard to create a macho image. He saw himself as a kind of Clint Eastwood figure—in the days when Eastwood was making spaghetti westerns. He affected an outfit that would have been almost laughable if he hadn't taken it so seriously and if he hadn't been such a large and threatening man: black shirt, pants, and boots; a black leather jacket; and a wide-brimmed black hat with a fuchsia band.

At least one woman, Brenda Simms,* a lovely blonde, said that Bennett simply could not believe she didn't want him as a lover. He even insisted that she leave her husband and come to him. She also said that he once forced himself on her. But she nonetheless continued to work with him at the Cash Card Company.

Nancy Brooks knew Bennett LeClerk and Rose Stahl, but they did not know each other. Nancy had met them in entirely different phases of her life. In 1974 all three of them just happened to live in Washington State. Two Bellevue housewives and a businessman–kung fu instructor–Buddhist priest. They sounded like the cast of an experimental theater play.

Early in November 1974, Sara Talbot, a teacher in Everett, Washington, twenty-six miles north of Seattle, was very troubled. After debating what she should do, she decided she had to go to the police, even though she was afraid they would think she was crazy. Finally she approached Officer Donald Rasmussen of the Everett Police Department and haltingly told him an incredible story.

It concerned a man named Bennett LeClerk, who, she said, had once been a jailer in the Snohomish County Jail in Everett. (Rasmussen checked; *that* much was true.) Sara Talbot said that LeClerk was living with his second wife, although he'd never divorced his first.

Sara Talbot said she had met LeClerk during a legitimate business deal. She described him as a very large man who seemed to be a confirmed philanderer. While she had avoided any personal relationship with him, she had observed him coming on to women, and she said he almost mesmerized them with his manipulative manner and his eyes.

She told Rasmussen about the kung fu classes LeClerk taught and about his Buddhist temple. "He can speak many languages," she said. He is an expert in explosives, a Special Forces veteran, and he has an IQ of 170."

If even half of what she was saying was true, she was certainly drawing a picture of an interesting character. Rasmussen explained that he still couldn't see that this Bennett LeClerk had done anything illegal—unless he had, indeed, committed bigamy. He asked Sara Talbot why she was so concerned.

"Because now he says he's been hired to kill someone," she blurted. "He says he's a hit man and that he has to kill two men. The first one's going to be next Tuesday. He says he's doing it as a favor for a friend because the man is a sadist who's cruel to his children. He says he usually gets $5,000 to hit somebody but that he will do this for only $1,000 because his friend asked him to do it."

Now Sara Talbot had Rasmussen's full attention. LeClerk might be a braggart, but no law enforcement officer could look the other way when murder for hire was mentioned.

"I didn't pay too much attention to Bennett the first time he told me this assassin story—he does like to tell grandiose stories," Sara said. "But now I'm frightened. He keeps insisting that I go with him and do the driving. I'm actually beginning to think there's some truth to it."

Sara said she had stopped by the Iron Horse Tavern to pick up some fried chicken and Bennett had said in all seriousness, "What are you doing next Tuesday?"

"I told him that I'd be off work at noon," she said, "and he said, 'Good. You will be with me on my hit next Tuesday.' I actually think he meant it."

Rasmussen conferred with his superiors, and they set up a meeting with Detective Sergeant Don Nelson of the Snohomish County Sheriff's Office. The investigators were in a bind. First of all, they could not arrest this LeClerk before the fact—for something he *might* do. Secondly, Sara Talbot had no idea who the purported murder victim was, so they couldn't warn him or her.

If Sara Talbot refused to go along with Bennett LeClerk's plans and it turned out he *was* serious, he would probably find someone else to aid and abet him, and *that* someone might not contact the police. It was a lot to ask of a woman who was as frightened as Sara appeared to be, but the authorities asked Sara to go along with LeClerk and make him think she was a willing accomplice.

"Do you know where this person is supposed to be killed?" Nelson asked her.

She shook her head. "But I got the impression that it's to be at a community college about ten minutes' drive from downtown Everett," she said. "The only community college that close would have to be Everett Community College."

"You'll have to go along with him," Nelson said. "But *we'll* be along with you."

Sara told the detectives that she was supposed to pick LeClerk up at his home at 6:30 P.M. on Tuesday, November 5. The hit was supposed to take place at 9:30.

As she drove up to LeClerk's home, Everett detectives Thomas Anglin and Truman Hegge, Rasmussen, and Snohomish County detectives Don Nelson, Don Slack, and Dick Taylor waited nearby in unmarked vehicles. They weren't sure in whose jurisdiction the hit was supposed to occur, so both city and county detectives were part of the task force that would follow Sara's car.

Sara Talbot parked in front of the expensive home where Bennett LeClerk lived. He jumped into her blue 1970 Toyota, and she saw that he was dressed in a bizarre costume. He wore an army fatigue jacket and trousers and a black navy watch cap.

He asked her to wait while he finished putting on what appeared to be theatrical makeup. His skin was naturally pale, and he darkened it until he was barely recognizable. To complete his disguise, he glued on a fake mustache and beard.

He had one gun tucked inside his belt at the small of his back, and he showed her where he carried another in his fatigue jacket.

The detectives, who were parked nearby, saw Sara's

blue car pull away, and one by one they fell in behind her, often changing places with one another and occasionally passing her car so that it would not become apparent to LeClerk that he was being followed. From time to time one car would turn off on a side street, only to rejoin the covert convoy later.

Almost from the beginning, nothing went as planned. They had expected the blue Toyota to head for Everett Community College. Instead, it gathered speed after it pulled onto the Interstate 5 freeway.

"They're heading for Seattle," someone said on the radio. "They've passed the community college."

Once Sara's car picked up speed, it was quickly swallowed up in traffic. Even she didn't know which of the cars behind her held police, and Bennett seemed perfectly calm. He obviously had no idea that he was being tailed.

They passed Lynnwood, and then Mountlake Terrace. In a few minutes, they would be crossing the northern boundary of Seattle. The Everett detectives radioed Seattle police and informed the dispatcher that a threatened hit was headed into their jurisdiction. They gave their location and asked for backup.

The way Sara was changing lanes told the police that her passenger was giving her directions. Then suddenly they were caught in a traffic jam, and they could no longer see the blue Toyota. For a few heart-stopping minutes the sneaker cars from the north found themselves in a morass of unfamiliar streets along the west side of the University of Washington campus. LeClerk had lots of places in which to get lost here.

The Everett and Snohomish County cars fanned out and, to their vast relief, spotted Sara Talbot's car. She was just parking it, and, although they didn't realize it at the moment, she and the hit man were only two blocks from the north end police precinct in Seattle. The stakeout team had the car in sight again, but where was the hit to take place, and, more important, who was the potential victim?

Seattle Police detectives Gene Birkeland and Doug Fritschy and officers Mike Crist, Jim Devine, and Sergeant Gerald Taylor joined the cops already waiting.

The blue Toyota moved frequently from one parking spot to another, settling for a time near an apartment building and then moving on to a tavern. At one point it drove away from the area entirely and, with a police tail, circled a plush residential area and then came back to what Seattleites call the Wallingford District.

This time the Toyota stayed in one spot. Don Nelson placed two of his deputies—Don Slack and Dick Taylor—on the roof of an automotive shop where they had a bird's-eye view of the area, and the other police personnel found spots where they could watch the activity in the blue car but still be out of sight.

The watching policemen tensed as a tall man wearing fatigues and makeup left Sara Talbot's car, but he only walked back and forth, peered around buildings, and then came back to her car.

He repeated his forays several times during the two hours the officers waited. They were at an impasse. They tensed each time the man got out to prowl the quiet residential streets and alleyways. They couldn't arrest him; there was no reason to. He had committed no crime.

The minutes ticked by, and Nelson reminded everyone by police radio that the hit was supposed to take place at 9:30 P.M. "We decided to confront the man," Nelson recalled. "But that's when he crossed the street and was momentarily out of our view."

Suddenly, at a few minutes after nine, LeClerk left the

car again, and things began to happen fast. Once the hit man could no longer see her, Sara Talbot pulled slowly along the street craning her neck until she spotted an Everett officer she knew. "Now!" she mouthed frantically. *"The time is now!"*

The officer spun around and headed for LeClerk. Mike Crist, a Seattle patrolman, had decided at almost the same instant that they had waited long enough. The men felt as if they were moving through molasses as they ran to catch up with LeClerk.

And then they heard a sound that made their hearts convulse. Before they could reach the tall man in disguise, a single shot echoed in the chill November night. Almost immediately they heard a man's voice screaming, "Help me! Somebody help me!"

Crist dropped to one knee at the exit to the alley where LeClerk had disappeared. Holding his .38 Police Special in both hands, Crist leveled the weapon and pointed it at a tall figure running toward him. Six more shots rang out as Slack and Taylor on the garage roof fired at the fleeing gunman. He slowed but didn't stop.

The man in fatigues was visible to Mike Crist in the yellow glow of a streetlight now. He whirled toward Crist, prepared to shoot it out with him, but Crist never wavered. "Drop your weapon," he ordered, aiming at the gunman's heart.

There were a few tense moments, and then Crist heard the clatter of a gun hitting the pavement. He had not had to fire his weapon. Slack's and Taylor's shots had struck the suspect.

The man, presumed to be Bennett LeClerk, was already wounded in the side of his neck and bleeding profusely. It was difficult to tell if he was seriously injured, but he was still on his feet. He was handcuffed and placed in a police unit to wait for paramedics, as the detectives who had pursued him and the Seattle officers rushed into the alley to check on the man who had screamed.

The target of the assassination plot lay in the alley, terribly wounded. He was conscious, though. He gave his name as Art Stahl. Stahl gasped that he had just walked out of a class on reflexology at the Acadia Health Center. He was in critical condition from a bullet that had pierced his chest at the midpoint of the breastbone and passed through his body, missing his spinal cord by a fraction of an inch. Seattle Fire Department Medic One paramedics rushed to stabilize his condition. When they tore open his shirt, they saw that the shot that hit him was a near-contact wound: the shooter had been standing less than a foot away from Stahl when he fired.

Before they could begin work, however, they had to shoo off members of Stahl's reflexology class, who had removed his shoes and were applying pressure to his feet in an area that they insisted would help heal his chest wound.

The scene was chaos. The gunman was bleeding more heavily than his victim, but Bennett LeClerk was in no danger. Police bullets had merely torn away some of the soft fleshy part of his neck. As a Medic One rig raced Art Stahl to the ER at Harborview Hospital, Sara Talbot sat in her car trembling. She had attempted to pull away from the scene before LeClerk could run back to her car, and Seattle police had arrested her as an accomplice.

"No," the Everett detectives said. "She's with us. She's a police informant." Her handcuffs were removed, and she waited to give a statement.

Bennett LeClerk was taken to the Wallingford Precinct for questioning, complaining all the while about his wound. Deputy Dick Taylor informed him of his rights under *Miranda,* and he admitted orally that he had shot a man named Art because he was "trying to help a friend solve a problem. The best solution was to shoot the person causing the problem."

LeClerk said he had been offered $1,000 to do the shooting, but he hadn't taken it.

"Who asked you to do it?" Taylor asked.

"I can't tell you," LeClerk said. And he refused to put any statement in writing. He said he couldn't answer any more questions because he could feel his throat swelling closed on the inside and he was having trouble breathing.

All questioning stopped—for the moment—and LeClerk too was transported to Group Health Hospital.

The mysterious hit had occurred in the city of Seattle. Seattle homicide detectives Sergeant Bruce Edmonds, Benny DePalmo, and Duane Homan were about to embark on one of the strangest investigations of their careers, and they were starting from scratch.

They retrieved and bagged LeClerk's clothing from the hospital. They found a clump of artificial hair from the beard in his pants pocket, two black leather gloves, a black "Jawa" stick, two rounds of .38 bird shot, and a paper napkin. The napkin was covered with notes and doodles. Among the doodles was a swastika, which—given the crime—was not surprising.

The paper napkin had come from the cocktail lounge of the Holiday Inn in Everett, and on it was written all the vital information a hired killer might need to identify Art Stahl: "52, Art and Rose, L.D. Dogs, $3,000 5'9 150."

On the lower half of the napkin was even more information that indicated that Bennett LeClerk knew exactly where to find his target: "Tuesdays only—Nov. 26, Acadia Health Center, 7–9 p.m. 1220 N. 45th, OTV-940, Black 2-door Dart 70, Bounty Tavern (next to the health center)."

The Seattle detectives knew already that Bennett LeClerk hadn't known Art Stahl even well enough to recognize him by sight. Witnesses who had walked from his reflexology class with him said that the gunman had walked up to him and asked, "Are you Art?" When Stahl said yes the stranger pulled the trigger. The first shot misfired, but the shooter instantly fired again, and Art Stahl fell to the ground and began to scream.

Stahl, who was fighting for his life in the hospital's critical care unit, could not be questioned. His estranged wife, Rose, was home when she was notified that he had been wounded. She told detectives later at the hospital that she was shocked and at a loss to explain the shooting. Yes, they'd been having marital difficulties, but violence had never been involved. She said they had been seeing a counselor and their friend Nancy Brooks, a registered nurse, was also helping them.

As soon as Rose Stahl got word that Art was in the hospital and might be dying, she called Nancy, who rushed over to baby-sit for the Stahls' little boys. She would spend the night at the Stahl home so that Rose could stay at the hospital with Art.

Detectives Benny DePalmo and Duane Homan asked Rose if she knew anyone named Bennett LeClerk, and she shook her head.

"Does your friend Nancy know him?"

"I don't know. . . . I don't think so. She's never mentioned him."

Several seemingly unrelated events occurred the next day, November 6, while Art Stahl remained in the ICU.

Claire Noonan called Nancy Brooks and asked her if she knew anything about Bennett's shooting some man named "Stowe."

"No," Nancy replied.

"Have you seen Bennett lately?"

"Not for a long, long time, Claire," Nancy said, adding that she had no idea what Bennett had been doing and she knew nothing of a man named Stowe being shot. Although her friend from California had misunderstood Stahl's name, Nancy certainly *had* heard of the shooting, but she didn't admit that to Bennett LeClerk's mother.

At this point the Seattle police were working without a number of pieces of vital information. They knew that their victim was a University of Washington instructor, that he had been having trouble in his marriage, and that he had been shot by someone who was apparently a stranger to him. They did *not* know yet that Art Stahl was worth almost a million dollars.

The Seattle Homicide Unit commander, Captain Herb Swindler, received an anonymous call at home that day, however, that filled in a lot of the blank spots. "Stahl's worth a bundle," the voice said. "Nancy Brooks may know something about all of this."

Detectives Duane Homan and Benny DePalmo learned that Art Stahl was out of surgery and awake. He was alert but clearly very frightened. He asked them if the police guard outside his hospital room could be kept there indefinitely. He didn't say who he was afraid of, and the detectives got the idea that he didn't really know. "I don't know who to trust," he said quietly, "but I have confidence in you two. I want to give you something. Hand me my trousers, would you?"

DePalmo got Stahl's trousers from the closet, and the injured man fished in his pocket until he came up with a key ring. He took a small key off the ring and handed it to the detective. "Here, this is for my desk drawer in my office at the university. I have a private journal that I've been keeping there for a year. Get it and read it. Maybe you'll get an idea of why this happened."

They retrieved Stahl's journal from his office and sat down to see if it held any clues to the shooting. As they read the running record of a loveless marriage, the two homicide investigators sympathized with Art Stahl. He'd had good reason to move out of his house. But even though Rose Stahl had threatened Art with a butcher knife, she wasn't a viable suspect. They could definitely place her at home in Bellevue miles away across a floating bridge from the alley where the shooting occurred.

Rose had a motive for wanting her estranged husband dead; the investigators checked and found that Stahl *was* wealthy, that his $780,000 plus was tied up in a trust, and that if he died before his will was finalized, Rose would become the beneficiary of the trust.

By November 13 Art Stahl was recovering well, although he still wanted a police guard twenty-four hours a day. Homan and DePalmo couldn't really blame him. They had attempted to learn more about his bleak marriage from the couples' friend Nancy Brooks. But she told them she had been in still another automobile accident, which had aggravated her already delicate spine. "I just can't come into Seattle to talk with you," she said. "Could you come here? And I know you won't mind, but I'd feel better if my attorney was present while you were here."

Homan and DePalmo had no problem with that, although it seemed a little peculiar that Nancy Brooks would take such a precaution when she was only an outside witness—someone they hoped knew both Art and Rose Stahl well enough to throw a little light on their investigation.

The two detectives drove to the Brookses' comfortable Bellevue home. They found Nancy to be a tall, somewhat fragile-looking woman, who seemed bemused by the news of Art Stahl's shooting. She told them she knew Bennett LeClerk but did not mention any recent contact with him.

"Did LeClerk know Rose Stahl?" DePalmo asked.

Nancy Brooks shook her head. She didn't think that he knew Rose, but said it was possible because they all raised dogs. "Rose and I raise poodles, but Bennett has German shepherds. I suppose she might have met him at a dog show or something."

Nancy Brooks seemed slightly ill at ease when she spoke about LeClerk, but the detectives could not be certain why; it was almost as if she feared him. But this was a shocking situation, and the woman before them seemed refined and unused to violence. Nancy volunteered that she had last seen Bennett in Everett sometime around the latter part of October. She had gone there to "counsel" him because he was upset, but she hadn't mentioned the visit to her husband.

"Why not?" Homan asked.

"My husband's an engineer," she said, wryly, "and he thinks like one."

While that remark might have gone over the heads of anyone outside the Seattle area, Homan and DePalmo understood. "Boeing engineer jokes" were always making the rounds. The jokes ridiculed engineers for having no imagination and showing no emotion, for wearing pocket protectors full of pens, and for thinking only in mathematical terms.

Homan and DePalmo wondered about the relationship between Nancy Brooks and Bennett LeClerk, and they discussed it as they drove back to town. Were they lovers? It hardly seemed possible. Nancy was eleven or twelve years older than Bennett and had known him since he was a kid. She seemed like the complete housewife, modestly dressed to the point of being prim; it was almost impossible to picture her in a love nest with a man as flamboyant and peculiar as Bennett LeClerk. No, Nancy appeared to be the kind of woman who was always trying to help people—listening to their problems, offering solutions.

Still, there had to be *some* connection. No matter how they tried to reconstruct the events leading up to the shooting, Nancy Brooks was the link—seemingly the only link—between Bennett LeClerk and Art Stahl. The two men had not known each other even by sight, but Nancy knew both of them well.

It would be almost four months later before Bennett LeClerk was ready to give a full statement about the shooting on November 5. His story was so incredible that it was difficult to believe him, and yet it was the only explanation that made any sense.

Bennett LeClerk said he had known Nancy Brooks for many years, ever since he was a teenager in California. When he moved to Washington and learned that she and her husband lived within thirty miles of him, he had reestablished his friendship with her, and she had become his confidante.

LeClerk told police that Nancy had called him in late October 1974 and asked to meet him in the cocktail lounge of the Holiday Inn in Everett. There Nancy told him how worried she was about a "terrible" situation in her friend Rose's home: Rose's husband was a sadist, a child-beater, and an abuser. This was about the worst thing that Bennett LeClerk could imagine, he said. He himself had a blank space of several years in his memory of his early childhood because he had been physically abused by a stepfather. He deplored the thought that anyone could harm a child, and Nancy was telling him that this guy named Art was making his and Rose's children's lives hell.

"I asked her," LeClerk said, "if divorce wouldn't be the answer to saving the children from this guy, but Nancy said it wouldn't be good enough."

Nancy Brooks was asking him to kill Art so that her friend and the children wouldn't have to be afraid any longer.

"I told her I'd think it over," LeClerk said.

On Halloween, LeClerk and Nancy Brooks had had a second meeting at the Holiday Inn, this time in the parking lot. She seemed distraught and told him that the situation in Rose's home was "deteriorating rapidly" and that he must do "it" as soon as possible. The children were suffering terribly.

He didn't feel comfortable sitting in the hotel parking lot discussing murder, LeClerk said, so he drove Nancy to his own home, where they talked for about two hours, weighing the pros and cons of blasting Art off the face of the earth. There were two little boys in Art and Rose's family, Nancy said—babies really—as well as some older children. Their father made them suffer, she said, very much as Bennett had suffered when he was a child.

LeClerk said Nancy promised to pay him $1,000 if he killed Art, but he said he wouldn't take money from her; the money should come from Rose. "She shouldn't be uninvolved emotionally or morally," he told Nancy. After all, they would be doing it for her and her children.

Nancy had convinced him, finally, that someone had to kill Art—and soon. "I told her I would do it," Bennett said, "probably [the] next Tuesday."

He then asked the woman who had been like an aunt to him, "But what if I get caught?"

"I hadn't thought of that," she reportedly said. "Then I would have to deny everything."

She showed him some small pictures of Art so he would know what his target looked like—but she took them back, LeClerk said.

LeClerk said he had then figured that if he wasn't caught in the first ten minutes after the shooting, he would be home free. Police would not be able to connect him to Art, any more than they could connect two strangers passing on a busy street. He didn't even want to know Art's last name.

Bennett just knew he had to kill him. It had to be done to save the children.

The detectives realized that if their prisoner was telling the truth, Nancy Brooks had been an integral part of this murder for hire. Quite possibly she was the instigator. She was the sole connection between LeClerk and Stahl; she was the only one who knew exactly which buttons to push in the complex mind of Bennett LeClerk; she knew all about his childhood; and she knew that he lost it when he heard about kids being abused.

Once he had agreed to do what Nancy Brooks asked, LeClerk said he began planning. He needed Sara Talbot to drive him to the address Nancy had given him—the place where Art went every Tuesday night. Sara's car wasn't nearly as recognizable as his own fleet of flashy cars. "I planned to find Art's car and clip the ignition wires so he couldn't drive away from that health center," he told the detectives.

He spent Tuesday morning, November 5, looking at houses "because I planned to go into the real estate business with Sara," he explained. "I ate lunch with her. Later I had supper—what little I managed to get down."

He said he owned three complete theatrical makeup kits, and he made himself up to look like a South American revolutionary, with dark makeup, the false facial hair, and the fatigue jacket and pants. "I took two guns with me—one a drop gun [an untraceable gun left at the scene to confuse police] and the attack weapon that I tucked into my belt."

He said he hadn't worn his glasses for fear he might drop them and his prescription would be traced to him. "I'm nearsighted in one eye," LeClerk said, "and farsighted in the other. My night vision in the medium range is poor."

Duane Homan and Benny DePalmo stared at the hit man. He seemed to be living in a fantasy world—with his elaborate makeup—but he was not as clever as he pretended to be. To go out on a murder-for-hire mission half blind without even knowing what his quarry looked like seemed less than clever. And yet this man in front of them was supposed to be a genius.

"I deliberately had no identification on me," LeClerk said, "just that napkin that Nancy gave me at the Holiday Inn on Halloween."

They had arrived near the Acadia Health Center around 7:00 P.M., Bennett unaware, of course, that they were tailed by a caravan of law enforcement officers. "I figured Art would park his car near the Bounty Tavern," he explained. "I found the 1979 Dart and I tried to clip the wires, but it was too dark to find the leads, so I gave up, for fear I might be noticed.

"I asked Sara to move her car several times, and I made several reconnoitering trips around the neighborhood on foot. I saw the alley between the health center and the Bounty Tavern and figured that would be the best place. . . . I would just stand there and wait for Art. Sara would wait for me at the other end of the alley. After the shooting, I was going to take off my makeup as we drove away."

"Why did you leave the area that one time and drive

through Windermere?" Homan asked, curious. Windermere is one of Seattle's poshest neighborhoods.

"Oh, that?" LeClerk said. "Well, this woman who worked for me had relatives there. I told Sara, 'It should be *him* I'm killing.' See, this Brenda left the week before, and she took money from my tavern and left a note. It said, 'Try to understand—this is all I can do. I'll get in touch.' "

(Bennett LeClerk certainly led a complicated life. Two wives, numerous mistresses, and one woman he wanted as a mistress, Brenda Simms, who would one day give detectives a good deal of background on him.)

"Tell us about the shooting," Homan said.

"Well, the class got out a little after nine. I saw the man I'd seen in the photographs Nancy showed me. He was talking to other people in his class. I walked up to him and said, 'Are you Art?' and he said, 'Yes,' and I fired. It was a misfire, and I fired again. But at the last minute, I turned the gun to avoid a fatal shot."

DePalmo and Homan looked at each other. Since Art Stahl had suffered a through-and-through wound to the dead center of his chest, it was hard to believe that Bennett LeClerk had *really* turned his weapon away. You couldn't aim with much more fatal intent than he had.

Bennett LeClerk pleaded guilty to first-degree assault and on March 5, 1975, was sentenced to up to twenty years in prison by Judge William C. Goodloe. Deputy Prosecutor Lee Yates had recommended that LeClerk be sentenced for "up to life" in prison, and Goodloe suggested that the minimum should be the same as the maximum—twenty years. "You are not a contract man flown in from Chicago with a violin case," he said scathingly to LeClerk. "You are a citizen of this state who made a decision that turned to mud."

LeClerk was uncharacteristically humble. "There is no question that my judgment was poor beyond description.

The act is repugnant to me and leaves scars I am going to bear for a very long time."

It was a classic sociopath's statement; those with this personality disorder *always* think of events in terms of themselves. While Art Stahl had barely escaped with his life and bore *real* scars on his neck and chest, Bennett LeClerk talked of *his* scars.

LeClerk remained in the King County Jail so that he could serve as a material witness against another suspect. The investigation, of course, was far from over. That very afternoon after the sentencing of her old friend, Nancy Brooks was arrested.

Detectives Homan and DePalmo obtained a warrant for her arrest on suspicion of conspiracy to commit first-degree murder. They arrived at the Brookses' Bellevue home at 4:17 P.M. Nancy Brooks seemed only a little surprised when she saw the warrant for her arrest. Otherwise, she maintained the same calm demeanor they had always seen. She quickly made arrangements to have her children and her dogs cared for and then walked with the Seattle investigators to their car.

She talked a little with detectives Homan and De-Palmo at headquarters.

She told them that Bennett LeClerk had "haunted" her since 1970, remarking, "I don't know why I am even telling you this, because you won't believe me. LeClerk is so *strange* you will think I made it all up."

They knew LeClerk was strange from personal experience with him, but the fact remained that Nancy Brooks was the thread that bound shooter and victim together.

Nancy denied any connection to Art's shooting. She told Homan and DePalmo that she did go to Bennett's house on Halloween and that he had insisted on giving her a "tour" that included even his shower. "I was afraid," she said, "because I kept thinking of that movie, *Psycho*. But I only met him, as I told you before, because he was upset and said he needed to talk to me."

Nancy Brooks was released a few hours later on $10,000 bond. A week later she pleaded innocent to the charges against her.

For three months the Stahl-Brooks-LeClerk case faded from the media. Nothing would be happening, at least on the surface, until Nancy Brooks's trial in June. Chief Criminal Deputy Prosecutor Roy Howson and Deputy Prosecutor Les Yates would represent the state, and Defense Attorney Gerald Bangs would attempt to show that Nancy Brooks had no connection to the near-murder of Art Stahl.

It was ironically fitting, perhaps, that Bennett LeClerk was the first witness for the prosecution. He made a striking figure as he left the jail elevator. His wrists were manacled, but he wore an expensive suit, a crisp white shirt, and a silk tie. His head was shaved, and he had grown a goatee and mustache. (This time, his facial hair was real.)

As he was led toward the courtroom through the marbled corridors of the courthouse, LeClerk passed his would-be victim, Art Stahl, who by now had recovered. Suddenly LeClerk whirled, and the court deputies' hands moved to their guns. They need not have been concerned. LeClerk merely leaned down and presented a very surprised Art Stahl with an expensive book about Buddhist philosophy. He had carried it in one hand, ready for this meeting.

Stahl, bemused, accepted it and thumbed through it as he waited to testify.

As a witness, LeClerk seemed intelligent and responsive, if more than a little eccentric, as he discussed his wives, mistresses, Buddhism, the temple of worship in his basement, and his small collection of *shrakin* (Japanese weapons), which included a *manreiki,* a chain with weights on the end.

"The Imperial Guards used [the chain] on assassins," he explained to the jury, "so that they could disarm them of samurai swords without spilling blood in the palace."

LeClerk spoke of his long friendship with Nancy Brooks and of his revulsion when she told him about a man named Art who was cruel to his children. Nancy had told him that Art was a sadist. He testified that she had finally convinced him that Art would have to die so that the children could be safe.

The jury would have to choose between this flamboyant witness and the prim, sweet-faced woman at the defense table whose skirts hung discreetly below the knee, whose makeup was barely visible, who was a registered nurse, and who had no criminal background at all.

Defense Attorney Bangs hit hard on LeClerk's many affairs and his religious "disciples," but the witness appeared to enjoy jousting with Bangs. He went into minute detail about his Buddhist shrine and the Buddhist symbol—a water dragon, or *miziechi.* He denied that he considered himself the eye of the dragon, or *so-ryugn.*

The words might as well have been Greek, but the man on the stand radiated charisma, and something more—perhaps a thin sheen of madness? Nevertheless, his genius was apparent to the jury and the gallery. No one listening would have denied that.

Nancy Brooks, sitting at the defense table, showed no reaction at all as LeClerk gave his version of the events of the previous fall. He said that his "conscious intent was to kill the man" but that a "subconscious intent" had made him attempt to turn the gun. So, in effect, he had saved Stahl's life.

LeClerk's mother, Claire Noonan, testified that she had called Nancy Brooks as soon as she read about the shooting in the newspapers. That would have been the day after—November 6. She said Nancy claimed to know absolutely nothing about it. Next, Claire had called her son in the hospital, where he was recovering from his neck wound.

"Why did you shoot that man?" she asked, and he replied that he "had done it for a friend of mine."

The witness said the only friend she had in Seattle was Nancy Brooks. "I asked my son if Nancy was the friend, and he said, 'That's right.' "

Art Stahl, the intended victim, was the last witness for the state. He recalled that the "violence" in his marriage had come not from him but from his estranged wife, Rose, who was furious over the way he spent his trust fund. No one except Rose and two friends at the university had known that he attended reflexology class on Tuesday evenings.

Stahl testified that he didn't see the stranger with a gun until a moment before he was shot in the chest. He also said he had filed for divorce from Rose as soon as he was well enough to leave the hospital.

Sara Talbot, the young woman who had driven the hit car, testified for the defense, but not in person: she had been diagnosed with terminal cancer in the months between the crime in November 1974 and the trial in June 1975. Her image appeared in the courtroom on videotape as she recalled the frightening evening she had spent with Bennett LeClerk. She had been told he had cut his "kill fee" because he was going to shoot a man "for a friend," but she had never heard the name Nancy Brooks.

Rose Stahl testified in support of her close friend Nancy. Rose admitted that she and Art had had a marriage marked by ups and downs, but she denied ever threatening to kill him. She certainly had not offered to pay

$1,000 to have him shot. She had never discussed any of her financial problems with Nancy. "My husband would not have approved of that," she said calmly.

Although it is rare for defendants in cases of murder or attempted murder to take the witness stand, Nancy Brooks's attorney evidently felt she would make a good impression on the jury. Dressed modestly, as always, Nancy Brooks squeezed her husband's hand as she rose to defend herself.

She testified in a soft voice, recalling that Bennett Le-Clerk had come back into her life a few years before. She had met him at a shopping center in 1973 and gone to see his house. She'd met "both his wives." They had confided that they had difficulty deciding who should answer when a caller asked for "Mrs. LeClerk."

Nancy Brooks said that the last time LeClerk had come to her house he'd worn all black and had carried a gun and a syringe full of poison meant, she said, for the husband of one of his mistresses.

Bennett's lengthy visits to the Brookses' Bellevue home had become a nuisance. She said she'd finally had to tell him not to come again because the neighbors were talking, but she said he could phone her. "You're making it up because your husband is jealous," she said LeClerk had raged. "All men are jealous!"

Asked by her attorney to try to remember all her contacts with twenty-eight-year-old Bennett LeClerk, Nancy Brooks said he had called her in the fall of 1973—twenty months before this trial—and he had said that one of his wives was pregnant and the baby was due in January. He thought Nancy might like to come and visit his mother when she came to Washington.

"And the next time?"

"It was probably in May—May of 1974." Nancy Brooks said she was just out of the hospital after having a neck fusion. Bennett was once again calling her and begging her to meet him, asking if he could come over and see her. "I told him he would have to call first—but he never called." She said he was very upset over a woman named Brenda Simms—"the one woman he could really love."

In September 1974, Nancy Brooks said, Bennett called again. He told her he had been drinking saki and taking Valium, Empirin, and codeine for a back injury. He asked her if she wanted to invest in something, and she had said no.

In October he called again, threatening suicide because everyone had deserted him.

"I believed him," she told the jury earnestly. "He was begging for just one hour of my time." She testified that she had agreed to meet him in Everett on October 25 only because he told her he was so depressed that he would kill himself if she refused. "I didn't want his suicide on my conscience."

Bennett wanted her to intercede with Brenda, who was leaving him. Nancy refused, but suggested he get counseling. She mentioned the name of a psychiatrist, she testified, and he became enraged. She then said she had friends who had gone through counseling and that it had helped them a great deal. No, she said, she "thought" she had not mentioned the Stahls by name.

Oddly, though, Bennett had referred to the Stahls as if he knew them.

Nancy Brooks blushed as she said LeClerk "got fresh" and put his hand beneath her blouse during the meeting in the cocktail lounge. After three hours he walked her to her car and threatened her by saying: "I'll run the show. You will meet me again. I know where your daughter rides, and she's beautiful. If you want to keep her face in that condition, you'll meet me."

He also threatened her husband, she testified. "He told me that if he couldn't get him, someone else would."

She had been terrorized by Bennett LeClerk, she told the jury. But had she told her husband—or the police or her attorney? No, she had not. "I was so scared," she explained to Prosecutor Roy Howson.

Asked if LeClerk had scribbled notes on a cocktail napkin during their meeting, she said she could not recall.

Despite her terror, Nancy Brooks said she had met LeClerk again on October 31. This time, she embellished what she had told Duane Homan and Benny DePalmo. They listened, amazed. They had been led to believe her visit to LeClerk's home had happened much earlier and in the presence of his wives.

Now she said that Bennett had forced her from the Holiday Inn to his home at gunpoint. He had shown her his shrine, his shower, and his bedroom. He had subjected her to sadistic teasing, laughing hysterically. He had shown her the Buddha downstairs and told her the orange dragon was modeled after him.

"He wrapped the chain . . . around his arms, legs, waist," she told the jury, "and he did barefoot karate kicks. He threw the chain toward me, and I jumped back and it fell on the floor."

As the jury leaned forward, Nancy Brooks continued her story of her secret visit to the home of a man she claimed to be afraid of. She said he took her into his bedroom and then into the shower, explaining how "sexy" it was. He told her, she said, that he had brought "many women" there. He'd asked her if she could tell what was so special about the shower. When she shook her head in bewilderment, he showed her how he'd had the shower head mounted so that he could direct the spray wherever he wanted it.

Hesitantly, Nancy said that Bennett had pushed her

down on the bed and tried to kiss her. She looked beseechingly at her attorney, "Do I have to say it all?"

"Try to paraphrase," he said gently.

"He pushed me on the bed and tried to kiss me. He told me over and over what an exciting lover he was . . . a lot of rubbish like that. He showed me a bottle of cinnamony liquid and put liquid from it on his finger and made me taste it, and he said it was part of his sex rituals."

The defendant insisted that she had not had sex with LeClerk. Finally, she said, he let her go and drove her back to her car. Again she failed to tell her husband of her frightening ordeal.

She was positive that she had never mentioned the Stahls while she was with Bennett. Positive that she had not said a word about Art's being brutal to his children.

She certainly had never contracted to have Art killed.

As Prosecutors Lee Yates and Roy Howson questioned Nancy, there was a hard edge to her answers. The softly modulated voice was gone now. She denied over and over again that she had been a go-between for LeClerk and Rose Stahl, the facilitator of a planned murder. She refused to look at the attorneys for the state as she answered them.

It was a lengthy trial. In his final arguments, Yates pointed out that Washington statutes declared that anyone who "aids, assists, abets, encourages, hires, counsels, induces or procures another to commit a crime is guilty and shall be treated the same as the person who actually commits it."

Yates stressed that Nancy Brooks had known exactly what strings to pull to make LeClerk do what she wanted. She was Rose Stahl's close friend. The women shared every confidence with each other. Nancy Brooks had known about the inheritance and the threatened divorce.

And she had also known just where Art Stahl would be on the night he was shot. She had known all the facts found on the napkin that Bennett LeClerk had carried. Who else would have provided him with the address and the description of the intended victim, right down to his license-plate number?

In the end, Yates asked the most salient questions: "Why Art Stahl? Why would LeClerk shoot Stahl, a man he didn't even know?"

And that was the question that the jury could not answer satisfactorily without finding Nancy guilty. There was no other way to fit the pieces of the puzzle together. Rose didn't know Bennett. Bennett didn't know Art Stahl. But Nancy Brooks knew everyone, and she knew just which buttons to push. The prosecution team didn't deny that Bennett LeClerk was a bizarre man, a man who professed to have great power and strength, but he was also a man who could not stand rejection from women.

Nancy Brooks had known him since he was a disturbed teenager; she knew all his vulnerable places. Whatever her attachment to Rose Stahl was, it was intense. Nancy wanted Rose to be happy—and rich. The only way to facilitate that was for Art to be gone. Really, really gone. When all the circumstantial and physical evidence was evaluated, the only conclusion to be drawn was that Nancy Brooks, the sweet mother and wife, had manipulated eccentric Bennett LeClerk into within a fraction of an inch of outright murder. And she had done all of this as a favor to a friend.

The jury of eight men and four women, after deliberating for less than five hours, found Nancy Brooks guilty of attempted first-degree murder. The penalty for attempted murder was the same as it would have been if the murder plot had succeeded. Judge James Mifflin sentenced Nancy Brooks to up to life in prison.

At this writing, both Nancy Brooks and Bennett LeClerk have served their prison terms and been paroled. They have not come to the attention of Washington State authorities again. Like Nancy and Bennett, Rose Stahl has disappeared from the public eye. Art Stahl recovered completely from his gunshot wound and is alive and well two decades later.

In the end, the argument for the healing powers of reflexology may have been strengthened. Art Stahl received what should have been a fatal—or at least a paralyzing—wound. But immediately after he was shot in the chest, a classmate removed his shoes and massaged the "heart healing" area of his feet. Who is to say that, at least in Stahl's case, it wasn't reflexology that saved his life?

The Most Dangerous Game
(from *In the Name of Love*)

When I was in high school, our English teacher assigned us a short story that has become a classic. "The Most Dangerous Game" was the story of a millionaire whose private island was his personal hunting preserve—only he hunted humans, not animals. It left a lasting impression on me and gave me a view of cruelty and manipulation I had never imagined. Many years later I came across a case that made me remember that troubling story. I have chosen the title of that short story for this Snohomish County, Washington, case. There are many dark similarities between the fictional story and the true case.

The victims in this case were very young and naive, full of the spirit of adventure and in search of a perfect world and perfect love. They were the age that I was in high school, and they had the same innocence. The peace and love and joy of Woodstock was only two years past, and many young people were still captivated by the concept the flower children had embraced: "All you need is love."

The girls in this case had never encountered pure, distilled evil before, and they did not recognize it for what it was until it was too late.

This true case has always reminded me of a Stephen King book or a "Jason" or "Freddie" movie. It's much like a ghost story as it plays out in the dark short days and endless nights of winter in the Northwest. Blizzards obliterate everything that once seemed familiar. Something scratches and bumps against a thin-walled cabin as two terrified young women huddle inside.

What was it knocking and scraping on their door? What followed them as they tried to escape, the presence they could feel but could not see, even when they whirled around to try to catch it unawares?

This case still gives me goose-bumps.

As terrifying as this encounter in a howling blizzard was, the ending was not as tragic as it seemed destined to be. For those who believe in miracles—or in angels—the astonishing denouement of "The Most Dangerous Game" will only strengthen that belief.

Washington is bisected by the Cascade Mountains. The state is rainy and mild on the Pacific coast and prone to hot dry summers and freezing winters on the eastern side. The mountains themselves often have snowy peaks year round. Skilled highway engineers have cut routes through the mountain passes, so that it is possible to cross the Cascades in all but the wildest of winter storms: White Pass, North Cascades Highway, Snoqualmie Pass, and Stevens Pass. The North Cascades Highway tends to close down for the winter first, and Snoqualmie Pass is the easiest route. Success for those who attempt to cross White Pass and Stevens Pass depends on the depth of the snowdrifts, the threat of avalanches, and the accuracy of weathermen.

None of these routes east from the Washington coast should be chosen by ill-prepared youngsters bent on running away—not in winter. Never in winter.

Maeve Flaherty* was sixteen years old in the winter of 1971. She lived in Seattle with her parents and brothers and sisters. Her father was a doctor, and the family lived in a more-than-comfortable home in one of Seattle's nicest neighborhoods. Maeve was a pretty girl, short and a little plump. She had a pixyish sense of humor, and like many teens in the early seventies, she was caught up in a world where the young were protesting what they saw as the sins of adults. The Chicago Seven, the Beatles with their long hair and their message-filled music, and the National Guard shootings at Kent State were in the news. While their parents were listening to Dinah Shore and Lawrence Welk, teens were buying Janis Joplin, Three Dog Night, and Simon and Garfunkel—music that sounded like cacophony to the older generation. It has always been so, and it always will be, but the youth revolution of the sixties and seventies was stronger and more visible.

Maeve liked to think she was a rebel—but she wasn't, really. She was a dreamer whose fantasies far outweighed her common sense. She was restless—eager to try her own wings. Whenever things didn't go well in her life, Maeve ran. She had run away often enough so that her parents, at their wits' end, considered putting her in a private girls' boarding school. Although they would miss having her at home, they hoped that she would get strict supervision there.

Maeve was adamant that she would not go away to school. She would rather run away than wear a uniform and observe a curfew and go to a stuffy school. She began to formulate a plan. She didn't tell her parents, of course; she needed time to prepare. By February 20, 1971, she was ready to leave. Maeve "triple-dressed"—and then some. She piled on layer after layer of clothes and jeans. That way, she wouldn't have to carry a suitcase, which would certainly have sounded automatic alarm bells.

Maeve wouldn't be running away alone. She had a friend whose views were much like her own. Kari Ivarsen* was eighteen—two years older than Maeve—and had lived away from her family for months. They both felt they were perfectly capable of taking care of themselves. They saw their parents as having morals and rules right out of the Stone Age. They both believed that the world was a good place, that you could trust strangers because all people were good if they were shown love, because love transcended all danger. If they could have, Maeve and Kari would have journeyed to Woodstock in 1969 and participated in that giant muddy love fest where everyone got along wonderfully despite the dire predictions of adults.

Where Maeve was a cute and cuddly girl, Kari was absolutely beautiful. She was slender and graceful with the perfectly symmetrical facial features that made men swivel their heads to look at her. Having already proved she could get by very well without parental supervision, Kari assured Maeve that they would be perfectly fine once they hit the road. They would have fun and interesting adventures, and when they were ready, they would come back home.

The two girls arranged to meet away from Maeve's home. They knew if they were to evade Maeve's parents and the authorities, they had to avoid all their usual hangouts and get out of Seattle as soon as possible. They had saved some money, but not enough to rent a room or an apartment. If they ran out of money for food, they could work as waitresses or dishwashers. Figuring out how to survive would be part of the adventure of their new life.

Someone had told them that there were scores of summer cabins around the Cascade foothills and the isolated lakes in Snohomish County just north of the King County line. Reportedly those cabins sat there empty during the off-season; their owners rarely, if ever, used them in the winter time.

Kari brought it up first: why couldn't they "borrow" a cabin for a while? She envisioned a cozy hideaway with a roaring fire where no one would find them or bother them. They wouldn't really be hurting anything; maybe later they could repay the owners for whatever canned goods or supplies they used. It wouldn't be stealing—not really—since they intended to replace everything.

Neither girl knew anything at all about mountain survival. They figured they would learn as they went along.

One thing about Washington State that its residents appreciate is that they can leave Seattle and be in the mountains in an hour—or on a Pacific Ocean beach in an hour and a half. One can actually stand in the middle of Seattle and see the snowcapped mountains in the distance; tricks of depth perception make them seem close enough to reach out and touch.

Maeve Flaherty and Kari Ivarsen decided to head for those deceptively safe-looking mountains. They had enough money to take a bus twenty-six miles north to Everett, the Snohomish County seat. They knew how to make their way to Stevens Pass from Everett, hitchhiking through the little towns of Monroe, Sultan, and Startup, where Highway 2 began to climb toward the summit of the towering mountain range. They passed through Gold Bar and Index, and then stood beside the highway. They needed to find shelter before dark. Kari and Maeve had no real plans at all after that; that was half the fun—waiting to see what would happen.

The dream sounded good, and they fueled each other's enthusiasm.

Almost three weeks earlier and some eighty or ninety miles south of the hideaway Maeve and Kari sought, a young man had also made plans to run away. But he didn't run away from his parents and the boredom of school. He was escaping from the U.S. Army. He used the name Al, although that wasn't his real name. The less people knew about him, the better he liked it. Al was twenty-one. He had been confident that joining the army would be the answer to all of his problems, but he found the rigors of basic training at Fort Lewis, south of Tacoma, more than he'd bargained for. He didn't like getting up before dawn, he didn't like hikes in the rain, and he didn't like being told what to do every waking moment. Most of all, he didn't like the idea of being shipped to a war in Vietnam.

Another soldier, who was from Washington State, had told Al about the cluster of empty cabins near Index in Snohomish County. He said that lots of the places up there were too deep in the woods to appeal to their city-dwelling owners in the winter. He directed Al toward Stevens Pass in the snowy foothills of the Cascades. From what Al could gather, a lot of people showed up there in the wintertime for reasons of their own.

The deserted cabins would be only the first phase of Al's plan. He had studied maps to find a place where he could cross the Canadian border without a lot of questions from the border patrols. Once free of the United States, he hoped to get on a plane or a boat to Sweden. Reportedly, many American draft dodgers and servicemen like him, who were absent without leave, had taken refuge in Sweden. He had picked up on rumors that an active underground, run by conscientious objectors, would shelter runaways from military service.

Al figured he'd blend in—protective coloration, as it were—in Sweden. He was blond with a crisp wave of hair that fell over his forehead, and he had dark eyes under heavy brows. He was a handsome young man, six feet tall, broad-shouldered, and trim but muscular. He was also outgoing and convincing. People liked him and were drawn to him—especially women, whether they were little old ladies or young girls. All he had to do was

grin. If there was rage just beneath his attractive facade—
and there was—he hid it completely.

Al hitched a ride north to Seattle and beyond. He visited with some relatives near Everett and then rode with a
truck driver through Sultan, Gold Bar, and Startup. He
was looking for a place called Mineral City.

The truck driver shook his head. "Never heard of it,"
he said, "and I've been driving Stevens Pass for years."

That shook Al a little. According to rumor, Mineral
City was a ghost town, a regular Shangri-la, with everything a man needed to live. Miners had abandoned the
settlement decades before, but the buildings were still
there. Al hadn't located it, but he figured it was too small
to show up on the map he'd bought at the service station.
In truth, there was no such place.

There *was* an area called Garland Mineral Springs, or
Garland Hot Springs. It had once been a mecca for those
who believed that the minerals in the spring water would
cure all manner of physical ills. The springs were fourteen miles east of Index on the Index-Galena Road. The
road wound north from Index and then east along the
north fork of the Snohomish River and past the Troublesome Creek Campground and the San Juan Campground
to Garland Mineral Springs before it meandered tortu-
ously south back to Jack Pass and Highway 2. The road
was used mainly by loggers. Garland Mineral Springs, a
scene of former grandeur, was now in disarray. Lodges
and buildings designed to attract health pilgrims had long
since fallen into skeletal ruins.

In summer, the area Al sought was verdant and invit-
ing to experienced hikers who were trail-wise and willing
to venture so far from civilized roads. In February, however, it was buried in snowdrifts, and icy tentacles clung
to the 100-foot fir limbs and the few buildings that still

had roofs. The foothills were over 5,000 feet high here: Troublesome Mountain, Bear Mountain, Frog Mountain. This was no place for amateurs.

It was sometime around February 2 when the tall young man known as Al lowered himself from the cab of the logging truck and headed into the tiny town of Index. Beyond his clean-cut handsomeness, he was not particularly unusual-looking, but there are so few strangers in Index in midwinter that almost any newcomer is noted and remembered. In the summer, things are a bit different; vacationers come and go for a week's hiatus from the city noise in the jerry-built cabins that dot the hills around the village. Strangers are commonplace in Index in August; they stand out in February.

Al had stopped for a beer in an Index tavern and made small talk with the bartender as he drank. The bartender noted that the stranger carried a duffel bag and wore jeans that had been slit up the outside leg seams and then laced together with rawhide. The young man, who said his name was Al, obviously wasn't a complete novice about winter survival; he wore an orange-and-green field jacket, gloves, a scarf, a sweater, and heavy-duty brown boots.

He said he was from California and he carried a map, which he said would lead him to Mineral City. The bartender had never heard of such a place, but he nodded noncommittally. Fantasies are not unheard of in taverns and he had heard a lot of stories in his job. If the stranger thought he was going to find some magic place up in the woods, let him dream.

Some distance out of Index, two young men occupied one of the rustic cabins that were sprinkled through the woods. They had come by it honestly; they paid rent on it every month. The men, known as Handy* and Digger,* were conscientious objectors. By inclination and principle, they were opposed to violence in any form. Because of their pacifist beliefs, they were involved in the underground passage system that smuggled draft evaders into Canada. Although many would find fault with their activities, few would argue that their participation in the underground was for any personal gain. Handy and Digger took risks to help other young men who felt the way they did about war. In return, they received nothing more than the knowledge that they were following their consciences.

The man named Al wandered up the Index-Galena Road to Handy and Digger's cabin a few days later. They gave him a place to sleep, fed him, and listened as he explained that he could not bear to hurt or kill anyone.

"I can't go to Vietnam," he said hoarsely. "I can't shoot someone. I have to get to Canada."

"We'll help you," Digger said. "We'll get you there." He and Handy explained that a lot would depend on the weather. Until they could assure him of safe passage into Canada, they would see that he had enough to eat and a place to stay.

The temperature dropped and the drifts grew deeper, and Al became something of a familiar sight around Index.

A few weeks later, Maeve Flaherty and Kari Ivarsen hitchhiked into Index. They were carrying supplies that they naively believed would see them through the mountain winter: several changes of clothing, a hammer, some nails, matches, and their eye makeup.

The two girls started walking up the Index-Galena Road away from civilization, looking for a cabin where they could settle in for the next few months. But night fell and caught them far from shelter. They managed to find a lean-to where they huddled together for the night, curling up spoon fashion to share their body heat. But it wasn't enough as the night deepened and the temperature plunged lower and lower. In desperation, the girls managed to set fire to the shelter, and the hard wood burned long enough and hot enough to keep them from freezing. They were grateful to see a pale sun come up, saving them from what had seemed like an endless night.

With the resiliency of youth, Kari and Maeve pushed farther into the woods. Eventually they came to Handy and Digger's cabin. They could see that someone probably lived there, although no one was home at the moment. They found a vacant cabin nearby, and Kari and Maeve used their hammer to break into it.

They were like little girls playing house. They swept the floor, started a fire in the fireplace, and prepared to settle in. Later that day, they met Handy and Digger, their "old ladies," and Al, their houseguest. Al smiled widely and held out his hand. Maeve and Kari liked him. He made them laugh and they thought he was awfully good-looking. After walking away from Fort Lewis, Al had grown a mustache and a Vandyke beard, which gave him a rather exotic appearance. His dark eyes were compelling as he stared at Kari and Maeve; he seemed fascinated by their story of running away to find a mountain hideaway.

The two teenagers felt as if the adventures they sought were beginning. They had met two genuine hippies, their girlfriends, and Al, who seemed concerned about them and who was very helpful and attentive.

After Maeve and Kari had spent a few nights in the cabin, Al came to them and suggested that perhaps the three of them should move farther into the woods. Handy and Digger were paying rent for their cabin, but the three of them were not. "I'm afraid somebody's going to show up to evict us," Al said worriedly, "or worse. You know, strictly speaking, we're breaking the law by being here. We could be in big trouble if they found us."

As the girls listened nervously, Al said he had heard that police were planning to move into the area and flush out squatters who didn't belong in the summer cabins. He would end up in jail, and they might have to go to juvenile hall. Kari said she was eighteen, but Maeve looked anxious. Juvenile hall would be even worse than a private girls' school.

Al had an air of authority about him, and Kari and Maeve realized that he was probably right about moving deeper into the woods. They had managed to walk into these cabins easily. The police could show up at any time; they weren't really very far from town. After a short discussion, they agreed to pack up and join Al in hiking farther from the highway as soon as he was ready.

They had known Al for several days, but they felt as if they had known him longer. He seemed a lot wiser about the world than they were and Kari and Maeve had come to count on him. It felt safer to have a strong man to look after them. It had been so scary the first night when they had to burn their shelter to survive. With Al leading the way, they wouldn't have to worry about being caught in a snowstorm again.

The trio started out the next morning. The Index-Galena Road grew narrower until it seemed to disappear completely in huge waves of white as they neared the Troublesome Creek area. There they had to break through drifts and wade through waist-deep snow. They were vastly relieved when they finally came to several habitable cabins standing side by side in a narrow clearing that had been hewn from the thick forest. It was almost like seeing a mirage in the desert, but this was real, the little cabins placed improbably in a nearly impenetrable forest of towering fir trees.

The snow on the tiny cabins' roofs was five or six feet deep, and drifts nudged so close to the doorways that they had to scoop the snow away with their hands before they could force the doors open. The cabins were only about ten feet by fifteen feet, and, of course, there was no electricity or running water. Still, with the sun shining down on it, the whole setup looked like a scene from the Swiss Alps. The girls half expected to see Heidi come leaping through the snow.

They would be safe here. The owners wouldn't come to check on their cottages—not with all those snowdrifts they had waded through. And the police couldn't drive this far; the road was drifted over for miles behind them.

Maeve and Kari took one cabin; Al chose one right next door. They filled lamps with coal oil and were delighted to find the cupboards stocked with enough canned food and staples to last them until spring.

Their first few days in the cabins were idyllic. They popped corn, played in the snow, and rearranged the rustic furniture in their cabins. Maeve and Kari felt good about joining up with Al. He was just a nice guy. He hadn't made any sexual overtures. It hadn't taken them long to find out that girls on the run had to expect men to come on to them, but Al wasn't like that. He was kind of like a big brother.

It was lonely way back there in the woods, though, and quieter than they had ever imagined it could be, with no television or radio, only the wind in the trees, a few birds calling, and crashes in the forest when a load of snow slipped off a tree branch high in the air. Maeve and Kari weren't afraid, but they *were* grateful for Al. They were especially thankful for him when they began to hear frightening noises—sounds that they couldn't identify.

One night the three of them were spending an evening in front of the fireplace in the girls' cottage. The coal oil lamps and the fire on the hearth sent flickering shadows on the rough walls, and the wind whistled against the frosted windows. It seemed as if they were the last people alive on the planet. And then suddenly there was a harsh scratching noise against one wall. It sounded as if an animal was trying to claw his way in.

Kari and Maeve had confided to Al that they worried about wolves and coyotes—and bears. Most of all, they were terrified of the Sasquatch—the legendary half-man, half-beast rumored to rove free in among Washington's mountains. There are those who swear they have seen the Sasquatch and his mate. The girls had even seen a blurred photograph that someone took of a creature who walked upright with a face that was half human and with thick, straggly hair sprouting from his body.

"The Sasquatch is ten feet tall," Kari whispered, "and they say he leaves a footprint eighteen inches long. If he wanted to get in, he could."

They listened, their voices hushed, to the scrabbling sound against the wall. After a while, the scratching stopped, but sitting around the fire wasn't much fun anymore, and the girls didn't feel like laughing at Al's jokes. When Al left to return to his cabin, Maeve and Kari bolted their door and decided to leave the lamps burning all night.

Just as they began to feel a little less frightened, they heard a shout and a cry for help. Shaking, they forced themselves to open the door. They found Al in the snow where he had fallen from a footbridge. He said he didn't think he could walk, so they lifted him and helped him to his cabin. Once they got him there, he didn't seem to be badly hurt, just shaken up. The girls scampered back to their own cabin.

They had scarcely gotten the door bolted when there was a tremendous, violent scratching and clawing against the wall. Whatever was out there had to be huge. They heard a powerful thump, as if something was hurling itself at their fragile cabin in an attempt to break through the wall. When the thumps grew louder, Kari screamed and Maeve sobbed in panic as they ran to Al's cabin, hysterically crying for his protection. But he wasn't there.

They screamed his name for several minutes, afraid to stay on his porch and afraid to go back to their cabin. Finally he came limping up, a dim figure in the dark.

"Where were you?" Kari demanded.

"I was chasing rabbits," he said. "Somebody has to get us some food."

"Did you try to scare us?" Kari asked accusingly.

Al shook his head and looked hurt. "You know me better than that. I wouldn't ever try to frighten you. But maybe you two had better bunk over here tonight just in case there *is* something out there trying to get in."

If they had any qualms about sharing a one-room shack with Al, they needn't have worried. He was a perfect gentleman. He slept in his bunk, and Kari and Maeve curled up in their clothes in the other. There were no more animal sounds, and gradually they all fell asleep.

Still, with the morning light, Kari and Maeve made a decision. Life in the deep woods was not the picnic they had pictured. They were afraid something "out there" was trying to get them. Also, it was still snowing, and they were fearful that the snow would cause their roof to collapse. Then they wouldn't have anything between them and the creatures that came out at night. The sky looked as if another snowstorm was on the way. If they didn't leave now, they might miss their last chance to get through the drifts to the road.

Al tried to talk them out of leaving. They had all been having a great time, he said, and they shouldn't let some branch scraping the cabins in the wind scare them away. "I have a gun," he said.

"Where did you get a gun?" Maeve asked, surprised.

"From this woman who lives down near Index," he said. "She loaned it to me. If anything happens, I can take care of you."

"You can stay if you want to," Kari said, as she stuffed her belongings in her backpack. "We are getting out of here while it's not snowing and it's still daylight."

Maeve nodded. "Come with us, Al," she said. "There *is* something dangerous out in the forest. You heard it last night just as much as we did."

Suddenly even homework seemed okay. Maeve thought longingly of her family's warm house and her own bed.

"I can't change your minds?" Al said with a smile. "Aren't we the Three Musketeers?"

"Nope," Kari said. "We're out of here."

Finally, grudgingly, Al agreed that maybe they *should* go. "But if you're going down to town, I'm going too. I don't want to be up here all alone."

Maeve and Kari didn't have adequate clothing or boots. They put on all five of their shirts and three pairs of jeans. They looked at their cabin for the last time and began to plow through the deep snow, headed for Index. They had almost ten miles to go, and they wanted to be sure they took the right fork in the road so they would head south past Snowslide Gulch and follow the river down to town. Al told them to go ahead. They moved slower than he did, anyway, and he would catch up with them. "I'll just get all my stuff in my duffel bag," he promised. "And I'll be along before you know it."

It was Saturday, February 27, although Kari and Maeve had just about lost track of the days of the week. There was no time up in the forest. No clocks. No radios to remind them. They slogged ahead, already feeling the snow seeping into their shoes.

The girls looked back to see if Al was following them, but they didn't see him as they rounded the first bend in what they hoped was the road. It was hard to tell.

It was midafternoon on Sunday when Handy and Digger heard someone frantically pounding on their door. They opened it to find Al, exhausted and disheveled. He was babbling something about a girl "being hurt" way back in the woods.

"You've got to get help!" he shouted. "She's way up there, and it's really bad. *Really bad.* Call the sheriff—or somebody."

Digger didn't stop to ask questions. He hurried out to where he knew there was a pay phone and called the Snohomish County Sheriff's emergency number.

The dispatcher gave the call to Deputy Allen Halliday who was on patrol in the Index area. He soon got backup from Deputy Frank Young. All the deputies knew was that someone was hurt—"possibly shot"—and the general location of the cabins up near Troublesome Creek Campground. But they realized almost at once that snow and ice prevented them from driving their patrol cars in to aid the injured girl.

Because its boundaries encompass so many perilous areas, Snohomish County has maintained one of the country's top search-and-rescue units for many years. Now Young and Halliday called Inspector C. R. "Bob"

Fisher, and he sent Deputies Don Daniels and Bob Korhonen in a four-wheel-drive vehicle that had snowmobiles aboard.

At the same time, Young called Detective D. C. "Doug" Engelbretson at home, where he was on call for the weekend.

"We don't know too much now," Young said, "but there's something strange going on here; maybe you'd better come up, Doug."

Fisher and his crew joined Deputies Young and Halliday. Digger and Hank told the rescue men that they thought a man they knew only as Al and two young women named Kari and Maeve had left several days before to go up the Index-Galena Road almost to Garland Hot Springs.

"I think they must have hiked a long way," Digger said, "maybe eight or ten miles. Al came down and said there was trouble, and one of the girls was injured."

"Where is he?" Fisher asked.

Digger shook his head. "I don't know. He's gone. He was gone when I got back here from phoning you guys."

Fisher's men, who had made almost a thousand rescues since their unit was mobilized, looked in the direction Digger gestured. A road—if it could be called that—extended at least partway through that area. After that they would be searching through a forest so deep in snow that any trail or road would be obliterated. Moreover, it was dark. Fisher had gotten the call at 2:30 P.M. Even though his group had gotten up there in record time, he estimated it might be after six before they could find whatever lay ahead in the black woods.

Halliday, Young, and Engelbretson waited anxiously as the four-wheel vehicle disappeared into the drifts. At Troublesome Creek, Fisher, Daniels, and Korhonen abandoned the rig and moved forward aboard snowmobiles.

At one point, their powerful lights played over bright crimson stains in the snow. It didn't look good.

It was 7:50 P.M. when the mobile radio at the base camp crackled. "We have the girls," was the terse message. "Have an ambulance waiting."

Doug Engelbretson, whose area of expertise was homicide investigation, waited anxiously, straining his eyes for the sight of lights coming back down the road from Troublesome Creek. Finally he hurried forward as the search-and-rescue rig emerged from the woods with two passengers on board.

Both were girls, but there was no time for Engelbretson to get much information about what had happened. One girl—the sixteen-year-old, whose name was Maeve Flaherty—was loaded at once into the waiting ambulance, which headed toward Providence Hospital in Everett. Kari Ivarsen, who said she was eighteen, seemed to be in shock but otherwise uninjured. She was taken where she could get warm and have some food.

Doug Engelbretson learned that Maeve Flaherty was alive when she reached Providence Hospital, but that she was in critical condition from a gunshot wound and was undergoing surgery.

Engelbretson waited until Kari Ivarsen was finally able to talk. He assured her that Maeve was alive and receiving expert care, but he did not mention how critical Maeve's condition was. Even though time was of the essence in finding the person who had shot Maeve, Engelbretson could see how delicate Kari's grip on reality was. He questioned her gently about what had happened up there in the deserted woods. As she spoke haltingly, he listened, horrified. Kari Ivarsen spun out a tale of twenty-four hours of shattering terror.

Kari recalled how she and Maeve had planned to walk

out of the woods to Index the afternoon before. "Al didn't want us to go, but we were afraid to stay," she said.

"Afraid?" Engelbretson asked.

"The snow—it was so deep—and we thought we might freeze. And there were funny scratching noises on our cabin at night."

Kari said that she and Maeve had put on as many clothes as they could to protect them from the freezing temperatures and had begun the nine-mile hike toward town. "We must have been walking for about an hour and a half when all of a sudden Maeve just fell forward into the snow. She just kind of keeled over.

"She seemed to be kind of out of her head," Kari remembered. "I didn't know what had happened, but I was scared. I started crying and screaming for Al, because I knew he would help us if he was around."

She said that Al was supposed to be following them into town, but he had sent them on ahead. She was relieved when Al heard her screams and caught up with them.

"I saw Al coming, hurrying to help," she said. "But before he got to us, he turned around and fired his rifle at something behind him."

"What was he shooting at?" Doug Engelbretson asked.

"He said there were two men on the ridge who were shooting at us. He shot at them to drive them off," Kari said.

Kari said that she and Al considered trying to get Maeve down to Index for help, but they knew it was too far. Somehow they managed to get her on her feet, and, half-carrying her between them, they finally made it back to the cabin.

Kari closed her eyes, remembering a nightmare. "I remember saying, 'Maeve, you're in shock,' and she said, 'Yes, yes, I've been shot.' And I said, 'No, no: *you're in shock.*' But then I undressed her and I held the flashlight over her back, and I said, 'My god, Maeve, you *have* been shot!' "

Kari said that she and Maeve had been so thankful to have Al there. "He said he had worked for a veterinarian in Kansas," Kari told Engelbretson. "He said that he knew enough about medicine to get the bullet out."

Al had taken complete charge of the situation, according to Kari Ivarsen. "He told me to get clean snow to pack the wound in Maeve's back to kill the pain. Then he took this huge bread knife from the kitchen table, and he cut a large *X* across the wound."

Kari had watched him work over Maeve. He seemed to know what he was doing, but he couldn't find the bullet. She didn't know why they had to take the bullet out right away, but Al said they had to.

"Every time Maeve moaned from the pain, Al packed more snow on the wound to freeze the area," Kari said. "And then he said he needed something sharper," Kari recalled. "He got a piece of glass—"

"Glass?" Engelbretson asked quickly.

"Yes . . . just a piece of broken glass, and he filed it down until it was pretty sharp, and he started probing with that."

Next, Kari said, Al took a broken pool cue and stuck it in the ugly bullet wound, saying he could feel the bullet but that he needed tweezers to get it out.

Kari told Doug Engelbretson that she had begun to sense that something was not right. A growing horror had risen in her, she said, as she watched Al working over Maeve, who was in and out of consciousness at this point.

"He was enjoying it," Kari said.

"What do you mean?"

"Her pain was turning him on," she said. "I realized he wasn't trying to help her—not really. He was enjoying sticking the knife and the glass and that pool cue into her."

With that awful knowledge, Kari said she had begun to wonder who had really shot Maeve. They hadn't seen anyone except Al. They had only his word that snipers were firing at them. Al had a gun, and she had learned that he was behind them all the time they were walking, although they had not heard or seen him. It was as if he was stalking them like deer or rabbits.

Kari said she thought as fast as she could. If she panicked, she knew that neither she nor Maeve would get out of that cabin alive.

"I told him that maybe we'd better let her rest awhile," Kari said. "I told him I would fix her some hot soup, and maybe that would give her some strength."

To her great relief, Al had agreed. Maeve couldn't eat much, but Al stopped trying to operate on her. She tossed and fretted, but occasionally she was able to take a few sips of soup. Kari said she felt a little more confident that Maeve would survive, because she could see very little blood from the wound, except for the irritation Al had caused by probing for the bullet.

"Still," she told Englelbretson, "I was afraid that Maeve might be bleeding internally. I thought about walking down to town by myself to get help, but I couldn't leave Maeve alone in the cabin with Al, and I didn't know if I could find the road in the dark. Besides, if Al really had shot Maeve, what was to stop him from discovering Kari was gone, shooting Maeve again—and then tracking Kari down in the night?"

It was full dark by then, and Kari knew that none of them would be able to get out of the woods until morning. She was frightened that Maeve wouldn't live that long, but she didn't know what she could do to save her.

"I sat up all night, watching over Maeve," Kari said. "I watched Al, too, and it looked as though he was sleeping. His gun was on the other side of the cabin. I wondered if I could reach it before he did if I went for it."

At 7:30 A.M., it began to get light outside. Maeve was still alive, and Al didn't seem to suspect that Kari no longer trusted him. From time to time he said he probably should go for help. When she heard that, hope rose in Kari, but two hours passed and Al made no move to leave.

Finally, at nine-thirty, Al did put on his coat. Kari waited for him to pick up his rifle, but he left it leaning against the wall. He promised to come back with help as soon as he could. Hours passed, with no sound but the crackling of the fire and the wind whistling around the cabins. It was bitter cold, and Kari expected that it would start to snow again at any time.

"Finally I said, 'Maeve, we've got to try to walk out, or we might be here all winter.' And I got her on her feet and dressed, but the minute I got her out the door, she fell down and couldn't move. She said one of her arms didn't have any feeling."

Kari would not leave her friend alone. So the two girls went back into the cabin, which had become their prison. They waited. And waited. And waited.

Kari said she realized that she had been a fool to believe that Al would send help. If he had shot at them—and she believed now that he had—why would he send someone to rescue them?

Kari admitted to Engelbretson that she finally began to panic. Maeve would die up there, and then she might, too. She didn't know where Al was—maybe hiding outside, waiting to play some more of his sick games. Still, she felt she had to do *something*. Another night was coming on, and the icy cold had already begun to creep into every corner of the cabin. No longer thinking clearly herself, Kari said she tried once more to get Maeve on her feet and moving toward Index.

"And then," the pretty girl said, smiling faintly, "we went outside, and the snowmobiles found us."

While Engelbretson awaited word from the hospital, he talked to a young boy who lived near Handy and Digger. The youngster said his mother had loaned Al the .22 rifle. "I got that gun in a trade," the boy said. "It was an Ithaca Model M49 that fired .22s short and longs."

In Providence Hospital, doctors worked desperately over Maeve Flaherty. She needed surgery, but they had to get her strong enough to withstand it. When she was stabilized, they rushed her into the operating room.

Maeve was in surgery for hours. As the surgeon probed, he was astounded to find that only a miracle had kept her alive so far. A .22 caliber bullet had entered her back. If it had traveled in a straight line, it would have pierced her heart. But .22 bullets travel at high speed, and if they hit a bone, they are deflected and their paths altered. This bullet had hit one of Maeve's ribs and changed course. The impact had caused the bullet to "mushroom" before it entered one of her carotid arteries—arteries present on either side of the neck that provide oxygenated blood to the brain. By a freak of fate, the mushroomed bullet had formed a crudely effective plug to prevent hemorrhaging. Had the bullet bisected the carotid artery instead of becoming stuck in it, Maeve Flaherty would have bled to death within three to five minutes.

As it was, the stoppage of blood to the brain on the affected side had acted like a small stroke. This explained why Maeve had complained of a lack of feeling in one

arm and hand. Whether it would be permanent could only
be determined by time.

Maeve's doctors cautiously predicted she would
live—*if* infection or complications didn't develop.

Surgeons wondered why that tiny mushroomed bullet
had not been jarred loose during Kari's attempts to walk
her friend out of the woods or during the rough snowmo-
bile ride down through the drifts. And they thanked God
that Al had not been able to reach it as he tried to remove it.
The bullet that almost killed Maeve had also saved her life.

Detective Doug Engelbretson issued a wanted order
on a young white male, five feet eleven to six feet tall,
twenty-three to twenty-six years of age, with medium
blond hair two or three inches long, brown eyes, a three-
week growth of beard, and a heavy mustache. The man
might be called Al. Kari Ivarsen remembered that he had
a scar on his right thumb.

Early Monday morning the investigative team from the
Snohomish County Sheriff's Office went back into the
wilderness where they had rescued Maeve Flaherty. They
found tracks in the snow, all leading toward Index. They
found the ridge with the platform where Al had said he'd
seen men shooting, but there were no footprints indicating
that anyone had been there recently. There had been no
snowfall since Maeve was shot, so the unbroken snow on
the ridge pretty well wiped out Al's story about snipers.

They did, however, find other tracks—tracks indicating that a lone stalker had trailed the two teenage girls as
they headed for town and safety. Someone had moved
stealthily along a creek bed just below the road the girls
walked on. From time to time the tracks went up the
banks of the creek bed, suggesting that the stalker had
climbed to a spot where he could take a bead on the road.

Just as a hunter stalks an animal, a man alone had obviously stalked the helpless girls. Evidently he had waited until the opportunity for a perfect shot presented itself. Then he had fired.

Back at the cabin, the sheriff's men found several knives sharp enough to probe for a bullet. Why, then, had Al used a dull bread knife, a piece of glass, and a pool cue?

"This man is a sadist," one investigator said. "He wanted to hurt her as much as possible. If we don't find him, I have a terrible feeling he'll do it again."

Deputy Frank Young, who was fairly new in the department, offered his time—on-duty and off—to Doug Engelbretson. Engelbretson, a former assistant police chief of Snohomish, Washington, and a seventeen-year veteran in law enforcement, was glad to have the help; they had at least twenty-five cabins to check.

It was almost March, and down in Everett, where their offices were, crocuses, daffodils, and pussy willows were budding out, but it was bitter winter in the mountains. Their breath froze and hung in the air as the investigators tromped through the drifts. They questioned every resident they could locate. Some locals had seen the elusive Al, but he had been very careful not to reveal anything at all about his plans or his background.

Doug Engelbretson talked again with Handy and Digger. They, of course, had every reason not to want to talk in any depth with a lawman. But Engelbretson knew they were opposed to violence of any kind.

"This man we're looking for," he began, "isn't the nonviolent type he told you he was. He shot that little girl, and then he operated on her just to hurt her more. I don't think he's the sort of person you want to protect. You think about it. If you can help me, call me at home any time. Leave your first name or don't leave any name at all. I'll know."

Handy and Digger nodded. "We'll see what we can do."

A day later an anonymous informant called Engelbretson. "The man you're looking for is named Daniel Albert Prentice.* He's AWOL from Fort Lewis, and he came from Salem, Oregon, to begin with."

Before Engelbretson could ask more, the phone went dead.

Armed with this information, however, the Snohomish County detective was able to locate Oregon records on Prentice. The suspect was on probation out of Reedsport, Oregon, charged with assault with a deadly weapon. He had apparently managed to hide that fact from army recruiters, but Daniel Albert "Al" Prentice had shown a predilection for violence in the past. Oregon authorities promised to co-operate completely in locating the missing man.

Doug Engelbretson had assured Handy and Digger that they could trust him, and his word was good. It paid off several days later. He received a phone call at home that spurred him into action.

"Listen," the voice began. "The man you want is being shuttled up to Canada after midnight tonight. He's going out of Redmond on 405 to Bothell and then north to the border at Sumas. We know now that he's not one of us—he wanted to kill that girl—and we won't cover for him. He's yours if you want to stop us along the road."

"What will you be driving?" Engelbretson asked.

"A dark blue Chevy van—license number J78862. There'll be three of us. He'll be the short-haired man in the middle. Me and Digger will be the long-haired hippies."

"Okay," Engelbretson said. "We'll intercept between Everett and Arlington. I won't tell you where—you'll act too nervous if you know. But we'll be all around you."

Engelbretson contacted Detective Sergeant Tom Hart at home in Arlington, and Hart said he would approach

Highway 9 from the north. Detective Jerry Cook would come in from the east. A patrol car would approach from the west, and Doug Engelbretson and Frank Young would head toward Arlington from the south.

Sometime before dawn, Hart radioed that he had the van in sight.

"We're moving in," Engelbretson responded. "We should intercept at Frontier Village."

It happened fast. One minute Prentice was relaxed and confident that he was almost free and clear in Canada. The next moment the van was surrounded by Snohomish County sheriff's vehicles, marked and unmarked. Digger and Handy bailed out of either side of their van and out of the line of fire. But the officers didn't have to shoot. Prentice was ordered out and told to lean against the van while he was frisked. He obeyed meekly.

"You're under arrest for first-degree assault with intent to commit murder. I must advise you of your rights," Engelbretson said, and he read Prentice his *Miranda* rights.

"What's it all about?" Prentice asked casually.

"A sixteen-year-old girl," Engelbretson answered tersely.

Prentice gave his name as Frank Fink.

One of the deputies, a man who had not been briefed on all the facts, moved in to arrest the long-haired duo who accompanied the suspect. Digger and Handy looked at Doug Engelbretson, a question unspoken in their eyes.

"They're with us," Engelbretson said. "Just let them move on."

The deputy did as he was told, but he stood shaking his head as Digger and Handy drove off.

At sheriff's headquarters, Engelbretson again informed "Frank Fink" of his rights. The suspect gave a statement, repeating his story of the unknown snipers who had shot at Kari and Maeve.

Engelbretson held up his hand and said quietly, "Dan, you're not telling me the truth. You stalked those girls as if they were deer, didn't you? . . . And then you shot Maeve."

Suddenly Prentice shuddered, drew a deep breath, and blurted, "Yes!"

Although he claimed to have no explanation for why he had attacked the girls who thought he was their friend, he admitted that he had hunted them, stopping from time to time to draw a bead, and then dropping back until he got a better shot. He said that he had shot Maeve through the back because he'd figured the bullet would go right through her heart. If she had died, he planned to shoot Kari dead too.

After the first shot, he said, he came to his senses. He fell to the snow and asked himself why he had done it. Finally he made himself get up and go to them.

Master criminalist George Ishii, who headed the Washington State Police Crime Lab, did ballistics tests on the bullet taken from Maeve Flaherty's neck and the .22 rifle Prentice had abandoned in the cabin. Under a scanning electron microscope, all the lands and grooves matched perfectly.

Daniel Prentice went on trial in Snohomish County Superior Court on August 5, 1971. Deputy Prosecutor David Metcalf presented the almost unbelievable case to a jury of Prentice's peers. Maeve Flaherty and Kari Ivarsen took the stand to recall the frigid night when their trust in Prentice turned to terror.

The jury quickly returned a verdict of guilty, and on September 17, Prentice was sentenced to twenty-five years in a Washington prison.

Doug Engelbretson had found his man, beginning

with only a description and a false name: Al. Amid those endless acres of snowdrifts he had found one of the most dangerous criminals he had ever hunted. Handy and Digger had held the key, and while they had no reason to trust cops, they *had* trusted Doug Engelbretson and he had kept his word to them. They would return to what they did, and the quiet-spoken detective would go back to his work.

Handy and Digger, the conscientious objectors who knew they were placing themselves in jeopardy but felt Prentice was so dangerous they had to take the chance, have long since moved on from Index to an unknown destination. The war in Vietnam that they deplored is over. For a short time, they fought a different kind of violence.

Maeve Flaherty recovered from the bullet wound that almost killed her, but she was left with semiparalysis in one hand and memories of terror that never quite went away. She and Kari had believed in a kind of love that was idyllic but dangerous—a love that included a trusting acceptance of everyone they met. They were ultimately disillusioned by Al. And yet they found the purest, most selfless kind of love in Handy and Digger.

And, I might suggest, in Doug Engelbretson who would not rest until their attacker was safely behind bars.

One question has always puzzled me. On the first night that Maeve and Kari heard an animal thrashing and scratching against their cabin, Al was *inside* with them. He could not have made the initial noises they heard, although it was certainly Al who made noise later that night when he said he was hunting rabbits. Who—or what—was outside their cabin? Could it have been the dread Sasquatch who scrabbled at the walls of the girls' cabin that wintry night in February? No one will never know.

In retrospect, Maeve Flaherty and Kari Ivarsen came to

realize that the monster they tried to escape from was not nearly as dangerous as the one they ran to for protection.

Today Kari and Maeve are women nearly fifty. Maeve suffered permanent physical damage from her bullet wound; both of them still carry a heavier emotional burden.

The Killer Who Never Forgot . . . or Forgave
(from *In the Name of Love*)

Of all the emotions humans feel, love may be the most confusing—and the easiest to misidentify. Infatuation, possessiveness, sexual attraction, jealousy, and passion have often been mistaken for true love. One of the strangest, saddest, and longest *cases I ever covered dealt with a married couple who had separated, reunited, and separated again. Their final "separation" brought one of them into court in a series of trials that seemed endless. I spent two Christmas seasons on the hard benches of a King County Superior Courtroom, taking copious notes.*

And so did the defendant in a double murder trial.

And so did the deputy prosecuting attorney.

Every morning we passed a huge Christmas tree in the lobby of the courthouse, but inside the courtroom, there was no holiday season.

The defendant was attractive, charming, and so at ease it seemed impossible that he was on trial for the premeditated murder of two members of his own family.

And yet he was *on trial—not just once but twice. If what the deputy prosecutor said about him was true, love had disintegrated into blind jealousy and then murderous hatred until finally the most innocent victim of all was killed because of an erroneous assumption.*

The trials culminated at Christmas, but the case had begun close to another holiday weekend. The tragic story of Jody* and Arne Kaarsten* first made headlines on July 6, 1966, the Wednesday after a long Fourth of July weekend. It was only a little over two weeks past the summer solstice, and the sun rose early in the Northwest that morning. Although dew still clung to the grass, it had been daylight for more than three hours when twenty-three-year-old Arne Kaarsten appeared at his next-door neighbor's house in the suburb of Kent, where the one-story homes were built close together. It was typical sixties mass-produced construction where the same three or four floor plans were repeated in every third or fourth house; only different colored paint and varied landscaping made the homes individual. For the most part, this was a neighborhood of young married couples.

It was a little before 8:00 A.M. when Arne Kaarsten pounded frantically on the kitchen window of Ted Pearce's home. Pearce looked up, startled, to see Kaarsten, dressed in a bathrobe, carrying his two-and-a-half-year-old daughter, Terry.*

"There's something the matter with Jody," Kaarsten gasped.

Pearce took the little girl and handed her to his wife.

317

Then he followed Kaarsten, who was already running back toward his own home. Arne entered his house through the sliding glass doors at the back, which Pearce knew opened into the dinette.

Pearce stepped inside and waited for his eyes to adjust to the dim light. "There," Arne said, pointing to what looked like a mound of blankets in the living room. "There she is."

Pearce moved closer until he could make out tufts of blond hair protruding above the blankets. He shoved away an overturned coffee table and snatched the covers back.

Twenty-two-year-old Jody Kaarsten lay absolutely still beneath them. She was face down and wore only a pair of bikini panties and a short quilted robe that was bunched up around her shoulders. Her panties had been pulled down just below her buttocks.

Numbly, Pearce touched her wrist. It was still warm, but he couldn't feel any reassuring pulse to show that her heart was still beating. He knew that she needed a doctor, but he could not imagine what might have happened to her. He wondered if she had somehow injured herself falling off the couch. While Arne stood there silently, Pearce ran to the phone and picked up the receiver.

There was no dial tone.

"Stay here, Arne," he said. "I'll run next door and call an ambulance."

Pearce was back within minutes. Arne hadn't moved. He seemed to be in shock.

"Ted, I think there's something around her neck," Kaarsten said quietly.

Pearce looked, but he couldn't see anything. He had to pull the blankets down and lift Jody's long blond hair away from her neck before he saw the man's necktie that cut deep into the tender flesh there. He tried to loosen it, but the garrote had been twisted around her throat so tightly that he could not even get his fingers beneath it.

Suddenly Arne cried out, "I forgot about the baby!" Pearce knew he was speaking of seven-month-old Peri Lynn, whose room was just down a narrow hallway leading from the living area. Arne ran now toward his younger daughter.

"Oh, my god!" Kaarsten's voice chilled Pearce. "The baby, too!"

Hoping against hope, Pearce ran to the nursery. He found Arne staring down at the motionless baby. "No, no," Pearce began, "she's just sleeping." But then he saw the pink satin ribbon—the kind used to decorate stuffed toys. It was embedded in Peri Lynn's neck just as the necktie encircled her mother's throat. Instinctively he reached out to get it off the baby's neck. But like the necktie, the ribbon was cinched too tightly for him to remove it by hand.

"Quick, get me a knife," he said to Arne Kaarsten. Understandably, Kaarsten seemed to be too stunned to help much. Instead, he led Pearce into the kitchen and pointed at the cabinets. Pearce rummaged through unfamiliar drawers until he came up with a paring knife. He ran back to the baby and cut the ribbon. Still, Peri Lynn did not move.

Now Pearce returned to Jody Kaarsten. He sliced once, twice, and once again at the tie that was wound three times around her neck. Finally it fell free.

But Jody Kaarsten did not move either.

Pearce knew that they needed all the help they could get. Again he ran home and called the Kent Police. However, the dispatcher determined that the Kaarsten home lay outside the boundaries of the small Seattle suburb and transferred the call to King County Police. He learned that the county police had been dispatched at the same time the ambulance call was logged and were already on their way.

It seemed as though hours had passed, but it had only been five or ten minutes. Ted Pearce returned to his stricken neighbor. He noted idly that Arne Kaarsten wore trousers, a T-shirt, and a bulky plaid robe. Arne kept repeating a litany: "Why did it have to happen to her? Why did it have to happen to *her?*"

Pearce didn't know if Arne was talking about his wife or his baby. Despite his neighbor's pleas that he go next door, Arne was adamant about remaining in his own home. He stared at his dead wife fixedly, as if he could will her back to life.

Two ambulance attendants came hurrying up the front walk, carrying a resuscitator. Skillfully the EMT turned Jody Kaarsten over and fitted an airway into her throat so that they could force air into her lungs. The machine made her breasts rise and fall artificially as air filled her lungs. Arne stood nearby and watched, transfixed, as his wife seemed to have miraculously come back to life.

"Is she breathing? *Is she breathing?*" he asked sharply.

The EMT shook his head, explaining that the breathing was really just an illusion, dependent on the machine. There were no signs of life at all. Arne sighed deeply.

Neither Jody nor Peri Lynn responded to the desperate efforts of the rescue team to save them. They had been dead too long before their bodies were discovered.

No one yet had asked why or how. It was hard enough just to accept that it had happened at all.

King County Patrol Officer Bill Gorsline arrived at the neat ranch home a moment later, followed shortly by fellow Patrolman Ken Trainor. Both urged Arne Kaarsten to leave his home. Finally he agreed to go next door with Pearce.

Gorsline glanced around the living room and saw that it was basically clean—the carpet vacuumed, the furniture dusted—but now it was in disarray. A woman's purse, its contents spilled out, lay on the floor beside the overturned coffee table; the change purse appeared to have been opened and pawed through. A diaper bag rested untouched on one chair, but a can of baby powder lay on the floor next to Jody Kaarsten's head. A copy of a book, *The Hospital War,* was on the floor nearby.

As Gorsline and Trainor waited for detectives from the Major Crimes Unit in downtown Seattle to respond, they moved carefully around the house. They saw that the bathroom floor was littered with curlers, bobby pins, and a diaper pin; the bathroom rug was twisted and had been pushed or pulled partway into the hallway.

Ken Trainor posted himself at the front door of the Kaarsten home to keep anyone from contaminating the crime scene. He heard a loud rapping sound and turned around. He was startled to see that Arne Kaarsten had returned to the house and was knocking on the living room window to attract his attention. Fighting exasperation because he knew the distraught widower was probably not responsible, Trainor beckoned to Kaarsten to come outside. But Kaarsten shook his head and signaled for Trainor to follow him.

"I've got something important to show you in the backyard," Kaarsten insisted.

"Look here," Kaarsten said, as they walked over the damp grass. "I was walking toward the house and I dropped my cigarette lighter. Then I kicked it accidentally, and it slid up against the house."

Trainor nodded, perplexed, wondering what Kaarsten was trying to say.

"So I bent over," Kaarsten said excitedly, "and when I

looked up I could see the reflection of broken wires in the telephone connection into the house. See?" He pointed toward the lower part of the home's siding.

Trainor didn't see. The wires were protected by a cover, and he couldn't see any break at all. Only when he placed his fingers beneath the plastic box and pulled it clear of the house a bit was he able to discern a break.

"I'll point that out to the detectives," Trainor promised, leading Kaarsten away from the home once more. "Now, I think you'll be more comfortable next door."

Kaarsten left, but he came back several times, anxious to assist the investigators in their assessment of what had happened. Every time they turned around, he seemed to be in their way. It was a hell of a thing, they realized, for a man to lose his wife *and* one of his children like this, and he had to be in shock, but neither of them had ever seen a family member so determined to be part of the investigation.

Detective Sergeant George Helland and Detective Robert Andrews reached the Kaarsten home shortly before 9:00 A.M. They saw that the 1,000-square-foot house was built on an open plan: the kitchen, dining area, and living room were actually one large room partially divided by counters. A door to the garage from the dining area stood half open. So did an outside door leading from the garage to the backyard.

A short central hallway led from the living-dining room to the nursery and then to Terry's room on the right. The bathroom and master bedroom were on the left. Someone, probably Jody Kaarsten, had apparently been sleeping on the convertible sofa in the living room, because it was folded down to the bed position.

The bed in the master bedroom was unmade, and a man's plaid bathrobe had been tossed across the end. A clock showing the correct time hummed away beside the bed.

Dirty glasses and ashtrays covered the tabletop in the dinette area. A single bowl half full of cereal stood amid the clutter.

Andrews photographed the interior while Helland made triangulation measurements. By measuring from Jody Kaarsten's body to fixed points in the house, he could establish exactly where the body and pertinent evidence had been found—if he ever needed to do so—even after her body was moved to the medical examiner's office. The two investigators dusted the exposed surfaces for prints.

They knew already that they were dealing with a case that defied any predictable pattern. A woman and a baby had been strangled in their own home—while an adult male and a small girl slept only a few feet away. While it was certainly possible for an intruder to enter a home and commit such brutal killings, the immediate question dealt with motive. The Kaarsten home was like any subdivision home a young couple just starting out might buy. The furniture was neat but inexpensive. There were no objets d'art, no jewels, furs, stereos, cameras—nothing to lure a burglar. Yes, Jody Kaarsten's purse had been rifled, but they wondered how much money the young wife could have had?

If the motive had been a sexual attack, surely Jody Kaarsten would have cried out to her husband for help. But Arne Kaarsten hadn't mentioned hearing screams. At this point, it didn't look like a rape that had progressed to murder. Jody's clothing was in disarray, but it had not been removed.

The clutter in the bathroom was odd. The rug rested halfway into the hall, and the curlers had been knocked to the floor, making it look rather as if she had been attacked while she was putting up her hair and then dragged to where she lay.

Even if rape *had* been the original motive, why would the killer have strangled little Peri Lynn? A seven-month-old baby could hardly have been a threat; she wasn't even old enough to stand up in her crib, much less crawl out of it. She couldn't talk. How could she have identified a killer?

Two-and-a-half-year-old Terry would have been more dangerous as a witness, but not much more. Two baby girls. Why would the murderer have killed the baby and left the toddler sleeping? Why hadn't Arne Kaarsten heard anything during the night?

Helland and Andrews went over the exterior of the home meticulously to see if any doors or windows had been jimmied or forced. None of them bore any marks. Sergeant Helland knelt to examine the cut telephone line. Like Trainor, Helland was unable to see the severed wires until he lifted the plastic cap that covered the terminal ends. As the single lead from the outside wall entered the plastic cap, it split into two segments, each leading to a terminal. One of these leads had been cut a few inches from the terminal. This would have caused the phone inside to go dead instantly.

Helland carefully cut this segment at the terminal end so that the severed end could be examined by the FBI laboratories. Then he made a temporary connection so that detectives could use the phone during their preliminary investigation. It had already been dusted for fingerprints.

The bodies of Jody and Peri Lynn Kaarsten were removed to the King County Medical Examiner's Office to await autopsy. The detectives stayed behind to bag and label everything in the house that might bear some trace evidence left by their killer.

As the morning progressed, more and more King

County detectives spread out over the area, questioning neighbors in an ever widening circle around the Kaarsten home. The Pearces, living right next door, were the first people interviewed. They were almost as shocked as Kaarsten himself; they said they had seen Jody Kaarsten at midnight the night before. They could scarcely believe that she was dead.

"Jody was over last night," Patti Pearce said. "They'd all gone down to Oregon for the Fourth of July. While she was down there, she had her hair bleached really blond, and she wanted to show us. Besides that, their phone was out of order, and she wanted to report it and call for the exact time because Arne said that all the clocks in the house had stopped."

It seemed that the Kaarstens' first day back from the long weekend had been marked by several unusual circumstances. The Pearces recalled Jody saying that Arne had told her he'd seen a man peering through their glass patio door earlier in the day. Arne Kaarsten evidently had not seen the man's face—only his legs. Then the peeper had run to the fence around their backyard and disappeared.

Patti Pearce said that Jody had arrived at their home about 10:00 P.M. Tuesday night and stayed until midnight.

Detective Ted Forrester was assigned the task of getting a statement from the widower. He offered to drive Kaarsten downtown to King County Police headquarters in the courthouse where he could give a formal statement about the events of the night and early morning. The Pearces volunteered to care for Terry, and Kaarsten rode into Seattle with Forrester.

Forrester is a kind, low-key man, and he was sympathetic to the young husband who had awakened to inexplicable horror. During the forty-five-minute drive to Seattle, Kaarsten spoke over and over about his loss. He explained that he and Jody had had a wonderful marriage. "We were the perfect family," he said. "I can't understand why she's been taken from me—in such a terrible way."

At headquarters, Chief of Detectives T. T. Nault talked with the grief-stricken young husband. Handsome, almost boyish-looking Arne Kaarsten had thick brown hair combed in a smooth pompadour. He told Chief Nault that he and Jody had been high school sweethearts. He had been nineteen and she a year younger when they married in November 1962. The teenage couple became parents the next year, when Terry was born.

"When was Peri Lynn born?" Nault asked.

Kaarsten looked down and bit his lip. "She was born on December 16, 1965. Last year."

Kaarsten said he was employed as a draftsman for a concrete conduit company. His avocation and his main interest, however, was race-car driving. Although he could not afford to own one of the expensive cars he raced, he said he drove for the president of a manufacturing firm who owned several cars.

Nault asked Kaarsten to recall the events leading up to the murder of half his family. Kaarsten sighed and began.

He recalled that the weekend just past had been particularly pleasant for his family. They had rented a car so they could drive to southern Oregon to spend the Fourth of July with Jody's relatives. The trip had been relaxing and fun, and he said he had been pleased when one of Jody's relatives bleached her hair for her. He said he loved the way she looked as a strawberry blonde.

They had driven home on Monday because Kaarsten had to work Tuesday. That afternoon—July 5—Jody had phoned her husband at work and asked him to pick up some supplies at the drugstore and bring them home on his lunch hour. He had gone to pick up Terry first, made the pharmacy trip in fifteen minutes, and come home to find that the door was locked.

"Locked?" Nault said.

Kaarsten nodded. "This was strange. Jody never locks the door in the daytime." He went on to say that she was very frightened. While he was gone, she had seen a man "in his twenties" and wearing work clothes prowling around outside their home.

Kaarsten said he went at once to the sliding patio doors to the backyard. He caught just a glimpse of a man's legs outside the patio doors, but the man disappeared before Arne could get outside and give chase. Pressed for more details, he shook his head. The glare of the sun on the glass doors had kept him from seeing more than the prowler's legs.

"Did you go back to work yesterday afternoon?"

"No, Jody was frightened, and both she and the babies were sick," Arne Kaarsten said. "I decided to take a half sick day from work so I could stay home and take care of them."

Later in the afternoon his wife and daughters apparently felt better. Kaarsten said they visited relatives, ate supper at a restaurant, and did some shopping at a discount store before returning home around 10:00 P.M.

It was only then, he said, that Jody had picked up the phone to call her family in Oregon and discovered the line was dead. She decided to run next door to the Pearces' and report it.

Kaarsten was struggling to recall the evening before in sequence. "I began to feel sick myself at that point," he said. He and Jody had agreed they would get a better night's sleep if he slept alone in the bedroom and she slept on the fold-down couch in the living room. They thought they had probably picked up some kind of twenty-four-hour flu while they were in Oregon.

He said one of his relatives was a nurse and had given him some sleeping pills. They had worked so well that he fell asleep almost immediately. He didn't know what time Jody had come back from the Pearces', and since she planned to sleep in the living room, she didn't disturb him when she got home.

"You hear anything last night?"

Kaarsten shook his head. "Nothing. I even slept past my usual wake-up time of six forty-five. I didn't wake up until a quarter to eight. Usually Peri Lynn wakes us at six forty-five."

But of course Peri Lynn did not wake up. Kaarsten said he had been half asleep when he wandered down the hall toward the living room. He had seen the pile of blankets on the floor, but he didn't immediately register what he was seeing. Only when he saw the blond hair poking out of the bedclothes did he realize that Jody was underneath.

He said he pulled the blankets back, then panicked at what he saw. "I grabbed Terry and ran next door to get help."

Nault wondered why Kaarsten had not grabbed Peri Lynn, too. Maybe he'd been afraid that Terry would wander out of her bedroom and find her mother dead. Maybe he just hadn't been thinking straight.

Arne Kaarsten told Nault that he was quite sure burglary had been the motive; Jody had had $100 in cash in her purse, and it was missing.

Nault wondered aloud why burglars had neglected to take Jody's diamond ring and her expensive watch. She was still wearing both when detectives arrived.

Kaarsten said he had no idea. None of this made much sense. But he was sure it had to do with the prowler who had been watching Jody though the patio doors. "I saw him," he said again. "I saw his legs. If only I'd managed to catch him . . ."

Arne Kaarsten thought the voyeur must have been the one who cut the phone line—so no one could call the police if he was caught inside the house. But the grieving widower was at a loss to understand why a burglar had picked his modest home.

Nault was puzzled, too—more than puzzled. There were elements here that made the skin prickle at the back of his neck. Burglars didn't break into little ranch houses when people were sleeping inside. It wasn't worth the risk. Also, burglars rarely killed when they were discovered; they ran. And burglars would have had no reason to kill a little baby. Furthermore, why would Kaarsten have bothered to check his wife's purse to see if the cash was missing? Wouldn't the motive for her murder have been the last thing on his mind when he was so filled with shock and grief?

Tactfully Nault questioned Kaarsten further about his marriage. He wondered if it was really the perfect union that Kaarsten had described. And slowly the picture of unblemished wedded bliss began to crumble. Kaarsten admitted that it had not been as idyllic as he had first described it.

Perhaps they had married too young; perhaps Jody had needed to know she was still attractive to other men. He said she had been unfaithful to him—something that he was embarrassed to admit but felt he had to explain, since her adultery might have had something to do with her murder.

Kaarsten said that Jody took a vacation—alone—to Oregon in April of 1965. While she was there she met another man. She spent a weekend with him. Her physical attraction to him was so consuming that she changed from the faithful wife she had always been. It was not like Jody to be unfaithful, but it happened. A week later, Kaarsten said, she flew back to Oregon to meet the man again. Her lover, Jack Kane,* seemed to have an almost hypnotic hold over his wife. In July, Jody actually left Arne and moved in with Kane in Oregon.

But Jody didn't stay long with Kane. She discovered she was pregnant. The baby would have been conceived in March—before she met Jack Kane; it was clearly Arne's baby. When Jody told her husband she wanted to come home and try again, he said he welcomed her with open arms. They reconciled, and according to the distraught man in front of Nault, their renewed marriage had been perfect ever since. Peri Lynn had been born six months later.

Nault had to ask an obvious question: "Did you ever think that Peri Lynn might not be your child?"

Kaarsten said the thought had crossed his mind several times. But he had decided it was destructive to worry, so he'd put it out of his mind. Born in mid-December, Peri Lynn was a full-term baby; that meant she had been conceived in March. As far as Kaarsten was concerned, Peri Lynn was his, and he accepted her just as he'd accepted Terry. Once he did so, the marriage had seemed to get better and better.

When he was asked to take a lie-detector test, Arne Kaarsten agreed readily. However, when the polygrapher, Norm Matzke, started to attach the leads of the machine that would register blood pressure, respiration, galvanic skin response, and heart rate, he could see that Arne Kaarsten was much too nervous and emotionally upset for his responses to be registered and evaluated accurately. It was just too soon. They would have to try again at a later date.

* * *

Kaarsten told the detectives that the necktie used to strangle Jody had been one of his own. It had to have been a weapon of opportunity. He remembered that he had taken it off, along with his sweater and jacket, when they came home the night before. He had draped the tie and his other clothing on the railing of Peri Lynn's playpen, which sat next to the couch.

Nault noted that Kaarsten had a Band-Aid on the back of his right hand. "You hurt your hand?" he asked casually.

"Yeah, I was roughhousing with Terry last night, and she scratched me accidentally."

"Can I take a look at it?"

When Kaarsten took the bandage off, Tom Nault could see that Kaarsten had two deep fresh scratches along the tendons between his middle and ring fingers. He jotted the information down but said nothing more.

It was noon—four hours after the bodies were found—when King County Medical Examiner Dr. Gale Wilson began the autopsies on Jody and Peri Lynn Kaarsten.

Jody was very slender at five feet six inches and 100 pounds. As Wilson had suspected, she had died of asphyxia by ligature. There were cruel bruises and indentations on the flesh of her neck where the necktie had cut in, and she had the characteristic pinpoints of petechial hemorrhages on her face and in her eyes, which were common to strangulation victims. The only other marks on her body were a bruise on the lower left side of her chin and vertical splits in the two middle fingernails of her left hand. It looked as if she had tried to fight off a hand that held the garrote that squeezed out her life. By measuring the degree of rigor mortis, lividity, and loss of body heat, Dr. Wilson determined that Jody Kaarsten had died between midnight and 2:00 A.M. the previous night.

Peri Lynn had died of the same cause, but she had no broken fingernails. She had probably been sound asleep when the ribbon from her teddy bear was placed around her neck and tightened.

The Kaarsten investigation was to become one of the strangest marathons King County Police detectives had ever participated in. They never fell victim to the tunnel vision that affects some departments. They eliminated all possible suspects, winnowing their theories down until there was only one possibility left.

They compiled a thick case file on every aspect in the double murder. They located Jack Kane, Jody's ex-lover, and Detectives George Helland and Len Randall brought him to Seattle for a secret preliminary hearing. The results of that hearing were announced through local news media, leaving the public even more bewildered than before.

It was a perfectly legal finding, though it was rarely used: "The deceased were killed by person or persons *known.*" People were accustomed to hearing that victims of unsolved murder cases were "killed by person or persons *unknown.*" That phrase was often used on television mysteries. If the police and the prosecuting attorney *knew* who the killer was, why hadn't they arrested someone?

Not surprisingly, murder cases are the most difficult to try; the defendant's life—either literally or figuratively—is in the hands of twelve jurors. If he or she is convicted, he will either be sentenced to death or be sent to prison for life. Ideally, the prosecution team wants to have a plethora of physical evidence to show the jury—something they can see, feel, hear, touch, or have explained to them by an expert witness.

Circumstantial evidence is helpful, but it is most effective as an adjunct to physical evidence. With only circumstantial evidence, the most confident prosecutor may have a few pangs of anxiety. If a defendant is acquitted of a crime, he cannot be tried again—other than civilly, as in the O. J. Simpson case—because double jeopardy will attach. Otherwise, defendants could be tried over and over and over for the same crime, and that would not be fair.

Most prosecutors prefer to play a waiting game, gathering as much evidence—both physical and circumstantial—as possible before they bring charges. Prosecutors often become the target of brickbats from reporters, who respond to a public demanding action.

An agonizing decision had been made in the case of Jody and Peri Lynn Kaarsten. Initially, there was not enough evidence to win a murder case. That did not mean the case was over, however, or that the victims had been forgotten by the detectives who had worked many overtime hours. They knew the name of the "person known," and they were biding their time until everything came together.

Three-year-old Terry Kaarsten went to live with relatives in another state. Arne Kaarsten picked up the threads of his life. He lost himself in his obsession with racing cars. He soon became better known as a racing celebrity than as the tragic widower who had lost his wife and infant daughter in a double homicide. Driving an English-built Chevrolet-powered Lola Formula A racer that cost $30,000, Arne Kaarsten became well known in racing circles in the Northwest. For true racing buffs, his fame extended to the rest of America. Arne wasn't the best, but he was good. He was described as a "fierce competitor" but a "temperamental loser."

The memory of the Kaarsten murders faded from the minds of the public, but not from the minds of King County detectives and prosecutors. George Helland, who had been promoted to lieutenant, often dropped into the Pacific Raceways track, where Kaarsten raced. There seemed to be no overt enmity between the two men. Kaarsten always greeted Helland with a grin and a handshake. If there was something beneath the surface of the greetings exchanged, it would have taken more than a casual observer to detect it.

Four years passed, and county elections brought a new King County prosecuting attorney and a new regime. A grand jury probe took the wraps off a number of cases that had lain dormant and almost forgotten in dusty King County files. The Kaarsten murders were among the cases that were reviewed.

Grand jury testimony is secret. Even the suspects' attorneys are not allowed into the inner sanctum where witnesses give testimony that may or may not lead to indictment. Among the witnesses called when the Kaarsten case was reopened was a married couple who had been extremely close to Arne Kaarsten. Knute Martin* owned Martin Marine Supplies and a stable of expensive racing cars; his much younger wife, Lily,* was an enthusiastic racing buff too. They had employed Arne to drive their Formula A, and he also worked in their marine products firm. Although they would continue to stand behind him both financially and emotionally, the testimony they gave behind the doors of the grand jury chambers was electrifying.

Twenty-nine-year-old Special Prosecutor Richard Mc-Broom and his associates, Gary Wagner and Jack Merrit, now urged that Arne Kaarsten be indicted for the murder of Jody and Peri Lynn Kaarsten. (Tragically, McBroom, a brilliant young special prosecutor, would not live to see the denouement of the indictment he had spearheaded; he died of a rare blood disease a year after the grand jury hearings of 1971.)

Deputy Prosecuting Attorney Jim Warme conferred with Lieutenant George Helland, and the two men agreed that they were morally bound to go into trial, even if the King County Prosecutor's Office had to do so armed only with the circumstantial evidence available.

Physical evidence that would have been invaluable if they were prosecuting a stranger for the murder of Jody and Peri Lynn was useless when the suspect was their own husband and father. Hairs, fibers, body fluids, and finger-prints found at the crime scene and traced to Arne Kaarsten meant nothing. He had lived in the same house with the victims. It was to be expected that he had left traces of himself there. Unless Kaarsten had left his fingerprint in his victims' blood, it would be of no evidentiary value. And his alleged victims had not bled. They had been strangled.

With his necktie. With the ribbon from Peri Lynn's own teddy bear.

On August 30, 1971—more than five years after the crimes of which he was accused—King County Detectives George Helland and Ted Forrester arrested Arne Kaarsten. He was charged with two counts of first-degree murder. He quickly posted $10,000 bail (10 percent of the $100,000 bail ordered) and walked away free. Although he was facing the most serious charge possible, Kaarsten would spend most of his time outside jail in the years to come. If he began to feel invincible, it was not surprising.

Arne Oscar Kaarsten's trial date was set for December 13, 1971.

A huge Christmas tree glittered in the lobby of the King County Courthouse as participants and spectators flocked to Kaarsten's trial. It was a bizarre trial. The defendant was not led into the courtroom in leg irons and handcuffed. He was not in jail during his trial. Instead, he was free to go to lunch at a local restaurant with his relatives and friends, and free to sleep in his own bed each night. Detectives, reporters, and the defendant often nodded across their lunch plates before returning to the courtroom.

Arne Kaarsten appeared to view his trial on two murder charges as only a slight interruption in his usual pursuits. He was confident and expansive—the very picture of a man who had been placed in a ridiculous position by some accident of fate. His attitude suggested that he would surely triumph. He smiled often and took voluminous notes during testimony. He betrayed neither dread nor sorrow.

The testimony elicited, however, was reminiscent of the classic film noir starring Barbara Stanwyck and Fred MacMurray, *Double Indemnity*. There was a story here— a story far more convoluted than the arguments between a young husband and wife living in a little ranch house in Kent, Washington.

Warme and his fellow prosecutor, Lee Yates, presented Arne Kaarsten in a new light. He was not, they suggested, the poised defendant the jury saw before them, not a man who allowed nothing to ruffle him or anger him. Instead, they described him as a man who was so enraged by his wife's infidelity that he had vowed to kill her for it. Moreover, they maintained that he had accomplished his revenge with a careful plan to gain financially from Jody's and little Peri Lynn's murder.

According to the prosecution, Jody Kaarsten's affair with Jack Kane was not as brief as Kaarsten had said it was. It was far from over when she returned to Kaarsten in June of 1965. Arne Kaarsten had been consumed with rage toward the couple who had cuckolded him. During a period when the Kaarstens had separated again, Jack Kane had the effrontery to come to Washington and actually spend several days with Jody in the home Kaarsten had provided for her. When Arne Kaarsten found them together, he was enraged, and he shouted, "One day I'll get you both!"

Even after Jody had returned to Kaarsten, ostensibly for good, she met with Jack Kane one last time, and they made love. By carefully backtracking her movements in 1965, the King County detectives had uncovered this information. Whether Kaarsten had found out about this final tryst before he learned of it in his murder trial was a moot question.

Had he ever forgiven Jody for betraying him? Warme and Yates suggested that he had not. He was, they said, a man who could put on a mask—a mask that hid his real feelings so flawlessly that Jody believed they had begun their married life again with a clean slate.

But Arne Kaarsten had wanted something far more than he wanted Jody. And the prosecutors said he had left a paper trail that detailed a meticulous plot to achieve two goals.

On March 27, 1966—little more than three months before Jody and Peri Lynn Kaarsten were murdered—Arne had answered an ad in a Portland, Oregon, paper. The ad offered a 1957 300SL Mercedes-Benz for $3,500. On March 29, Knute Martin, Kaarsten's racing sponsor, took out a note to buy that car. The car was for Arne, who would somehow have to come up with the money to pay off the note.

Ten days later, on April 6, Arne Kaarsten bought insurance policies on the lives of his wife and two daughters. Jody was insured for $7,500 and the youngsters for $15,000 each. The insurance was double indemnity. In case of accidental or other violent death, the policies would pay off twice as much.

During that period in 1966, Arne Kaarsten made slightly over $700 a month as a draftsman, adequate in that era to support a small family. But a salary of $9,000 a year could not satisfy a taste for expensive cars. And Arne Kaarsten had come to care for flashy cars far more than he cared for Jody.

On June 24 he attempted to borrow $3,800 from a bank. He explained to the loan officer that he wanted the money to exercise an option on a piece of property. As collateral, he listed a 1957 Mercedes-Benz, the car that he did not yet own. His listing of his assets continued as a work of fiction. He confided that he was being groomed for the presidency of his company, a blatant lie, and that he was a partner in another business, which had netted him $9,400 in 1965—another lie. To cinch the loan, he explained that he would receive a large bonus from his company within a month and could pay off the loan then—yet another lie.

The loan was denied when the bank found that the Mercedes did not belong to Kaarsten. Indeed, he wanted the loan to *buy* the car.

Twelve days after Kaarsten attempted to borrow $3,800 and three months to the day from the time he bought the insurance policies on their lives, Jody and Peri Lynn Kaarsten were dead.

An old friend of the Kaarstens testified for the prosecution. She had known Arne and Jody Kaarsten since they were newlyweds. They had been very happy then. Arne had been in her home, the woman said, on the day he found his murdered wife. He'd had a handkerchief folded over two deep scratches on his hand, which were still bleeding. When she asked what had happened, he told her that little Terry had accidentally scratched him. The next day Kaarsten had asked this female witness not to talk about the case to anyone but his attorney. She had found this request oddly troubling.

Even more troubling, however, was a conversation she had with Arne Kaarsten on the evening after they had attended the double funeral for Jody and Peri Lynn. Arne had suddenly pulled his insurance policies out of his coat pocket and said, "Hey, I didn't know it was double indemnity."

The witness had been shocked that he would actually be carrying the policies in his suit jacket when half of his family was being buried. She was even more shocked when he seemed so elated to find that they had double indemnity clauses.

Arne Kaarsten had filed his claims quickly and had collected an initial payment of $16,722.26 in insurance money.

Deputy Prosecuting Attorney Warme spoke to the jury and reconstructed the murders as he had deduced the sequence of events from the investigation.

"Jody Kaarsten returned from her neighbors' at midnight and went to the bedroom where Kaarsten slept," Warme explained. "She took off her dress, put on a robe, and then went to the bathroom to fix her hair. In the small bathroom a man came up behind her. She didn't scream. That man put Arne Kaarsten's necktie around her neck. She reached up with her hands to save her life—she split two fingernails fighting to breathe. She fell then . . . striking her chin, probably on the vanity. . . .

"Then she was possibly dragged or carried to the living room and covered with blankets. Maybe she was already dead; maybe she was still unconscious and dying. Seven-month-old Peri Lynn Kaarsten slept in her nursery. Someone's hand took a pink ribbon from a stuffed toy and put it around that baby girl's neck and strangled the life from her body."

The young deputy prosecutor didn't name names; he didn't have to—every eye in the courtroom was on Arne Kaarsten. But Kaarsten remained serene. When he looked up, he could see the photographs of Jody's and Peri Lynn's bodies; prosecutors had pinned the pictures to a corkboard at the front of the courtroom. Still, he continued to smile and chat with his coterie of supporters during breaks.

Other witnesses from the Kaarstens' neighborhood testified. It soon became clear that the "prowler" had been spotted by Arne and Arne alone. The jury had only his statement that Jody had seen the window-peeper too; Jody was dead and could not testify about what she had and had not seen.

The detectives who had been at the crime scene on that long-ago July morning testified that Arne Kaarsten had been "overly" helpful in providing them with information about peculiar events around his home prior to his wife's murder. It was Arne Kaarsten who saw the prowler's legs outside the patio doors. It was Arne who had led Ken Trainor to the severed phone wires. Although two detectives had to get down to ground level and lift the opaque cover over the wires, Arne had somehow been able to tell they were cut without raising the lid. Arne Kaarsten was the only one who knew how much money Jody had had in her purse. He was the one who said $100 was missing.

There were other bits of circumstantial evidence that marked Arne Kaarsten as a liar. Jody Kaarsten had told her neighbors that Arne said all the clocks in the house had stopped. Arne said that he had overslept because his alarm didn't go off. Why, then, had detectives found the clock in the master bedroom working perfectly the next morning? Jody had allegedly come home and gone to sleep in the living room without even going into the master bedroom. Had Kaarsten himself stopped to reset the bedroom clock in the morning before running to the Pearces for help?

A neighbor living directly across the street testified that he had been up preparing for work at 6:45 A.M. on that Wednesday in July. When he glanced through the front window of the Kaarsten house he saw a man wearing a bulky coat or robe in the Kaarsten living room. That was more than an hour before Arne Kaarsten, wearing his bulky bathrobe, ran for help to the Pearces' home shortly before 8:00 A.M. And even though detectives found that robe on the end of the bed in the master bedroom, Kaarsten insisted he had not worn it in months. Was it within the realm of credulity that an intruder—a man who had killed a woman and a baby—would still be lingering in the house long after daylight?

And who had prepared a bowl of cereal that morning and eaten half of it—only feet away from the body of Jody Kaarsten? Would a burglar-killer have been so brazen?

One of Arne Kaarsten's acquaintances testified about a strange conversation. When Arne learned that scrapings had been taken from Jody's nails, he had explained to his friend, "They'll probably find some of my skin. Terry scratched me, roughhousing, and then Jody cleaned Terry's nails with her own when she put her to bed."

This statement was inconsistent with his earlier statements. He had told police that *he* had put Terry to bed.

There were other discrepancies. Taken singly, they didn't mean that much. Considered all together, they suggested that Arne Kaarsten had concocted a plan that didn't fit, and so he had made it fit by continually changing his explanations.

If Arne Kaarsten's family had been sick enough for him to take a half-day off from work, why did he take them out to dinner, shopping, and visiting on that same day?

Even more difficult to understand was Jody's change in attitude. According to Arne, Jody had been so terrified of the prowler that she had locked her doors in the middle of the day. Wasn't it peculiar, then, that she had gone outdoors and through the dark yard to visit the Pearces? She had come home alone at midnight, too; she didn't ask Ted Pearce to see her safely home. She hadn't been at all afraid. And if Kaarsten had seen a prowler's legs and attempted to chase him earlier that day, why had he gone peacefully to sleep while Jody was out there in the dark?

When the defense began its case, Kaarsten's attorneys, Carl Richey and Larry Barokas, presented a number of character witnesses who attested to the harmony in the Kaarsten marriage at the time of the double murder. They also presented witnesses who said that Kaarsten was known to be a very sound sleeper. Again and again the defense attorneys stressed the fact that there was no physical evidence linking the twenty-three-year-old widower to the crime. Under the laws of the United States, Richey and Barokas were not saddled with the burden of proof. They did not have to prove that Arne Kaarsten was innocent; it was up to the prosecutors to prove beyond a reasonable doubt and moral certainty that he was guilty.

Richey and Barokas threw down their ace card when they called Jody's alleged lover, Jack Kane, to the stand. He was an attractive man in a carny-cowboy kind of way whose testimony often made jurors and the gallery smile.

Kane was only too happy to go into detail about his affair with Jody Kaarsten. He was obviously a ladies' man, and he admitted that he had been married several times. He also acknowledged that he had once been a patient in a mental facility. But he certainly did not appear at all deranged on the witness stand, and he told his story in a straightforward—albeit colorful—way.

Kane said he had first met Jody in April of 1965. "I fell somewhat in love with her that weekend," he testified. "The next Friday she called and said she was flying to Eugene [Oregon]. I met her, and we spent the weekend in a motel room. I saw her again at the Kaarsten home in May of 1965. I was shaving in the bathroom when Kaarsten came in. We shook hands and started making small talk. Terry came in and ran to me and said, 'Hi, Daddy!' "

"And what happened then?"

Jack Kane testified that Arne Kaarsten had stopped being civil at that point. "Kaarsten said, 'What the hell's going on?' Then he left and said, 'Okay. You guys go back to your funny little games. Someday, I'll fix both of you.' "

Larry Barokas focused on Kane's history of mental illness: "Didn't you tell your psychiatrist that you planned to blow up your in-laws with a detonator?"

"I may have," the witness admitted casually, explaining that he was angry with them at the time, but he insisted that he wouldn't really have harmed them.

"What was the reason you went to the hospital in the first place?" Barokas pressed. "Wasn't it for rape?"

Kane wriggled uncomfortably in his chair. "Well . . . I was only sixteen, and this older woman invited me over. When I walked in . . . well, she came out in hardly any clothes and I was scared . . . so I . . . Well, I just hit her."

It was clear that Barokas was attempting to set Jack Kane up as a viable suspect in the murders. But Kane insisted that he was not angry when Jody left him to go back to Kaarsten. He testified that she was pregnant and needed a husband to take care of her and that he was in no position to marry her. They had parted reluctantly but by mutual agreement.

"Where were *you* on July 6?" Barokas asked suddenly.

"I was working in the woods in Casper, Wyoming," Kane answered. He admitted that he had been on a drinking binge during that whole week. Jack Kane, as charming a rogue as he appeared to be, was clearly not blessed with good judgment. He confided to an utterly fascinated jury that his memory had failed him during that time. One of the main reasons he had been unable to marry Jody Kaarsten was that—in the summer of 1966—he was already married to one of his many wives. But on July 16 he had completely forgotten he was currently married, and he had wed a beautiful teenage girl. So he had become a bigamist.

He continued his testimony, which sounded like nothing so much as a cross-country movie comedy script. He and his new, if bigamous, bride were headed for their honeymoon in South Dakota's Badlands National Park when they had a mishap.

"A buffalo attacked my sports car," Kane testified.

"I beg your pardon," Barokas said.

"He came at us and crushed both doors, and we couldn't drive it, and we couldn't get out of it, either. We had to wait until the state police found us."

After a long uneasy time trapped in the battered little car, Kane said he and his teenage bride were rescued by a highway patrolman. The incident got much tongue-in-cheek coverage in local papers and hit the AP wires. It was a natural for human interest: "Buffalo Attacks Sports Car of Honeymooning Couple."

Unfortunately for Jack Kane, the parents of his latest *legal* wife read the news stories with interest. They learned that their son-in-law had remarried without benefit of divorce and then had been roughed up by a buffalo. They didn't find it as funny as the reading public. When they told their daughter, she brought charges against Jack Kane and had him arrested for bigamy.

The double murder trial, which was now edging dangerously close to Christmas, continued through Saturday, December 18. On the advice of counsel, defendants in murder cases rarely take the witness stand. But Arne Kaarsten insisted on testifying. His demeanor continued to be that of a supremely confident man. He might well have been the toastmaster at a banquet for close friends. He smiled and spoke easily to the jury, turning often to include them in his answers to questions. After the lunch break, however, Kaarsten seemed a changed man. Either he'd had time to think about the enormity of the charges against him or his legal counsel had suggested that he should act a little more somber, considering the occasion. Now his face sagged, and he spoke in a low, almost humble tone.

"What happened to that smile?" Deputy Prosecutor Lee Yates asked with a bite in his voice.

"I guess I'm just surprised at being called to the witness stand today," Kaarsten responded weakly.

When he was shown a picture of his wife, Kaarsten broke into sobs. That seemed peculiar, since it certainly wasn't the first time he had seen the photograph. Kaarsten had gazed at pictures of the bodies of Jody and Peri Lynn on the corkboard in front of the courtroom through most of the trial and had never shown a trace of emotion. Now it was as if he were seeing for the very first time this picture of his wife lying dead in a tangle of blankets.

It was late afternoon on December 21, 1971, when the jurors retired to begin deliberation. It would not be a quick verdict. The rule of thumb that attorneys and court watchers live by is that a quick verdict is a guilty verdict; the longer a jury stays out, the more likely it is that there will be an acquittal. When the jurors were still weighing the testimony and evidence more than forty hours later, the defense camp felt optimistic. In the end, it took Arne Kaarsten's jury almost forty-eight hours to reach a verdict. It was two days before Christmas when Kaarsten walked into the courtroom to hear the jury's decision. He walked arm in arm with one of Jody Kaarsten's closest relatives; her family was supporting his innocence. If Jody's own family believed in him, how could a jury find otherwise?

Arne Kaarsten was shocked and turned stark white when the jury foreman read the verdicts. In the death of Jody Kaarsten: "Guilty of murder in the first degree."

In the death of Peri Lynn Kaarsten: "Guilty of murder in the first degree."

The jury did, however, recommend against the death penalty. Arne Kaarsten was sentenced instead to two concurrent life sentences; with good behavior, he could be out of jail in thirteen years and four months.

The Kaarsten saga was far from over. Arne Kaarsten's legal team appealed the guilty verdicts on the basis of prejudicial testimony by a witness. The witness in question was the owner of a Kent ambulance service, also an EMT, who was the man who had tried in vain to bring Jody Kaarsten back to life. He had testified that, in his opinion, Kaarsten had not seemed as concerned or as grief-stricken as other husbands he had observed when he worked over their stricken mates. He said that Kaarsten grew concerned only when it looked as if Jody was breathing—when her chest began to rise and fall as a result of air being forced into her lungs by the resuscitator.

At that point—and that point only—did the ambulance owner detect panic in Kaarsten.

The prosecution had inferred that Arne Kaarsten was afraid his wife was still alive and might tell who had choked her.

The defense attorneys claimed that the ambulance driver was not an expert in human behavior and that his testimony should have been deemed prejudicial and should have been stopped, or else the jury should have been advised to disregard it. Although the EMT had seen scores of worried relatives in accident and sudden death situations and had become a kind of intuitive judge of human nature in such cases, he was not—in the accepted legal sense—an expert witness.

On March 5, 1973, the Washington State Court of Appeals reversed Arne Kaarsten's convictions and ordered a new trial. Kaarsten had been released from the Monroe, Washington, Reformatory on a $35,000 appeal bond on July 31, 1972, pending a State Supreme Court hearing on the issue of whether or not he should be allowed bond. The state subsequently ruled that Kaarsten could not be freed because of the capital nature of the crime, but, ironically, that decision did not take effect until his convictions had been reversed.

Arne Kaarsten remained free for sixteen months.

In December 1973, almost exactly two years after his first trial, Arne Kaarsten once again went on trial for the murder of his wife and baby. Once more, a Christmas tree dominated the lobby of the courthouse. The courtroom was different, and the judge and jury were different, but one got a feeling of déjà vu. It seemed that all of this had happened before. As indeed it had.

Kaarsten himself, still a popular race-car driver, appeared scarcely changed. His hair was a bit grayer, but his full face was unlined. Interestingly, the strain of the marathon legal ordeal showed strongly on relatives and friends of Jody and Peri Lynn, both now dead for seven years. Little Peri Lynn would have been in the fourth grade by now. Terry was in the sixth.

Some of the witnesses had died, although the ones whose testimony was vital to a conviction had been located and brought to the trial.

Carl Richey once again represented Kaarsten, and Lee Yates would again prosecute for the state. The mere passage of time had made the Kaarsten case less newsworthy. This time there were no headlines on the front page—only short articles in the back sections of local papers. Kaarsten spoke expansively to an attractive television newswoman and was filmed smiling broadly as he strode into the courtroom. One reporter studied the jury and remarked, "It's possible that Kaarsten may seem innocent now just because so much time has gone by since they died. That alone might be enough to sway a jury."

Lieutenant George Helland once again sat behind the prosecutors to aid in the case as a "friend of the court." Those of us who had been there for the first trial felt that we were seeing a movie for the second time.

The testimony was repeated. Everything was the same—except for one thing. Lee Yates had felt there was one loose end dangling in the first trial. That raveling concerned Jody Kaarsten's lover, Jack Kane. The defense had done its best to plant a veiled implication that Kane might have been the killer—that Jack Kane, consumed by jealousy, might have come skulking around the Kaarsten home and then attacked Jody and the baby after Kaarsten was asleep. Had it not been for Jody's discovery that she carried Arne's baby, Peri Lynn, she might have continued her affair with Jack Kane. That was something the defense had run with as a motive to suggest Kane was the killer.

Yates was sure that the defense would employ the same tactics this time. Kane had testified he was "working in the woods in Casper, Wyoming," but the prosecution had been unable to locate a witness who could substantiate this in the first trial.

Now Yates undertook an all-out campaign to find someone who could place Kane several states away from Washington on the day of the murders. Kane had mentioned that he'd gotten paid on July 6 and that his boss would remember he was there. But efforts to find the boss, Arnold Schillings, had always resulted in blind alleys.

Yates figured that a contractor with a business as large as the one Kane had described was probably a fairly solid citizen. It was likely that Schillings still maintained a business somewhere in the western states. "Arnold Schilling" wasn't the most common name in the world, but it wasn't that unusual, either. The young prosecuting attorney decided to forgo a night's sleep and search for Schilling.

Lee Yates began calling information operators in Wyoming, Montana, and Idaho. He called every town in each of the three states and inquired about a listing for "Arnold Schilling," "A. Schilling," "Schilling Construction," or anything similar. With the cooperation of patient information operators, Yates found that Schilling did not live in Wyoming or in Montana.

Then Yates hit it lucky. An operator checking in a statewide directory for Idaho found a listing for an Arnold Schilling in Twin Falls. He was the only Arnold Schilling in the state. Holding his breath, Yates asked to be put through to the number.

Lee Yates was elated when he realized he had found the right Arnold Schilling. Surprisingly, Schilling said he had heard about the Kaarsten murders. He happened to have been traveling through Washington State on vacation a few weeks after the homicides, and he remembered hearing about it on a radio news broadcast. But of course, he'd had no reason to connect the killings to Jack Kane, the man who worked for him.

"Could you tell me if Kane was working for you in Wyoming on July 6, 1966?" Yates asked. It was such a long shot. The IRS wouldn't require Schilling to keep employment records for seven and a half years.

"Sure . . . sure," Schilling said. "You know, I think he was. I could check some pay records."

In the end, Schilling's records verified that he had handed Jack Kane a check on July 6, 1966. The check itself, returned after cancellation, had been lost in a flood. But Schilling was prepared to swear on the witness stand that he had seen Kane on that day, paid him, and that Kane could not have been in Kent, Washington, at the time of the murders.

This may have been the turning point in Arne Kaarsten's second trial.

Once again, as Christmas lights twinkled outside, a jury found Arne Kaarsten guilty on two counts of first-degree murder. Judge Janice Niemi allowed Arne Kaarsten to remain free on his $35,000 appeal bond when his lawyers said he would appeal yet again.

Lee Yates moved that the bail be revoked, however, and six days later Judge Niemi ruled that criminal procedure guidelines prohibited bail for a person convicted of capital offenses.

Kaarsten was ordered back to jail.

On January 21, 1974, Arne Kaarsten was once again

sentenced to two concurrent life terms. On February 5, he was again denied bail pending appeal—with the court citing, ironically, the case of *The State vs. Kaarsten* as a precedent.

The State Supreme Court released Kaarsten from the Washington State Reformatory on March 14, pending the appeal of his conviction, with the posting of $10,000 in cash and a $100,000 appearance bond. The court action followed a recent statute issued by the U.S. Supreme Court, which gave trial judges discretion in granting bail in capital crimes such as murder. Immediately he was rearrested and was back in the King County Jail on March 15.

On December 23, 1975, Arne Kaarsten was sent to the Washington State Reformatory in Monroe to begin serving his life sentence. He was later transferred to a federal prison on McNeil Island, Washington. He was paroled to a halfway house on April 11, 1989, and discharged from parole permanently on July 26, 1993—twenty-seven years after his wife and baby were murdered. His conviction for the double murder had kept him in prison for only the standard "life sentence" of that era: thirteen and a half years.

More than two decades after Arne Kaarsten's conviction, Senior Deputy Prosecuting Attorney Lee Yates—who is now assigned to the Appeals Division of the King County Prosecuting Attorney's Office—remembers Kaarsten's two trials as if they had happened only last week. He was not surprised to learn that Kaarsten was out of prison. "He was lucky in his timing," Yates said with acceptance tinged with a trace of bitterness. "If he committed the murders of his wife and baby today, he would be charged with aggravated murder and he would have received a mandatory sentence of life without parole."

Yates was, however, a bit startled to hear that Arne Kaarsten was living a highly successful post-prison life. He served three years as president of a local Sons of Norway Lodge. In that position, Arne Kaarsten was the chosen escort for the king and queen of Norway when they visited Seattle a few years ago. Kaarsten remained as charming, personable, and confident as he appeared in his two trials. Although his hair turned white in the years since 1966, Kaarsten was still handsome and wore the same perfect pompadour that he did then. He had a successful career and, presumably, a good life with a woman he knew before he went to prison.

Ironically, although Arne Kaarsten was the race-car driver in the 1970s, it is Prosecutor Lee Yates who races today—in his classic Porsche.

Had she lived, Jody Kaarsten would be sixty today. Peri Lynn would be thirty-seven in December. A necktie and a pink ribbon ended their future three decades ago.

Update, December 2003

Arne Kaarsten never lost his taste for rare, expensive cars. He now owns a silver Mercedes, an M-100, 6.9, one of the rarest, most powerful and luxurious automobiles ever produced. During their eighteen year reign as Mercedes-Benz's flagship sedans, fewer than 17,000 M-100's came off the assembly line. Only 1816 of the 6.9's that Kaarsten owns were sold in America.

At the age of sixty-one, Kaarsten belongs to a very exclusive club of M-100 men, who love the speed, power, and cachet of their celebrated cars.

Tragically, the young family of four who lived in a

neat tract house in Kent, Washington, thirty-seven years ago has only one survivor today—Arne Kaarsten himself. Terry Kaarsten, Jody and Arne's first child, who was raised in California by her mother's family, died at almost the same age as her mother did.

Terry was twenty-three when she was killed in an automobile accident in April 1986, in Southern California.

seat that (in)front Kent, Washington (they) were but
my raising one summer today — Amy Kayleen Russell
Jerry Rockwell Jone, and Anne... Jerry child, Stephanie
moved to California to be her mother's family, and started
life anew in her mother life.

There was twenty-three years old, she was arrested on
gasoline at work in April 1986, in Fresno, California.

The Lost Lady
(from *A Rage to Kill*)

Thousands upon thousands *of adults disappear in America every year. Some go because they choose to; the stresses and disappointments of life can make the concept of "running away" seem very appealing. Some actually do suffer from amnesia, that much beloved plot device of the television soap opera writer, but it is an exceedingly rare psychological phenomenon in real life. Lots of people vanish because they are victims of foul play. And some human beings actually seem to evaporate into the mist that forms between midnight and dawn, gone forever without explanation.*

I have never researched a police case as unearthly as the story of Marcia Moore. Marcia was an altogether beautiful woman, a psychic of international reputation, an heiress to a large fortune, and a well-published author. And at the age of fifty-one, she had found the kind of perfect love that all women long for in their secret hearts.

Years before I ever wrote about Marcia Moore, she was familiar to me. I first saw her image in the seventies when so many of us were caught up in the yoga craze, hard on the heels of the study of reincarnation and astrology. The lithe, gorgeous woman who demonstrated yoga positions in Jess Stearn's books was Marcia. She seemed to all of us in that bemused decade to be the very essence of perfection. My friends and I would have been shocked to know that her life had been as beset by heartbreak as it had been blessed by wealth and genetic gifts.

Seeing her then as she posed in leotards and tights, a study in grace and beauty, no one could ever have imagined the tragedy that lay ahead of her.

In 1928, Marcia Moore was born into a family of high achievers. She was the cherished daughter of Robert Lowell Moore, a thirty-two-year-old Bostonian with a scrupulously blue-blooded background. Undeterred by the financial climate of the Great Depression, Marcia's father founded the Sheraton Hotel chain in the 1930s and his business knowledge made the luxurious hotels flourish. The Sheraton Corporation stayed in the family until it was sold to ITT in 1968 for an estimated $20 million.

Marcia's parents were involved in the New England Theosophical Society, which she always called laughingly, "kind of blue-blooded spiritualists." Later, they built a "meditation mount" in Ojai, California, where they often joined friends who were interested in the same spiritual pursuits.

One of Marcia's brothers became a successful attorney in Greenwich, Connecticut. The other was Robin Moore, whose books *The Green Berets* and *The French Connection* stayed at the top of the best-seller lists for months and then were made into blockbuster movies.

Marcia herself was a talented writer, but her field of expertise was far more ethereal than her brother's. She saw beauty in nature, secrets of life beyond the veil of reality, and she trusted more than the average human, using her special sense to guide her. She was considered a true psychic by those who believed that the mind was capable of perceiving far more than the concrete things that can be rationally explained.

Marcia Moore's life story and her expertise in the mystic arts of yoga became familiar to a million readers when Jess Stearn wrote a book about her in 1965: *Youth, Yoga, and Reincarnation.* Stearn, who also published *Edgar Cayce, The Sleeping Prophet* and *The Girl with the Blue Eyes,* spent three months with Marcia Moore and her third husband at their Boston home, and he, too, became a devotee of the yoga philosophy.

Marcia appeared in the picture section of the book, wearing leotards and demonstrating the complicated yoga positions or "asanas," her body so perfect that there wasn't a hint of cellulite or the slightest bulge of fat. She was almost forty, but she was completely flexible, her muscles elastic and trained. Indeed, she appeared to be a girl in her teens. That was important to her; she had a fear of growing old.

Oddly, although Marcia was a brilliant woman with an exceptionally strong mind, she had never been successful at choosing men. By the time she was fifty, she had four husbands. The first three were men who had disappointed and hurt her. Though she charted her life through her knowledge of astrology, letting the stars guide her, they often failed to guide her well when it came to romance.

There were dark sides to the men she chose. "Marcia was drawn to brutal men," a friend said sadly. "She was so lovely and so good—she deserved better."

Marcia Moore referred to her first three marriages as "unfortunate," and didn't say much more. "She felt her first husband treated her like a writing machine," her friend recalled. "She was basically kept behind the type-writer—being a little 'word merchant,' as she called it."

When Stearn wrote about her in the mid-sixties, Marcia Moore was in the midst of her third marriage—to a man who was twelve years younger than she. He was also an astrologer, but their marriage was to be no advertisement for selection by the stars. Marcia probably knew that when she spoke with Jess Stearn. He quotes her in the book as saying that her destiny and her husband's might not always lie together. She told him that she only knew that it was meant for them to be together at that point in their lives.

After the excesses of the sixties, America was ready for a lifestyle that was pure and healthy. Marcia Moore was right at the forefront of all the new fads. She espoused vegetarianism as well as yoga. Except for her relationships with men, it all worked for her wonderfully well. She had everything, seemingly, that anyone might need to be happy—beauty, intellect and vibrant health. Indeed, Marcia had such control over her body and mind that she could actually control her heartbeat, her breathing and her blood pressure. She taught these techniques to her then-husband. By following her directions, he was able to beat a lie-detector test in a clinical situation by controlling those responses that would indicate he was not telling the truth. With his mind alone, he stopped perspiring, slowed his heartbeat, and lowered his blood pressure.

Marcia Moore's whole life was directed toward learning as much as she could about the other side of reality. She believed there were hidden doors she might step through, ways to step beyond her physical body into a world most people never glimpsed. Even as a young woman attending Radcliffe College, Marcia had been fascinated with the world of the occult. She took correspondence courses in meditation and traveled to India to study yoga. Blessed—or cursed—with psychic ability, she searched for keys to open doors to the "other" world.

Despite the bitter disappointment she felt when her marriages failed, Marcia Moore continued to believe she had the ability to make the right choices about her future through astrology charts and her psychic gift.

Initially, and despite urging from associates who had taken pharmacological shortcuts to enlightenment, Marcia found nothing that convinced her that drugs were the answer. Later, she reluctantly tried marijuana, mescaline, LSD, and even ingested seeds from the heavenly blue morning glory, but she was not impressed. None of them expanded her mind enough.

She wrote that ". . . these endeavors left me with the tantalizing sensation of having caught a few sneak previews of a show that never came to town."

Always seeking, Marcia Moore wrote or co-authored seven books dealing with the psychic world, including the popular *Diet, Sex, Yoga and Reincarnation,* and *Key to Immortality.* She coined the term "hypersentience" for a technique she had discovered that seemed to open her mind and let her get in touch with other lives she had lived before her current existence on earth.

Reincarnation as a philosophy is as old as mankind. It predicates that all of us have lived many times before. Proponents believe that souls choose each life as a vehicle that will help them refine and perfect their souls to a point where utter bliss, purity, and Nirvana are reached. Believing in reincarnation allows believers to deal with the tragedies and disappointments in life, because they can be seen as being preordained by karmic design. Sadness and disaster give the believer the opportunity to cope in order to achieve spiritual growth.

The Lost Lady

There was a tremendous interest in reincarnation in the seventies. Even the Beatles were spending time with gurus and mystics. With deep hypnosis, many people said they had been able to go back far beyond birth to recall past lives. Interestingly, the most vocal of the previous life travelers had all been someone famous—or *infamous*—in their earlier lives.

Marcia Moore took reincarnation more seriously than most. She believed that while hypnotized, she had gone back into Egypt, back to the days before Christ. She described former lives and deaths. It was a fascinating theory that could not be proven or disproven.

Marcia Moore, in her present life, resembled Cleopatra. Her silky black hair was cut in a sleek cap; her features were perfectly symmetrical. She had many suitors. Although her first three marriages fell apart, Marcia bore and raised three children to adulthood. She rarely spoke of them to her friends on the West Coast. Sometimes even *her* life seemed mundane and disappointing, but she searched continually for answers to questions that most of us never think about seriously.

Marcia didn't have to worry about money; there was the trust fund set up by her family plus the money that she received from her lectures and books. She was involved with groups who were searching for meaning, just as she herself was.

Marcia had a talent for friendship; she was sincerely concerned about her women friends and kept in touch with notes and cards, always urging them on to better things. She often drew pen and ink sketches of flowers on her cards and included quotations from Thoreau and Emerson.

One of Marcia's dearest friends was Elise Devereaux* who was president of the Seattle Astrological Society. The two women had met through a mutual friend, a psychologist in San Francisco, who had known Marcia since the sixties when he was in college. Elise was responsible for bringing Marcia to Seattle in 1975 to speak to the Astrological Society. "She was a most gracious and professional guest speaker," Elise would recall. "She helped the society significantly."

In 1976, Marcia wrote to Elise:

Dear Elise,
    Delighted to have your letter of May 23, and especially to hear that you are regressing people. As for the truth or falsity of the material in terms of scientific validation, it is still too early to judge. All we know is that some of them do check out. . . . Interesting about your life as a monk who ran an orphanage in the valley. But actually these *were* the ones who did such fine work in raising abandoned children. It is easy to imagine you in such a situation.

Marcia wrote that she hoped to come back to the Northwest, but would have to wait until she had a paid book tour. "But I'd love to plan on the regional conference in the summer of '77. That sounds a long way away, but it isn't really. By then, I should have some genuinely new conclusions and not just a bunch of case histories as I have now. I have a fairly long story with the astrological correlates in the September Bulletin. In fact, I plan to give more space to Karmic Astrology from now on . . ."

Marcia Moore and Elise Devereaux had become fast friends, even though they didn't see each other in person that much. Elise was living in the foothills of the Cascade Mountains and Marcia was either traveling or headquartered in Ojai. They kept in touch by letter and the occasional phone call. "Marcia was very reserved," Elise said.

"If it had not been for my friend [who introduced them] I would never have guessed there had ever been anything seamy in her life. She was just attracted to the wrong men. Marcia was like a princess, small, beautiful and wealthy; there was a sadness about her. I think she was always looking for a 'Bright World.' She was very eloquent and educated, and somehow she could make the damndest things seem reasonable."

Sometime after she posed for the pictures in Stearn's books, Marcia had a face lift. She was nearing fifty, and she had the kind of fragile thin skin that showed wrinkles early. The operation was a complete success, and she looked under forty again, although she never actually admitted to having had plastic surgery. One thing that Elise noticed was that Marcia never showed her legs; she wore either long flowing skirts or slacks. Elise remembers that Marcia was in a fire as a child, and suspected that her legs were badly scarred as a result. She never spoke about it, though.

After three marriages, Marcia Moore was essentially alone. She still hoped to find the man in the world she was destined to be with. Elise Devereaux was alone too, divorced and raising her small daughter. She was giving astrological readings, and an older woman who was cutting down on her clientele sent Elise several referrals. One of them was a handsome, dark-haired man named Steve Monti*. Monti was an anesthesiologist who was on staff in a Seattle hospital. Although he was awfully good-looking and masculine, Elise was somehow not attracted to him.

"I did his chart," Elise said. "And gave him a reading in my home. Dr. Monti recorded the reading. But then I received a call from him saying that the recording was blank—and he asked if I would do the reading again."

She told him that, of course, she would. At the time Dr. Monti was going through a divorce, and talked to

Elise about it. He showed her pictures of a very pretty blonde woman and explained that this was his *second* divorce from the same wife. There were children from their marriage, and Monti said that his family lived in North Bend, Washington.

It wasn't unusual for Elise's clients to confide their most intimate concerns. Steve Monti told Elise that he hated his name—that he had always hated it because it was his stepfather's name. He said the man had sexually abused him when he was small, and he was going to get rid of the name as part of a healing process for the scars left behind. Henceforth, he would be known as Walter "Happy" Boccaci*.

Monti-Boccaci had had a life full of catastrophes, it seemed. He told Elise that he had survived a terrible car accident a few years before. He had been driving his Volkswagen which was crushed by a larger vehicle. "I think the only reason I survived," he confided, "was because the doctors knew I was a physician, too, and they went to extraordinary effort to save me."

Dr. Boccaci said that his aorta had burst, which was usually a "death sentence." Indeed it was; unless a patient is actually on the operating table when the main artery of the body tears or bursts, death by exsanguination almost always follows. But Happy Boccaci had survived, although he was in sorry shape. He showed Elise pictures of himself on crutches. His legs seemed to be limp and paralyzed.

However, by the time he'd come to her for an astrological reading, he looked to be in perfect health. The only sign that he'd been in an accident, he said, was that he could no longer drum or roll his fingers on a hard surface. He had lost control of those nerves.

If Elise had begun to wonder if Dr. Boccaci was full of tall stories, she soon had proof that he *was* on the staff of a highly respected hospital. "I have a genetic bone disease," she said. "One morning, I woke up with stress fracture of my knee. Happy had me come to his hospital and I was given the royal treatment. I didn't have to pay for anything. I really felt that Happy took a real, altruistic interest in my health."

Elise was in her thirties and attractive; Dr. Happy Boccaci was about forty and newly single. Soon he began to visit her on a social basis, although she tried to keep their relationship platonic. It wasn't that he wasn't attractive because he *was*. But there was something that put her off.

"He began buying my two-year-old daughter gifts," she said. "This was making me uncomfortable and I tried to make some distance. I remember my daughter crawling on his lap once and asking, 'Are you nice or are you mean?' He told her he was a nice Italian man."

The question of Dr. Boccaci's interest in Elise Devereaux soon became moot. Marcia Moore came back to Seattle to speak for a second time in the summer of 1977. Happy Boccaci was in the audience and was totally taken with the fragile heiress. He learned that Elise was a friend of Marcia's and began a campaign to get an introduction to Marcia.

Something made Elise hold back. She knew that Marcia was involved with a young man, whom Marcia sensed to be a reincarnation of Lord Byron. She had always been fascinated by Lord Byron, and felt they had had a connection in another life. Although the man she was seeing was much younger than she was, she was drawn to him. He had a lot of medical problems, and Marcia was taking care of him. He was her "Lord Byron."

Even so, Elise knew that Marcia was often lonely, and so was Happy. There was no real reason they shouldn't meet, although Marcia was about a dozen years older than Happy. "He kept badgering me to introduce them,"

Elise recalled. "I was reluctant. He actually called me on the phone and had a temper tantrum. I must have felt intimidated because I invited him to a private reception. The rest is history. Marcia and Happy were drawn to each other immediately."

Anyone could see that they made a striking couple—the big bear of a man with thick dark hair, beard and mustache, and heavy features, and the petite woman with the features of a porcelain doll. Dr. Happy Boccaci swept Marcia Moore into his arms and she felt, finally, as if she had come home.

Walter "Happy" Bocacci at forty was the deputy chief of the anesthesiology department at Seattle's Public Health Hospital. He had held that highly responsible position for ten years. Until his second divorce from his wife, his interests had been in the scientific world where everything was explainable. It would seem that he would be an unlikely mate for the ethereal Marcia Moore, but he had already plunged into the world of astrological projection by the time he met Marcia.

They both felt a karmic link. Who could argue that the meeting of Bocacci and Marcia Moore did not seem preordained? It *did* seem as if they were meant to be together.

Happy always told the story of their meeting in a way that did not include Elise Devereaux. He explained that he had been browsing in the Quest Bookstore in Seattle, a shop specializing in works on the psychic world, in late May 1977, when he picked up a volume titled *Astrology, the Divine Science.* "I was mesmerized by the picture of a woman on the dust jacket."

It was Marcia Moore.

As he confided to Marcia later, "It flashed through my mind. Wow! Would she make a perfect wife! I actually felt some electrical impulse coming off the page and penetrating me—such as we visualize with magnetism."

And so when Marcia came to Seattle to lecture, Dr. Happy Boccaci was there, sitting in the front row, taping her remarks so that he wouldn't lose the sound of her voice or her insights into this new world that enthralled him. He knew that he would see her again, that he was already half in love with her.

After Elise's private reception, Happy invited Marcia to walk with him. They strolled through the fragrant summer night and talked until the sun came up.

Marcia had to leave Seattle for lectures in Vancouver, British Columbia, but Happy Boccaci pressed his suit with letters he had a friend hand-carry to Marcia in the Canadian city. He invited her to visit him in Seattle, saying, "Marcia, I know my destiny is either with you or through you."

She agreed with him. She had missed him terribly, and they spent a week together and, as Marcia wrote later, took "two incredible mind trips together." Marcia Moore had been traveling for five years, never spending more than three months in one place before moving on.

Certainly, a lot of men had come on to her, had desired her, but this was the first man in a long, long time who had seemed right for her. With him, she'd felt that she had "come home" at last.

Marcia and Happy were married on November 25, 1977. Two days later, she wrote to Elise Devereaux, "Little did you know what forces you set in motion when you invited me to stop off in Seattle this last July! Anyway, here I am married to Walter, and very much enjoying life in our clean, fresh, and shining new home near Lynnwood. We would both love to see you! Do come by whenever you can. Also, we are having an open house on Friday night, December 23. So much news to catch you up on . . . You won't believe what we are doing!"

One would never expect to find a woman like Marcia Moore living in a duplex apartment in Alderwood Manor, Washington. She had always seemed to belong in Los Angeles or Shanghai, or, even India, studying the masters of the occult.

But Marcia's own particular karma had intervened. The man she had fallen in love with lived in Washington and, when she joined her life with his, she, too, would settle in the principally rural area of Snohomish County. Fir forests, lumber mills and farms instead of incense, tapestries, and mystery.

One of the subjects Marcia and Happy discussed at length was the capability of drugs to alter the mind. Marcia was still trying to find a way through the looking glass of life. She mentioned a relatively little known drug, ketamine, to Happy and he surprised her with his familiarity with it. She shouldn't have been so surprised; as an anesthesiologist, he had used it on children and in animal experiments.

Normally, ketamine was used in such strong doses that it would produce unconsciousness, but Marcia felt ketamine had properties that could unveil age-old secrets of the psyche if it were taken in much smaller quantities.

Happy wondered if she might be right. She was exquisite, brilliant, and she seemed to have, almost within her grasp, the answers he sought.

Marcia Moore became more and more convinced that ketamine was the answer to what she was seeking, and Dr. Boccaci soon was almost as enthusiastic about the mind-expanding properties of the drug as she was. Boccaci was convinced that ketamine would one day be recognized as one of the brightest tools in psychotherapy. He called it "ketamine psychotherapy." He left behind the job at the hospital that was paying him $47,000 a year, to prove his theories.

Walter and Marcia received government approval to research ketamine. They called their research "the samadhi therapy." They set up a foundation and lived off the $1,400 a month that Marcia received from the family trust fund. They began to call ketamine hydrochloride "the goddess Ketamine."

Marcia charted their experiments, and wrote of her reactions to her first 50-milligram injection of ketamine.

". . . I became aware of a tingling warmth and a sense of relaxed well-being . . . In this and subsequent ketamine voyages, my impression was one of making the circuit of a vast, multi-dimensional wheel. *Walter!* I repeated the name and the syllables shone forth like a glowing crown of light . . . 'Walter, flower, power.' I kept on chanting the words, watching the equivalent images blossom forth."

Both Happy and Marcia were injected with the drug daily for about six months, but Boccaci soon found that he wasn't getting the insights that Marcia was. He said later that he felt he didn't have her mind, her psychic capacity or the spiritual growth that she had possessed before he met her. So he stopped.

But Marcia Moore continued. For fourteen months, Marcia took the drug daily—the only human on earth known to have ingested it with such regularity.

One of Marcia's friends, an author himself who had written a number of books about the human mind, begged her to stop. He told her that he had experimented with it, too. He warned her that he had become addicted to it. "Marcia," he pleaded, "my wife found me face-down in the swimming pool. I barely survived. I'm telling you, you are a damned fool to mess with ketamine . . ."

Marcia wouldn't listen. She was even able to convince

a few of her close friends to try ketamine, but none of them liked the sense of falling away from themselves that resulted.

Marcia and Happy invited Elise to spend the night with them in their duplex. "It was a small town house," Elise remembered, "but it was attractively decorated with all the treasures that Marcia had purchased on her travels to the East."

Although she had never been much of a homemaker before, Marcia cooked a lovely meal of stir-fried vegetables and tofu. "The two of them were just like little kids telling me about their plans with ketamine," Elise remembered. "They felt that they were a perfect duo—he an anesthesiologist, and she with her background in psychology. It was as if the sixties had passed them by and they thought that ketamine could do what Leary thought acid would do with psychotherapy."

Elise didn't want to hurt their feelings, but she felt they were deluded. "I thought it was all nonsense."

Undeterred, in 1978 Happy and Marcia published *Journey into the Bright World,* a book about ketamine. Everything seemed to be working beautifully for them. Marcia's capacity for creative work had always been high, but now she had multiple projects going. She was writing a book using astrological projections about the Kennedy family for her brother's publishing company. It would be timely, considering the upcoming presidential elections. Marcia confided to her brother that Ted Kennedy must not run for president, that his karmic involvement was such that he didn't deserve to win, couldn't win, and would be destroyed trying.

She was also working on another book that unveiled the beauty secrets of Cleopatra, whom Marcia felt she had known in a past life.

Marcia Moore was thrilled with what she had discovered; she felt she had something to tell the world, and wondered, "Can it be that the so-called common man is as deserving of a mystical experience as he is of the opportunity to take a plane trip?"

And so, by January 1979, Marcia Moore appeared to finally have reached the happiness that she had sought for half a century. She was fifty-one, still beautiful, wealthy, married to her one true love for fourteen months, and engaged in work that consumed her.

What happened on January 14 is as inexplicable and eerie as anything Marcia Moore ever visualized as a psychic or experienced under the effects of ketamine.

On that Sunday evening, Happy Boccaci asked his wife if she cared to see a movie with him. She shook her head and smiled, he recalled, saying that she was going to get up early the next morning to begin work on a new book. He left her cozily ensconced in their apartment and went to the show alone.

When he returned at one A.M., he was a little alarmed to find that Marcia was not in their duplex. Her purse, her wallet, and all of her cash were there. Her passport was still in their home too. He expected her to pop in at any moment; perhaps she had gone to visit a neighbor in one of the other units. Boccaci searched the place inside and out, and then, even though it was a bitterly cold night, he walked over to the nearby Floral Hills Cemetery to look for her there. Unlike less hardy and more fearful women, Marcia often enjoyed solitary walks in the huge, well-kept cemetery. But she was not there. She wasn't anywhere that Happy Boccaci looked.

Early in the morning, Boccaci called the Snohomish County Sheriff's Office, and reported that his wife was missing. Sheriff Bob Dodge, a retired long-time Seattle police officer, dispatched investigators to check the Boccaci duplex. There was no sign that anything criminal had taken place. The doors and windows showed no evidence that they had been forced, and there was absolutely nothing that would indicate a struggle. The ground outside was frozen hard, and would not have held any impressions from shoes or tire treads.

Dr. Boccaci wasn't sure what clothing his wife was wearing, but detectives found her kimono lying on the floor of her closet, something friends would say wasn't at all like her. She was almost compulsively neat.

Marcia Moore became a "missing person." Lieutenant Darrol Bemis took over the probe personally, assisted by Detective Doris Twitchell. For detectives trained in scientific investigation, the search for Marcia Moore would be a whole new experience.

It was not out of the scope of rational reasoning to suspect that Marcia Moore might have been kidnapped. Her family was both well-known and extremely wealthy, but no requests for ransom money came in. And kidnapping the woman without trying to collect for her safe return didn't make sense.

Suicide? How? And where?

A woman whose life's work involved writing about life and those areas beyond life would certainly have left a note. Moreover, Marcia Moore believed devoutly in reincarnation. And for believers, suicide is the worst possible death. Suicide destroys the natural karmic pattern. At best, the individual would have to come back again and start all over, making the same mistakes, suffering the same disappointments and agonies of the life they have just left. At worst, some proponents of reincarnation believe that a suicide is doomed in every life hereafter. Moore's friends said that Marcia had espoused the latter theory. For her, suicide would be sentencing herself to endless lifetimes of misery, with no hope of spiritual growth.

Could she have been abducted by a killer? Possibly. It was unlikely that she would have allowed a stranger into her home, but she could have gone for a walk in the cemetery and been attacked there. But, if that were the case, where was her body? Most murder victims turn up sooner or later. Most—not all. Snohomish County was full of rivers, lakes, much of it on the shores of Puget Sound. There were abandoned mine shafts, and mountain passes covered in deep snow.

Could Marcia have decided to leave of her own accord? Neither her husband nor her brothers felt she would do that. She was happily married, involved in her work. And she was very considerate of her elderly parents. "She would communicate with us if she were able," attorney John Moore insisted. "She wouldn't do that to the folks."

Robin Moore concurred. "My sister and I were quite close. She would not have disappeared without letting me know. She was writing a book for my publishing company. If there's one thing she had, it was a very strong sense of deadlines. She would have called."

Most of her friends were baffled by Marcia's disappearance, but Elise felt an ominous cloud that had nothing to do with her skill at astrology. "I watched Marcia deteriorate very rapidly after she started experimenting with ketamine," she said. "She had complained of pain in her hip. That was why she took walks around Floral Hills. The paths were a flat surface on which to walk. She didn't want to talk about her hip, but she did say that someone was 'bewitching' her . . ."

But Elise didn't think Marcia would have gone walking in the cemetery at night.

Robin Moore's wife had spoken long-distance with Marcia on Saturday, January 13. She had found her sister-in-law very enthusiastic about her new projects, if a little repetitive and "slightly confused" about her theories.

Robin Moore, himself familiar with police investigations and mysteries from research on his books, had two theories about his sister's fate. "I really think it's at least a fifty-fifty chance she was kidnapped, but not by an ordinary kidnapper. It would be a grotesque kidnapping by one of the people who knew [of] this very unorthodox spiritualism she was involved in.

"Then maybe her husband is right. Maybe the ketamine caught up with her. Maybe something snapped and she took off walking."

Agonized, Dr. Boccaci said he had come to that theory as a possibility. Although he had never seen any profoundly detrimental effects from the drug, he realized that Marcia was a special case—the only human in the world known to have ingested so much for so long.

Could she have suddenly been gripped by amnesia without his seeing its approach? The *PDR (Physicians Desk Reference)* warned that a side effect of ketamine is "confusional states" during a patient's recovery from surgery. Temporary amnesia was a possibility.

But Marcia's dosage had been far less than that used for surgical anesthesia. If she had been building cumulative residuals of ketamine, a physician of her husband's experience would surely have noted it.

Boccaci described the immediate effects of the drug in small doses by injection. "After the first two or three minutes, you begin to feel the initial effects, like hearing the chirping of crickets. Then, after five minutes, you begin to leave your body behind. There is no cognition of the fact that you have a body, but you are aware that you are still alive. You have a center point of consciousness. You go out of the planet of Earth and into the astro planes."

This is the opposite reaction to the street drug known as "angel dust." With angel dust, the ingester feels dead and those who have overdosed are convinced that they are, indeed, dead.

Some of Marcia's friends told the Snohomish County investigators that, with deep meditation, there were documented cases where the "soul" had gone so far out into the astro planes that the body left behind had died. But, even if it had succumbed without its "soul," it was still there. Marcia Moore's body was nowhere—nowhere where anyone could find it.

Lieutenant Darrol Bemis had to take a crash course in the psychic world, spending half his nights reading Marcia Moore's books and others like it, "so I can understand the terminology psychics use," he told reporters.

He was deluged with tips from mystics who believed they knew what had happened to Marcia Moore. In a case with no clues, the investigative team tried to remain open-minded and consider every possible source of information carefully, no matter how far-fetched it might be.

The phone bills run up in the probe were astronomical. Lieutenant Bemis and his team called every telephone number they could locate in the missing woman's duplex, without finding anyone who had heard from Marcia. Marcia Moore's family on the East Coast never heard from her. No one in Ojai, California—where she had scores of friends—heard from her.

There was one strange incident that might have had bearing on her disappearance. On either January 15 or 16, the twelve-year-old daughter of one of Marcia's closest friends answered the phone and a woman with a Boston accent like Marcia's asked, "Is your Mummy there?"

The child said she was not and there was no number where she could be reached, and the caller said she would call back later. She never did.

"If she were in trouble, that would be the time she would call me," the friend offered. "She has called me to her side several times in the past when she needed me."

The search for Marcia Moore grew eerier and eerier. Some psychics maintained that the ghosts of the dead were able to use phone lines to get messages through, even years after they passed over. Was it possible that Marcia Moore would try to contact someone from the other side? Bemis and his fellow investigators found themselves considering the most bizarre possibilities when regular detective work netted them nothing at all.

Marcia and Happy Boccaci were to have attended the International Cooperation Council's Rainbow Rose Festival in Pasadena, California, on the weekend of January 27 and 28 as featured speakers. This was America's largest gathering of psychics and it was a function that Marcia would never have missed if there was any way she could be there.

One of the festival organizers had a theory on Marcia's disappearance. "I guess this sounds kind of far out, but a lot of psychics here think she dematerialized. In the Indian philosophy, you can raise your consciousness, keep developing yourself like Jesus Christ and some of the gurus, and reach a point where you just zap out."

Bizarre? Of course. But then the whole of Marcia Moore's life had bordered on the bizarre, and there were no rational explanations about where Marcia had gone.

Marcia had also written a speech that she planned to present at the World Symposium on Humanity in Los Angeles in April. Happy Boccaci went in her place. He wrote to Elise, "I just got back from L.A. where I delivered Marcia's brilliant speech, entitled, 'Where is the reincarnation movement heading today?' And I got a lot more people praying. I don't have much to say except I am terribly depressed and ever so lonely. I do cry a lot. Again, thank you for your note and do keep praying . . . Light and love, (not so) Happy."

The husband of a missing woman is always suspect. So was Dr. Walter "Happy" Boccaci. Marcia's family considered him the prime suspect in her disappearance, although he stood to gain nothing financially in case of her death. He would actually be poorer because her trust fund wouldn't go to him—but to her three children.

Boccaci seemed remarkably sanguine about the suspicions of the Moore family. "I realize that if my daughter were suddenly to marry somebody on the East Coast that I had never met—and six months later she disappeared, I would say, 'Damn it. It's the husband who did it. He's the culprit!' That's just a natural thing to believe."

Her family used Marcia's trust fund to hire private detectives. They came to the Northwest, and had no better results than the Snohomish County investigators. Although they looked hard at Dr. Happy Boccaci, and reportedly tried to trick him into believing he would get an inheritance if Marcia's body was found, he told them what he had told everyone: "I wish I knew where her body was, her soul, whatever. But I don't."

Because Marcia Moore was herself a psychic, I consulted two psychics whom I knew to be amazingly accurate in their assessments and predictions. What would happen when the cards were thrown down a year after her disappearance and questions were asked about Marcia?

Would there be two diverse opinions—or would they agree?

Barbara Easton, a well-known Northwest psychic who reads ordinary playing cards, did several spreads on Marcia Moore. She knew only a little about the case. She was asking the question, "What were the circumstances around Marcia Moore's disappearance?"

The answers came swiftly. "Just before she vanished," Barbara said, "she received a long-distance phone call from a woman concerning a contract in which a lot of money was involved. There is a man involved, too—a man concerned about a real estate contract on which a great deal of money hinged."

According to the cards, Marcia Moore's marriage had been in trouble, and she was in the process of making a decision to get rid of emotional ties that had never worked. She had been very disappointed and frustrated. Moreover, she had recently heard from a man out of her past and received an invitation which had made her happy.

"The cards tell us that she wanted a divorce—even if no one was aware of it," Easton said, shaking her head.

Easton spread the cards four times, and each time the ace of spades (the death card) appeared side by side with the nine of hearts (the wish card).

"I think she's dead," Easton sighed. "Someone wished her dead, but the cards indicate that she was also blessed with very good women friends who were lucky for her, women she had turned to in the past for help."

Easton also picked up repeatedly on "hospital" and "court (or trial)" as she did further spreads of cards. Could Marcia Moore be in a hospital some place where no one knew who she was? Could there eventually be a trial for her murder?

The blonde psychic explained that, although death

showed repeatedly in Marcia's cards, these could also be interpreted as the death of the personality as it has been known. "She could have been so enlightened by the drug that her known personality died—leaving her body. There's possibly a five percent chance that she's hospitalized or sitting on a mountain top some place—meditating," Easton said. "It's called going to the void."

The elements of Marcia Moore's disappearance, then, that Easton elicited from the cards again and again were:

1. Marital problems, disappointments, frustration.
2. A renewed relationship with an old love.
3. A real estate transaction involving a lot of money.
4. Concern over another woman.
5. Phenomenal success ahead for Marcia in her work.
6. A hospital.
7. Death. Violent death.
8. A court trial.

"I think the decision was made for Marcia Moore to die," Easton summed up flatly.

Another popular psychic based in the Northwest, Shirley Teabo, read Tarot cards. Like Easton, she had a high success rate.

Shirley Teabo was not told about Barbara Easton's reading on Marcia Moore, nor did she know more than the bare facts about the woman's disappearance.

Could a second psychic home in on whatever astral projections Marcia Moore's entity was sending? Would Teabo's interpretations be entirely different from Easton's?

Teabo was able to pinpoint the date of Moore's disappearance (without knowing when it was) as between December 20 and January 20, 1979. "At that time, there was a passage away from difficulties—a journey over water," she said. "A journey over water far enough to leave the state of Washington. I see her on a ferry boat and I see the rays of a lighthouse crossing over her. She has—or had— a woman friend who was very good for her, someone from the past."

Teabo picked up a "retreat, a meditative state, a convalescent state after much anxiety."

"For some reason, I pick up the San Juan Islands. She has ties there, but I pick up a sunny day and she is happy. It may be something that has happened in her past."

The next card was not so cheerful; it was a coffin, a sarcophagus—a sign that someone is buried. "Sheets and things are wrapped around her," Teabo said. "Her 'fear' card revolves around a real estate transaction—something involving a great deal of money."

The psychic spread cards asking about what had happened in Marcia Moore's home on the last day she was seen. These cards showed the end of a cycle, a finishing-up. "She was preparing for a change, and she was well able to protect herself."

Oddly, Teabo, too, saw trouble with another woman— a woman of a violent nature who could have caused Moore real problems. "One woman is her friend—the other was a danger to her."

According to Teabo's reading, Marcia Moore had been about to advance tremendously in the world of her art. The books she was working on would have been highly successful. "But I see an illness . . . a hospitalization. She may be in an institution."

According to Shirley Teabo, Marcia Moore had been subjected to great stress. "Quarrels over money, over land, and someone was trying to make away with something that belonged to her."

Marcia's brother Robin had theorized that, if she had been kidnapped, it would have been because of the "unorthodox spiritualism" she was involved in. Teabo turned up cards that indicated that this might very well be true. Twice in succession, the anti-religion and cult cards turned up side by side. "She was at a crossroads and the path she chose was faulty, dangerous."

Marcia's marriage had not been serene, according to the Tarot cards; the couple had each felt bondage and restriction, frustration in the marriage.

As Barbara Easton had, Shirley Teabo saw violence on the last day of Marcia Moore's known existence. She picked it up again and again. "Oddly, I don't think she's dead . . . but I don't see her alive, either. It's as if her mind isn't hers any longer. If she is dead, she's earthbound."

A summary of Teabo's reading has many points of similarity with Easton's.

1. Trouble in the home.
2. A real estate transaction involving a lot of money.
3. Great success ahead in Moore's career.
4. Concerns about another woman who was dangerous to her.
5. Hospitalization.
6. Violence.
7. A "death" state.

If Marcia Moore was alive, the cards of both psychics suggested that she was incapacitated to the degree that she couldn't let anyone know where she was. If she was dead, her body had been secreted so carefully that it might never be found.

While Lieutenant Darrol Bemis and Detective Doris Twitchell worked the case from the scientific viewpoint of trained police officers, Dr. Walter Boccaci tried to reach his wife through less orthodox methods. After fasting all day and doing yoga, he injected himself with ketamine at midnight.

"The sole purpose of this is to reach my wife. We were telepathic. We were soul mates. Ketamine is the only way I can get out of my body. And I have been reaching her. I see her so clearly. She's sitting in a lotus position, lovely and beautiful. But she doesn't talk to me. I know why. She's amnesic. That's the only possibility, don't you see. The only way that makes sense."

Dr. Boccaci published one last issue of "The Hypersentience Bulletin," the newsletter he and Marcia had mailed to their followers. He wrote a "Final Note" to Marcia: "When you walk along the beach and listen to the sound of the waves, listen also to the roar of my voice, reverberating, 'Marcia, I love you. I'll always love you . . .' "

Despite his protestations that his life was over now that his wife was gone, Boccaci remained a suspect in her disappearance—or death . . . or transformation, whatever had happened. He told Erik Lacitis, a *Seattle Times* columnist, about his troubles. "The tragedy of this whole thing is what's happened to me. I am just hanging on by the skin of my teeth. I am destitute. I'm surviving by selling furniture and other personal possessions.

"I just spent a whole year of my life devoting all my energy to trying to find my wife . . . I tried everything. There's nothing more I can do to find my wife. Now, I'm trying to pick up the pieces of my life. I am forty-two, and I have another forty-two years ahead of me. And I can't get a job. I have been blackballed."

Although Boccaci said he had never lost a patient because of anesthesia or even had one with an adverse reaction, he felt he had been unable to find work in his profession because of all the publicity about Marcia's disappearance, and, perhaps, their ketamine research.

Boccaci left Washington State and took a residency at a Detroit hospital where his story was not so familiar. At length, he *did* find a job as an anesthesiologist at a tiny hospital on the Washington coast. Happy Boccaci wrote to Marcia's friends that he was finally doing well, jogging five miles a day, and feeling much better.

Marcia Moore's family members were divided in their opinions of what had become of her. Her daughter recalled how often Marcia had spoken of her dread of growing old. "It bothered her a lot. What do *I* think really happened?" she asked. "I would have to say that she committed suicide in some way."

But committing suicide without leaving a body behind is not easy to do. If Marcia Moore had leapt from a ferry boat on its way to the San Juan Islands, her body might have sunk—but, more likely, it would have eventually washed up on some spit of land.

It would be two years after Marcia Moore vanished before those who loved her and those who sought her would have at least a partial answer to a seemingly incomprehensible mystery.

A property owner was clearing blackberry vines from a lot he owned near the city of Bothell on the first day of spring 1981. He reached down and almost touched a partial skull that lay hidden there. There was another bone, too. The site was less than fifteen miles from the town house where Marcia and Happy had lived. The skull had well-maintained teeth, and that would help in identifying the remains.

When the Snohomish County investigators asked a

forensic dentistry expert to compare Marcia Moore's dental records with the teeth in the skull, they knew, at long last, where she was.

A meticulous search of the area produced nothing more, however. No clothes. No jewelry. No hiking boots.

Could Marcia Moore have walked so far on the freezing night she vanished? Possibly. But she would have had to skirt a busy freeway and pass any number of areas where people lived, shopped, and worked, and no one had ever reported seeing her. Could she have been murdered, and taken to this lonely lot? Possibly. Although the detectives didn't release the information, there was profound damage to the frontal portion of her skull.

One of Marcia's close women friends made a pilgrimage to the spot where her last earthly remains had lain. She wrote to a mutual friend who also mourned for their dear friend, and it was both a comforting and a disturbing letter.

"I went over and saw the exact spot where the skull was located," she wrote. "And it was a beautiful place, on top of a bed of soft, dry leaves, encircled by some very large trees. And growing all around the circle were trilliums beginning to come up. Of course not in bloom yet. My first thought was, 'Marcia would have loved this place!' It was almost like a gigantic fairy ring, those big trees in a circle. A little boy showed me the place; he is the son of the man who found the skull. The little boy said there was a hole right in the front of the skull, and I said, 'That sounds like a bullet hole,' and he agreed."

But he was only a little boy, and the investigators were never convinced that Marcia Moore had been shot in the head; her skull was so fragile and it had lain out in the elements for more than two years.

To this day, no one really knows what happened on

that Sunday night in January 1979—no one but her killer, if, indeed, she *was* murdered. Marcia had always longed for a glimpse into another, brighter, world. Once there, she sent no messages back to the friends who waited for some sign.

No one has heard from Dr. Happy Boccaci for a long time.

Update, December 2003

Twenty-five years ago, Marcia Moore's and Dr. Walter "Happy" Boccacio's experimentation with the drug ketamine seemed harmless enough—if a bit eccentric.

Today, ketamine (ketamine hydrochloride) is a drug that is being abused by an increasing number of young people who use it as "club drug." It is often handed out at "raves" and parties, sometimes with tragic results.

Street names for ketamine include: "Special K," "Vitamin K," "Kit Kat," Green," "Blind Squid," "Purple," and "Special La Coke." It is a rapid-acting dissociative anesthetic used medically on both animals and humans (for pediatric burn cases). Ketamine usually comes in liquid form and the most potent way to use it is by injection. The human response to ketamine occurs so quickly that there is a risk of losing motor control even before the injection is completed. Users respond in different ways—from rapture to boredom. Its hallucinogenic effects impair perception, and it's quite common for those using ketamine to relate out-of-body or near-death experiences.

The drug prevents all pain, so it is possible for the user to be injured and completely unaware of it. The effects of a ketamine "high" usually last for four to six hours, but may last from twenty-four to forty-eight hours. Hearts seem to beat normally after the user is injected with ketamine, but their breathing can be suppressed.

Marcia Moore's daily dose of 50 mg was in the low range—which would rapidly have produced psychedelic effects. However, if her use increased, she would have gone into the convulsions, vomiting, and oxygen starvation of the brain and muscles that follows large doses.

As dangerous as ketamine is, it has become the emerging top choice as a club drug in New York, Miami, and San Diego. With the new information about a drug that is legal *only* for medical use, it is clear now that Marcia Moore and her husband were playing with fire. With her long history of daily use of a drug now known to be very, very hazardous, she was undoubtedly psychologically and physically addicted.

Unable to feel or acknowledge pain, Marcia might well have left her home on a freezing night and been unaware of the cold as she wandered miles away. But the hole in her skull has never been explained. In all likelihood, someone *did* shoot her or strike her with a blunt weapon, whether it was a wicked stranger who picked her up on the road or someone who knew her well.

Marcia Moore would have been seventy-five by now, possibly still searching for answers to age-old questions of this world and the next. Dr. Happy Boccaci has disappeared. If he is alive, he is close to sixty-five.

The Stockholm Syndrome
(from *Empty Promises*)

There is a time-worn belief among lay people that murder will out—that all homicides will eventually be solved and that killers will eventually be prosecuted and found guilty. That is perhaps a comforting thought, but it isn't true.

Two bizarre and inexplicable deaths in an isolated forest in Oregon were almost written off as accidental. It was only through the efforts of some of Oregon's top criminal investigators and prosecutors that the killer was found and convicted.

The investigation began with a paucity of physical evidence, a witness who had been brainwashed, and two deaths that certainly appeared to be tragic accidents. But when it was over, a team from the Oregon attorney general's office uncovered a story of horror and violence that made even the most experienced detective's flesh crawl.

I must confess that, in a sense, I have written this case before. To protect the female victim from public scrutiny and to avoid invading her privacy, I fictionalized this case in my only novel Possession, *first published in 1983.* The young woman was a teenager then and a widow when she should have still been on her honeymoon. My conscience wouldn't let me write her story as nonfiction,

387

and I have never regretted that. Possession*'s characters are not real, but composites of the people who lived through this case. In that book, I moved the crimes' location from Oregon to Washington, and actually created a fictitious county that people have been looking for for twenty years! I still get letters from readers asking why there isn't any photo section in the novel!*

Now, with the survivor's permission, here is the actual case and the true location of the crimes: the Mount Hood National Forest in Oregon. All the details are factual. And there are photographs, but I will never publish the female victim's picture or use her true name.

She has lived through an ordeal that few women could and she still deserves confidentiality.

I cannot count the number of readers who have contacted me to say that they never go camping in the woods now without thinking of this case. It doesn't stop them from going, but it reminds them to be more cautious.

Until the Patty Hearst kidnapping, the mass suicides of Reverend Jim Jones's followers in Guyana, and, more recently, the cult deaths in Waco and southern California, people thought of brainwashing as something that happened only in Korean or Vietnamese prison camps. It's easy to be smug and confident in the safety of one's own living room or at a cocktail party and say, "I could never be programmed to do something like that. There are just some things I would never do."

But the mind is an incredibly complex entity and, given the right circumstances, virtually any mind will crack and begin to believe that black is white, that wrong is right, and that reality no longer has any validity. Brainwashing can take place in an hour or over many days. It is a strategy used in many hostage situations. When ordinary people are held prisoner in banks or planes, some of them will eventually begin to think their captors are good and kind people *simply because they haven't killed them.* When their plans are interrupted, captives move from outrage to fear to passivity and finally to a belief that their captors must possess at least a few tender places in their hearts. When they survive, many hostages feel they owe their lives to the bank robbers or skyjackers. This curious phenomenon is known as the Stockholm Syndrome.

For brainwashing to occur, a human being must be exposed to four basic elements:

1. A severe traumatic shock
2. Isolation—being taken away from the people and surroundings where the person feels secure
3. Programming—hearing what the mind controller wants the subject to believe, over and over and over and over
4. The promise of a reward—often the subject's very life

When all four of these components come into play, the stage is set. Every one of these elements is vital in unraveling the story of Robin* and Hank Marcus* and their seemingly benign meeting with a stranger in the woods.

It was Thursday, July 22, 1976, when Robin and Hank set out from their home in Canby, Oregon, for a camping trip along the Clackamas River near the foothills of Oregon's majestic Mount Hood. The trip was to be a celebration of their first wedding anniversary. Robin was only sixteen, her husband five years older, but they were so much in love that her family didn't object when their beautiful raven-haired daughter wanted to marry. They knew Hank loved Robin and would take care of her. The young couple's happy first year of marriage showed everyone that their decision had been the right one. The trip into Oregon's idyllic wilderness would be like a second honeymoon for the couple.

Hank and Robin lived on a shoestring. They had only sixty dollars to spend on their trip; that immediately eliminated motels and restaurants. They would have to sleep out under the trees or in their car and cook over a campfire. At first they planned to leave Rusty, their collie, with

Robin's grandmother, but she was ill. They certainly couldn't afford to put him in a boarding kennel, so they decided to take him along.

A sense of fatalism would run through all of Robin's eventual recollection of the events of that bizarre weekend. Call it karma, destiny, or what you will. If they had made even some small decisions differently that weekend, Robin's and Hank's lives might have gone on without incident for another fifty years.

Robin initially wanted to go to the Oregon coast, where she and Hank had spent their honeymoon, but Hank chose Austin Hot Springs in the Oregon mountains instead. He wanted to teach her how to fish; it was one of his passions, so she finally capitulated. That made him happy, and they could always go to the coast another time.

But Robin had terrifying dreams the night before their trip. Something indefinable frightened her and she woke knowing only that her nightmares had something to do with their planned outing in the mountains. The next morning she mentioned her fears to a girlfriend, who suggested she take her Bible with her on the trip. "If you have your Bible with you," she said, "you know everything will be all right."

Robin tucked her much-read Bible into her backpack, but she was still afraid. She told Hank about her dreams, and he too admitted that he felt a presentiment of danger, something that was totally unlike him. Just to be on the safe side, he suggested they stop and ask a friend of his to go along with them for the weekend, but the friend wasn't home. They left him a note which read, "We were by to ask you to go to the mountains with us. Sorry you missed the fun!"

The sun was shining, the weather was perfect, and Robin and Hank tried to shake off their forebodings.

They bought fishing licenses and canned food, and they gassed up their car. That left them with about twenty dollars to cover any emergencies.

They drove the twenty miles from Molalla to Estacada, and headed south. Somehow though, they missed the turn leading into the Austin Hot Springs campground and turned instead into the road leading into Bagby Hot Springs. They drove deep into the wilderness before they realized they were heading in the wrong direction. "This road is so much spookier than I remember it," Hank commented when he failed to recognize any landmarks. "In fact, it's so spooky, it gives me the creeps. It's like no other road I've ever been on."

Once they realized they'd taken a wrong turn, they retraced their path. By then they had used up a quarter of a tank of gas, they were running late, and they finally arrived at the Austin Hot Springs campground just as the gates were being locked for the night. All the camping spots were taken.

The park ranger told them they could park outside and walk back in. "You can cook your supper, take a dip in the hot springs, and you can fish, just so long as you don't camp inside the park tonight."

Robin and Hank cooked dinner, laughed at some people who were skinny-dipping, and took Rusty for a walk in the woods. They felt better and their spooky feelings now seemed silly.

Still, they didn't want to camp alone; they wanted to park near other campers, and they finally found an enclave of Russian families and parked their sedan close to them. They slept in the car with the doors locked. They were having a restless night with Rusty jumping on them and whining. They finally got up, made their way down to the Clackamas River by flashlight, and gave the dog a drink of water. Then they returned to the car and settled down for the night.

They woke at six the next morning. It was Friday, July 23. The park ranger said there was a spot available inside the park now and he directed them to the campsite. Robin cooked breakfast while Hank fished. But he had no luck, and they swam in the hot springs instead. There were people all around them, including the families they'd met the night before, and Robin felt safe enough when Hank headed farther upriver to try his luck again.

The only bad moment she experienced was when a man yelled at her for letting Rusty swim in the springs. "They're for people, not dogs," he complained. "You could get slapped with a $500 fine."

"He's probably cleaner than you, most likely," she'd called back, as she tugged the collie out of the water.

Hank was gone fishing a long time, at least two hours, and Robin began to worry. When he finally showed up, he was grinning and soaked to the skin. "You almost lost me," he laughed. "I was helping some of those Russians ford the river with a rope and I hit a sinkhole and started going under some white water—until I grabbed a branch and got my footing."

Robin had been so worried that she was mad at him at first, but she relented. "I'm sorry I yelled at you," she apologized. "I thought something had happened to you, and I got scared."

Hank Marcus was a big man—6 feet tall, 185 pounds. He was fully capable of taking care of both of them. He soothed Robin, pointing out all the people around them, saying there just wasn't anything for her to be so afraid of. She was timid without him, though, and tended to worry far more than she needed to.

It was a good afternoon. They frolicked in the hot

springs and talked to the Russian families. One of the men made a pass at Robin as he carried her across the river and she deliberately stepped on his boat, swamping it. Later, Hank laughed when she told him what she'd done. He wasn't jealous of her; he had no need to be.

But Hank was disappointed with the trip so far; he still hadn't caught any fish, so they broke camp and headed up the road to give it another try. Robin cooked a late lunch while Hank tried out the new fishing spot. They said grace before they ate, as they always did.

That evening, while it was still light out, they drove farther and farther downstream looking for signs of fish in the river. They passed a lone man fishing and asked him if the fish were biting. He shrugged and said, "I haven't caught anything all day." So they kept on driving.

They came upon another fisherman, who told them he had only caught three fish all afternoon, "and they weren't keepers." But he told them he'd heard that a truckload of fish had been dumped into the Colawash River earlier in the week. "Ask about that up at the ranger station," he suggested.

Hank and Robin were undecided whether to stay or head home. Their gas was getting dangerously low now, and they hadn't found any good fishing at all. For Hank's sake, Robin suggested they try just one more spot before going home.

The road they chose took them deep into the woods as the long shadows of evening closed over them. They came upon a small boat-launch area near the North Fork Dam and stopped to watch some children playing in the river. They were parked at the side of the road when a red pickup pulled up. It was an old truck, road-worn and mud-covered, with a broken tailgate and a crumpled bumper. The lone occupant was a short youngish man. He left his engine running as he got out and ran up the fish ladder.

Hank Marcus went over to talk to the stranger. Robin waited in their car; the windows were open, and she could hear snatches of their conversation. Hank was telling the man that the fishing prospects seemed to be nil in the area. "All we found were a couple of suckers," he said.

The stranger didn't even turn to look at Hank. He mumbled something and kept staring out at the river. But when Robin got out of the car and walked toward the two men, the man turned to look at her and she felt his eyes burning into her. "It was almost as if he'd never seen a woman before," she recalled. "He lit up like a Christmas tree."

Suddenly he smiled and turned back to Hank. "I know where they just dumped a whole truckload of fish," he said. "I was just up there working when they dumped them off the bridge. That's where I'm headed."

Since the other fisherman had also told them about the fish dump, it seemed reasonable that this stranger, who said his name was Tom, was telling the truth. Hank was really tempted, but he worried about his nearly empty gas tank. Tom told them that it wasn't that far—they had more than enough gas to make it, adding, "Besides, I can go to town in the morning and bring back gas if you run low."

They decided to follow Tom to the place where he said he'd seen the fresh dump of fish. The two-vehicle caravan wended its way slowly down the deserted road. At one point, Tom pulled the truck over and suggested that they ride with him so that they wouldn't run out of gas, but Robin shook her head, and Hank shrugged. She wanted to stay in their own car; the feeling of uneasiness that had plagued her for the past two days had returned.

"Just where is this spot?" Hank asked.

"Just beyond the Bagby Hot Springs Road."

Hank and Robin looked at each other; that was the road that had frightened them when they'd taken it by mistake the day before. It had given them both goose pimples on a hot day. They whispered to each other about turning back, but they finally decided to go on. "It's silly for us to be afraid of a road," Hank reassured Robin.

They passed a man and his daughter they'd camped with the night before, and Robin felt better; they were nice, normal people and seeing them here on this road allayed her fears.

Hank looked over at Robin and grinned. "See, things always work out. It's neat that we met Tom. If we hadn't been at the dam at that precise minute, we wouldn't have had this chance to catch some fish. We probably would have just gone home and lost the whole weekend."

Up ahead, Tom turned onto an old dirt road that was bumpy and deeply rutted. They could no longer see much of the landscape because the sun had dropped below the horizon, and it was that time of evening between dusk and full dark. They pulled in behind the glowing taillights of Tom's red pickup.

They lit a fire, and Tom pulled out a bottle of liquor and offered them a drink. To be polite, they each took a little sip. Then Tom pulled something out of his truck. It was a milk carton with a dead bird in it. "See this?" he bragged. "I picked it off on the way down here."

Robin felt her stomach turn over. "We don't believe in killing things for sport," she murmured. "Not unless you have to—for food."

"Oh, don't worry," Tom said. "I plan on eating it."

After they ate, Tom grabbed a rifle from his truck and called to Hank and Robin to join him on a walk. They came to a clearing in the midst of the lowering pine and fir forest and Tom told them that this was where he did his hunting. "If we got a deer, we could eat only the hindquarters. We could be wasteful masters," he said. It was an odd term. Robin had never heard it before.

"That's illegal," Hank said.

Tom only laughed and shrugged.

They shared Tom's binoculars, and there was just enough light to see a deer foraging in the clearing and, farther on, some bear cubs playing. Tom raised his gun, sighting in on them, but he didn't shoot. Robin heard him cock the gun, and she quickly turned her back in disapproval and horror. She tugged on Hank's arm and pleaded, "I want to go back to camp right now. If he shoots a cub, the mother will kill all of us!"

Tom smiled, his teeth white in the dusk, and lowered the gun. They made their way back to the campfire.

Hank and Robin prepared to sleep in their car again.

"I'll rap on your hood in the morning when I get up," Tom said, "about five."

Alone in their car, with Rusty tied outside, Robin told Hank she didn't like Tom. "He seems to enjoy killing for its own sake," she whispered.

Hank held her close and said softly, "You just have to understand everyone in his own way, honey."

Hank was like that. He didn't judge people—he accepted them, but Robin felt an overwhelming rush of fear that she couldn't shake. She clung to Hank all night. While she watched him as he slept, she had a numbing thought. What would she do if something took him away from her? She loved him so much, but she knew that sometimes there was nothing she could do to stop whatever Fate had planned for them.

At dawn on Saturday, July 24, they awoke to Tom pounding on the hood of their car. They'd slept in their clothes, and now they hurriedly pulled their shoes on. The three of them agreed they would fish before breakfast and

Tom drove them in his truck deeper into the woods to a large clearing. He had trouble finding the trail, and Robin found this odd since he'd told them that he came here to hunt every weekend.

They finally found the path and headed up the overgrown trail. Robin ran ahead with Rusty and waited for Tom and Hank to catch up. The sun was shining now, and there were field daisies and wildflowers growing everywhere. The night's dread began to recede.

They had to climb over logs and rocks to reach the riverbank. Once there, Robin and Hank sat on a rock, and Tom stayed behind them. They all threw lines in, but their luck was no better here than it had been anywhere else. None of them caught anything.

Suddenly Robin felt prickles running up and down her spine and she sensed that Tom was pointing his gun at them. But when she turned to look, he was staring elsewhere, his gun cradled carelessly in his arms.

They decided to go back to camp and fix breakfast. They wouldn't have the fresh fish they'd counted on, but Robin would manage to throw something together. They were tired from tromping through the thick woods and climbing over deadfalls, and so they rested on a log along the trail. Robin whistled, and a bird flew close to them, checking to see if she was a bird, too.

She started to make a joke about her name being appropriate when Tom's rifle roared. He fired repeatedly at the birds all around them. Eerily, the more he fired, the closer the birds came.

"Why do they do that?" Robin asked. Tom seemed to have some weird aura about him.

"They're curious about the sound," he explained.

"Haven't you got better things to do than try to kill poor little birds?"

Tom didn't answer. In the sunlight when he squinted, he had eyes like a fox or a ferret; they seemed to see everything between his half-closed lids. He finally stopped firing at the birds, but he held his gun so that it appeared to be pointing at Hank, who didn't notice. Now Tom looked at their Rusty. He was stroking the dog as he said, "There're only two things wrong with Rusty," he said. "He's alive and walking."

It was a sick joke, and neither Hank nor Robin laughed.

Robin studied Tom. She couldn't figure him out. When he'd first seen her, his eyes had practically undressed her and he'd smiled broadly. She recognized male interest, but he'd barely glanced at her since, talking only to Hank.

Still, Hank told her he didn't trust Tom around her. When they got back to the truck in the thick early morning heat, Robin unbuttoned her blouse, revealing her bikini top, and Hank quickly told her to button it up again. Then Hank gave her a kiss, smiled, and walked away with Tom. They each carried a gun and were headed back toward the clearing.

Robin was alone now. She could hear the birds chirping and Rusty panting in the heat. She knew she should fix breakfast, but she was immobilized with a dread that was much worse than before. She tried whistling loudly but no one responded, not even the birds.

And then she heard the shot. Only one shot. It reverberated through the woods until the echoes diminished into dead silence.

She waited, wondering what the men had shot at. After a time, Tom came strolling back. "We got us a deer," he said laconically. "I need a knife to gut it out."

Something wasn't right. Hank would have been the one to come back and tell her. He wouldn't have sent Tom back. With Rusty close beside her, she began to run toward where she'd heard the shot.

Tom's gun roared again behind her and she looked back to see Rusty falter and fall dead in the path, his blood staining his silky sable fur. Horrified and sobbing, Robin turned toward Tom with a question on her lips. But now Tom was leveling the rifle at her.

"You shot my dog!" she screamed.

"Yeah, I know," Tom smiled. "I shot your husband, too."

Tears coursed down her face, and she pleaded, "Oh, God . . . please don't hurt me!"

She believed Hank was dead. She knew Rusty was dead. Robin Marcus was sixteen years old, and she was alone in the wilderness with a killer. She fully expected to die, but it didn't seem to matter much at that point; she had lost the two beings who were closest to her.

It would be three days—Saturday, Sunday, and Monday—before Robin would get the chance to tell anyone what had happened up there in the woods near the meadow. When she did, she appeared rational—in shock, certainly—but basically lucid.

The detectives and attorneys who listened to her story took her at her word. They didn't understand then that they might as well have been listening to a programmed robot.

On Tuesday, July 27, Robin Marcus and Tom Brown entered the offices of an Oregon City attorney, James O'Leary. O'Leary, who had served as Tom Brown's attorney in the past, listened while Tom and Robin explained that Brown had accidentally killed Robin's husband in the Bagby Hot Springs area on Saturday, July 24. Robin sobbed as she recalled witnessing the accident. She said that she wanted to go with Brown to talk with the Clackamas County sheriff about the incident. She didn't want him to be blamed for something that wasn't his fault.

O'Leary contacted Detectives Hank Reeves and Lynn Forristall and they listened to the incredible story that Tom Brown and Robin Marcus gave. On the face of it, it seemed to be a tragic story about the accidental discharge of a gun. According to Brown, he and Hank Marcus had been looking for deer when they decided to exchange rifles. Brown said that one was a Winchester lever action and the other a .22 caliber high-power Savage. As they had passed the guns between them, Brown said one of the guns had gone off, fatally wounding Hank Marcus in the head. He died in an instant.

Tom Brown said that after Hank died, the Marcuses' pet collie, Rusty, went wild and attacked him. Robin nodded as Tom explained that he had no choice but to shoot Rusty. In the shocked aftermath of what happened, he said he and Robin wandered the wrong way in the forest and lost their bearings for three days.

Brown admitted that he had an extensive prior record, and conceded that this made him reluctant to report the accident. But then Robin promised to go to the authorities with him and confirm what had happened. She told him she would explain to the police that she had witnessed her husband's death, and she would verify that Tom was telling the truth.

The cops separated the strange pair, and each gave a formal statement. The two statements matched in every detail. Then Robin, exhausted and covered with scratches and insect bites, was driven back to her home in Canby. Tom Brown agreed to accompany the Clackamas County investigators into the wilderness to show them where the bodies of Hank and the dog lay.

Medical Examiner Ken Dooley would join the detectives for a cursory examination of the bodies. It was 5:45 p.m. on July 27 when the group left headquarters; they reached the Buckeye Creek Road at 8:20. It was dark and they needed high-powered flashlights as they moved along the trail looking for the dead man and his fallen dog. They found the remains of the trio's campsite, and 200 yards farther on, they came across Hank Marcus's body.

Fully clad in jeans and hiking gear, the dead man lay 30 feet from the logging road, his body partially covered with ferns. From the position of the body, it appeared that he had rolled over an embankment and landed 8 feet below. He lay on his face as if asleep, his left arm tucked under him. According to Tom Brown and Robin, Hank Marcus had been there for almost four days in the baking July heat. Decomposition was advanced, particularly in the area of the head wound.

The investigators took photographs in the twilight of that Tuesday night, and Detective Forristall placed stakes at the edge of the road to mark the probable site of the actual shooting, where dried blood stained the earth about four feet from the edge of the bank.

Tom Brown had voluntarily turned over the Savage rifle, saying it was the gun he had used to kill Rusty, the collie. He told them he had discarded the other weapon—the one that had fired unexpectedly, killing Hank Marcus. He didn't know if he'd be able to find it again; it was in a heavily wooded area much farther away.

They found Rusty's body along the trail. The huge collie was also covered with vegetation and he too had suffered a single gunshot wound in the head. Someone had apparently made an attempt to protect the two bodies. Or perhaps to hide them.

Tom Brown, age twenty-nine, seemed both cooperative and contrite as he told the investigators about the fatal accident. They put him up in a motel for the night, and he agreed to come to sheriff's headquarters the first thing in the morning to help them find the missing rifle.

Detective Sergeant Bill Werth and Forristall and Reeves, met with Thomas Brown early the next day. They went with him again into the Mount Hood National Forest in the Colowash River area to recover the gun.

They took more photos of the campsite, the Marcuses' car, and the scene where Hank had died. Then they hiked into the wilderness beyond. They crashed through underbrush for a mile to the banks of the Colowash, where they walked upstream for three miles, then crossed the river and came to a smaller stream. There Werth noted footprints that appeared to match Brown's shoes and much smaller footprints in the soft sand. Both sets were headed in the opposite direction from where Brown was leading the investigators.

In the heat of the day, the pace was rapid and wearying. The group walked three more miles upriver and then cut away from the riverbank again and moved into the woods in a northerly direction. They were now so deep into the forest that civilization seemed not to exist at all. Indeed, the terrain here had changed little since pioneers first came to Oregon almost 140 years before. Lost in these woods, a novice hiker might never find his way out. It was easy to understand why Tom Brown and Robin Marcus had become disoriented. But now Brown led the group, pointing out landmarks as they moved along. All of this was beginning to look familiar to him.

He pointed to a very heavily vegetated area. "We spread our sleeping bags out here on the night of the twenty-fifth," he said. "There it is! There's my rifle. It's a .22 high power with lever action. I had about eleven bullets left in a plastic bag. I tossed them out into the brush."

The gun was there all right, but even when they dropped to their hands and knees and searched through the undergrowth, the detectives could not find the bullets. To preserve any latent prints, they fashioned a sling in which to carry the rifle.

Back down along the creek bed, Brown showed them where he and Robin had dumped a sleeping bag when they had finally found their way to the trail head. The sleeping bag was literally torn to pieces from being dragged through the underbrush.

The exhausted search party got back to the campsite at 9:35 P.M., after more than ten hours of slogging through the forest. Packing the two bodies out along the trail for postmortem examination was extremely difficult. When they returned to the sheriff's office, the investigators secured the .22 rifle in the property room to await ballistics tests and dusting for fingerprints. They had also retrieved blood samples from the dirt near Hank's corpse, and from Rusty's body.

On July 29, Tom Brown gave a more detailed statement of the accident. He explained he hadn't known either of the Marcuses before he met them near the dam; they decided to join up for a fishing trip. The next morning he and Hank Marcus took a hike before breakfast.

"Hank and I walked up to the clearing the morning of the twenty-fourth. He was looking through my binoculars and he spotted a deer. He handed the binoculars to me so I could see, and I handed the rifle over to him at the same time. Then, after I got a bead on the deer, I gave the glasses back to Hank and he handed the gun back. As it was being passed to me, I grabbed it by the balance with my finger on the trigger. It fired . . . and the bullet hit Hank in the head."

"And his wife saw this?"

Brown nodded. "Like she said, she was standing a couple feet behind us. Hank fell to the ground, and I scooped up both the rifles. Robin started screaming. I ran toward the campsite."

Brown said that Rusty had been asleep back at the site and came running toward him, snarling as if he was about to attack. "I had to shoot him."

Brown said he'd been in shock. He sat around the campsite for several hours trying to decide what to do. "I finally knew I had to split—that no one would believe me. I told Robin she could do what she wanted, but that I was going to head to the mountains. She said I couldn't leave her there, that I had to take her back to civilization, but I said, 'No way. I'm going.' I told her she could go with me if she wanted, but she'd better hurry and get her stuff together."

It was obvious that Brown lacked gallantry, but it was easy to imagine that Robin Marcus, lost in the woods, in deep shock after seeing her husband killed, *might* have chosen to stay with the only other human being around.

She told the investigators she had witnessed the accidental shooting. And then, she said, Brown told her that he was afraid no one would ever believe him—not with his record. He was panicking and determined to head up and over the mountain. He said he knew the woods; she didn't. She decided, Brown said, to go with him rather than wander around in the wilderness where she probably would have died of fatigue or starvation or as prey for a bear or a cougar.

Brown acknowledged that he had dragged the collie's carcass off the trail and that he'd rolled Hank's body off the bank and then covered both bodies with sword ferns to deter the ravages of animals. That stamped him as a novice in the woods, the detectives thought. A few ferns wouldn't keep animals away, but they might hide the bodies from a human hiker.

So Tom Brown took off into the deep woods, with Robin trailing behind. He said he spent the next three days trying to calm himself down, and he finally decided the best thing to do was to turn himself in. Robin promised him that she would stand by him, and tell the cops she was a witness to her husband's death. "Then we headed back to Oregon City."

On July 29, a polygraph expert from the Oregon State Police gave Tom Brown a lie detector test. All the tracings of his body's reactions indicated that he was telling the truth. The victim's own wife was supporting Brown's story, all the evidence had been turned over by Brown himself, and he passed the polygraph test. It was tragic that the young husband should have died on his first wedding anniversary, but it clearly wasn't a homicide.

Tom Brown vacated the motel room and disappeared. There was no reason to require him to stay around.

The postmortem examination of Hank Marcus confirmed that he had died of a single gunshot wound to the head with the bullet entering the right cheek and traveling out the left side of his neck. The path of the bullet had been almost horizontal, indicating that he was standing next to someone of similar height when he was shot. Unfortunately, because of the extreme decomposition of the tissue, there was no way to determine if there had been any blotching or stippling of powder burns around the wound. That eliminated their chance to establish how far the shooter had been from the victim.

However, because the Oregon State Crime Lab was doing a special study on lead traces in bullet wounds, two fragments of Hank Marcus's tissue—each no more than an inch or so in diameter—were excised from the site of the entrance and exit wounds so they could be examined under a scanning electron microscope equipped with a laser beam.

Because of an oversight, Rusty's body was buried before the direction of the wound to the dog's head could be determined. And he wasn't buried in a single grave, but in a mass grave at the city dump with several other dogs.

Hank Marcus was buried, too, and Robin and their families tried to pick up the loose threads of their lives.

Everyone thought Robin was going through normal, predictable grief. In truth, Robin Marcus was suffering through her own private hell, something far beyond normal grief. There was something just below the surface of her mind that kept bubbling up, no matter how hard she tried to keep it submerged. As the days passed, it grew stronger and stronger.

Her memory was playing games with her. It was very odd. She could remember everything about preparations for their trip, remember the day they spent before they met Tom, and even recall how she'd been afraid of him at first. But the three days after Hank and Rusty were shot were all a blur. For the life of her, she could not pull those memories into focus.

She liked Tom. She *thought* she liked Tom. She could remember riding to the sheriff's office with Mr. O'Leary, Tom's attorney, and telling him Tom was a nice person. They asked her a lot of questions in the Clackamas County sheriff's office about why she'd gone up into the woods with Tom. Could she have escaped from him? She said yes—yes, she could have. She could have left when they got to Mr. O'Leary's office, but she promised Tom she would stick by him and tell them about how he'd shot Hank accidentally. The gunshot haunted her. She kept hearing the *boom* in her head and seeing Hank's blood.

And it frightened her. But she couldn't bring the actual shooting back. When she talked to the detectives, she believed she had seen it. But now she could not remember it.

Although she didn't realize it, Robin Marcus was beginning to come down from the intensive brainwashing she had undergone for three days after Hank's death. Whenever she began to go over the events in her mind the way Tom told her they happened, a very clear picture kept getting in the way—a picture that warred with Tom's words. She kept seeing his smile as he told her that he had shot Hank as well as Rusty. Why *did* he smile? It was such an odd smile, like the grimace on a devil's mask. But then she recalled that Tom had smiled when he was talking with detectives, too. Even though tears were running down his face when he told them about the accident, he'd had that same peculiar grin on his face. Maybe that's just the way he was.

As the days passed, Robin began to remember what had happened more and more clearly. She'd told the detectives what Tom wanted them to hear; she'd even told her family and Hank's that his death had been an accident. And she had believed it herself. Now she no longer did; her memory was coming back.

On August 2, Robin and her parents appeared at the sheriff's office again. "I want to tell you what really happened," Robin blurted. "It wasn't an accident. Tom Brown killed Hank."

She seemed so positive about what she was saying that the detectives immediately ushered her into an interview room where she gave a second statement. There were to be five more statements as her memory fought its way to the surface.

Robin explained that she had gone with Tom after Hank was killed, but only out of fear for her life. Tom had not been her savior in the woods. He had raped her again and again. She still didn't understand how but Tom had somehow managed to convince her that she was there when Hank died, that the killing had been an accident, and that she should return to town with him to verify his story. At the time it seemed the most natural thing in the world.

This new version was hard to swallow, and the detectives interviewing her looked at each other doubtfully. Robin Marcus was given a polygraph exam—and failed.

Indeed, Robin Marcus would fail more lie detector tests, but the investigators came to believe her even though they couldn't say why. She agreed to talk with a psychiatrist in the hope that it would help her explore which memories were real and which had been planted there by Tom Brown.

The forensic psychiatrist talked with Robin at length and reported his findings. He explained that Tom Brown had played such tricks with her mind that it would be a long time before she would be able to remember exactly what had happened. She wasn't lying; she had been very skillfully brainwashed.

At this point, the Clackamas County sheriff's office didn't have much of a case to take into court. Conflicting statements. Conflicting polygraphs. Nothing tangible to work with. Worse, Tom Brown was gone. He was a drifter; he could be anywhere. He might never be found.

The case, however, was taken to a grand jury, which would decide if the death of Hank Marcus had been a murder or an accident. The case remained there for some months. In the interim, Brown's lawyer, James O'Leary, ran for district attorney of Clackamas County and won. Even if the grand jury decided that Brown should be charged, there was no way O'Leary could prosecute a case in which he had originally been the defendant's lawyer.

The grand jury ultimately agreed that Tom Brown should be tried for the murder of Hank Marcus. An indictment charging Thomas Brown with murder, forgery, and car theft was handed down by the grand jury in late December, five months after Hank Marcus died; it was not going to be an easy case to prosecute. (The latter two charges were from another state, and both crimes had occurred before the events of July 24.)

James A. Redden, Oregon's attorney general, maintained a special Criminal Justice Division. It was manned by assistant attorneys general and investigators who were available to help county D.A.s prosecute cases if they requested assistance. Small counties often had complicated cases that required more manpower than they had on staff. Most of the attorney general's lawyers and several of the investigators had years of experience in criminal investigation. The investigators were once the cream of the detectives in the departments from which they were recruited.

Assistant Attorney General Stephen Keutzer was from the Lane County district attorney's office in Eugene, and Assistant Attorney General Robert Hamilton had once been on staff in the Marion County D.A.'s office in Salem. Between them, they had a great deal of experience in prosecuting homicide cases. Now they responded to Clackamas County's request for help in the investigation and prosecution of Tom Brown.

Robin Marcus's many statements suggested that she might be a good candidate for Sodium Amytal (truth serum) and the grand jury requested an examination by Dr. J. H. Treleaven, head of the Psychiatric Security Unit of Oregon State Hospital, to see if the drug might unveil hidden areas in her mind.

Treleaven's conclusion was that the young widow

would probably reveal nothing more under truth serum. He determined that she had been subjected to classic brainwashing during the time she was held captive after her husband's murder. All the elements were there: psychic shock, isolation, programming, the promise of reward and, for Robin, the need to alleviate her guilt that she had been responsible for Hank's death.

The shock of hearing her husband was dead and seeing her dog shot before her eyes would have been profound. The wilderness of the Mount Hood National Forest was as isolated as a place could get. And over the three days Robin was held captive, Brown systematically programmed her to believe whatever he told her about the "accident." Robin's promised reward was that she might escape with her life. Perhaps more important to her, she wanted to believe it had all been accidental. That would relieve her of the burden of knowing Hank had died because this stranger desired her sexually and was willing to kill to get her. In her mind, she would have felt responsible for the death of the man she loved more than anyone on earth.

Robin Marcus was, after all, only sixteen years old. She was suggestible and pliable. Before her ordeal, she had been an exceptionally trusting person. She was deeply religious, and she had only her Bible for protection against the stalking killer.

Now Keutzer and Hamilton and their team of investigators would start from the beginning, reviewing all the evidence on the case, the conflicting statements, and the circumstances of the killing. Optimally, a homicide case is easier to prepare when the prosecution team has been at the crime scene within hours of the event, just as the time element in solving a murder is so vital. The more time that passes after a killing takes place, the less likely investigators are to solve it.

Hank Marcus's family was distraught, crying for justice. Robin Marcus only wanted to forget. What she had experienced was so disturbing that she could not bear to go over it again. She was distraught that she had been asked so many questions, and forced to relive her terror so many times. She was jittery at the thought of testifying before a jury.

Robin had been hammered with questions and linked to the leads of lie detectors so often because her original statement was in direct opposition to what she had later told the Clackamas County detectives. They had no choice but to keep questioning her. Predictably, she was not the most cooperative witness a prosecuting team could hope for.

One of the first things the team from the attorney general's office did was to review the past record of Thomas Brown. When he said he had a long criminal history, he hadn't been exaggerating. Brown had an incredible background of violence—seemingly for its own sake. He had first come to the attention of Oregon lawmen when he was barely sixteen years old, after a wild shooting incident. The Clackamas County sheriff's office had been called after a young man was critically wounded by a gunshot while he was standing in the window of his own home. Witnesses had identified the gunman as Tom Brown, who was arrested almost immediately by a deputy who saw Brown as he was getting out of a pickup truck with a rifle in his hand.

With Brown in custody, the deputy raced to the house of the victim, who was only nineteen. He was still standing, but his hand was pressed tight over his stomach in a vain attempt to hold back the blood that gushed out between his fingers. The wounded man was taken to the hospital while Brown was questioned.

"Did you shoot him?"

"Yeah," Tom said. "I wanted his car, and I was willing to kill to get it."

Tom said that he and a friend had decided at school that day that they needed some money. Brown borrowed a rifle and five bullets from a friend, picked up the sixth at home, and the teenagers headed for a gas station near a junior high but "there were too many people there for a single-shot weapon," the cocky kid explained.

Then they headed for Canby, Oregon. They only had a little gas, so they ran a woman motorist off the road, demanding money when they ran up to the car. The quick-thinking woman quickly locked her doors, but the two teenagers fired anyway. "The expression changed on her face," Tom said, smiling at the memory. "We thought we'd hit her."

They had run into the woods, but they came back to where the woman had abandoned her car and run for help. Their plan to find someone else to shoot ended when they saw a police car approaching with the colored beacons on its light bar circling.

"Jim hit the gas pedal," Tom had told the deputy. "I told him to turn off at Clackamas. I knew we could make a standoff because there was only one cop. We hit a truck, slid sideways, and flipped. I was in the backseat, aiming out the back window, and let the cop have it. The next thing I knew I was out in the weeds."

Luckily, Tom's shot missed the officer—but the two wild teenagers weren't done. They were going to show the world.

Next, Tom ran along a log boom and approached a man, demanding his car keys. The man said he didn't have any. Then Tom had gone to a nearby house and threatened a girl there. Panicked, she ran across the street to the house where the nineteen-year-old shooting victim lived. "I ran to the girl's house. There were windows in every room and I figured if a cop came after me, I could pick him off."

It was at that point that Tom Brown shot the man in the stomach, and commandeered a pickup truck to make his escape. "But there wasn't enough room in the cab to aim my rifle—that's when you got me," he finished, evidently proud of his shooting spree. He believed he had shot at least two people. In truth, he had critically injured just one man, who eventually recovered.

Tom Brown was sentenced to the MacLaren School for Boys, Oregon's reform school. The man who liked to shoot birds and cubs and deer out of season—the "wasteful master"—had started his violent career fourteen years before he met Robin and Hank Marcus.

Upon his release from the MacLaren School, and after an interim period of petty crimes, Tom Brown committed a crime that sounded like a rehearsal for what he'd done to the Marcuses. He had been going with a woman who had two young children, and she'd rejected him. He kidnapped her and her children at gunpoint and took them into the mountains, where he kept them overnight.

After he released his hostages, Tom told police: "I was going to have her one way or another. I would have burned down her house, used a gun, whatever it took, so no one else would ever have her either."

That Milwaukee, Oregon, case never went to trial. The woman victim refused to file charges, grateful for her life and afraid of reprisal from Tom Brown.

After that kidnapping incident, Brown had gone to Nebraska, where he worked on a farm. His boss allowed him to use a red GMC pickup truck. One day in early summer, Tom said he was going into town. He just kept on going all the way to Oregon, however, taking the truck and his employer's rifles with him.

Brown's Nebraska boss was considerably disappointed in the man he'd trusted. He filed a stolen car report, and that warrant out of Nebraska was still in force. Several other friends in the Clackamas County area were also disappointed when they had cashed checks for Brown and they came back bouncing.

This was the man Hank and Robin had met in the woods. Although he was now indicted for murder, it might be months, even years, before Tom Brown could be arrested and brought to trial. Bob Hamilton and Steve Keutzer went ahead and built the foundation of their case. They would be ready whenever Brown resurfaced.

And then, surprisingly, Tom Brown himself strolled into the Clackamas County sheriff's office one day. He said he'd heard there was a murder warrant out for him and he "wanted to get it all straightened out." He didn't seem worried or even mildly upset. He looked, indeed, for all the world like a man who had an ace up his sleeve. He was booked into jail to await trial.

The Oregon State Police Crime Lab's study of gunshot residue turned out to be a godsend for Keutzer and Hamilton. It gave them solid physical evidence they badly needed. Laser evaluation of the two tiny exemplars of the tissue from Hank Marcus's wounds revealed no gunpowder residue at all. That meant that Hank could not have died the way Tom Brown said he did. He said they were exchanging rifles when the gun went off. For this to be true, the rifle would have been so close to Hank's face that his wound would be near-contact and gunshot residue would certainly have been present. The crime lab tests proved that Tom Brown must have been standing at least a foot and a half away from Hank when the gun went off, and probably even farther away.

Secondly, if the shooting happened the way Brown described it, the trajectory of the bullet would have been at an upward angle. It was not; autopsy findings indicated that the wound was almost horizontal, with a variation of only an inch or so from a straight, flat path.

Unfortunately, Rusty was long buried in a mass grave, and they would never be able to find out whether the bullet had entered the dog head-on, as Brown said, or from the rear, as Robin claimed.

There were no bullets to test, only fragments. Bob Hamilton spent two weeks trying to find similar ammunition for the near-antique 1932 rifle and finally came up with a precious few from a gun buff. Their makeup matched the fragments found in Hank's neck.

Robin Marcus's polygraph tests had gone from "failed" to "inconclusive" to the point where she passed cleanly. After profound brainwashing, psychiatrists explain that memory returns slowly, but it *does* come back. Finally, Robin knew exactly what had really happened. But how would a judge or jury react to the information that it had required a series of polygraph tests to elicit the truth from Robin? And even if she did make a believable witness, she had not actually seen the killing; she had only heard the gunshot that killed her husband.

Jim Byrnes, one of the attorney general's criminal investigators, was given the task of obtaining the seventh, and final, statement from Robin Marcus. Byrnes was the chief of detectives of the Marion County sheriff's office when he was asked to join the A.G.'s staff. He was a highly skilled interrogator, and if anyone could gain Robin's trust, it would be Jim. He knew he would have to spend days with her as he explained why it was essential she give just one more statement.

Finally he hit on the right approach. "Robin, I won't ask you to give me a statement," he said. "I want you to write it out yourself. Take as much time as you want. You write exactly what happened, everything you remember, and when you're ready, call me."

Robin had not been in control of her own life for a long time. And Byrnes believed that, for a time, she had actually allowed Tom Brown to take over the thought patterns in her very brain. By letting her write her own statement, he was allowing *her* to ask herself the questions and to pick the time when she was willing to hand her statement over to Jim Byrnes. She liked him—he had daughters close to her age. She wanted to trust him, but it was hard for her to trust anyone anymore.

Byrnes had guessed right. Robin Marcus wrote an eighteen-page statement from her own memory and it was one of the most frightening and incredible statements Jim Byrnes, Bob Hamilton, and Steve Keutzer had ever read. Robin Marcus had forgotten nothing. The truth had been locked up in her subconscious mind and now came spilling forth. Her statement detailed exactly how her husband's savage killer had brainwashed her, causing her to forget her ordeal.

Robin wrote how she begged Tom to leave her in the woods after he killed Hank and Rusty, but he answered, "If I leave you here, it won't be alive."

Then he forced her to drag Rusty off the trail and wipe the dog's blood off her hands with dirt and ferns. She thought Rusty might still be alive because his feet were still moving, and she wanted to take care of him. But Tom told her, "Those are his reflexes. I never have to shoot anything more than once. I don't like to see anything suffer."

Tom told Robin it wouldn't do her any good to run. His gun could shoot 500 yards. She didn't know anything about guns, and she believed him. She pleaded with him not to kill her, but all he did was smile that same odd grin. He then explained he couldn't trust her and had to tie her hands. Then he led her to her husband's body.

"Don't look. You wouldn't want to see him," he warned, leaving her tied a short distance away. He returned with Hank's watch. "Now," he ordered. "You're not allowed to cry. I'm going to tell you a story. You'll have your time to cry, but I'll tell you when it's time."

He washed any residual blood off her hands with a bottle of water and then took a swig of water as he began his story.

"You and your husband were dumb to believe I was a logger who worked up here. You can see my truck's from Nebraska. I've killed five or six people, and I'm wanted for murder in several states. My name is Kent, not Tom, and I'm a hit man for the Organization, but I've killed one man too many, and now they're after me. I had to kill your husband because I wanted to take you into the mountains to live with me. I need companionship.

"If they come after us, you are to run in one direction and I'll run in another so I'm the one who'll be killed."

He explained that he had been watching her and thought she was fit enough to make a mountain woman. She stared at him, dumbfounded. He was like someone from another planet to her. She could barely believe what he was telling her. "Now, now," Tom said, "you can cry."

Finally, Robin let her sobs out, crying brokenheartedly. When she was empty of tears, she tried everything she could think of to convince him that he didn't want her. She told him she was really a city girl who couldn't last on the mountain trails. She told him she was sick; she would be a drag on him. She even told him she was a "slut who gets it on with everyone," hoping this would turn him off and make him afraid she might infect him with something. But he only kept smiling that fixed grin. "I was so afraid to be up there with him," she wrote. "He tried to comfort me and hug me, but I wouldn't let him."

Then Tom instructed her to gather her belongings and some food and follow him. He allowed her to take her Bible. She pleaded with him to let her leave a note for her family, but he said they couldn't leave a trail.

Laden down, they headed into the woods. When the trees closed off behind them Tom had her change into army pants so that she would be camouflaged from the "hit men who are after us." She went into the bushes to hide herself from him as she changed. Strangely, Tom dumped articles along the trail as they went. At first, she thought he was being careless, but then, when he cut through the brush, she knew he was leaving a false trail. They went down a steep rocky bank to the river's edge, and headed upriver. "If you see an airplane or a helicopter, duck," he warned, "that will mean they've found us."

Robin wrote, "He was bossy and always telling me to hurry. He told me only to step on rocks—never mud, sand, moss, or bark or anything else that would leave footprints. He said we were going way over to the other side of the mountain, and if anyone did come across us, I was to keep quiet and pose as his wife."

Robin recalled that a small plane flew overhead and they'd hidden. Then they cut over to the smaller tributary of the river. She asked Tom if they had brought her grandmother or their friend along, would he have killed them too? He said, "Yes, but I don't really like killing. We do it only if we have a good reason."

He didn't look like a hired assassin, she thought; he was slightly built and his swaggering seemed to be an act, but he certainly talked like a member of a sinister organization. And he had the cruelest eyes she'd ever seen, deep-set and full of hate. After hours of crashing through the brush, Tom told her they could take a rest. He lay on the sleeping bag while she went into the water to cool off.

"I went in the water in my bikini with my back to him. I wasn't even thinking of sex, so I figured he wasn't either. All of a sudden, I felt him staring at me. He ordered me to come over to him. I got out of the water with my hair over my cleavage, and then he told me to take my top off. I begged him to wait a few days. I said, 'You've just murdered my husband. Please don't do this.' "

Tom took the knife from his belt and put it on the ground next to him, and said, "Remember what I told you?"

She took off her top, but left her long black hair covering her nakedness.

"Now take off the bottoms and pull your hair back," he ordered. Trembling, she was forced to stand naked in front of him.

Tom expected romance because he had chosen her to be his woman, his companion in the woods, but Robin broke into tears of fear and embarrassment. Her terror didn't bother him at all. He forced himself on her and raped her.

When he finished, he allowed her to get dressed. Robin begged Tom again to just leave her in the woods, telling him that she would somehow find her way out. But he refused.

They continued along the river, climbing over logs and rocks. Tom grudgingly helped Robin over difficult spots when she couldn't keep up with him. That night they made camp and ate. Robin felt like gagging on her food, but she knew she had to keep up her strength. Tom bragged to her that he could have killed Hank with a knife or with his bare hands since he was trained in hand-to-hand combat. "But of course, a gun is much less messy and painless," he finished, "if you know how to use it."

Robin told him she'd been ill and that Hank had considerately avoided having sex with her. Tom shrugged and said, "I was going to kill him last night, but I thought I'd be a sport and give you one more night together."

Tom explained to Robin that *he* was trying to protect her. After all, he hadn't killed Hank in front of her. "I tried to make it easy for you."

"How did you kill Hank?" she asked.

"I just pointed at something and gave him the binoculars, and I stepped back and fired."

As Robin's long, handwritten statement continued, a reader could track the points where her mind had gradually began to bend under the combination of grief, fear, guilt, and the persuasive words of her captor. She submitted to more sex acts, things Hank had never asked her to do. She learned to turn her mind off and not think about what he was doing to her. She just wanted to get it over with, and now she no longer fought him. "I cried myself to sleep," she wrote. "I've never felt so alone before. The next morning I woke up, forgetting that it wasn't Hank beside me but the man who had killed him. It was a nightmare. I didn't want to believe he was a murderer, though, because he was the only person on earth I had to talk to."

The brainwashing process intensified. The world Robin knew was far behind her, and she was so frightened. All the time, Tom talked on and on and on. The second day wasn't as bad for her; she began to get used to plunging mindlessly through the woods. Whenever they rested, she read her Bible and prayed.

"I used to be religious myself," Tom commented, "but God gave up on me a long time ago."

Robin assured him that God didn't give up on anyone, not even him.

Tom shook his head. "I've killed too many people—a

lot in the army and five or six for the Organization. That's all I know how to do."

Tom embellished his story of Mafia connections. He told Robin he had been betrayed by a girlfriend who was in the Organization, and Robin believed him. She knew he could kill, and she believed now that he was an expert in survival. Now he was letting her see the pain he had known in his life. It was important for her to see him as something other than a murderous monster.

Tom didn't like to see Robin cry. "You should be getting over it by now," he complained. But Hank had only been dead for twenty-four hours. How could he expect her to get over it so soon? She would *never* get over it.

"He was hard to figure out," Robin wrote. "One minute, he'd be rough and mean, and the next he'd be kind and gentle. We talked about the human mind a lot. He said the mind contains a lot of little doors and that you could open and shut them when you wanted to. He said, 'When I kill someone, I open a door.' He said someday the doors in his head might all open and let the bad things loose and he might go crazy, but until then he had no guilt feelings."

Robin read the Bible aloud to Tom until he asked her to stop. It helped her to hear the words aloud. When she began to cry again, Tom got angry and yelled at her.

All along, he assured Robin that he was her protector. She had to remember that he was saving her from the men who were hunting them.

"Why didn't you just tie Hank up," she asked. "Then you could have taken me away."

He explained why he hadn't done that. "That would have been mean," Tom said. "[To leave him] In the hot sun with no food or water."

His reasoning was bizarre, but somehow he made it seem believable. He said he had killed Rusty out of kindness, too, because the dog would never have made it in the wilderness with them. It was far better to eliminate him humanely. "Rusty never knew what hit him."

Robin was getting mixed up. There was no one but this man beside her, and she wanted so much for him to tell her it had all been a terrible accident. She couldn't bear to think Hank had died only because Tom wanted her.

They camped out for a second night.

"What will you do if you tire of me?" she asked.

"I don't see how I could. You're the only person here."

They talked about books and movies. He told her he admired Adolf Hitler. She asked him about his family and he said he hated them. She had to be careful about the subjects she brought up. Things could make him so angry in an instant. Gradually, however, Robin's fear lessened and she prayed, asking God to somehow allow her to get home.

The next day, July 26, they didn't travel at all. Tom was sick, coughing and pale. He thought he might have pneumonia. He ranged around, checking the area, asking her how far away she could spot him. He wanted to be sure they would see anyone looking for them so they wouldn't be ambushed. He came back and asked for some paper, and he then sat down to write three notes to friends in which he apologized for the "accident."

"I'll probably be dead soon," he said.

Robin started to cry, and suddenly Brown began to cry, too. "I knew that one of those doors in his head had finally opened," she wrote. "He told me that if I would mail the letters for him, he would tell me what had really happened. He told me that killing Hank was an accident. When he said that, it was just what I needed to hear. He said he didn't remember how it happened."

Seeing Robin coming around to his thinking, Tom

pressed on, telling her the sad story of how the woman he loved had rejected him. He said he'd gone to Nebraska to forget her, and he was treated well there. He admitted his name was really Tom, after all. He promised to walk Robin to the river and let her make her way home. He even went so far as to take her there, telling her that he was sick and was better off dying alone in the woods.

"I felt so sorry for him," Robin wrote. "Deep inside, I knew it was no accident, but I told myself he was telling the truth. I couldn't just let him die up there. After all, he was nice enough to spare my life and let me go."

Tom was now all generosity. He offered her the sleeping bag and the water, and he told her sadly that no one would ever believe him about the accident. He had no choices left.

"And you're sure it was an accident?" Robin asked.

"Yes. I'm sure."

"If you're sure," Robin said, "I'll go to the police with you and tell them I saw it."

Tom smiled then, as if this was exactly what he wanted her to say. He led Robin all the way back to the camp she and Hank had set up—how long ago? The days were beginning to blur. She knew she could easily find her way out of the forest from here. Then Tom told her that he was heading back into the woods. "All I ask is one hour."

Robin's essay for Jim Byrnes continued, detailing her day with Tom. She wrote that she hated the thought of leaving a sick man all alone deep in the woods. She insisted she would be his alibi. At this point, she'd honestly believed he was a nice person, that he was a victim of a terrible mishap. Her brainwashing was complete. He allowed her to "persuade" him to accept her help. Finally he agreed to go with her so she could explain that she had seen the shooting, that it had all been an accident.

Tom went to where Hank's body still lay and brought

back his wallet. Meekly, he asked if it was all right that he'd taken two dollars out for gas, and Robin said it was. She didn't want to see Hank dead. The sun was setting by the time they reached Tom's truck.

They headed for Estacada, and Robin noticed that Tom was driving erratically. He actually *was* ill and had a high fever, so she told him they should wait until morning to go to the police. They spent the last night in a park, going to Tom's lawyer's office to talk to James O'Leary the next morning.

Although Robin had not seen Tom shoot Hank, it seemed now that she had. Tom had explained it to her often enough. "He told me how it was supposed to have happened, what to say, and I believed that story. I heard it so often, I really believed it was true."

And, according to Dr. Treleaven, she did indeed believe the story she had told the Clackamas County sheriff's detectives was true. At that time, she had been methodically and thoroughly brainwashed.

Tom Brown was now in jail. Criminal Investigator Paul Keller spoke with him, and he glibly went through the same story he'd told before. The shooting was an accident, and Robin had seen it. That was all there was to it. If the dead man's wife backed him up, he couldn't understand why the police were harassing him. Then, on the advice of his lawyer, Tom stopped talking. He had nothing more to say.

As Tom Brown's trial approached, Steve Keutzer and Bob Hamilton acknowledged that they had some problems with their case. They were absolutely convinced that Brown was a merciless killer, but would a jury believe the victim's widow? The defense would certainly bring up the undependability of her memory. Was the evidence enough? And would a jury understand the gunshot-residue evidence?

Knowing Brown's potential for violence, they didn't

want him out on the streets. Could they gamble on a win in court? It might be safer to agree to a plea bargain, allowing him to plead guilty to a lesser charge. That would ensure he was locked up for a little while at least.

The two state attorneys were conferring with Brown's defense team about the possibility of reducing the murder charge to negligent homicide when a grinning detective walked up. "Don't agree to anything," he whispered. "I've got somebody you might like to talk to."

At this point in the case, a colorful witness named Wendell Stokeberry* came forward. He had never been known for his cooperation with the police; Stokeberry had a rap sheet that went so far back that even he wasn't sure just what he'd done and what he hadn't done—although if he was pinned down, he could usually sort it out. He was bright and silver-tongued, and he would make one of the best—and one of the most flamboyant—witnesses Hamilton and Keutzer had ever brought into a courtroom.

Wendell Stokeberry was currently a resident of the Clackamas County jail and had recently renewed a friendship with Tom Brown, an old schoolmate from the MacLaren School for Boys. Brown was so positive that he was going to walk free that he had spent hours bragging to Stokeberry about how he had convinced Robin Marcus to go to the police with him.

Jim Byrnes taped Stokeberry's statement. Stokeberry wanted little in return. He wanted a simple escape charge erased from his record, and he wanted to be sent to an out-of-state prison after he testified. That wasn't unreasonable; snitches didn't live long inside the walls. Jim Byrnes knew Stokeberry was risking more than he might gain. Still, he agreed to give information without any promises being made to him. Even with his many walks on the wrong side of the law, Stokeberry felt Tom Brown was too dangerous to be turned loose on society.

"I been knowing this cat since the early sixties, even before we went to MacLaren," Stokeberry said. "Once we got there, we were in the same cottage. We was good friends. So I get booked into jail here, and there he is. I tell him what I'm in for and he tells me he's in for first-degree murder and a couple of sex things."

"Did you ask him any questions?" Byrnes asked.

"Yeah, about the murder charge."

Tom Brown had explained who the Marcuses were but had not given their names. He just told Wendell Stokeberry he'd met them only the day before the killing. "He said they all went fishing and that they had a big collie with them. He said he shot the guy in the face."

"Did he say it was an accident?"

"He said, 'I killed him,' but that his story to the police was that it was an accident that happened when guns were being exchanged. He said he had used an odd kind of gun. The casing of the bullets was extra long with a heavier powder charge than usual."

"Did he tell you the reason for killing this man?"

"Later he did. He said he was paid to kill him, and he said the police didn't have a case against him, because of the girl involved. He says it's just his word against hers, and he said the girl wasn't even there. Then he said he just leveled the gun down and blasted the dog. Then he said he got together with the girl for four days. He said he was going to beat the case because the girl was so nervous and the jury wouldn't believe her. Then he said he was going to kill her, too, as soon as he got out."

"Did he say why?" Byrnes asked, keeping his voice calm.

"Yeah, because she won't corroborate the lie he made her tell police in the first place. He told me how he beat the polygraph. He said you just have to tell yourself the same story over and over, and then you get to believe it yourself. Then you have no worry, no stress at all when you take it yourself. Then he showed me how to breathe and all when you take it."

Stokeberry said that Tom was sure a jury wouldn't believe Robin because she looked about twenty-four or twenty-five. "She's a Jezebel type," he says. "They won't believe her."

Tom added that he'd been 8 or 10 feet away from the victim when he shot him. "Tom says powder burns won't show from that far away, and he's worried about that now."

"Did he say why the girl gave the wrong statement?"

"Yeah. He says he convinced her that the police wouldn't believe her." Then Brown explained to Stokeberry how he'd worked on the girl's mind until she believed him.

Jim Byrnes knew there was no way Stokeberry could have known certain details about the case unless Tom Brown had told him. No one beyond Robin and the investigators knew all these details. Wendell Stokeberry was clearly telling the truth.

With the added impact of this witness, Steve Keutzer and Bob Hamilton felt they had more than enough to go ahead with a first-degree murder charge against Tom Brown. There would be no jury. The case was to be heard in front of a judge only—Judge Winston Bradshaw.

Two days before the trial, Tom Brown scraped up enough money for bail and walked out of jail. He had threatened to kill Robin Marcus, so the attorney general's office put her into a motel under guard until the trial. She was petrified with fear even though they assured her that

Brown couldn't find her. She was registered under a fake name and a police officer would always be there to ensure that no one could approach her.

When the time came for trial, the smug defendant wasn't nearly as confident as he had been. As the eight-day trial progressed, Robin testified for a day and a half. Wendell Stokeberry testified, too, although he drew giggles from the gallery as he swaggered to the witness chair. He adeptly parried defense efforts to discredit him by saying, "If you say I got busted for something, then I guess I must have. My record is *ex*-ten-sive."

He might not have been a law-abiding citizen, but he was telling the truth—and it showed.

Prosecutor Bob Hamilton presented expert testimony on the fact that there were no lead particles in the tissues around Hank Marcus's wounds. Using a long wooden dowel, he demonstrated just how far the killer had to have been away from Hank so that a shot wouldn't leave gunpowder stippling on his skin. There was no way that it could have happened as Tom Brown said.

Hamilton showed the judge the angle of the wound. Again, it contradicted Brown's version. Brown had even forgotten which side of the victim's head the bullet entered.

After hearing his story riddled with errors, Tom Brown insisted on testifying. Now he gave a different version of his recall of the gun exchange, but his efforts were feebly transparent.

Over defense objections, Judge Bradshaw allowed testimony on the mechanisms of brainwashing into the record. This was a major coup for the prosecution. As Dr. Treleaven explained it, the brainwashing of Robin Marcus was a classic example of mind control. Her mind literally became evidence in the case.

As the trial wound down, it was apparent that the attorney general's prosecutors, Bob Hamilton and Steve Keutzer, had presented a brilliantly organized case—a case that had begun with all the earmarks of a loser.

Judge Bradshaw retired to make his decision. Three days later, he came back with a verdict of guilty. Thomas Leslie Brown was sentenced to life in the Oregon State Penitentiary. His motion for a new trial was denied on July 19, 1977.

The testimony in the Marcus-Brown case on brainwashing was something of a landmark in legal precedent. Bob Hamilton pointed out that, although such testimony is generally not admissible, furtive conduct to cover up a crime is evidence of guilt. In this instance, the evidence that Tom Brown covered up was Robin Marcus's memory. If he could have permanently changed the "computer" of Robin's brain, the crime might never have been discovered, much less successfully prosecuted.

The long ordeal of Robin Marcus seemed to be over. At the time Hank Marcus was murdered, however, life sentences in Oregon were not what they seemed to be. Some lifers got out in ten to twelve years. And by the late 1990s Tom Brown began to appear periodically before the parole board, asking to be released.

The victims or the victims' families usually appear at these hearings, standing in a small room with the felon who terrorized them as they give their reasons why the prisoner should *not* be released. To protect Robin, Bob Hamilton stands in as the victim. "It would be too hard on Robin to have to see Tom Brown again," Hamilton explains. "So I'm there in her place, and Brown and I engage in what's basically a long staring contest."

Thus far, Brown has failed psychological tests that

would indicate he was safe to move about in society. He is still in prison, but he will continue to come up for parole, and it's quite possible he will one day be released from the Oregon prison system.

Robin Marcus is over forty now; she has remarried and has children. In her new, happy life she now lives thousands of miles away from Oregon. Only a handful of people know where she is and what her name is, and she is grateful for that. She is still afraid of the man who hunted humans rather than animals, and she dreads the day he is paroled.

ACKNOWLEDGMENTS

We try to give readers at least one new book a year, and I couldn't possibly do that without the super-efficient help I get from my friends at Pocket Books! I'd like to thank them, the team that stands behind me—and sometimes tugs me forward: Louise Burke, Executive Vice President and Publisher; Mitchell Ivers, my editor; Josh Martino, Mitchell's very able assistant and the man who edits my newsletters; Steve Llano, Copyediting Supervisor; Donna O'Neill, Managing Editor; Hillary Schupf, Publicity Director; Louise Braverman, my longtime publicist; Paolo Pepe, Art Director; and Felice Javit, Vice President and Senior Counsel.

As always, I received encouragement from my first-reader, Gerry Brittingham Hay, and my literary agents, Joan and Joe Foley of The Foley Agency. Ron Bernstein of International Creative Management is my theatrical agent and makes my books turn into miniseries and movies, although it isn't as easy as simply waving a magic wand!

And a big hand and thank you for my readers. I am more grateful for you every year. I enjoy your letters and emails and read every one—even when I can't always write back.